Introducing .NET 4.0

With Visual Studio 2010

Alex Mackey

Apress®

Introducing .NET 4.0 with Visual Studio 2010

ISBN-13 (pbk): 978-1-4302-2455-6

ISBN-13 (electronic): 978-1-4302-2456-3

Printed and bound in the United States of America 9 8 7 6 5 4 3 2

Publisher and President: Paul Manning
Lead Editor: Matthew Moodie
Technical Reviewer: Stefan Turalski
Editorial Board: Clay Andres, Steve Anglin, Mark Beckner, Ewan Buckingham, Gary Cornell, Jonathan Gennick, Jonathan Hassell, Michelle Lowman, Matthew Moodie, Duncan Parkes, Jeffrey Pepper, Frank Pohlmann, Douglas Pundick, Ben Renow-Clarke, Dominic Shakeshaft, Matt Wade, Tom Welsh
Project Manager: Anita Castro
Copy Editors: Damon Larson, Kim Wimpsett, Nancy Sixsmith, Tracy Brown Collins, and Mary Ann Fugate
Compositor: Lynn L'Heureux
Indexer: BIM Indexing & Proofreading Services
Artist: April Milne
Cover Designer: Anna Ishchenko

Distributed to the book trade worldwide by Springer-Verlag New York, Inc., 233 Spring Street, 6th Floor, New York, NY 10013. Phone 1-800-SPRINGER, fax 201-348-4505, e-mail orders-ny@springer-sbm.com, or visit hwww.springeronline.com.

For information on translations, please e-mail rights@apress.com, or visit www.apress.com.

Apress and friends of ED books may be purchased in bulk for academic, corporate, or promotional use. eBook versions and licenses are also available for most titles. For more information, reference our Special Bulk Sales–eBook Licensing web page at www.apress.com/info/bulksales.

This book is dedicated to my wife Sharyn whom without life would be a lot less interesting.

Contents at a Glance

Contents

About the Author

I have always had an interest in computers and started out programming with a hobbyist language called Amos on the Amiga. I had originally wanted to be a games developer, but this never happened as I instead found myself drawn to internet development. I think I blame books such as William Gibson's *Neuromancer*. *Neuromancer* contains a fantastic quote that I'll always remember:

"The Matrix unfolds like neon origami beneath clusters and constellations of data."

Fantastic stuff—although Gibson's world didn't contain the wonder that is IE6.

My first commercial development experience was at university (Business Computing with Psychology, first class honors) where I worked for a small consultancy creating applications using ASP and VB6. Shortly after that, .net arrived and I moved into ASP.net/SQL server development, where I have remained for the last eight years or so.

I have worked in a development/consultancy capacity in the fields of healthcare, government, CRM, finance, and the automotive industry and have been lucky enough to work around the world in the UK, Ireland, the Middle East, America, and Australia.

I currently live in Melbourne, Australia, where I work as a senior developer. I am occasionally exposed to sophisticated Australian "pom" humor, which is inevitably delivered with a bad 1820s cockney London accent. Australians are, however, some of the most welcoming, friendly, and fun people I have met, so I am thankful to the new friends I have made here who have made the transition easier.

I am active in the programming community and have spoken at a number of conferences and user-group events. In the UK I set up and ran the Surrey-based .net user group DevEvening.co.uk. I was awarded the MVP C# award in October 2008. I am currently working to bring the DeveloperDeveloperDeveloper day conference format to Melbourne (dddmelbourne.com) and set up DevEvening.com.au.

Outside of work I enjoy running and weight training, and I have an interest in artificial intelligence. My website is at simpleisbest.co.uk and you can follow me on twitter at twitter.com/alexjmackey.

About the Technical Reviewer

 **Stefan Turalski** is a nice chap who is capable of performing both magic and trivial things, with a little help from code, libraries, tools, APIs, servers, and the like. Wearing many hats, he is experienced in most phases of the software life cycle. Stefan is especially skilled in business analysis, design, implementation, testing, QA, and small, agile teams management.

His area of interest is quite wide and could be summarized as emerging technologies, with a recent focus on RIA (Silverlight, AIR), cloud computing, functional programming, and software engineering principles. Before he realized that he enjoys criticizing other people's work more than his own, Stefan published several technical articles, mainly about .NET technology, SOA, software engineering, and mobile development.

For last ten or more years he has built solutions ranging from Perl scripts, through mid-size websites, to distributed C++ or highly scalable .NET & COM+ enterprise class systems. Developing software for embedded or mobile devices and playing with Python web frameworks, F#, Closures, Azure (or EC2, depending on the weather) in his spare time, he earns a living optimizing Oracle and SQL Server-based systems, maintaining ancient code and recently building on top of Microsoft Office SharePoint Server and Dynamics CRM.

Feel free to contact him at stefan.turalski at gmail.com, especially if you need an inquisitive technical reviewer.

Acknowledgments

A book like this would not be possible without the assistance of many different people. I would particularly like to thank the following:

- Simon Pease, for his assistance, encouragement, and development of initial concept
- Mike Ormond and Eric Nelson at Microsoft, for their assistance and contributions
- Stefan Turalski, for his excellent technical review skills, assistance, encouragement, and late night discussions!
- Matt Moodie and Anita Castro, for their editing skills and minimizing my crimes against grammar (and, yes, I did notice the removal of some of my jokes!)
- Matt Lacey, for reviewing my early drafts, and everyone at DevEvening.co.uk, for proving my wife wrong—yes, people do want to talk about programming at the pub (but we all knew that beer, food, and programming was a good combination)
- John Sanderson, Bruce Richards, Chris Canning, and Pat Simons—I learned a lot from working with you guys.

Contributors

When covering a huge spectrum of technologies there is a very real danger that no subject is given sufficient coverage to be of any real use to anyone. It is also impossible for one developer to be an expert in all the areas that we will be covering. I am no exception, so I am very grateful to have had the assistance of those who *are* experts in their various fields.

I am grateful to the following people (in no particular order), who have assisted with answering queries, correcting mistakes, or providing contributions:

Jon Skeet, Andy Britcliffe, Ray Booysen, John Mcloughlin, Rusty Johnson, Jeremy Skinner, Sebastian Lambla, Dane Morgridge, Barry Dorrans, Craig Murphy, Julie Lerman, Daniel Moth, Danny Shih, Shawn Farkas, Chris Hay, Phil Winstanley, David Sussman, Michael Foord, Jonathan Keen, Gabriel Torok, Tarek Mahmoud Sayed, Rene Schulte.

Also, thanks to Kimberlee Kessler Design for allowing the use of her image in Figure 3-2.

Introduction

Many developers are too busy (or lazy!) to learn new technologies and skills. This is a shame, as they miss out on

- Producing better software
- Making their lives easier through better and easier-to-maintain code
- Opening up new promotion and job opportunities
- Impressing people

First of all, let's get out of the way what this book is not…

This book is about breadth rather than depth, so it may not cover some areas in as much detail as you would want. Secondly, this book is written for the professional edition of Visual Studio 2010, so we will not be covering some of the great new features available in Premium and Ultimate editions of Visual Studio. It's not that these features are not important—it's more that I believe the majority of developers utilize the professional edition and there's more than enough to cover already.

…But We Will Give You All This!

This book will get you up to speed quickly on what's new, in just enough depth to get you going, but without getting bogged down with too much detail. When something big like Visual Studio 2010 is released I believe developers need and want an overview of what's new. Most of us have been developing software long enough now that we just need a lead-in to a new technology and can explore it in further detail ourselves. I don't believe it is necessary to read an entire 600-page book to begin benefiting from new technologies (although big tomes do look rather good on your desk).

This book will make you aware of the opportunities available in .net 4 & VS2010, with the assumption that you will want and need to explore these further on your own.

When writing this book I tried to keep in mind the following ideas:

- Give the reader an introduction to new technologies
- Show the basics
- Don't get too bogged down in detail so the book can still be easily read
- Produce examples that are as simple as possible but not polluted with unnecessary detail

Code Examples

One of the things I find irritating about code examples in MSDN and some books is they often contain unnecessary code that obscures key concepts. When you are following an example, you don't care if it looks nice. The examples in this book are kept as short as possible, which, I hope, makes concepts easier to understand and reduces the amount of typing you have to do!

The other side of this, however, is that code in this book should definitely not be used as an example of good practice (e.g., the MVC chapter). You should make sure that your code includes proper error handling, closing of connections, etc.

Danger—Work in Progress!

Much of this book has been written using pre-release versions of Visual Studio and .net 4, which are, of course, subject to change. At the time of writing, documentation in some areas was very limited and some features didn't work, which limited the depth I could go into.

It is also likely that come final release, some of the code examples may need minor amendments and some screens may look slightly different. We will aim to update these in the future, but in the meantime errata will be made available on the Apress website at `http://www.apress.com/book/errata/1247`.

If you do find any omissions or errors, I would appreciate you letting me know by going to `http://simpleisbest.co.uk/Home/VisualStudio2010/`, and I'll aim to let people know via my website at `simpleisbest.co.uk`.

CHAPTER 1

■ ■ ■

Introduction

These are exciting times to be a .NET developer, and Visual Studio 2010 (VS2010) and the .NET 4.0 framework have brought a bewildering number of changes. But fear not! In this book I will be getting you up to speed on these enhancements, and also taking a brief look at some of the important out-of-band releases, such as ASP.NET MVC, Silverlight, and WCF Data Services. There is some cool stuff in this release, and most of it is not that tricky (with the exception of variance and parallelization) to get to grips with.

Versions

Visual Studio 2010 is available in five main versions:

- Express
- Professional ($799)
- Professional with MSDN ($1199 new or $799 renewal)
- Premium with MSDN ($5,469 new or $2,299 renewal)
- Ultimate with MSDN ($11,924 new or $3,841 renewal)

Note that these editions also come with free Azure time (Chapter 16).

It is likely that the Professional edition will fulfill most developers' needs, but to see what you are missing, I have summarized some of the additional functionality found in the Premium and Ultimate editions in Table 1-1. For a full comparison of features please consult: www.microsoft.com/visualstudio/en-us/products/2010/default.mspx.

Table 1-1. *Simplified Comparison of Advanced Version Features*

Item	Premium	Ultimate
Code coverage	X	X
Coded UI test	X	X
Web performance testing and load testing		X
DB deployment, change management, unit testing, and test data generation	X	X

(Continued)

Table 1-1. *Continued*

Item	Premium	Ultimate
Static code analysis	X	X
Code metrics	X	X
Profiling	X	X
Intellitrace (historical debugger)		X
Test management		X

What Is .NET 4.0 and VS2010 All About?

VS2010 and .NET 4.0 lay the foundations for the next epoch of .NET development and correct a number of omissions. I consider that we can divide the changes under four main headings:

- Efficiency
- Maturation of existing technologies
- Extensibility
- Influence of current trends

Let's take a whirlwind tour of these now.

Efficiency

One of the first things you will notice in VS2010 is the shiny new WPF-based IDE. The IDE contains some great features available previously only in add-on products such R# and Refactor (note there is already a VS2010 version of R#, yay!) IDE highlights include box selection, snippets, class stub creation, call hierarchy, and quick search; we will look at these features in Chapter 2.

There are also some great language enhancements that can make code cleaner, such as optional and named parameters, dynamic functionality, and changes to variance that will be covered in Chapter 3. Some of these changes will also assist developers working with COM, who frankly need all the help they can get, poor guys and gals (a moment of respect, please).

Maturation of Existing Technologies

Many .NET-based technologies, such as ASP.NET, have been around for some time now and haven't changed hugely in this release. Microsoft has, however, fixed a number of long-term omissions in ASP.NET and introduced some useful tweaks, which I will cover in Chapter 10.

Toward the end of 2008, Microsoft announced that future versions of Visual Studio would include the popular JavaScript library, jQuery. Although not strictly a .NET change, jQuery is a very useful framework that you will defiantly want to make use of in your web applications. I cover it in Chapter 12. In Chapter 11 we'll look at the enhancements to Microsoft's own Ajax libraries, which make it very easy to bind to data with client script.

Windows Workflow Foundation (WF) and Windows Communication Foundation (WCF) are much more closely integrated in this release. WF undergoes a radical overhaul with a much-improved designer, introduction of new activities, and easier customization (Chapter 6). WCF becomes simpler to use and also introduces new service discovery functionality that I will examine in Chapter 7.

WPF has some great additions, with an improved designer, multi-touch, and Windows 7 task bar support that I will look into in Chapter 15. I will also be taking a quick look at Silverlight 3 in Chapter 15. Even through Silverlight is not a .NET 4.0 technology, I believe it is an important release. If you have never used Silverlight before, then take a look at Chapter 14, which contains a brief introduction to Silverlight.

Entity Framework received much criticism when it was first released, and the team has attempted to address these criticisms in .NET 4.0. Find out if they have in Chapter 8.

Extensibility

VS2010 is your flexible and extensible friend. You may have already heard that much of the IDE is now written using WPF and can be customized with the Managed Extensibility Framework (MEF). I will look at IDE customization and MEF in Chapter 2.

Influence of Current Trends

Software is not developed in a vacuum, and certain trends have undoubtedly influenced VS2010 and Microsoft's product line.

Multicore Shift

Due to various physical limitations, CPU manufacturers are now concentrating on releasing multicore processors. Writing programs to run in parallel is difficult, but fear not: VS2010 and .NET 4.0 have fantastic new parallelization constructs and debugging facilities, both of which will be covered in Chapter 5.

Unit Testing and Test-Driven Development

Unit testing and test-driven development are becoming increasingly popular in software development. VS2010 contains a number of IDE enhancements to assist with these strategies. I cover these in Chapter 2. Other related changes that may be of interest are the new dynamic features and the DLR (Chapter 3) and ASP.NET MVC (Chapter 13). OK, ASP.NET MVC isn't .NET 4.0, but again it is an important interim release.

Cloud Computing

Cloud computing must win the buzzword of the year award for 2009. It is becoming an increasingly popular way to reduce costs and simplify management of infrastructure. Windows Azure is Microsoft's entry to this area, and I take a look at its capabilities and potential uses in Chapter 16. Note that if you purchased Visual Studio with MSDN, you even receive free Azure time.

What Do Others Think About .NET 4.0?

Throughout this book I have tried to include interviews with developers and companies that are lucky enough to be developing with some of these new technologies to gain their insight into potential issues and opportunities.

I asked a number of experts what they were excited about in VS2010 and .NET 4.0.

Mike Ormond (Microsoft Evangelist)

http://blogs.msdn.com/mikeormond/

What am I excited about? There's a truckload of productivity enhancements in VS2010, like snippets for Visual Web Developer. At last, snippets for ASP.NET, HTML, and JavaScript! Reference highlighting and generating types from usage are two other productivity enhancements I'm looking forward to, as well as the Intellisense enhancements (I no longer need to remember the exact member name and the improved JavaScript support is awesome).

I dabble in Office development from time to time and have a tendency toward C#, so I'm really pleased to see the language embrace the likes of optional and named parameters as well as the new dynamic type, which will make COM interop that much easier. Office development in C# is going to be a dream from now on!

From a web perspective, I love the new features in Web Forms. Many of them are small, but they are crucially important enhancements to the platform, as well as the new kid on the block: ASP.NET MVC. Choice is always good, and ASP.NET now offers two great choices. Add into the mix the Microsoft Ajax enhancements such as client-side templates/databinding and jQuery integration, and you have a killer web application platform. And of course there's the Web Deployment Tool and web.config transforms that allow you to automatically ready and package your applications for deployment."

Eric Nelson (Microsoft Evangelist)

http://blogs.msdn.com/ericnel/

For me .NET 4.0 represents a turning point in how we will develop database applications in the future. With .NET 4.0 we get a great Object Relational Mapping (ORM) technology in the ADO.NET Entity Framework 4.0, which will significantly simplify the effort involved to work with RDBMS from .NET applications. I have been really impressed with how the product team listened to feedback from the community on the initial release of the Entity Framework and went on to deliver significant new functionality in version 4.

Craig Murphy (MVP and developer community organizer)

http://www.craigmurphy.com/blog/

Every so often the computing sector goes through a paradigm shift. Programmers have gone through many such shifts, many of which are the result of a change in design techniques or in some cases changes in the way we think. The leap from procedural programming to object-oriented programming is an example of a paradigm shift. More recently, with functional programming becoming part of the mainstream Visual Studio product, programmers are offered another shift.

Advances in hardware has meant that even entry-level laptops are now being supplied with dual and multicore processors. This leap in hardware technology has positive implications for programmers. It also means another shift in the way programmers think about their applications; more so, it affects application design. Working with a single CPU in a multi-threaded fashion is no longer the challenge: working with a single CPU with 2 or more cores, each capable of performing a unit of work, is the new challenge.

Writing applications that are capable of targeting the specific cores on a CPU presents programmers with the challenges associated with deadlocks, race conditions, scalability, lockout, and determinism. On the upside, applications that share their workload over manycore become more responsive and are more efficient.

The Parallel Extensions and understanding manycore are other paradigm shifts for programmers. However, it's a shift that doesn't just affect programmers: the deep-reaching positive effects extend into application performance and user experience. A well-designed application that takes advantage of manycore may even result in your end user's computer feeling more responsive: it's a win-win situation.

Visual Studio and .NET 4.0 offer programmers a solid framework for building .NET applications that target manycore. As far back as late 2007, Microsoft has been providing programmers with their Parallel Extensions, offering support for Parallel LINQ (PLINQ) and task parallelism via the Task Parallel Library. Programmers need to understand .NET 4.0; this book will give them an excellent understanding of how to use VS2010 to take advantage of the .NET 4.0 feature set, including the Parallel Extensions.

Phil Whinstanley (ASP.NET MVP and author)

weblogs.asp.net/Plip/

ASP.NET 4.0 has the benefit of hindsight. With the integration of both the Web Forms and MVC rendering engines, developers are free to express themselves as they choose while still benefiting from the underlying ASP.NET Platform. To support developers in the building of rich powerful ASP.NET applications, VS2010 has streamlined its approach and is focusing on those areas that matter to developers. Speed, efficiency and ease of use.

Dave Sussman (MVP and author)

www.ipona.com

One of the things I love most about .NET and Visual Studio is the teams themselves and their openness to the community. Sure, they keep certain things hidden and have private betas, but much of what they do is public and open to comment, which makes the product improve in ways that we, the developers, need it to.

Much of the talk is about MVC, a great platform that has brought in new users, but I'm excited by the changes to Web Forms, MVC's mature elder brother. Web Forms are still supported and still being actively developed, and although the changes aren't as radical as MVC, they are far reaching. Many ASP.NET controls in .NET 4.0 now emit clean HTML (the Menu being a great example), and along with the control of client IDs, we have a far better platform for building Ajax based sites. Couple that with features such as the client templates and support for jQuery, and the platform is re-energized; I'm loving the thought of building Web Form sites without having to jump though so many hoops to produce standards compliant HTML that can be easily styled with CSS.

In Visual Studio itself the most exciting new feature is the potential that WPF brings. Using WPF for the code surface not only allows a UI refresh to make it look better, but opens up wonderful possibilities for tools to enhance the code editing experience. I think what we have now is just the tip of the iceberg in terms of what's possible for editing support.

Matt Lacey (Devevening.co.uk organizer)

blog.mrlacey.co.uk

www.devevening.co.uk

I meet lots of developers, and most of them don't have lots of time to learn new things or even an inclination to do so. For that reason I'm always excited to see features that need minimal training or explanation. Named and optional parameters are two such features. They're easy to explain and understand. Plus, they can allow for a dramatic reduction in the amount of code needed for some tasks. Needing less code to perform a task should lead to fewer bugs and more time to test and implement new features. Everyone wins!

The other feature I'm really excited to see is ASP.NET MVC. It's important for two reasons. Firstly, it's raising questions about the importance of having testable code. In turn this will lead to more developers using testing tools and techniques to improve their code. Secondly, it's causing developers to ask why it's needed and what's wrong with ASP.NET Web Forms. One key difference with ASP.NET MVC is that it's much harder to develop without having an understanding of HTTP. Whether using MVC or WebForms, having more web developers with a better understanding of HTTP can only be a good thing.

Alex Mackey (Author of this book and MVP)

simpleisbest.co.uk

For me the best changes in this release are the simple ones that will be utilized every day. I'm talking about changes such as the new `String.IsNullOrWhiteSpace()` or `Enum.TryParse()`. As a web developer myself, the ASP.NET changes fix some long-term annoyances, and the integration of jQuery is a smart move. I don't have to do much multithreaded work, but I really like the new Task model and find it much more intuitive to work with. Changes that make your applications run quicker without you having to do anything are always welcome, so am glad of the GC and threadpool enhancements in this release. I also really like the direction the security model is moving in, as I found the previous system overly complex. Perhaps one of the biggest surprises for me was how good Entity Framework now is, but I'm going to stop here as I have the rest of the book to tell you about all the great new features.

Future Trends

A big risk for software developers is learning and backing technologies that will quickly become obsolete. Of course, no one can know for certain what the future holds (no matter how much they claim to), but I think it can be useful to look at current recruitment trends when deciding on which areas to concentrate.

I spoke to Jonathan Keen, head of search practice at a UK recruitment agency, Cognitive Group (cognitive-group.co.uk), about trends he was seeing in .net development. Keen shared the following:

- Generally, companies are cutting back on new projects, so we are seeing less development roles.

- The most popular and highest paid skills in London at the time of writing (October 2009) are Sharepoint, Dynamics AX, and Dynamics CRM.

- There are many roles focusing on integration with existing applications such as Sharepoint and Dynamics suite.

- More competition for job roles places increasing importance on distinguishing yourself. Prove your passion for development. Get out there to conferences, user groups, and blogs. (And buy Apress books about new releases of .NET! – author)

- C#, ASP.NET, SQL Server remain core skills companies seek.

- There is some interest in "Agile" skills and SCRUM but less in TDD.

- Increasingly, WCF and WPF skills are expected on a developer's resume.

- Many public sector projects are still using .NET 1.1.

- There is an emphasis on web over desktop programming.

- Silverlight and MVC are not yet in demand (note many developers I spoke to disagreed and felt Silverlight is *the* current hot area – author).

- MVC has been used as hook to attract developers.

- Technologies such as BizTalk have decreased drastically in popularity.

My Own Subjective Opinion

WPF certainly seems to be a growth area. The highest .NET contract rates appear to be for Silverlight currently. My own subjective experience of the job market has shown ASP.NET remains popular, and jQuery is becoming a must-have skill. It will be interesting to see if ASP.NET MVC becomes mainstream, although I suspect many companies have too much investment in ASP.NET now, and that ASP.NET MVC will be too big a change in thinking for many developers.

The new parallelization functionality is interesting, but I suspect will not be utilized or needed in the majority of line of business applications. Developers skilled in threading and parallelization should always be able to command high salaries, so it will defiantly be worth looking into.

Summary

Enough of a high level overview, let's get started with the new IDE functionality–bring on Chapter 2!

```
static void Main(string[] args)
{
    dynamic alexBook;
    alexBook.Run();
}
```

Visual Studio IDE and MEF

This release of Visual Studio sees the IDE overhauled and much of it rewritten using WPF and managed code. The move to WPF allows Microsoft to make some stunning aesthetic additions to the IDE, and also opens up customization possibilities when combined with the new Managed Extensibility Framework (MEF).

Microsoft's use of WPF for a flagship product such as Visual Studio is important, as it demonstrates its commitment to the framework and confidence in its maturity.

In this chapter I will begin by looking at some of the new productivity enhancements in VS2010. I will then create a code snippet and customize the start page. Finally I will introduce MEF and take a look at some of the advanced customizations that it enables.

64-BIT VERSION OF VISUAL STUDIO?

A common question is whether Microsoft will release a 64-bit version of Visual Studio. At the time of writing, Microsoft has said it has no plans to do, so and that this is due to the following:

- Making use of lazy loading techniques would be a more cost-efficient way to improve the IDE's performance, and would benefit 32-bit users as well.

- A 64-bit version could adversely affect performance because data structures will use more memory.

- There are cost issues. Rico Mariani (see link below) considers the cheapest way to provide 64-bit support will be to incrementally convert the IDE to managed code, but this would break many existing extensions.

For a detailed discussion of this issue, please refer to the following link: http://blogs.msdn.com/ricom/archive/2009/06/10/visual-studio-why-is-there-no-64-bit-version.aspx.

General Improvements

VS2010 contains some long-awaited changes, including:

- There is now support for multiple monitors and the ability to drag windows outside of the IDE (see Figure 2-1).

- Intellisense is now 2 to 5 times as quick as previous versions.

- Readability of text is improved.

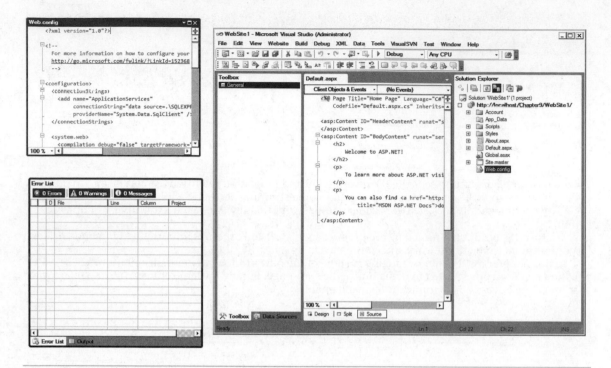

Figure 2-1. *VS2010 allows you to drag windows outside the IDE.*

Improved Multitargeting Support

When a new version of Visual Studio/.NET framework is released, it can take time to upgrade and test existing applications. This can prevent you from taking advantage of features such as IDE enhancements if you are not ready to upgrade your application yet. VS2010 contains improved support for targeting previous versions of the framework.

As per previous studio releases, the new project dialogue contains a drop-down menu that allows you to select the version of the framework that you are targeting when creating an application (see Figure 2-2). When you make a selection, Visual Studio will filter the project types you can create to those available in that version of the framework. Note that you can also select the framework version you are targeting in the project properties.

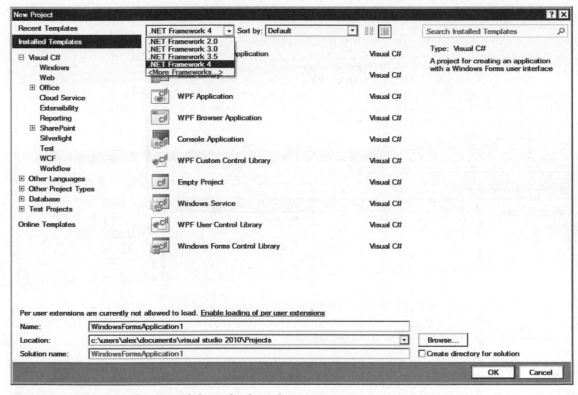

Figure 2-2. *Select your framework from the drop-down menu.*

In VS2010 the Toolbox and Properties windows are filtered to display functionality available in the targeted framework version. Previously, some properties that were not available in the targeted framework would still be exposed. VS2010 will even try to display the correct version of third-party components for the targeting framework version.

VS2010 emulates what is available in previous framework versions through reference assemblies. These assemblies contain metadata that describes functionality available in previous versions. VS2010 itself uses the .NET 4 framework, so when adding multitargeting support the team decided against running a previous framework version inside the same process. When your application is compiled to 100 percent guarantee application compatibility, previous compiler versions are used.

■**TIP** You may be interested in the ability to specify that your application should be run using a specific version of the framework. I discuss this in Chapter 3.

Intellisense

Intellisense will now perform partial string matching. For example, if you were to type the word SB, Visual Studio would display both the `StringBuilder` and `UrlBuilder` options (as shown in Figure 2-3). This can be very useful if you cannot remember the exact property or type name.

Intellisense also supports lookups based on capitalization. Because all .NET types are pascal-cased, you can simply enter just the uppercase letters of the type. For example, SB would return the type `StringBuilder`, among others with the same pascal-casing. Intellisense performance has also been improved particularly for JavaScript libraries.

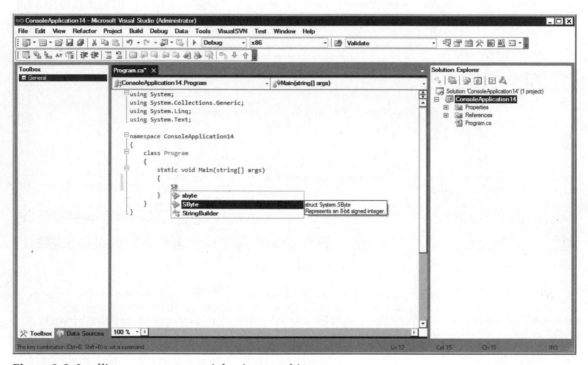

Figure 2-3. *Intellisense supports partial string matching.*

Add References

The add references functionality was previously slower than Mr. Slow in a slow town on a slow day while walking backward. Add reference in VS2010, however, is pretty quick. When the Add Reference dialogue first displays, the focus is set to the Projects tab while separate threads load up the .NET and COM tabs.

Web Development (Code-Optimized Profile)

VS2010 contains some environment profiles such as the Web Development (code-optimized profile), shown in Figure 2-4. This profile is optimized for code and hides design features. Code-optimized profile can be selected when you first load Visual Studio or by selecting Tools ➤ Import and Export Settings.

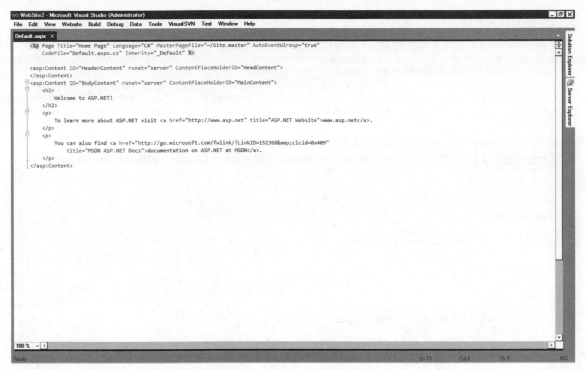

Figure 2-4. *VS2010 contains environmental profiles, such as the Web Development (code-optimized) profile.*

Zoom

As much of the IDE is written in WPF, it was easy for Microsoft to add functionality such as the ability to zoom into the code editor (as shown in Figure 2-5). To zoom into the code editor window, simply press Ctrl and use the mouse wheel to increase and decrease zoom level. You could utilize this feature in presentations/code reviews or to zoom out to help you navigate a lengthy piece of code.

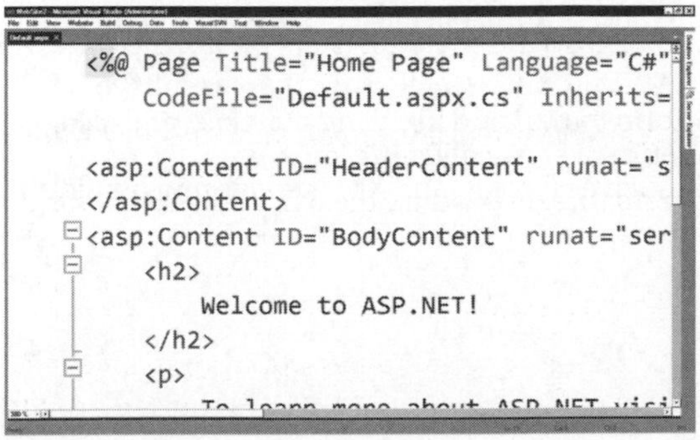

Figure 2-5. *VS2010 includes the ability to zoom into the code editor window.*

Highlight References

Highlight References allows you to quickly navigate through different instances of the same method call within a file. For example, if you want to navigate through all calls to the DoSomething method, then click once anywhere on the DoSomething method text (note you don't have to highlight the text) and you will find the IDE marks all the other DoSomething calls in the same file with a light grey background, as shown in Figure 2-6. You can then navigate to the next DoSomething method by pressing Ctrl + Shift + Down or Ctrl + Shift + Up to return to the previous instance.

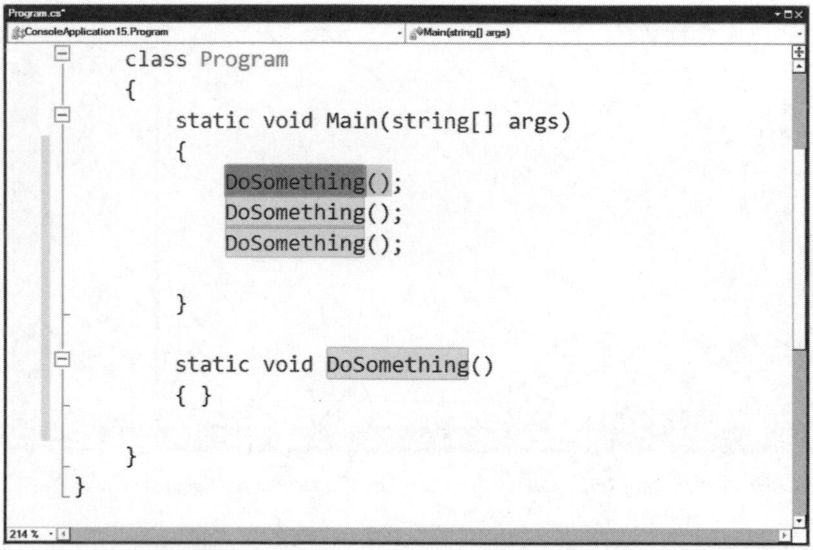

Figure 2-6. *Highlight References allows you to quickly move between calls to the same method.*

Navigate To

Sometimes if you need to find a specific piece of code it can be much quicker to use the search functionality rather than trawl through Solution Explorer. VS2010 improves on the existing "search" and "search in files" functionality with the Navigate To window.

To bring up the Navigate To window, simply press Ctrl and comma or select Navigate To on the Edit menu. You can then enter a phrase you want to search for in your solution, and Navigate To will immediately filter results as you type, as shown in Figure 2-7. You can then click on these results to be taken directly to the results location. Navigate To will perform partial and in-string matches, and also supports pascal-casing searches (for example, BT would return a class called BigTiger).

Navigate To supports all commonly used types of file such as C#, VB, and XML, and is much quicker and easier to navigate than previous search methods.

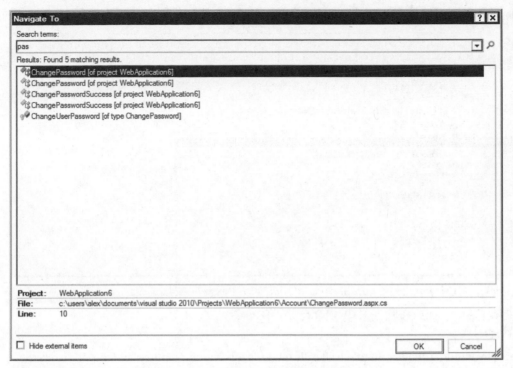

Figure 2-7. Search files in your project with Navigate To Window.

Box Selection

Box Selection is one of my favorite new features. It allows you to quickly perform the same change on many lines of code. To use box selection, place the cursor where you want to make the change, and then hold down Shift + Alt in combination with the arrow keys to create a "box" where the change will be applied. Finally, enter your change and it will be applied to all the selected lines.

Box selection could, for example, be used to refactor a number of class variables' access levels from `public` to `private` in one edit, as shown in Figure 2-8.

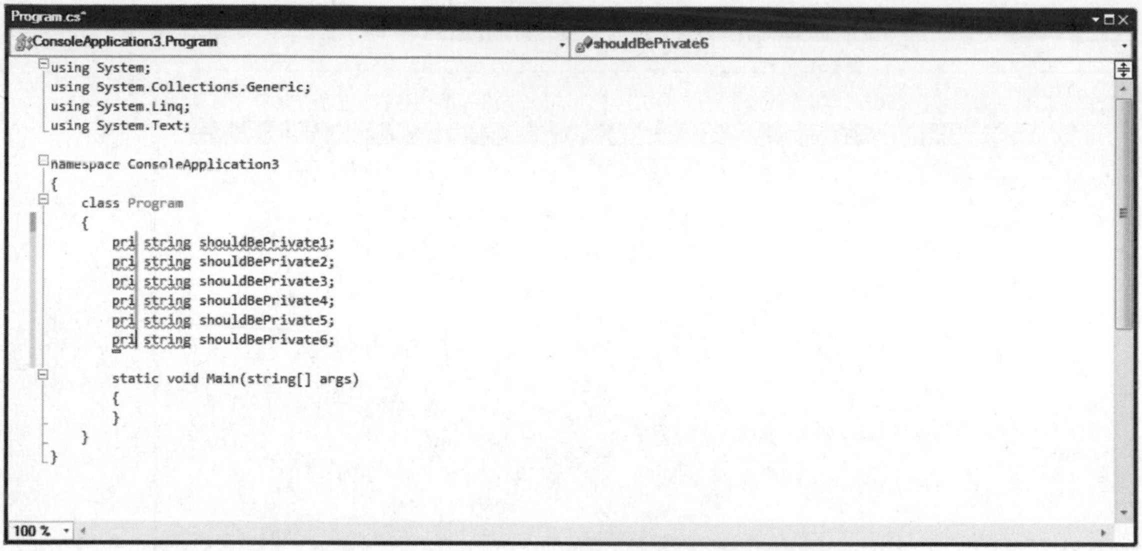

```
Program.cs*                                                                    ▾ □ ×
ConsoleApplication3.Program                              ▾   shouldBePrivate6          ▾
  using System;                                                                      ⊞
  using System.Collections.Generic;
  using System.Linq;
  using System.Text;

  namespace ConsoleApplication3
  {
      class Program
      {
          pri string shouldBePrivate1;
          pri string shouldBePrivate2;
          pri string shouldBePrivate3;
          pri string shouldBePrivate4;
          pri string shouldBePrivate5;
          pri string shouldBePrivate6;

          static void Main(string[] args)
          {
          }
      }
  }

 100 %  ▾
```

Figure 2-8. *Quickly make changes to multiple lines of code with Box Selection.*

Call Hierarchy

The Call Hierarchy window allows you to see all calls made to a particular method and all calls from the method. Call hierarchy is recursive. To open the Call Hierarchy window, right-click on a method, property, or constructor, and select View Call Hierarchy. The Call Hierarchy window will then open, displaying calls to and from the method (see Figure 2-9). Note that you can filter the Call Hierarchy window by solution, project, and document.

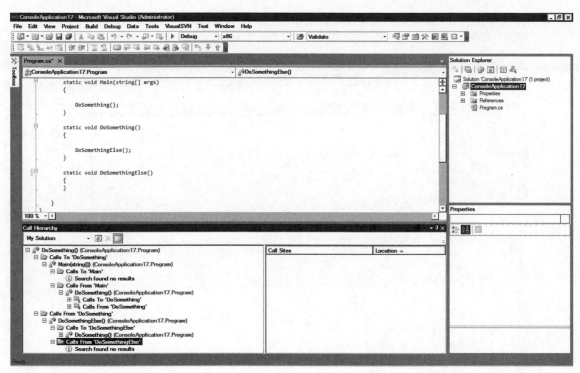

Figure 2-9. *See calls made to and from a particular method with the Call Hierarchy window.*

Code Generation

A great feature in VS2008 is that you can enter a new method name that doesn't exist and have the IDE create a stub of it for you (to do this enter a method name that doesn't exist, press Ctrl + . and select the Generate method stub option). VS2010 expands on this functionality and allows you to create classes, structs, interfaces, and enums in a similar manner. This is a great feature when you are starting the development of an application and particularly suitable for a TDD style of development. Let's try this out now.

1. Create a new console application

2. Enter the following code:

    ```
    Zebra MyZebra = new Zebra();
    ```

3. Either click the smart tag (fiddly) beneath the Z in zebra or press Ctrl + . (much better) to bring up the menu (as shown in Figure 2-10).

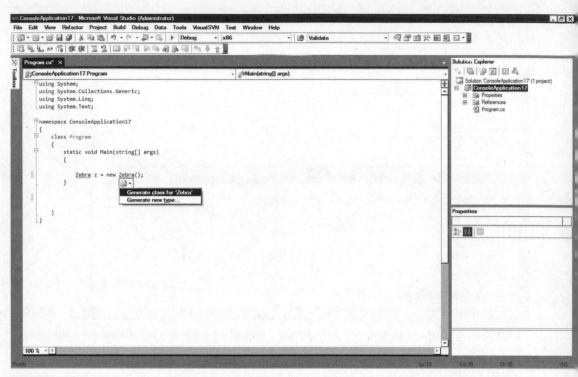

Figure 2-10. *There are new options available in VS2010 for generating classes and method stubs.*

4. You now you have the choice of creating a Zebra class in a separate file (Zebra.cs) by selecting "Generate class" or you can select "Generate new type" to bring up an options screen that allows greater control of generated type. In this example please select "Generate new type."

5. The Generate New Type screen (shown in Figure 2-11) will appear, allowing you to specify a number of options such as access level, file name, item to create, and so on. Select Class on the Kind drop-down menu and change the access level to Internal.

Figure 2-11. *Generate New Type allows you greater control over what is created.*

Visual Studio will then generate a new Zebra internal class.

Consume First Mode

Intellisense is a great feature, but can sometimes get in your way. For example, imagine an application where you have a class called `TigerCage` and you now want to create a `Tiger` class. If you want to use VS2010's new class generation features and start typing `Tiger` then Visual Studio's Intellisense will jump in and smugly change your code to `TigerCage`.

To resolve this issue Intellisense now operates in two modes: default and consume first mode. Consume-first mode prevents Intellisense from automatically completing a type or member that has not yet been defined. To switch to consume first mode press Ctrl+Alt+Space. You can enter Ctrl + Alt + Space again to switch back to the default mode.

■**NOTE** Intellisense is now programmed to switch automatically to consume first mode in common cases where it is known to be problematic.

Breakpoints

VS2010 allows you to export/import and label breakpoints. You can use this feature to share a collection of breakpoints with a colleague or quickly return to a previous debugging setup. Note that the exported file holds the breakpoint location by line number, so if you should modify your code and import breakpoints they will no longer be positioned correctly.

Individual breakpoints can be exported by right-clicking on them and then selecting the Export option. Or you can export all breakpoints (or those matching a specific search criteria) by opening the Breakpoints window (Debug➤Windows➤Breakpoints) and selecting the "Export all breakpoints" option. Breakpoints can be imported in the Breakpoints window.

VS2010 allows you to apply a label to a breakpoint, as shown in Figure 2-12. This may be useful to associate it with a particular issue or with grouping in the Breakpoints window. To label a breakpoint, right-click on one and select the Edit labels option. VS2010 will then give you the option of entering a new label for the breakpoint or reusing an existing one.

Figure 2-12. *Labelling a breakpoint*

Toolbox

If you start typing a letter, the toolbox will jump to items containing the letter typed. You can also tab through to the next item that matches.

Code Snippets

Previous versions of Visual Studio contained a feature called snippets that allowed you to save blocks of code for later insertion, saving you on the retyping (or remembering) them. VS2010 contains a number of new snippets (in particular for ASP.NET) and allows you to easily create your own. Although you can create your own snippets in VS2008, it wasn't an easy process without the use of third-party applications (e.g. Snippet Editor `http://msmvps.com/blogs/bill/archive/2007/11/06/snippet-editor-2008-release.aspx`).

This changes, however, in VS2010 and is now very easy.

- `Expansion` (the snippet is inserted at the cursor)

- `SurroundsWith` (wraps around existing code)

Let's take a look at this now and create a code file header snippet:

1. Add a new XML file to your project called `verHeader.snippet` (snippets always have the extension `.snippet`).

2. Right-click on the editor window and select Insert Snippet➤Snippet. VS2010 will then create a basic XML snippet template.

In this example we will create an expansion snippet so we need to remove the tag that reads:

`<snippetType>SurroundsWith</snippetType>`

3. Modify the `Title` tag to read "Code File Header."

4. Modify the `Author` tag to your name.

5. Modify the `Shortcut` tag (this is the trigger word that activates the snippet) to "codehead"

6. Enter a description for the snippet, such as "Adds a header to a code file"

7. Snippets can be created for different languages (such as VB & XML), but in this example we are creating a C# snippet. Change the `Language` attribute of the Code tag so it reads as follows:

```
<Code Language="CSharp">
```

8. We now need to alter the `Literal` section. Literals allow you to define editable values that are inserted into your snippet. We want the user to enter his or her own name in the author section, so change the `ID` value to `Author` and enter your name in as the `Default` tag.

9. The Code section contains what will be added when the snippet is inserted. Modify it to it looks like the following:

```
<Code Language="CSharp">
    <![CDATA[
    **********************************
    Author: $Author$
    Date:
    Version:
    Purpose:
    **********************************
    ]]>
    </Code>
```

Your finished snippet should end up looking like below:

```
<CodeSnippet Format="1.0.0"
xmlns="http://schemas.microsoft.com/VisualStudio/2005/CodeSnippet">
  <Header>
<Title>Code File Header</Title>
    <Author>Alex Mackey</Author>
    <Shortcut>codehead</Shortcut>
    <Description>Adds a header to a code file</Description>
    <SnippetTypes>
      <SnippetType>Expansion</SnippetType>
    </SnippetTypes>
  </Header>
```

```
<Snippet>
  <Declarations>
    <Literal>
      <ID>Author</ID>
      <Default>Alex Mackey</Default>
    </Literal>
  </Declarations>
  <Code Language="CSharp">
    <![CDATA[
    ********************************
    Author: $Author$
    Date:
    Version:
    Purpose:
    ********************************
    ]]>
  </Code>
</Snippet>
</CodeSnippet>
```

Loading the Snippet into Visual Studio

Before we can use our snippet, we need to load it into Visual Studio. Because snippets are pretty useful, you will probably want to create more than one. Follow these steps to create a new directory somewhere on your computer called MySnippets.

1. Copy the verHeader.snippet file in your solution to the snippets directory you just created.

2. On the main menu, go to Tools, then Code Snippets Manager and you should see a screen similar to Figure 2-13.

3. Select Import

4. Select the snippet you saved earlier

5. Click OK

6. Visual Studio will then confirm you want to place the snippet in My Code Snippets directory

That's it your snippet is ready to use. You can now use this snippet by typing "codehead."

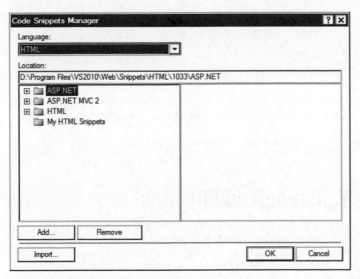

Figure 2-13. *Code Snippets Manager screen*

■**TIP** You can avoid the previous installation steps and have Visual Studio automatically pick up the snippet by saving it to VS2010's code snippets directory. Default location`C:\Users\<Username>\Documents\Visual Studio 10\Code Snippets\`. You will not even have to restart VS.

Using Snippets

There are a number of ways to add snippets to your code. No doubt the quickest way is to use the trigger word (such as *textbox* in an ASP.NET app), but sometimes you may not know the trigger word to use. In that case you can pick the word from the snippet dialogue.

To open the snippet dialogue, right-click on the editor, Select Insert Snippet, and you can then choose from either the ASP.NET or HTML snippets. You can also press Ctrl + K and then Ctrl + X to bring up the Insert Snippet enhancement, which allows you to navigate through them using the keyboard.

Creating Custom Start Pages

VS2010 allows you to customize the start page that is displayed when the IDE first loads. You could use this feature to display items such as current bugs, last night's build status, and so on. On my Windows 7 machine, this directory is held at the following path: `C:\Users\alex\Documents\Visual Studio 10\StartPages`.

1. Open the project StartPage.csproj and note how StartPage.xaml is a standard XAML page with some Visual Studio-specific controls to display items such as recently opened projects.

2. Perform a simple modification, such as altering some of the text content.

3. Save the file with a new file name, such as CustomStartPage.xaml, in the same directory.

Before you can use your new start page, you have to select it in Visual Studio options. Go into Tools➤Options then select the Startup node. Select the new custom start page from the Custom Start Page drop-down menu.

Close Visual Studio and reopen it. Your new start page should now appear the next time Visual Studio is loaded.

T4 (Text Template Transformation Toolkit) Files

A T4 template is a code-generation language that has been around since VS2005. You should be aware of them, as they are used in areas such as Entity Framework and MVC and can be useful for your own development. To see T4 templates in action, create a file with the extension .tt, add some text content, save the file, and note how Visual Studio will generate a code file from the template. You can apply complex logic using T4 templating language to change the output that is generated depending on various conditions.

T4 templates in VS2010 are compiled when they are saved (preprocessed). This means that they are another type that can be instantiated.

Scott Hanselman has some great and information on this area so please refer to the following article:

www.hanselman.com/blog/T4TextTemplateTransformationToolkitCodeGenerationBestKeptVisualStudio Secret.aspx.

T4 templates don't have Intellisense so your best bet is to download the Tangible T4 plugin:

http://visualstudiogallery.msdn.microsoft.com/en-us/60297607-5fd4-4da4-97e1-3715e90c1a23.

For more see:

http://code.msdn.microsoft.com/DslTools/Wiki/View.aspx?title=What%27s%20new

http://karlshifflett.wordpress.com/2009/10/30/t4-preprocessed-text-templates-in-visual-studio-2010/

VS2010 Premium and Ultimate

I will only be covering Professional edition in this book, but I want to make you aware of a couple of fantastic features available in more expensive versions.

Generate Sequence Diagram

Generate sequence diagram creates a diagram of a methods calls. To use generate sequence diagram, simply right-click on a function and select Generate Sequence Diagram.

Historical Debugging (Team System Edition Only)

Visual Studio Team edition contains a very cool feature called Historical Debugging. Ian Who, a developer on the profiler team, says:

> *The Historical Debugger plays a role similar to that of a black box in a plane. We keep track of important points in your programs execution and allow you to play back what happened at those points at a later time.*

For more information please refer to:

```
http://blogs.msdn.com/ianhu/archive/2009/05/13/historical-debugging-in-visual-studio-team-
system-2010.aspx
```

Static Analysis of Code Contracts

Code contracts (which I cover in Chapter 3) allow you to express constraints within code that can be analyzed at compile time to check if your code violates them. Although code contracts are present in all versions of Visual Studio, only Premium and Ultimate provide static analysis.

Customization of IDE

VS2010 allows you to create much more advanced customizations than changing the start page or creating snippets. VS2010 has been written from the ground up for extensibility and customization.

- Screens have been rewritten in WPF and managed code.
- The IDE API has been refactored for easier use.
- The IDE API is fully documented.
- New immutable text snapshots make it easier to obtain accurate snapshot of text editor.

Many areas of the IDE can be overridden by creating a MEF component (I will talk about MEF shortly).

So, what can you customize? VS2010 allows you to customize the following areas, among other things:

- Margins and scrollbars
- Tags
- Adornments (items painted on the editor surface)
- Mouse processors
- Drop handlers
- Options
- Intellisense and debugger

Before you can perform any of these customizations, however, you will first need to download and install the Visual Studio SDK.

Extensions in VS2010 make heavy use of a new technology called MEF. Before we create any customizations we need to understand a bit about MEF.

MEF (Managed Extensibility Framework)

MEF is a new framework for creating customizable applications that can be used by any .NET-compatible language. Glenn Block (PM for the new Managed Extensibility Framework in .NET 4.0) says:

> *Quite simply, MEF makes building extensible apps, libraries and frameworks easy. It shares some common characteristics of other frameworks out there, but it also addresses a whole new set of problems that arise in building extremely large scalable extensible systems.*

```
http://blogs.msdn.com/gblock/archive/2008/09/26/what-is-the-managed-extensibility-
framework.aspx
```

Let's say you have created a Tetris application and want to allow users to extend it by creating their own shapes of bricks. MEF enables you to do this by defining a brick interface and then dynamically loading and resolving the created extensions.

When creating a MEF application, take the following steps:

1. Define areas of the application that can be extended and decorate them with the [Import] attribute.

2. Determine a contract/interface that defines what your extensions must do/be (this could be a simple as they must of String).

3. Create an extension that meets these requirements and decorate it with the [Export] attribute.

4. Modify your application to load these extensions.

Why Use MEF?

Using MEF has the following advantages:

- Microsoft hopes that MEF will become the preferred <u>standard</u> method of creating extensions. By utilizing a standard plug-in model, your extensions could be used in many applications

- MEF provides a number of flexible ways to load your extensions.

- Extensions can contain metadata to provide further information about their capabilities. For example, you may only want to load extensions that can communicate securely.

- MEF is open source and works on VS2008 (www.codeplex.com/MEF).

BUT COULDN'T I ACCOMPLISH THIS WITH REFLECTION/DEPENDENCY INJECTION/IOC CONTAINERS/VOODOO?

There is overlap in the functionality provided by the above technologies and MEF. MEF and IOC do have some overlap, and many would classify MEF as an IOC. MEF's primary purpose is, however, creating extensible applications through discovery and composition, whereas IOC containers are generally more focused on providing an abstraction for testing purposes. It's not a discussion I want to get into, but Oren does, so please refer to: http://ayende.com/Blog/archive/2008/09/25/the-managed-extensibility-framework.aspx.

Hello MEF

In this sample application you will create two extensions that print out a message. You will then load them both into an IEnumerable<string> variable called Message before iterating through them and printing out the messages.

Create a new console project and call it Chapter2.HelloMEF.

1. Add a reference to System.ComponentModel.Composition.

2. Add a new class called MEFTest.

3. Add the following using statements to the class:

    ```
    using System.ComponentModel.Composition;
    using System.ComponentModel.Composition.Hosting;
    using System.Reflection;
    ```

5. Modify MEFTest class code to the following (note how we decorate the Message property with the [Import] attribute):

    ```
    public class MEFTest
    {
        [Import]
        public string Message { get; set; }

        public void HelloMEF()
        {
            CompositionContainer container = new CompositionContainer();
            CompositionBatch batch = new CompositionBatch();
            batch.AddPart(new Extension1());
            batch.AddPart(this);
            container.Compose(batch);

            Console.WriteLine(Message);

            Console.ReadKey();
        }
    }
    ```

We now need to create the extensions to load so create a new class called Extension1.

4. Add the following using statement:

```
using System.ComponentModel.Composition;
```

5. Amend Extension1.cs to the following:

```
public class Extension1
{
    [Export]
    public string Message
    {
        get
        {
            return "I am extension 1";
        }
    }
}
```

6. Finally open Program.cs and add the following code:

```
static void Main(string[] args)
{
    MEFTest MEFTest = new MEFTest();
    MEFTest.HelloMEF();
}
```

7. Press F5 to run the application, and you should see that both extensions are loaded and the Message property printed out, as Figure 2-14 shows.

Figure 2-14. *Output from HelloMEF application*

Congratulations you have created your first MEF application.

How Did This Example Work?

You started off by telling MEF that your Message property can be extended by marking it with the [Import] attribute. The [Import] attribute means "I can be extended" to MEF:

```
[Import]
public string Message { get; set; }
```

You then created an extension class and added the [Export] attribute. [Export] tells MEF "I am an extension":

```
class extension1
{
    [Export]
    public string Message
    {
        get
        {
            return "I am extension 1";
        }
    }
}
```

You then created a container (containers resolve MEF extensions when they are requested) to hold the extensions and added your extension classes to it using a CompositionBatch:

```
CompositionContainer container = new CompositionContainer();
CompositionBatch batch = new CompositionBatch();
batch.AddPart(new extension1());
batch.AddPart(this);
```

The Compose method was then called which caused MEF to load our extensions into the Message property.

```
container.Compose(batch);
```

MEF then loaded extensions into the Messages property decorated with the [Export] attribute that matched the contract. Finally, you printed out the message to the screen. In this example, you only loaded extensions contained within the project itself, which isn't too useful. Luckily MEF allows you to load extensions declared outside the project.

MEF Catalogs

MEF uses a concept called catalogs to contain extensions. Catalogs come in three different flavors:

- Assembly (extensions are contained in a .net assembly)

- Directory (extensions are in a physical directory)

- Aggregate (a catalog type that contains both assembly and directory extensions)

In this example you will use a directory catalogue to load an extension defined outside the main project. Directory catalogs will scan the target directory for compatible extensions when first created. You can rescan the directory by calling the Refresh method.

1. It is a good idea to declare MEF interfaces in a separate project to avoid circular reference issues and facilitate reuse so open the existing Chapter2.HelloMEF project and add a new class library project called Chapter2.MEFInterfaces.

2. Inside this project, create an interface called ILogger.

3. Replace the existing code in ILogger.cs with the following code:

```
using System;
using System.Collections.Generic;
using System.Linq;
using System.Text;

namespace Chapter2.MEFInterfaces
{
    public interface ILogger
    {
        string WriteToLog(string Message);
    }

}
```

4. In the Chapter2.HelloMEF project, add a reference to the Chapter2.MEFInterfaces project.

5. In the Chapter2.HelloMEF project, create a class called MoreUsefulMEF and enter the following code:

```
using System;
using System.Collections.Generic;
using System.Linq;
using System.Text;
using System.ComponentModel.Composition;
using System.ComponentModel.Composition.Hosting;
using System.Reflection;
using System.IO;
```

```
namespace Chapter2.HelloMEF
{
    class MoreUsefulMEF
    {
        [Import]
        private Chapter2.MEFInterfaces.ILogger Logger;

        public void TestLoggers()
        {
            CompositionContainer container;
            DirectoryCatalog directoryCatalog =
              new DirectoryCatalog(
                (Path.GetDirectoryName(Assembly.GetExecutingAssembly().Location))
              );

            container = new CompositionContainer(directoryCatalog);
            CompositionBatch batch = new CompositionBatch();
            batch.AddPart(this);
            container.Compose(batch);
            Console.Write(Logger.WriteToLog("test"));
            Console.ReadKey();
        }
    }
}
```

6.   Open `Program.cs` and amend the `Main` method to the following:

```
MoreUsefulMEF MoreUsefulMEF = new MoreUsefulMEF();
MoreUsefulMEF.TestLoggers();
```

You will now create a logging extension so add a new class library project to the solution called `Chapter2.EmailLogger`.

7.   Add a reference to the `Chapter2.MEFInterfaces` project.

8.   Add a reference to `System.ComponentModel.Composition`.

9.   Add a new class called `EmailLogger`.

10. Amend the code to the following:

```
using System;
using System.Collections.Generic;
using System.Linq;
using System.Text;
using System.ComponentModel.Composition;
```

```
namespace Chapter2.EmailLogger
{
    [Export(typeof(Chapter2.MEFInterfaces.ILogger))]
    public class EmailLogger : MEFInterfaces.ILogger
    {
        public string WriteToLog(string Message)
        {
            //Simulate email logging
            return "Email Logger Called";
        }
    }

}
```

11. When you use a directory catalog to load MEF components, you can either compile the Chapter2.EmailLogger project and copy the built assembly to Chapter2.HelloMEF's bin folder, or add a project reference in Chapter2.HelloMEF to the Chapter2.EmailLogger project.

Once you have done this press F5 to run the HelloMEF project. The Email Logger extension should then be loaded and "Email Logger Called" output to the screen.

Metadata

An important feature of MEF is that you can provide additional information about an extension's capabilities with metadata. MEF can then utilize this information to determine the most appropriate extension to load and query its capabilities. For example in the previous logging example you might specify whether the logging method is secure or not and then in high security environments only load extensions that communicated securely. Meta data can be defined at a class or method level.

To add metadata to a class use the [PartMetaData] attribute to your class:

```
[PartMetadata("secure", "false")]
[Export(typeof(Chapter2.MEFInterfaces.ILogger))]
public class EmailLogger : MEFInterfaces.ILogger
{..}
```

You can add metadata to an individual method with the [ExportMetadata] attribute:

```
[ExportMetadata("timeout", "5000")]
public string WriteToLog(string Message)
{..}
```

Metadata can then be retrieved using a part's Metadata property. The following code demonstrates retrieving metadata from a directory catalog:

```
CompositionContainer container;
DirectoryCatalog directoryCatalog =
  new DirectoryCatalog((Path.GetDirectoryName(Assembly.GetExecutingAssembly().Location)));
```

```
foreach (var Part in directoryCatalog.Parts)
{
        Console.WriteLine(Part.Metadata["secure"]);
}
```

Note that querying a method's metadata is slightly different and that you must instead use the `Part.ExportDefinitions` property.

What's This All Got to Do with Visual Studio Extensibility?

Visual Studio utilizes MEF in an almost identical way to the previous examples when it loads Visual Studio extensions. When Visual Studio first loads, it examines the extensions directory and loads available extensions. Let's now look into how these extensions are created.

Visual Studio Extensibility

After you install the Visual Studio customization SDK, a number of new extensibility projects are available for you to create. These projects are templates that demonstrate how to perform various "hello world" type customizations that you can then build on. Figure 2-15 shows these new project types.

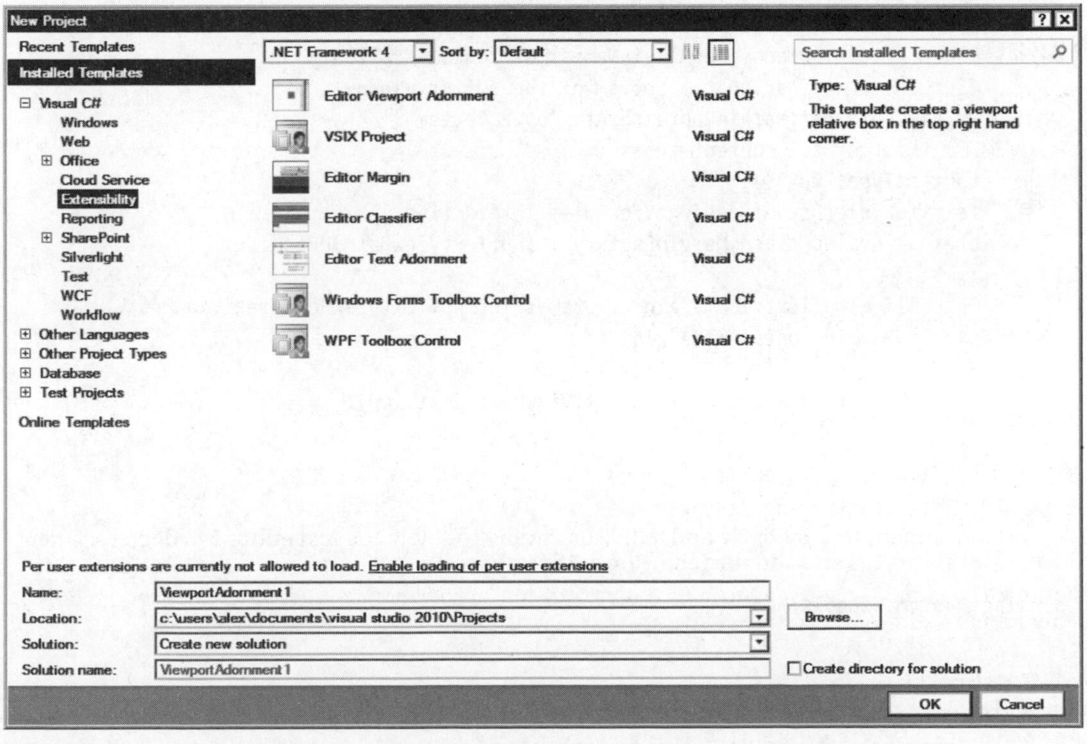

Figure 2-15. *New extensibility projects are available after installing customization SDK.*

The following extensibility projects are available:

- VSIX Project (empty extension that contains just the minimum references needed and a manifest file that describes the extension)

- Editor Margin (creates a green box down the bottom of code editor frame)

- Editor Classifier (formats types of text a blue color)

- Editor Text Adornment (template highlights all instances of the letter 'a')

- Editor Viewport Adornment (template creates a purple box in the top right corner of IDE) and a Windows Forms toolbox control

Let's take a look at the Editor Margin extensibility project.

Editor Margin

Open up Visual Studio and create a new Editor Margin project called Chapter2.EditorMargin.

1. Open MarginFactory.cs and note how it utilizes the MEF [Export] attribute (the other attributes contain various bits of metadata utilized by the IDE):

    ```
    [Export(typeof(IWpfTextViewMarginProvider))]
        [Name("GreenBar")]
        //Ensure that the margin occurs below the horizontal scrollbar
        [Order(After = PredefinedMarginNames.HorizontalScrollBar)]
        //Set the container to the bottom of the editor window
        [MarginContainer(MarginContainerAttribute.Bottom)]
        //Do this for all content types
        [ContentType("text")]
        [TextViewRole(PredefinedTextViewRoles.Interactive)]
        internal sealed class MarginFactory : IWpfTextViewMarginProvider
        {
            public IWpfTextViewMargin CreateMargin(IWpfTextViewHost textViewHost,
    IWpfTextViewMargin containerMargin)
            {
                return new GreenMargin(textViewHost.TextView);
            }
        }
    ```

2. Let's do something a bit crazy and tell Visual Studio to rotate the text editor 245 degrees. Open MarginFactory.cs and add the following using statement:

    ```
    using System.Windows.Media;
    ```

34

3. Inside the CreateMargin constructor above the line that reads return new GreenMargin(textViewHost.TextView); add the following code:

```
textViewHost.TextView.VisualElement.LayoutTransform = new RotateTransform(245);
```

4. Build and run this project and the IDE will launch a special test instance containing your extension (this may take a bit of time so be patient).

5. Once the test instance has loaded, create a new console project. Voila! As you can see, the text editor has been rotated and a green Hello world box created at the base of the editor (Figure 2-16).

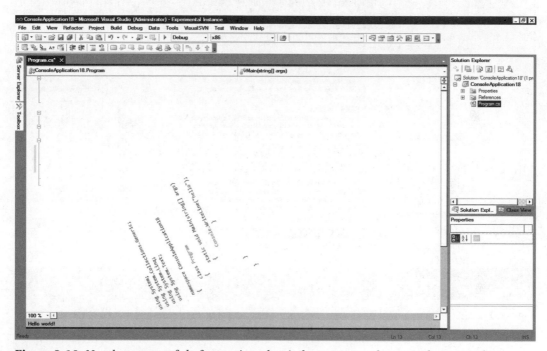

Figure 2-16. *Not the most useful of extensions, but it demonstrates the control you now have.*

A useful extension? No, but it demonstrates just how much control you have, and note how the text editor still works just as you would expect with syntax checking, intellisense, and so on (although the scroll bars behave a little strangely).

Distributing Extensions

So you have just created your very useful rotate text editor extension and want to share it with your friends/victims. When extensions are compiled they are built as .vsix files that can be installed by double-clicking them or copying them to the extensions directory at C:\Program Files\Microsoft Visual Studio 10.0\Common7\IDE\Extensions.

Extension Gallery

The Extension Gallery (see Figure 2-17) allows you to download a number of additions from new project templates to IDE customizations. A number of extensions for VS2010 are available already and some with source code. To open the extension gallery, select Extension Manager on the Tools menu and then the Online Gallery option.

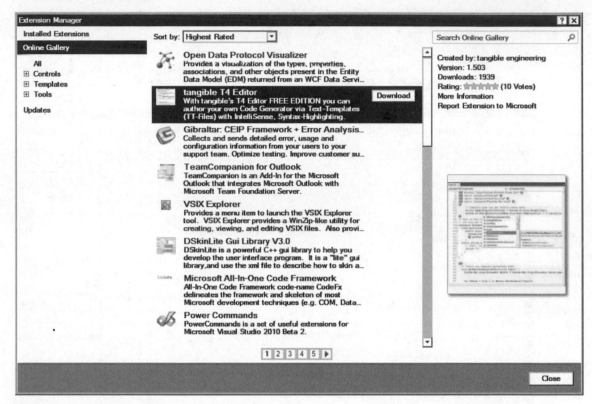

Figure 2-17. *Extension Gallery*

WHAT ABOUT EXISTING EXTENSIONS CREATED WITH PREVIOUS API?

Microsoft say that 80%+ of existing IDE customization will be supported through the use of shims (code that maps the old API methods to the new). It is important to note however that they plan to remove these shims in the next version of Visual Studio after VS2010.

Visual Studio Shell

It is worth noting that from VS2008 Microsoft opened up the ability to make use of the IDE for your own applications. This is called the Visual Studio Shell. A popular project using the Visual Studio Shell is the add-on studio for the online game World of Warcraft (http://addonstudio.codeplex.com).

For more information on the Visual Studio Shell please refer to: http://msdn.microsoft.com/en-us/vsx2008/products/bb933751.aspx.

Dotfuscator Changes

Dotfuscator is a post-build .NET hardening and instrumentation platform for protecting, measuring and managing .NET applications. Traditionally a reduced functionality version of Dotfuscator has been bundled with previous releases of Visual Studio and VS2010 is no exception. However, the new version of Dotfuscator Software Services CE contains Runtime Intelligence functionality and some great added features including:

- Tamper defense (detect modification of application)

- Application expiration (such as expire an application after 30 day trial period)

- Session and feature usage tracking (allows you to track what the user was actually doing within your application)

- Ability to send tamper and tracking usage to an end point of your choice for later analysis

To access Dotfuscator functionality within Visual Studio on the main menu, go to Tools and select Dotfuscator Software Services. For more information on Dotfuscator please refer to http://www.preemptive.com/dotfuscator.html and for more information on Runtime Intelligence see: http://en.wikipedia.org/wiki/Runtime_Intelligence.

Conclusion

Many developers were concerned at the prospect of Visual Studio's IDE being built using WPF, specifically that it would be slow and clunky. Microsoft has without a doubt demonstrated the flexibility and power of WPF and proved these doubters wrong! VS2010 has some great productivity enhancements in this release and with the improved multitargeting support even if you are not ready to move your code base to .NET 4 you can make use of many of these features today.

CHAPTER 3

■ ■ ■

Language and Dynamic Changes

There are some welcome changes to C# and VB.NET, and major enhancements to the Common Language Runtime(CLR) and Base Class Library (BCL) in .NET 4.0. I have separated these changes into two chapters:language (this chapter) and CLR and BCL (Chapter 4), although there is of course some overlap.

In this chapter I will be covering the following:

- Future co-evolution of VB and C#

- Changes to C# and VB

- Improved COM interoperability

- Variance

- Dynamic code

- F#

Future Co-evolution of VB and C#

All .NET languages compile to the same IL code, so there is really no reason a feature should be present in one language and not another. Traditionally, C# got most of the new features, but not anymore. Microsoft has stated that it will now aim to ensure that VB and C# contain the same functionality. VB.NET and C# will be kept in sync like an elastic band: when a new feature is introduced in one language, it will be brought into the other language in the next release pinging the two into line. There will of course continue to be style differences between the languages, so don't expect to see semi-colons appearing in VB because that would be very silly.

This release tries to sync the two languages, fixes an old constraint, and introduces some great dynamic functionality. No longer will VB.NET developers miss out on anonymous methods and C# developers will now benefit from named and optional parameters.

C# Enhancements

C# 2010 introduces two useful features that have been present in VB for a long time: optional and named parameters (technically two separate features but often found together).

Named and Optional Parameters

Named parameters allow you to pass parameters into a function in any order and are near essential when using C#'s other new feature: optional parameters. To use a named parameter, simply specify the parameter name followed by a colon and then the value you are passing into a function. The following code illustrates passing the value 1 to a method's Copies parameter, COLOR to the ColorMode parameter, and readme.txt to DocumentName:

```
Print(Copies:1,ColorMode:"COLOR",DocumentName:"readme.txt");

static void Print(string ColorMode, string DocumentName, int Copies)
{...}
```

Optional parameters are created in C# by specifying a default value and must appear after required parameters:

```
static void Print(int Copies=1, string ColorMode="Color", string DocumentName="") {...}
```

This method can then be called in a multitude of ways, some of which are shown here:

```
Print(1);
Print(1, "Color");
Print(1, "Color", "My doc");
Print(Copies: 1);
Print(ColorMode: "Color");
Print(DocumentName: "myDoc.txt");
Print(Copies: 1, ColorMode: "Color");
Print(Copies: 1, ColorMode: "Color",  DocumentName: "myDoc.txt");
```

Optional parameters can make your code more readable and easier to maintain, and can reduce the amount of typing you have to do. They also can make it easier to work with COM objects (see the following section). For example, if we were creating a Print() method that accepts a number of different parameters, we no longer have to overload it with a number of methods, such as:

```
public void Print(string DocumentName)
{
    Print(DocumentName, 1, "COLOR");
}

public void Print(string DocumentName, int Copies)
{
    Print(DocumentName, Copies, "COLOR");
}
public void Print(string DocumentName, int Copies, string ColorMode)
{}
```

Optional parameters allow us to refine this as:

```
public void Print(string DocumentName, int Copies=1, string ColorMode="COLOR")
{...}
```

Rules (Non-Optional)

There some rules you need to be aware of when working with named parameters.

- Non-optional parameters must be declared first.

- Non-optional parameters must still be specified when you call a method.

- Parameters are evaluated in the order they are declared.

- If two function signatures are equally valid for your input, then the one with no optional values is given precedence.

VB.NET Changes

Although in this book I am mainly covering C#, for completeness I will cover changes to VB.NET as well.

Line Continuation

One of the aspects of VB.NET I really hated was the line continuation character (an underscore with a space before it). This particularly annoyed me when writing LINQ queries, because it made them less readable and the underscore character is kind of awkward to type (okay that's not *that* big an issue):

```
Dim numbers() As Integer = {1, 2, 3, 4, 5}
Dim query = from n in numbers _
            Select n _
            Where n>5
```

In .NET 4.0, in the majority of situations, this will no longer be necessary, as the compiler is now clever enough to work out how lines will be split. This then allows the above LINQ query to be rewritten without the underscore character:

```
Dim query = from n in numbers
            Select n
            Where n>5
```

You can of course continue to use the line continuation character in your code so you will not have to do any modifications to existing projects. You may also need to use it in the unlikely situation the compiler cannot infer where a line break exists.

Inferred Line Continuation Rules

According to Microsoft, the inferred line continuation works in the following situations:

- After an attribute.

- After a comma.

- After a dot (such as for method invocation).

- After a binary operator.

- After a LINQ query clause.

- After a (, {, or <%=.
- Before a), }, or %>.

Anonymous Method Support

Anonymous methods allow you to declare an inline function and *can* make code more readable. This can be done as follows (note how we don't need line continuation underscores):

```
Dim add = Function(x as integer, y as integer)
    Return x+y
End function
```

Auto-Implemented Properties

It is very common to need to create private variables with public accessor methods. In VB.NET you probably have written something like the following (although bet you haven't had the need to create a Tiger class):

```
Public Class Tiger
    Private _Name As String

    Property Name() As String

        Get
        Return _Name
        End Get

        Set(ByVal Name As String)
            _Name = Name
        End Set

    End Property

End Class
```

You can now use the following syntax to get the compiler to generate a private backing field like in C#:

```
Public Class AdvancedTiger
    Property Name() As String
End Class
```

The old syntax is of course still supported.

Collection Initializes/From Keyword

Adding items to a collection in VB was previously slightly tedious, and would be done with code such as the following:

```
Dim ThingsNotFoundInEmploymentAgents As New List(Of String)
ThingsNotFoundInEmploymentAgents.Add("technical knowledge")
ThingsNotFoundInEmploymentAgents.Add("honesty")
ThingsNotFoundInEmploymentAgents.Add("a reflection")
```

Collections can now be initialized using the following syntax with the new From keyword:

```
Dim TraitsNotFoundInJobAgents As New List(Of String) From {
  "technical knowledge", "honesty", "a reflection"
}
```

Array Literals

Array literals allow the compiler to infer an array. In the following example the array will be automatically typed as an integer:

```
Dim myArray = {2, 3, 5}
```

Personally I prefer to specify the type, as I think it makes your intention clearer, but the decision is now yours.

New Syntax for Creating Jagged Arrays

Until this release you could not declare jagged arrays in VB.NET easily and would have to resort to code similar to the following:

```
Dim firstSetOfValues() As Integer = {1, 2, 3}
Dim seondSetOfValues() As Integer = {4, 5}
Dim allValues()() As Integer = {firstSetOfValues, seondSetOfValues}
```

However, you can now use the following syntax:

```
Dim allValuesNewWay = {(({"1", "2", "3"}),
  ({"4", "5"})}
```

Nullable Optional Parameters

Optional parameters can now be nullable:

```
Public Sub MyFunction(ByVal Val1 As String, Optional ByVal z As Integer? = Nothing)
End Sub
```

Easier COM Interoperability

Many of the language enhancements we have looked at so far can greatly ease working with legacy code such as COM objects.

Let's look in more detail as to by adapting an example from Scott Hanselman's blog (www.hanselman.com/blog/CLRAndDLRAndBCLOhMyWhirlwindTourAroundNET4AndVisualStudio2010Beta1.aspx).

In Scott's example, the Microsoft Office API is used to open an existing text file. To see this example, add the following code and a reference to `Microsoft.Office.Interop.Word` then take a look at the intellisense for the `Open()` method (see Figure 3-1: eek!):

```
using Microsoft.Office.Interop.Word.

var WordApplication =
  new Microsoft.Office.Interop.Word.Application();WordApplication.Visible = true;
object missing = System.Reflection.Missing.Value;
object file =@"c:\test.txt";
object visible = true;
object readOnly = false;

Document aDoc = WordApplication.Documents.Open(
ref file,ref missing,ref readOnly,ref missing,
ref missing,ref missing,ref missing,ref missing,
ref missing,ref missing,ref missing,ref visible,
ref missing,ref missing,ref missing,ref missing);
```

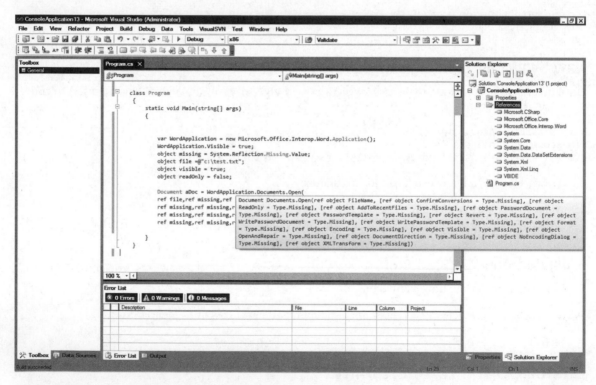

Figure 3-1. *Working with Microsoft Office Interop is fun honest*

.NET optional and named parameters make this much easier:

```
var betterWay = WordApplication.Documents.Open(file, ReadOnly: true, Visible: true);
betterWay.Activate();
```

The new dynamic functionality (which we will look at shortly) can also make your code more readable by allowing you to infer many casting operations. For example, the compiler can now work out the type of object you are using (duck typing) allowing code such as

```
((Excel.Range) excel.Cells[1, 1]).Value2 = "Excell-ent!";
```

… to be rewritten as:

```
excel.Cells[1, 1].Value = "Excell-ent!";
```

Not hugely different, but much more readable.

We're Out of PIA

Another COM-related change worth mentioning is that you no longer need PIA files. In previous versions of Visual Studio, when a COM component was referenced, Visual Studio would create an additional assembly to describe the COM DLL to the CLR (a PIA or Primary Interop Assembly).

Unfortunately, these PIA files could get pretty large as they described every method of the COM object even if you were not using them. In VS2010 to stop Visual Studio generating PIA files simply set the Embed Interop Types property to True in Solution Explorer.

Variance

Variance has changed in .NET 4.0. At the 2008 PDC Anders Hejlsberg (lead architect of C#) summarized the changes to variance as:

> *(Allowing) you to do things in your code that previously you were surprised you couldn't do.*

For those that are already comfortable with the concept of variance (stop looking so smug) here is the short version of what has changed in .NET 4.0:

- You can now mark parameters in generic interfaces and delegates with the out keyword to make them covariant, and with the in keyword to make them contravariant (In and Out in VB.NET).

- The in/out keywords have been added to some commonly used generic interface and delegate types to now enable them to support safe co- and contravariance (for example, IEnumerable<out t> and Action<in t>).

If this means nothing to you, read on. Variance is a confusing subject, and I suspect you can have a happy development career without it ever really affecting you. It is only applicable in a rare number of situations.

Don't feel bad if you have never heard of variance. I hadn't either, before researching this chapter. At WebDD09 conference in the UK, I asked who was familiar with variance in a room of 120 developers to find just 3 people put their hand up.

The Long Version for Everyone Else

To really understand variance, we need to go back in time to somewhere around the year 2000. Was the world a happier place? Who knows. But what's important for our discussions is that Java was pretty big around that time, and Microsoft wanted to lure Java developers over to C#. To ease the transition between the two languages, Microsoft brought some controversial functionality from Java to .NET and made arrays **co-variant**. Right, why is this bad?

Bad Arrays of Animals and Elephants

To demonstrate why co-variant arrays are bad, create a new console application called Chapter3.Variance.

1. Now create two classes, Animal and Elephant. Note that Elephant inherits from Animal - this is important:

    ```
    public class Animal { }
    public class Elephant : Animal { }
    ```

2. Enter the following code:

    ```
    class Program
    {
        public class Animal { }
        public class Elephant : Animal { }

        static void Main(string[] args)
        {
            Animal[] animals = new Elephant[10];
            animals[0] = new Animal();
        }
    }
    ```

3. Compile your code.

Everything should be fine but now run the application. An exception will be thrown on the second line:

```
Attempted to access an element as a type incompatible with the array
```

Whoa, but the compiler let us do this, and then complains about a type exception. What gives?

-   We are allowed to put Elephants in an Animal array, because Elephant inherits from Animal and it will also have all the properties of Animal.

-   Animals, however, will not necessarily have features specific to Elephants (such as trunks, tusks, and an enviable memory), so the reverse is not true.

-   This exception occurs because our Animals array actually consists of Elephants, so is essentially an Elephant array.

Code that compiles but throws type exceptions at runtime is bad news, so when Generics were introduced, Microsoft was not going to have this problem so made Generics **invariant**. The following will not compile for the previously stated reasons:

```
List<Animal> Animals = new List<Animal>();
//This will work fine as we can be sure Elephant has all Animal's properties
Animals.Add(new Elephant());
List<Elephant> Elephants = new List<Elephant>();
//This will not compile
Elephants.Add(new Animal());
This is further illustrated in Figure 3-2.
```

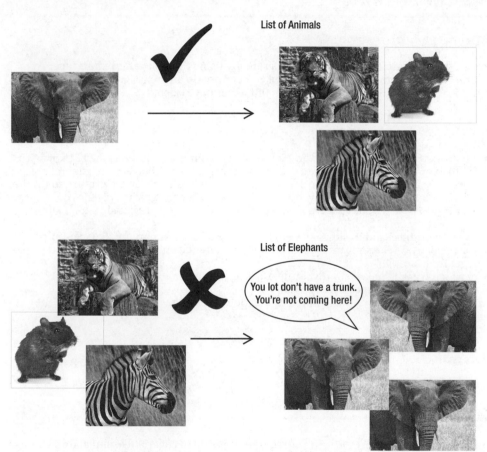

Figure 3-2. *Generic lists and variants, or why elephants are mean.*

So, What's the Problem?

Well, some folk found that .NET would stop them from writing code and modeling situations that *are* safe. For example, the following did not work prior to .NET 4.0:

```
IList<Elephant> elephants = new List<Elephant>();
IEnumerable<Animal> animals = elephants;
```

Here, the exception is:

```
Cannot implicitly convert type
'System.Collections.Generic.IList<Chapter3.Elephant>' to
'System.Collections.Generic.IEnumerable<Chapter3.Animal>'. An explicit conversion
exists (are you missing a cast?)
```

There is no reason this shouldn't work, as the code is safe. By using the IEnumerable interface, Animals are only ever returned in the output position, and you cannot do any reassignment. So the new variance changes are very much fixing a problem that should never have existed.

Out

The previous example works in .NET 4.0 because the IEnumerable<T> interface now has the out keyword in its parameter list, which enables us to use a more specific class (Elephant) when a more general class (Animal) should be used. The out keyword tells the compiler that Animal can only ever be returned (in the **out**put position), which keeps the compiler happy, because IEnumerable contains no way for you to add objects to it after IEnumerable is declared. This avoids the problems discussed previously and ensures type safety.

The term for this is *covariance,* and it allows an item to be treated as its supertype. For example, IEnumerable<string> can also be IEnumerable<object> (note that variance only applies to reference types so will not affect integer for example).

Contravariance, which we will look at shortly, is the exact opposite. It allows a type like Action<Object> to be treated as a subtype Action<String>.>.

You can add the out modifier to your own interfaces and delegates. It has also been added to the following generic intefaces:

- IEnumerable<out T>

- IEnumerator<out T>

- IQueryable<out T>

Contravariance

Related to covariance is contravariance. *Contravariance* is the opposite to covariance, and allows you to use a more general class when a specific class should be used. Contravariance uses the In modifier to specify the parameter can only occur in the **in**put position. You can add the In modifier to your own interfaces and delegates, and it has been added to the following generic interfaces and delegates:

- IComparer<in T>

- IEqualityComparer <in T>

- Func<in T,.., out R>

- Action<in T,..>
- Predicate<in T>
- Comparison<in T>
- EventHandler<in T>

Example of Contravariance

Let's say we want to create a common class that will sort animals by weight. It would be great if we could use this same class to weigh anything that had a base class of Animal, but as you can guess the code we will write won't work in VS2008.

We will add Weight and Name properties to the Animal class so we can easily identify individual Animal instances.

1. Modify the Animal class so it now looks like:

```
public class Animal
{
    public int Weight { get; set; }
    public string Name { get; set; }

    public Animal()
    { }

    public Animal(string InputName, int InputWeight)
    {
        Name = InputName;
        Weight = InputWeight;
    }
}
```

2. Now modify the Elephant class to the following:

```
public class Elephant : Animal
{
    public Elephant(string InputName, int InputWeight) : base(InputName, InputWeight)
    {
    }
}
```

3. To weigh all our animals, we will create a new class called WeightComparer that will implement the IComparer interface; implementing the IComparer interface will then enable us to use the Sort() method on the list object. Create the WeightComparer class with this code:

```
public class WeightComparer : IComparer<Animal>
{

    public int Compare(Animal x, Animal y)
    {
        if (x.Weight > y.Weight) return 1;
        if (x.Weight == y.Weight) return 0;
        return -1;
    }
}
```

ICOMPARER

IComparer accepts two parameters and will return an integer representing whether one object is greater, equal, or less than the other. In our example:

0 if x.weight equals y.weight

1 if x.weight is more than y.weight

-1 if x.weight is less then y.weight

---

4. We will now add some animals to sort so alter the Main method to the following:

```
static void Main(string[] args)
{
    WeightComparer objAnimalComparer = new WeightComparer();

    List<Animal> Animals = new List<Animal>();
    Animals.Add(new Animal("elephant", 500));
    Animals.Add(new Animal("tiger", 100));
    Animals.Add(new Animal("rat", 5));

    //Works
    Animals.Sort(objAnimalComparer);

    List<Elephant> Elephants = new List<Elephant>();
    Elephants.Add(new Elephant("Nellie", 100));
    Elephants.Add(new Elephant("Dumbo", 200));
    Elephants.Add(new Elephant("Baba", 50));

    //Doesn't work prior to .net 4
    Elephants.Sort(objAnimalComparer);

    Elephants.ForEach(e=> Console.WriteLine(e.Name + " " + e.Weight.ToString()));
}
```

5. Compile the code, and you should find that the elephants are sorted by weight; however, if you try this code in VS2008, you will find it will not compile.

Further Reading

Variance is a difficult subject, so for more information please refer to the following blogs and book:

- http://blogs.msdn.com/charlie/archive/2008/10/28/linq-farm-covariance-and-contravariance-in-visual-studio-2010.aspx

- http://blogs.msdn.com/ericlippert/archive/tags/Covariance+and+Contravariance/default.aspx

- Skeet, Jon. (2008) *C# in depth*. Manning Publications.

Dynamic Enhancements

The new dynamic functionality in .NET 4.0 allows us to work with types not known at compile time in an intuitive and easy to read way. Many of you may be wondering what can the dynamic changes do for you. The dynamic changes allow us to do the following:

- Write more readable code with fewer casting operations.

- Create new languages to utilize the .NET Framework, such as IronPython and IronRuby. Additionally, .NET's dynamic architecture allows these languages to automatically benefit from future framework advances.Utilize other dynamic languages and their libraries.

- Utilize other dynamic languages and their libraries from C# and VB.NET.

- Introduce customization/scripting and debugging/querying functionality within our applications.

- Work with COM objects more easily. Microsoft Office COM is going to be around for some time whether you like it or not.

- Many other cool uses we haven't thought of yet.

Can't We Do This Kind of Thing Already in .NET?

.NET has a number of classes and methods for working with types not known at compile time, such as reflection and expression trees. However, if you have spent much time with these technologies, you will known that they can make for some clunky and difficult to read code. As I will show you, the dynamic enhancements can make your life much easier.

Before we look at how to use the dynamic enhancements, we need to understand the difference between statically and dynamically typed languages.

Static Languages

In a statically typed language, such as C# or C, the compiler checks you are using types correctly at compile time. Compilation will fail, for example, if you assign a string to an integer or misspell a variable name. Statically typed languages can catch simple syntax errors and typos during development and as the compiler knows the types it will be working with static languages generally run quicker then dynamic languages (next) as optimizations can be performed on code.

Dynamic Languages

In contrast, dynamic languages, such as JavaScript, Python, Lisp, and Ruby, do not perform type checks on code until runtime. This can be a big advantage if you don't know the type of object you will be working with at compile time. These features can also make it possible to perform some interesting code tricks and reduce tedious casting operations if the language can work out how to use the type. Some developers feel dynamic languages can help them develop and prototype applications much quicker, and can be particularly suitable for testing and prototyping applications.

The main disadvantage of working with dynamic languages is they of course lack compile time checks and generally have inferior performance when compared to static languages. When working with dynamic languages, simple syntax errors and typos can stop your code working. I think anyone that has done any web development has spent much time tracking down such an error in JavaScript with its very helpful "object not set to an instance" message.

Dynamic Dangers

When working with dynamic types and the Dynamic Language Runtime (DLR) there are three considerations you should bear in mind.

- IDE support is limited

- Generally, performance is poor (although precompilation is sometimes possible), especially on the first call to a method where the DLR has not yet cached a method call.

- Using the DLR unnecessarily is not big or clever (more complexity = bad).

I'll cover the DLR in detail later in this chapter.

Type Dynamic

.NET 4.0 introduces a new type `dynamic` that allows you to tell the compiler to resolve a variable's type at runtime. Somewhat paradoxically the keyword `dynamic` statically types an object as `dynamic`.

To declare an object as dynamic, prefix the variable name with the type `dynamic`:

```
dynamic myDynamic="Something";
Console.WriteLine(myDynamic.GetType().Name);
Console.ReadKey();
```

What type will be output on the second line? `Dynamic`, `object`?

For those of you who said `String` you are correct (now stop looking so smug); I will explain why this is shortly.

Is dynamic the Same as Var?

No, `dynamic` is very different. When the var keyword is used the compiler infers the type of value you are using and writes the appropriate code for you when you compile the application. Variables declared using var benefit from type checks, Intellisense, and offer better performance than their dynamic equivalent. Types declared as `dynamic` are evaluated at run time and do not have these benefits.

Why Type Variables as Dynamic?

One advantage is that it can avoid some tedious casting and Reflection code. For example, let's say we want to create an instance of a type using a string and call a method on it at runtime. In our example we will create a StringBuilder instance and call the Append method on it using Reflection:

```
object UsingReflection =
  Activator.CreateInstance(Type.GetType("System.Text.StringBuilder"));
Type ObjectType = UsingReflection.GetType();
//Append has many overloads so we need to tell reflection which type we will use
Type[] TypeArray = new Type[1];
TypeArray.SetValue(typeof(string), 0);
var ObjectMethodInfo=ObjectType.GetMethod("Append", TypeArray);
ObjectMethodInfo.Invoke(UsingReflection, new object[] { "alex" });
Console.WriteLine(
  ObjectType.GetMethod("ToString", new Type[0]).Invoke(UsingReflection, null)
);
Console.ReadKey();
```

By using dynamic, however, we can make this simpler and more readable (and I know which bit of code I could remember):

```
dynamic usingDynamic = Activator.CreateInstance(Type.GetType("System.Text.StringBuilder"));
usingDynamic.Append("Hello");
Console.WriteLine(UsingDynamic.ToString());
Console.ReadKey();
```

■**NOTE** Technically you could do something similar in VB.NET by declaring UsingDynamic as object, so arguably VB.NET could be considered to contain dynamic functionality already.

Consider using dynamic types in the following situations:

- When working with COM, dynamic types allow a more concise syntax (we saw this earlier). Let the DLR do the work figuring out how to bind your method and property calls.

- When interacting with a dynamic language such as IronPython.

- When working with objects that have changing structures, such as HTML or XML documents (we will look at this shortly).

System.Dynamic.ExpandoObject

ExpandoObject is a strange new beast in the .NET Framework that allows you to add and remove properties, methods, and events at runtime. The following example demonstrates how to add two new values and a method:

```
using System.Dynamic

dynamic MyExpando = new ExpandoObject();
MyExpando.Value1 = "new value 1";
MyExpando.Value2 = "new value 2";

MyExpando.DoSomething = new Action(() => Console.WriteLine("DoSomething called"));
Console.WriteLine(MyExpando.Value1);
MyExpando.DoSomething();

Console.ReadKey();
```

ExpandoObject could be used for wrapping data and making it easier to work with and is included for interoperability with dynamic languages that support this concept.

System.Dynamic.DynamicObject

.NET 4.0 introduces a new class called DynamicObject that allows the definition of runtime behavior, offering a much greater level of control than ExpandoObject. It is important to note that DynamicObject is never instantiated directly but must be inherited from.

DynamicObject again is great for wrapping data and making it easier to work with, but offers a much finer level of control than ExpandoObject. If you just need to define parameters at runtime you will probably be adequately served by ExpandoObject (above) however DynamicObject allows you full control over various operations performed.

The following example shows how to query an XML document using properties to create more readable code:

```
using System.Dynamic;
using System.Xml.Linq;

class Program
    {
        static void Main(string[] args)
        {
            dynamic easierXML =
              new EasierXML(@"<test><node1>Alpha</node1><node2>Beta</node2></test>");
            Console.WriteLine(easierXML.node1);
            Console.WriteLine(easierXML.node2);
            Console.ReadKey();
        }

        public class EasierXML : DynamicObject
        {
            private XDocument _xml = new XDocument();

            public EasierXML(string Xml)
            {
                this._xml = XDocument.Parse(Xml);
            }
```

```
        public override bool TryGetMember(GetMemberBinder binder,
                                           out object result)
        {
            string nodeName = binder.Name;
            result = _xml.Element("test").Element(nodeName).Value;
            return true;
        }
    }
}
```

In this example, the TryGetMember() method intercepts the call to .node1 and .node2, thus allowing us to query the XML document and return the individual nodes.

IDynamicMetaObjectProvider

IDynamicMetaObjectProvider is an important interface in the dynamic world that represents an object that has operations bound at runtime. Both ExpandoObject and DynamicObject implement this interface. You can use this interface to add dynamic functionality to your own classes. IDynamicMetaObjectProvider requires you to implement GetMetaObject(),(), which resolves binding operations (for example, method or property invocation on your object).

Dynamic Limitations

When working with dynamic objects, there are a number of constraints you should be aware of:

- All methods and properties in classes have to be declared public to be dynamically accessible.

- You cannot use the DLR to create classes in C# or VB.NET. Apparently, the DLR does allow you to create classes, but this cannot be expressed using C# or VB.NET.

- Dynamic objects cannot be passed as arguments to other functions.

- Extension methods cannot be called on a dynamic object and a dynamic object cannot be passed into extension objects.

Annoyingly, these restrictions stop you calling an extension method on a dynamic object.

Dynamic IL

You may be wondering what code the C# compiler generates when you use the dynamic keyword. Let's take a look at the IL that is generated using ILDASM for a simple console application that declares and initializes a string:

```
string d;
d = "What do I look like in IL";
```

This will generate the following IL:

```
.method private hidebysig static void  Main(string[] args) cil managed
{
  .entrypoint
  // Code size       8 (0x8)
  .maxstack  1
  .locals init ([0] string d)
  IL_0000:  nop
  IL_0001:  ldstr      "What do I look like in IL"
  IL_0006:  stloc.0
  IL_0007:  ret
} // end of method Program::Main
```

Now we will alter d to be of type dynamic:

```
dynamic d;
d = "What do I look like in IL?";
```

This will generate the following IL:

```
.method private hidebysig static void  Main(string[] args) cil managed
{
  .entrypoint
  // Code size       8 (0x8)
  .maxstack  1
  .locals init ([0] object d)
  IL_0000:  nop
  IL_0001:  ldstr      "What do I look like in IL"
  IL_0006:  stloc.0
  IL_0007:  ret
} // end of method Program::Main
```

Note how the line locals init ([0] object d) replaces locals init ([0] string d) in the dynamic example. This is probably what you might expect to happen, but let's take another more complex example. Create a new console application called Chapter3.DynamicComplex and add the following code:

```
using System;
using System.Collections.Generic;
using System.Linq;
using System.Text;

namespace Chapter3.DynamicComplex
{
    class Program
    {
        static void Main(string[] args)
        {
            TestClass t = new TestClass();
            t.Method1();
        }
    }
```

```
    public class TestClass
    {
        public void Method1() { }
    }

}
```

Compile the application and examine the IL using ILDASM. You will find something similar to the following:

```
.method private hidebysig static void  Main(string[] args) cil managed
{
  .entrypoint
  // Code size       15 (0xf)
  .maxstack  1
  .locals init ([0] class Chapter3.DynamicComplex.TestClass t)
  IL_0000:  nop
  IL_0001:  newobj     instance void Chapter3.DynamicComplex.TestClass::.ctor()
  IL_0006:  stloc.0
  IL_0007:  ldloc.0
  IL_0008:  callvirt   instance void Chapter3.DynamicComplex.TestClass::Method1()
  IL_000d:  nop
  IL_000e:  ret
} // end of method Program::Main
```

However, if we alter our t variable to the following:

```
dynamic t = new TestClass();
t.Method1();
```

.. then the IL will look very different (I have removed some of the IL to save some trees):

```
class [mscorlib]System.Collections.Generic.IEnumerable`1<class
[Microsoft.CSharp]Microsoft.CSharp.RuntimeBinder.CSharpArgumentInfo>)
  IL_003a:  call       class [System.Core]
System.Runtime.CompilerServices.CallSite`1<!0> class
[System.Core]System.Runtime.CompilerServices.CallSite`1
<class [mscorlib]System.Action`2<class
[System.Core]System.Runtime.CompilerServices.CallSite,object>>::Create(class
[System.Core]System.Runtime.CompilerServices.CallSiteBinder)
  IL_003f:  stsfld     class [System.Core]System.Runtime.CompilerServices
.CallSite`1<class [mscorlib]System.Action`2<class
[System.Core]System.Runtime.CompilerServices.CallSite,object>>
Chapter3.DynamicComplex.Program/'<Main>o__SiteContainer0'::'<>p__Site1'
  IL_0056:  callvirt   instance void class [mscorlib]System.Action`2<class
[System.Core]System.Runtime.CompilerServices.CallSite,object>::Invoke(!0, !1)
```

Whoa, what is happening here? Well the short answer is that calls to dynamic methods are sent to the Dynamic Language Runtime for resolution. It is time to take a look into how the DLR works.

Dynamic Language Runtime (DLR)

The Dynamic Language Runtime (DLR) is behind all the cool dynamic functionality and sits just above the core .NET framework. The DLR's job is basically to resolve calls to dynamic objects, cache dynamic calls making them as quick as possible, and enable interaction between languages by using a common format. The DLR has actually been around a while, and was included in earlier versions of Silverlight. You can even view the source code behind the DLR at: `http://dlr.codeplex.com`. Note that this version contains a number of features not present in the framework version.

When discussing the DLR we need to understand five main concepts:

- Expression trees/Abstract Syntax Trees (AST)

- Dynamic Dispatch

- Binders

- IDynamicObject

- Call Site Caching

Expression/Abstract Syntax Trees (AST)

Expression trees are a way of representing code in a tree structure (if you have done any work with LINQ, you may have come across this before with the `Expression` class). All languages that work with the DLR represent code in the same structure allowing interoperability.

Dynamic Dispatch

Dynamic Dispatch is the air traffic control center of the DLR, and is responsible for working out what to do with dynamic objects and operations and sending them to the appropriate binder that takes care of the details.

Binders

Binders resolve classes from dynamic dispatch. .NET 4.0 currently supports the following binder types:

- Object Binder .NET (uses Reflection and resolved our earlier example to type string)

- JavaScript binder (`IDynamicObject`)

- IronPython binder (`IDynamicObject`)

- IronRuby binder (`IDynamicObject`)

- COM binder (`IDispatch`)

Note that dynamic objects can resolve calls themselves without the DLR's assistance (if they implement `IDynamicObject`), and this method will always be used first over the DLR's dynamic dispatch mechanism.

IDynamicObject

Sometimes you will want objects to carry out resolution themselves, and it is for this purpose the IDynamicObject exists. Normally dynamic objects are processed according to type, but if they implement the IDynamicObject interface then the object will resolve calls itself. IDynamicObject is used in IronRuby and IronPython.

Callsite Caching

Resolving objects is an expensive operation, so the DLR caches dynamic operations. When a dynamic function or operation is performed, the DLR checks to see if it has been called already (Level 0 cache). If it hasn't, then the 10 most recently used dynamic methods for this callsite will be checked (Level 1 cache). A cache is also maintained across all target sites with the same binder object (Level 2 cache).

IronPython

A similar process to this is used when languages such as IronPython interact with .NET. What follows is a high-level version of how the DLR processes an IronPython file:

1. The IronPython file is first compiled into intermediary IronPython AST. (Not all languages will necessarily create an intermediary AST, but IronPython's developers decided this would be a useful step for creating language-specific tools.)

2. The IronPython AST is then mapped to the generic DLR specific AST.

3. The DLR then works with the generic AST.

For a detailed look at how this works with Iron Python please refer to: http://msdn.microsoft.com/en-us/magazine/cc163344.aspx.

As all languages end up being compiled into the same common AST structure, it is then possible for interaction between them.

Embedding Dynamic Languages

One use of dynamic languages that really excites me is the ability to embed them within your C# and VB.NET applications. One possible use would be to use them to define complex business rules and logic. Dynamic languages are often utilized in computer game construction to script scenarios and logic (such as how Civilization IV utilizes Python). Let's take a look at how to work with IronPython in a C# application.

Calling IronPython from .NET

The following example passes a value into a simple IronPython script from C#. Note that you should have installed IronPython from http://ironpython.codeplex.com/. Now add a reference to IronPython.dll and Microsoft.Scripting.dll (at the time of writing these don't show up on the main Add Reference window but are located at C:\Program Files (x86)\IronPython 2.6).

```csharp
using Microsoft.Scripting;
using Microsoft.Scripting.Hosting;
using IronPython.Hosting;

namespace Chapter3.PythonExample
{
    class Program
    {
        static void Main(string[] args)
        {
            ScriptEngine pythonEngine = Python.CreateEngine();
            ScriptScope scope = pythonEngine.CreateScope();
            string script = @"print ""Hello "" + message";

            scope.SetVariable("message", "world!");

            ScriptSource source =
              scope.Engine.CreateScriptSourceFromString(script, SourceCodeKind.Statements);
            source.Execute(scope);
            Console.ReadKey();
        }
    }
}
```

IronPython is already in use in two real-world applications, so let's take a look at these now.

Red Gate Reflector Add-In

Many of you will be familiar with the tool Reflector (www.red-gate.com/products/reflector/). Reflector allows you to explore an assembly and view the IL code within it. C# MVP Ben Hall developed an add-in (Methodist) to Reflector that allows you to actually call the classes and methods within the type you are exploring using Iron Python. For more information please consult: http://mail.simple-talk.com/dotnet/.net-tools/methodist-make-.net-reflector-come-alive-with-ironpython/.

ResolverOne

One of the best know uses of IronPython is for ResolverOne (http://www.resolversystems.com). ResolverOne is an application that allows you to work with Excel's objects using IronPython. See Figure 3-3.

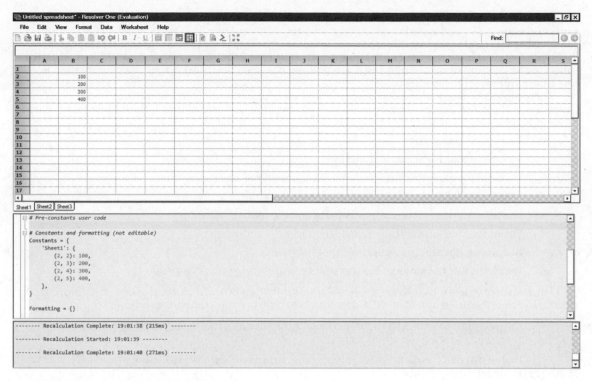

Figure 3-3. *ResolverOne application*

One of the developers on ResolverOne was Michael Foord, who is author of *IronPython in Action* (Manning Publications, 2009). I spoke to Michael about his experiences with working with embedding dynamic languages and IronPython.

Michael Foord

Why should VB.NET/C# developers be interested in IronPython?
Much of the discussion here applies to other dynamic languages, including IronRuby, but Python is my particular area of expertise.

IronPython is a .NET implementation of the popular open source programming language Python. Python is an expressive language that is easy to learn and supports several different programming styles, including interactive, scripting, procedural, functional, object-oriented, and metaprogramming. But what can you do with IronPython that isn't already easy with your existing tools?

The first entry in the list of programming styles is "interactive." The IronPython distribution includes ipy.exe, the executable for running scripts or programs that also doubles as an interactive interpreter. When you run ipy.exe, you can enter Python code that is evaluated immediately and the result returned. It is a powerful tool for exploring assemblies and learning how to use new frameworks and classes by working with live objects.

The second reason to use IronPython is also the second programming style in the list: scripting. Python makes an excellent tool for generating XML from templates, automating build tasks, and a host of other everyday operations. Because scripts can be executed without compilation, experimentation is simple and fast. Python often creeps into businesses as a scripting language, but beware it spreads.

One of the big use cases for IronPython is for embedding in applications. Potential uses include user scripting, adding a live console for debugging, creating domain-specific languages (DSLs) where rules can be added or modified at runtime, or even building hybrid applications using several languages. Python has several features, such as the ability to customize attribute access, that make it particularly suited to the creation of lightweight DSLs. IronPython has been designed with these uses in mind and has a straightforward hosting API.

There are many areas where dynamic languages are fundamentally different from statically typed languages, a topic that rouses strong opinions. Here are a few features of IronPython that make it easy to develop with:

- No type declarations

- First class and higher order functions

- No need for generics; it uses flexible container types instead

- Protocols and duck-typing instead of compiler enforced interfaces

- First class types and namespaces that can be modified at runtime

- Easier to test than statically typed languages

- Easy introspection (reflection without the pain)

- Problems like covariance, contravariance and casting just disappear

The best way to learn how to get the best from IronPython is my book *IronPython in Action*. I've also written a series of articles aimed at .NET developers to help get you started, including

- Introduction to IronPython (`http://www.voidspace.org.uk/ironpython/introduction-to-ironpython.shtml`)

- Python for .NET Programmers (`http://www.voidspace.org.uk/ironpython/python-for-programmers.shtml`)

- Tools and IDEs for IronPython (`http://www.voidspace.org.uk/ironpython/tools-and-ides.shtml`)

Happy experimenting.

What does Resolver One's Python interface provide that VBA couldn't?
The calculation model for Resolver One is very different from Excel. The data and formulae you enter in the grid is translated into an interpreted language and you put your own code into the flow of the spreadsheet, working on the exact same object model that your formulae do.

Having the programming model at the heart of Resolver One was always the core idea. When development started, the two developers (a few months before I joined Resolver Systems) evaluated interpreted languages available for .NET. When they tried IronPython they made three important discoveries:

- Although neither of them was familiar with Python, it was an elegant and expressive language that was easy to learn.

- The .NET integration of IronPython was superb. In fact, it seemed that everything they needed to develop Resolver One was accessible from IronPython.

- As a dynamic language, Python was orders of magnitude easier to test than languages they had worked with previously. This particularly suited the test-driven approach they were using.

So the main advantage of Resolver One is that programmability is right at the heart of the spreadsheet model. IronPython is generally regarded as being a much "nicer" language than VBA. Python is a dynamically typed, cross-platform, open source, object-oriented, high-level programming language. Python was first released publicly in 1991, making it older than C#, and is widely used in many different fields.

What do you think of the new dynamic features in .NET?
They're great, particularly for interoperating between C# and DLR-based languages. The dynamic features make this *much* easier.

The dynamic keyword also makes creating fluent APIs possible (like the way you access the DOM using the document object in Javascript). This is particularly useful for DSLs.

Duck typing is one of the features of dynamic languages that simplify architecture. I doubt that the dynamic keyword, will be used much for this however, as it doesn't gel well with the way most .NET developers use traditional .NET languages.

Apart from your book (obviously), any recommended reading on Python or dynamic languages?
The Python tutorial and documentation is pretty good. Unsurprisingly they can be found from the Python website at http://www.python.org/. There is an interactive online version of the Python tutorial created with IronPython and Silverlight at: http://www.trypython.org/.

For learning IronPython there is an excellent community resource called the IronPython Cookbook: http://www.ironpython.info/.

For more general Python resources I recommend *Dive into Python* and the *Python Essential Reference*.

F#

F# is a functional programming language for the .NET framework that was previously available as a separate download to Visual Studio but now comes included in VS2010. Some developers feel that functional languages such as F# can enable you to work in a more intuitive way (particularly for those with a mathematical background), and are very good at manipulating sets of data and for solving mathematical and scientific problems.

Interest in functional languages is increasing due to their absence of side effects (where an application modifies state as well as returning a value). The lack of side effects is vital in multithreaded and parallelized applications (see Chapter 5). Note that F# is not as strict as some functional languages and allows the creation of non-functional constructs, such as local variables.

So should you rush out and learn F#? Well it's not going to take over C# or VB.NET for developing line of business applications, but it is worth noting that functional languages have been influencing the development of C# and VB. An example is the recent addition of traditionally functional features, such as lambda expressions.

However, I do believe that looking at other languages can help make you a better programmer (I'm currently looking into Python). At a DevEvening user group presentation, Jon Skeet suggested to us that functional languages may help you become a better developer by getting you to think about a problem in a different way.

For a great introduction to F# view the presentation at: http://mschnlnine.vo.llnwd.net/d1/pdc08/WMV-HQ/TL11.wmv.

And then take a look at the official site at: http://research.microsoft.com/en-us/um/cambridge/projects/fsharp/default.aspx

Jon Skeet

For those developers who really want to delve into the details of a language, I don't think you can do much better than read Jon Skeet's *C# In Depth* (Manning Publications, 2008). A revised version for .NET 4.0 is currently on its way (http://csharpindepth.com/).

I spoke to Jon about his thoughts on C# 2010.

What Do You See as the Top Feature(s) in C#2010, and Why?

Named arguments and optional parameters, without a doubt. (That sounds like two features, but they naturally come together.) It's a small feature, but it's likely to be the most widely used one. Two of the others (better COM support and dynamic typing) are only likely to be used by a minority of developers, and while generic variance is useful and interesting, it's more of a matter of removing a previous inconvenience than really introducing something new.

Admittedly, to fully take advantage of optional parameters, you have to be confident that all your callers will be using a language supporting them. For example, suppose you wanted to write a method with five parameters, three of them optional. Previously you may have used several overloads to avoid forcing callers to specify arguments for parameters where they're happy with the default. Now, if you don't care about (say) C#2008 callers, you can just provide a single method. But that *would* force any C#2008 callers to specify all the arguments explicitly.

The biggest potential use I see for the feature is immutability. C#2008 made it easy to create instances of *mutable* types using object initializers, but provided no extra support for *immutable* types. Now with named arguments and optional parameters, it's a lot easier. For example, take the initialization of a mutable type:

```
Person p = new Person {
    Name = "Jon",
    Occupation = "Software Engineer",
    Location = "UK"
};
```

This can be converted into initialization of an immutable type without losing the benefits of optional data *and* explicitly specifying which value means what:

```
Person p = new Person (
    name: "Jon",
    occupation: "Software Engineer",
    location: "UK"
);
```

Are There any New Features in C#2010 That You Would Avoid Using or That Have the Potential to Encourage Bad Programming?

Well, dynamic typing is going to be really useful *when you need it*, but should generally be avoided otherwise, in my view. It's great for interoperability with dynamic languages via the DLR, some additional COM support, and occasional cases where you would otherwise use Reflection. But C# is basically a statically typed language. It isn't *designed* for dynamic typing. If you want to use dynamic typing widely throughout a program, write it in a dynamic language to start with. You can always use the DLR to work with C# code as well, of course.

What Would You Like to See in the Next Version of C#?
More support for immutability. For example, readonly automatic properties would be a simple but really helpful feature:

```
public string Name { get; readonly set; }
```

That would be backed by a readonly field behind the scenes, and the property could only be set in the constructor (where the assignment would be converted into simple field assignment). Beyond that, the ability to declare that a type is *meant* to be immutable, with additional compiler support and checking, would be great. But that's a bigger request.

If Code Contracts takes off, it would also be nice to embed the simplest contract, non-nullity, into the language, in the way that Spec# did. For example, instead of:

```
public string Convert(string input)
{
    Contract.Requires(input != null);
    Contract.Ensures(Contract.Result<string>() != null);

    // Do processing here
}
```

you could just write:

```
public string! Convert(string! input)
{
    // Do processing here
}
```

The handling of non-nullable local variables could be tricky, but there are smart people at Microsoft. I'm sure they could figure something out.

Admittedly I'm wary of anything that links the language too closely to specific libraries, but this would be a *really* nice win in terms of readability.

These may all sound like I'm lacking in ambition. After all, there are bigger ideas on the table such as metaprogramming. But I'm really keen on small, simple changes that make a big difference. I generally need to be persuaded more when it comes to large changes. The ones we've already had in C# have been very well designed, and I'm pleased with them. But the language is getting really pretty big now, and I think we need to make sure it doesn't become simply too hard to learn from scratch.

Future of C#

At the 2008 PDC Anders Hejlsberg noted that many developers were creating programs that created programs (meta programming). Anders considered it would be useful to expose compiler methods to developers to give them complete control over compilation. In a future version of .NET the compiler will be written in managed code and certain functions made accessible to the developer. Anders then demonstrated an example of this by showing a REPL (Read Evaluate Print Loop) C# application.

■ ■ ■

CHAPTER 4

CLR and BCL Changes

Availability: Framework 4

In this chapter you will look at the changes to the common language runtime (CLR) in .NET 4.0 that cover changes to security, garbage collection, threading, and internationalization. You will then look into the new types introduced in .NET 4.0 and the enhancements that have been made to existing classes. You will finish the chapter by looking at code contracts a great new feature allowing you to express assumptions and constraints within your code.

New CLR

The last two releases of.NET (3.0 and 3.5) have been additive releases building on top of the functionality available in CLR version 2.0 (see Figure 4-1).

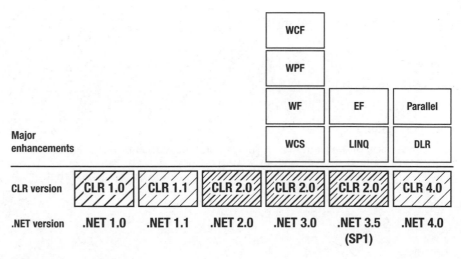

Figure 4-1. *CLR releases*

.NET 4.0 however has a new version of the CLR! So you can happily install .NET 4.0 without fear that it will affect your existing .NET applications running on previous versions of the framework.

ASP.NET

When using IIS7, the CLR version is determined by the application pool settings. Thus you should be able to run .NET 4.0 ASP.NET applications side by side without fear of affecting existing ASP.NET sites.

What Version of the CLR Does My Application Use?

It depends; applications compiled for earlier versions of the framework will as before use the same version they were built on if it's installed. If, however, the previous framework version is not available, the user will now be offered a choice about whether to download the version of the framework the application was built with or whether to run using the latest version. Prior to .NET 4.0, the user wouldn't be given this choice with the application using the latest version available.

Specifying the Framework to Use

Since almost the beginning of .NET (well, .NET Framework 1.1), you can specify the version your application needs to use in the App.config file (previously as requiredRuntime):

```
<configuration>
<startup>
  <supportedRuntime version="v1.0.3705"  />
</startup>
</configuration>
```

The version property supports the following settings:

- v4.0 (framework version 4.0)

- v2.0.50727 (framework version 3.5)

- v2.0.50727 (framework version 2.0)

- v1.1.4322 (framework version 1.1)

- v1.0.3705 (framework version 1.0)

If this setting is left out, the version of the framework used to build the application is used (if available).

When the supportedRuntime property is set, if you try to run the application on a machine that doesn't have the CLR version specified, users will see a dialog similar to Figure 4-2.

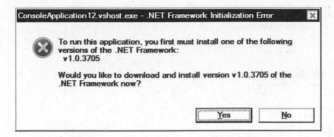

Figure 4-2. *Dialog showing application targeted for version 1 of the framework*

VB.NET Command-Line Compiler

The compiler has a new /langversion switch option that allows you to tell the compiler to use a particular framework version. It currently accepts parameters 9, 9.0, 10, and 10.0.

```
vbc /langversion:9.0 skynet.vb
```

Improved Client Profile

Client profile is a lean, reduced-functionality version of the full .NET Framework that was first introduced in .NET 3.5SP1. Functionality that isn't often needed is removed from the client profile. This results in a smaller download and reduced installation time for users. At the time of writing, Microsoft has reduced the size of the client profile to around 34 MB, although it intends to minimize it even further for the final release.

The .NET 4.0 client profile is supported by all environments that support the full .NET Framework and is redistributable (rather than web download only) and contains improvements to add/remove program entries, unlike the version available in .NET 3.5SP1.

To use the client profile in your application, open the project Properties page, select the Application tab, and on the Target framework drop-down menu select .NET Framework 4.0 Client Profile (as shown in Figure 4-3). Note that in VB.NET, this option is in the Compile➤Advanced Compile Options tab.

Client profile is the default target framework option in many VS2010 project types such as Windows Forms and Console. This is important to remember because sometimes you will need functionality not available in the client profile and be confused as to why various options are not available in the Add Reference menu.

For more information about client profile, please consult http://blogs.msdn.com/jgoldb/archive/2009/05/27/net-framework-4-client-profile-introduction.aspx.

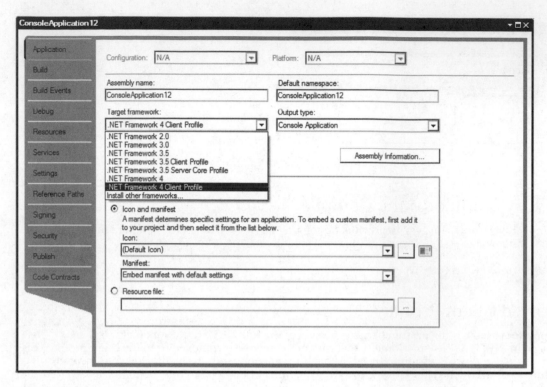

Figure 4-3. *Selecting client profile option*

In-Process Side-by-Side Execution

Prior to .NET 4.0, COM components would always run using the latest version of the .NET Framework installed by the user. This could cause some issues, for example at some of the PDC08 presentations Microsoft cites an Outlook add-in that contained a thread variable initialization bug. The add-in worked correctly in .NET 1.0, but after the clever guys in the CLR team made performance improvements to the threading pool in .NET 1.1, the add-in left many Microsoft executives unable to read their e-mail (some cynics argued that little productivity was lost).

Obviously you want to fix this bug, but it is vital to know that your application will run in the same manner as when you tested it. In-process side-by-side execution ensures that COM components run using the version of the framework they were developed for.

Prior to .NET 4.0, COM components would run using the latest version of the .NET Framework installed. You can now force COM components to use a specific framework version by adding the `supportedRuntime` section to `App.config`:

```
<configuration>
  <startup>
    <supportedRuntime version="v4.0.20506" />
  </startup>
</configuration>
```

You can also force components to use the latest version of the .NET Framework with the following configuration:

```
<configuration>
    <startup>
        <process>
            <rollForward enabled="true" />
        </process>
    </startup>
</configuration>
```

For more information, please refer to http://msdn.microsoft.com/en-gb/library/ee518876(VS.100).aspx.

Developers creating .NET components should note that their libraries will always run using the same framework version of the app domain they are running in if loading through a reference or call to Assembly.Load(). For example, libraries built in a previous version of .NET used in an application upgraded to .NET 4.0 will run using .NET 4.0. This might not be the case for unmanaged code, however.

Garbage Collection

Garbage collection is something you rarely have to worry about in our nice managed world, so before you look at what has changed in .NET 4.0, let's quickly recap how GC currently works to put the new changes in context.

Garbage Collection Prior to .NET 4.0

As you probably know, the CLR allocates memory for your applications as they require it and assumes an infinite amount of memory is available (you wish). This is a mad assumption, so a process called the garbage collector (GC) is needed in order to clean up unused resources. The GC keeps an eye on available memory resources and will perform a cleanup in three situations:

- When a threshold is exceeded

- When a user specifically calls the garbage collector

- When a low system memory condition occurs

To make this as efficient as possible, the GC divides items to be collected into "generations." When an item is first created, it is considered a generation 0 item (gen 0), and if it survives subsequent collections (it is still in use), it is promoted to a later generation: generation 1 and later generation 2.

This division allows the garbage collector to be more efficient in the removal and reallocation of memory. For example, generation 0 items mainly consist of instance variables that can be quickly removed (freeing resources earlier) while the older generations contain objects such as global variables that will probably stick around for the lifetime of your application. On the whole, the GC works very well and saves you writing lots of tedious cleanup code to release memory.

The GC operates in a number of modes: workstation, concurrent workstation (default for multicore machines), and server. These modes are optimized for different scenarios. For example, workstation is the default mode and is optimized for ensuring that your applications have a quick response time (important for UI-based applications) while server mode is optimized for throughput of work (generally more important for server type applications). Server mode does pause all other managed threads during a garbage collection, however. If server mode were used for a Windows Forms application, this collection could manifest itself as intermittent pauses, which would be very annoying.

Garbage Collection in .NET 4.0

So what's changed then? Prior to .NET 4.0, a concurrent workstation GC could do most but not all of a generation 0 and 1 collection at the same time as a generation 2 collection. The GC was also unable to start another collection when it was in the middle of a collection which meant that only memory in the current segment could be reallocated.

In .NET 4.0, however, concurrent workstation GC collection is replaced by background garbage collection. The simple explanation (and GC gets *very* complex) is that background garbage collection allows another GC (gen 0 and 1) to start at the same time as an existing full GC (gen 0, 1, and 2) is running, reducing the time full garbage collections take. This means that resources are freed earlier and that a new memory segment could be created for allocation if the current segment is full up.

Background collection is not something you have to worry about—it just happens and will make your applications perform more quickly and be more efficient, so it's yet another good reason to upgrade your existing applications to .NET 4.0.

Background collection is not available in server mode GC, although the CLR team has stated they are aiming to achieve this in the next version of the framework. The GC team has also done work to ensure that garbage collection works effectively on up to 128 core machines and improved the GC's efficiency, reducing the time needed to suspend managed threads

For more information and a detailed interview with the GC team, please refer to http://blogs.msdn.com/ukadc/archive/2009/10/13/background-and-foreground-gc-in-net-4.aspx and http://channel9.msdn.com/shows/Going+Deep/Maoni-Stephens-and-Andrew-Pardoe-CLR-4-Inside-Background-GC/.

GC.RegisterForFullGCNotification()

It is worth noting that from .NET 3.5SP1, the CLR has a method called GC.RegisterForFullGCNotification() that lets you know when a generation 2 or large heap object collection occurs in your applications. You might want to use this information to route users to a different server until the collection is complete, for example.

Threading

Threading has been tweaked in .NET 4.0, with the thread pool switching to a lock-free data structure (apparently the queue used for work items is very similar to ConcurrentQueue). This new structure is more GC-friendly, faster, and more efficient.

Prior to .NET 4.0, the thread pool didn't have any information about the context in which the threads were created, which made it difficult to optimize (for example, whether one thread depends on another). This situation changes in .NET 4.0 with a new class called Task that provide more information to the thread pool about the work to be performed thus allowing it to make better optimizations. Tasks and other parallel and threading changes are covered in detail in Chapter 5.

Globalization

Globalization is becoming increasingly important in application development. The .NET 4.0 Framework now supports a minimum of 354 cultures (compared with 203 in previous releases—now with new support for Eskimos/Inuits—and a whole lot more).

A huge amount of localization information is compiled into the .NET Framework. The main problem is that the .NET Framework doesn't get updated that often, and native code doesn't use the same localization info.

This changes in .NET 4.0 for Windows 7 users because globalization information is read directly from the operating system rather than the framework. This is a good move because it presents a consistent approach across managed/unmanaged applications. For users not lucky enough to be using Windows 7 (it's good; you should upgrade), globalization information will be read from the framework itself as per usual. Note that Windows Server 2008 will still use the localized .NET 4.0 store.

Globalization Changes in .NET 4.0

There have been a huge number of globalization changes; many of them will affect only a minority of users. For a full list, please refer to `http://msdn.microsoft.com/en-us/netframework/dd890508.aspx`.
   I do want to draw your attention to some of the changes in .NET 4.0:

- Neutral culture properties will return values from the specific culture that is most dominant for that neutral culture.

- Neutral replacement cultures created by .NET 2.0 will not load in .NET 4.0.

- Resource Manager will now refer to the user's preferred UI language instead of that specified in the `CurrentUICultures` parent chain.

- Ability to opt in to previous framework versions' globalization-sorting capabilities.

- zh-HK_stroke, ja-JP_unicod, and ko-KR_unicod alternate sort locales removed.

- Compliance with Unicode standard 5.1 (addition of about 1400 characters).

- Support added for following scripts: Sundanese, Lepcha, Ol Chiki, Vai, Saurashtra, Kayah Li, Rejang, and Cham.

- Some cultures display names changed to follow naming convention guidelines: (Chinese, Tibetan (PRC), French (Monaco), Tamazight (Latin, Algeria), and Spanish (Spain, International Sort).

- Parent chain of Chinese cultures now includes root Chinese culture.

- Arabic locale calendar data updated.

- Culture types `WindowsOnlyCultures` and `FrameworkCultures` now obsolete.

- `CompareInfo.ToString()()` and `TextInfo.ToString()()` will not return locale IDs because Microsoft wants to reduce this usage.

- Miscellaneous updates to globalization properties such as currency, date and time formats, and number formatting.

- Miscellaneous updates to globalization properties such as currency, date and time formats, and number formatting.

TimeSpan Globalized Formatting and Parsing

`TimeSpan` now has new overloaded versions of `ToString()()`, `Parse()()`, `TryParse()()`, `ParseExact()()`, and `TryParseExact()()` to support cultural sensitive formatting. Previously, `TimeSpan`'s `ToString()` method would ignore cultural settings on an Arabic machine, for example.

Security

In previous releases of .NET, the actions code could perform could be controlled using Code Access Security (CAS) policies. Although CAS undoubtedly offered much flexibility, it could be confusing to use and didn't apply to unmanaged code. In .NET 4.0, security is much simpler.

Transparency Model

The transparency model divides code into safe, unsafe, and *maybe* safe code (depending on settings in the host the application is running in). .NET has a number of different types of hosts in which applications can live, such as ASP.NET, ClickOnce, SQL, Silverlight, and so on.

Prior to .NET 4.0, the transparency model was used mainly for auditing purposes (Microsoft refers to this as *transparency level 1*) and in conjunction with code checking tools such as FxCop.

The transparency model divides code into three types:

- Transparent
- Safe critical
- Critical

Transparent Code

Transparent code is safe and verifiable code such as string and math functions that will not do anything bad to users' systems. Transparent code has the rights to call other transparent code and safe critical code. It might *not* call critical code.

Safe Critical Code

Safe critical code is code that might be allowed to run depending on the current host settings. Safe critical code acts as a middle man/gatekeeper between transparent and critical code verifying each request. An example of safe critical code is FileIO functions that might be allowed in some scenarios (such as ASP.NET) but not in others (such as Silverlight).

Critical Code

Critical code can do anything and calls such as `Marshal` come under this umbrella.

Safe Critical Gatekeeper

Transparent code never gets to call critical code directly, but has to go via the watchful eye of safe critical code.

Why Does It Matter?

If your .NET 4.0 application is running in partial trust, .NET 4.0 will ensure that transparent code can call only other transparent and safe critical code (the same as the Silverlight security model). When there is a call to safe critical code, a permission demand is made that results in a check of permissions allowed by the current host. If your application does not have permissions, a security exception will occur.

Security Changes

There are a number of security changes:

- Applications that are run from Windows Explorer or network shares run in full trust. This avoids some tediousness because prior to .NET 4.0 local and network applications would run with different permission sets.

- Applications that run in a host (for example, ASP.NET, ClickOnce, Silverlight, and SQL CLR) run with the permissions the host grants. You thus need worry only that the host grants the necessary permissions for your application. Partial trust applications running within a host are considered transparent applications (see following) and have various restrictions on them.

> ■NOTE Full trust applications such as ASP.NET application can still call critical code, so they are not considered transparent.

- Runtime support has been removed for enforcing `Deny`, `RequestMinimum`, `RequestOptional`, and `RequestRefuse` permission requests. Note that when you upgrade your applications to use .NET 4.0, you might receive warnings and errors if your application utilizes these methods. As a last resort, you can force the runtime to use legacy CAS policy with the new `NetFx40_LegacySecurityPolicy` attribute. For migration options, see `http://msdn.microsoft.com/en-us/library/ee191568(VS.100).aspx`.

> ■CAUTION If you are considering using the `NetFx40_LegacySecurityPolicy`, Shawn Farkas on the Microsoft Security team warned me that
>
> *"This will have other effects besides just re-enabling `Deny`, and `Request*` though, so its use should generally be as a last resort. In general, uses of `Deny` were a latent security hole, we've found that most people tend to need `LegacyCasPolicy` in order to continue to use the old policy APIs (CodeGroups, etc) before they cut over to the newer sandboxing model."*

- For *un-hosted* code, Microsoft now recommends that security policies are applied by using Software Restriction Policies (SRPs,), which apply to both managed and unmanaged code. Hosted code applications (e.g., ASP.NET and ClickOnce) are responsible for setting up their own policies.

SecAnnotate

SecAnnotate is a new tool contained in the .NET 4.0 SDK that analyzes assemblies for transparency violations.

APTCA and Evidence

I want to highlight two other changes (that probably will not affect the majority of developers):

- Allow Partially Trusted Callers Attribute (APTCA) allows code that is partially trusted (for example, web sites) to call a fully trusted assembly and has a new constructor that allows the specification of visibility with the `PartialTrustVisibilityLevel` enumeration.

- A new base class called `Evidence` has been introduced for all objects to be used that all evidence will derive from. This class ensures that an evidence object is not null and is serializable. A new method has also been added to the evidence list, enabling querying of specific types of evidence rather than iterating through the collection.

■**NOTE** Thanks to Shawn Farakas of the Microsoft security team for assisting me with this section.

Monitoring and Profiling

.NET 4.0 introduces a number of enhancements that enable you to monitor, debug, and handle exceptions:

- .NET 4.0 allows you to obtain CPU and memory usage per application domain, which is particularly useful for ASP.NET applications (see Chapter 10).

- It is now possible to access ETW logs (no information available at time of writing) from .NET.

- A number of APIs have been exposed for profiling and debugging purposes.

- No longer must profilers be attached at application startup; they can be added at any point. These profilers have no impact and can be detached at any time.

Native Image Generator (NGen)

NGen is an application that can improve the startup performance of managed applications by carrying out the JIT work normally done when the application is accessed. NGen creates processor optimized machine code (images) of your application that are cached. This can reduce application startup time considerably.

Prior to .NET 4.0, if you updated the framework or installed certain patches, it was necessary to NGen your application all over again. But no longer; through a process known as "targeted" patching, regenerating images is no longer required.

Native Code Enhancements

I will not be covering changes to native code, so I have summarized some of the important changes here:

- Support for real-time heap analysis.

- New integrated dump analysis and debugging tools.

- Tlbimp shared source is available from codeplex (http://clrinterop.codeplex.com/).

- Support for 64-bit mode dump debugging has also been added.

- Mixed mode 64-bit debugging is now supported, allowing you to transition from managed to native code.

Exception Handling

Exception handling has been improved in .NET 4.0 with the introduction of the System.Runtime.ExceptionServices namespace, which contains classes for advanced exception handling.

CorruptedStateExceptions

Many developers (OK, I *might* have done this, too) have written code such as the following:

```
try
{
// do something that may fail
}
catch(System.exception e)
{
...
}
```

This is almost always a very naughty way to write code because all exceptions will be hidden. Hiding exceptions you don't know about is rarely a good thing, and if you do know about them, you should inevitably be handling them in a better way. Additionally, there are some exceptions that should never be caught (even by lazy developers) such as lowdown beardy stuff such as access violations and calls to illegal instructions. These exceptions are potentially so dangerous that it's best to just shut down the application as quick as possible before it can do any further damage.

So in .NET 4.0, corrupted state exceptions will never be caught even if you specify a try a catch block. However, if you do want to enable catching of corrupted state exceptions application-wide (e.g., to route them to an error-logging class), you can add the following setting in your applications configuration file:

```
LegacyCorruptedStateExceptionsPolicy=true
```

This behavior can also be enabled on individual methods with the following attribute:

```
[HandleProcessCorruptedStateExceptions]
```

New Types

Now that the lowdown changes are out of the way, lets look at some of the new types in .NET 4.0 and modifications to existing classes and methods.

BigInteger

Working with really big numbers in .NET can get a bit strange. For example, try the following example (without advanced options such as overflow checking) and you might be surprised at the result you get:

```
int a = 2000000000;
Console.WriteLine(a * 2);
Console.ReadKey();
```

Surely the result is 4000000000? Running this code will give you the following answer:

```
-294967296
```

> ■**NOTE** VB.NET won't even let you compile the equivalent.

This issue occurs due to how this type of integer is represented in binary and the overflow that occurs. After the multiplication, the number gets bigger than this type can handle, so it actually becomes negative.

OK, so not many applications will need to hold values of this magnitude. But for those that do, .NET 4.0 introduces the BigInteger class (in the System.Numerics namespace) that can hold *really big* numbers.

BigInteger is an immutable type with a default value of 0 with no upper or lower bounds. This upper value is subject to available memory, of course, and if exceeded, an out-of-memory exception will be thrown. But seriously, what are you holding? Even the U.S. national debit isn't that big.

BigIntegers can be initialized in two main ways:

```
BigInteger bigIntFromDouble = new BigInteger(4564564564542332);
BigInteger assignedFromDouble = (BigInteger) 4564564564542332;
```

BigInteger has a number of useful (and self-explanatory) methods not found in other numeric types:

- IsEven()
- IsOne()
- IsPowerOfTwo()
- IsZero()
- IsSign()

Lazy<T>

Lazy<T> allows you to easily add lazy initialization functionality to your variables. Lazy initialization saves allocating memory until the object is actually used. So if you never end up accessing your object, you have avoided using the resources to allocate it. Additionally, you have spread out resource allocation through your application's life cycle, which is important for the responsiveness of UI-based applications.

Lazy<T> couldn't be easier to use:

```
Lazy<BigExpensiveObject> instance;
```

■**CAUTION** Lazy has implications for multithreaded scenarios. Some of the constructors for the Lazy type have an isThreadSafe parameter (see MSDN for more details of this: http://msdn.microsoft.com/en-us/library/dd997286%28VS.100%29.aspx).

Memory Mapping Files

A memory mapped file maps the contents of a file into memory, allowing you to work with it in a very efficient manner. Memory mapped files can also be used for interprocess communication, allowing you to share information between two applications:

Let's see how to use memory mapped files inter process communication:

1. Create a new console application called Chapter4.MemoryMappedCreate.

2. Add the following using statements:

    ```
    using System.IO;
    using System.IO.MemoryMappedFiles;
    ```

3. Enter the following code in the Main() method:

    ```
    //Create a memory mapped file
    using (MemoryMappedFile MemoryMappedFile = MemoryMappedFile.CreateNew("test", 100))
    {
        MemoryMappedViewStream stream = MemoryMappedFile.CreateViewStream();

        using (BinaryWriter writer = new BinaryWriter(stream))
        {
            writer.Write("hello memory mapped file!");
        }

        Console.WriteLine("Press any key to close mapped file");
        Console.ReadKey();
    }
    ```

4. Add another Console application called Chapter4.MemoryMappedRead to the solution.

5. Add the following using statements:

    ```
    using System.IO;
    using System.IO.MemoryMappedFiles;
    ```

6. Enter the following code in the Main() method:

```
//Read a memory mapped file
using (MemoryMappedFile MemoryMappedFile = MemoryMappedFile.OpenExisting("test"))
{
    using (MemoryMappedViewStream Stream = MemoryMappedFile.CreateViewStream())
    {
        BinaryReader reader = new BinaryReader(Stream);
        Console.WriteLine(reader.ReadString());
    }

    Console.ReadKey();
}
```

7. You have to run both projects to demonstrate memory mapped files. First, right-click the project Chapter4.MemoryMappedCreate and select Debug ➤ Start new instance. A new memory mapped file will be created and a string written to it.

8. Right-click the project Chapter4.MemoryMappedRead and select Debug ➤ Start new instance. You should see the string hello memory mapped file! read and printed from the other project.

The other main use of memory mapped files is for working with very large files. For an example, please refer to this MSDN article: http://msdn.microsoft.com/en-us/library/system.io.memorymappedfiles.memorymappedfile(VS.100).aspx.

SortedSet<T>

Sorted set is a new type of collection in the System.Collections.Generic namespace that maintains the order of items as they are added. If a duplicate item is added to a sorted set, it will be ignored, and a value of false is returned from the SortedSet's Add() method.

The following example demonstrates creating a sorted list of integers with a couple of duplicates in:

```
SortedSet<int> MySortedSet = new SortedSet<int> { 8, 2, 1, 5, 10, 5, 10, 8 };
```

ISet<T> Interface

.NET 4.0 introduces ISet<T>, a new interface utilized by SortedSet and HashSet and surprisingly enough for implementing set classes.

Tuple

A *tuple* is a typed collection of fixed size. Tuples were introduced for interoperability with F# and IronPython, but can also make your code more concise.

Tuples are very easy to create:

```
Tuple<int, int, int, int, int> MultiplesOfTwo = Tuple.Create(2, 4, 6, 8, 10);
```

Individual items in the tuple can then be queried with the Item property:

```
Console.WriteLine(MultiplesOfTwo.Item2);
```

Tuples might contain up to seven elements; if you want to add more items, you have to pass in another tuple to the Rest parameter:

```
var multiples = new Tuple<int, int, int, int, int, int, int,Tuple<int,int,int>>(2, 4, 6, 8,
10, 12, 14, new Tuple<int,int,int>(3,6,9));
```

Items in the second tuple can be accessed by querying the Rest property:

```
Console.WriteLine(multiples.Rest.Item1);
```

System.Numerics.Complex

Mathematicians will be glad of the addition of the new Complex type: a structure for representing and manipulating complex numbers, meaning that they will no longer have to utilize open source libraries or projects. Complex represents both a real and imaginary number, and contains support for both rectangular and polar coordinates:

```
Complex c1 = new Complex(8, 2);
Complex c2 = new Complex(8, 2);
Complex c3 = c1 + c2;
```

And I am afraid my math skills aren't up to saying much more about this type, so let's move on.

System.IntPtr and System.UIntPtr

Addition and subtraction operators are now supported for System.IntPtr and System.UIntPtr. Add()() and Subtract() methods have also been added to these types.

Tail Recursion

The CLR contains support for tail recursion, although this is only currently accessible through F#.

Changes to Existing Functionality

.NET 4.0 enhances a number of existing commonly used methods and classes.

Action and Func Delegates

Action and Func delegates now can accept up to 16 generic parameters, which might result in unreadable code. This reminds me of an API that a health care provider (who shall remain nameless) gave me that had a method with more than 70 (?!) parameters.

Compression Improvements

The 4 GB size limit has been removed from System.IO.Compression methods. The compression methods in DeflateStream and GZipStream do not try to compress already compressed data, resulting in better performance and compression ratios.

File IO

.NET 4.0 introduces a new method to the File class called File.ReadLines()(), which returns IEnumerable<string> rather than a string array. Reading a file one line at a time is much more efficient than loading the entire contents into memory (File.ReadAllLines()).

This technique also has the advantage that you can start working with a file immediately and bail out of the loop when you find what you are looking for without having to read the entire file. ReadLines()() is now the preferred method for working with very large files.

```
IEnumerable<string> FileContent=File.ReadLines("MyFile.txt");
foreach(string Line in FileContent)
{
    Console.Write(Line);
}
```

File.WriteAllLines()() and File.AppendAllLines()() now take an IEnumerable<string> as an input parameter.

System.IO.Directory has the following new static methods that return IEnumerable<string>:

- EnumerateDirectories(path)

- EnumerateFiles(path)

- EnumerateFileSystemEntries(path)

System.IO.DirectoryInfo has the following new static methods:

- EnumerateDirectories(path) returns IEnumerable<DirectoryInfo>

- EnumerateFiles(path) returns IEnumerable<FileInfo>

- EnumerateFileSystemInfos(path) returns IEnumerable<FileSystemInfo>

Enumerating files within a directory is also now more efficient than previously because file metadata such as a creation date is queried during enumeration. This means that Windows API calls should be unnecessary because the information is already retrieved.

Path.Combine()

The Path.Combine() method has new overloads that accept three and four parameters and an array of strings.

Isolated Storage

The default space allocation for isolated storage has now been doubled.

Registry Access Changes

The RegistryKey.CreateSubKey() method has a new option that allows the passing in of a RegistryOptions enumeration, allowing you to create a volatile registry key. Volatile registry keys are not persisted during reboots, so they are great for storing temporary data in. The following code shows how to create a volatile registry key:

```
var key = instance.CreateSubKey(subkey, RegistryKeyPermissionCheck.Default,
RegistryOptions.Volatile);
```

In 64-bit versions of Windows, data is stored separately in the registry for 32- and 64-bit applications. `OpenBaseKey()()` and `OpenRemoteBaseKey()` methods now allow you to specify a new enum called `RegistryView` for specifying the mode that should be used when reading. Note that if you mistakenly use the 64-bit option on a 32-bit version, you will get the 32-bit view.

Stream.CopyTo()

`Stream.CopyTo()` allows you to copy the contents of one stream to another, avoiding some tedious coding:

```
MemoryStream destinationStream = new MemoryStream();

using (FileStream sourceStream = File.Open(@"c:\temp.txt", FileMode.Open))
{
    sourceStream.CopyTo(destinationStream);
}
```

Guid.TryParse(), Version.TryParse(), and Enum.TryParse<T>()

New `TryParse()` methods have been added to `Guid`, `Version` and `Enum` types:

```
Guid myGuid;
Guid.TryParse("not a guid", out myGuid);
```

Enum.HasFlag()

Returns a Boolean value indicating whether one or more flags are set on an enum. For example, you could use the `HasFlag()` method to test whether a car has particular options set:

```
[Flags]
public enum CarOptions
{

    AirCon = 1,
    Turbo = 2,
    MP3Player = 4
}

static void Main(string[] args)
{
    CarOptions myCar = CarOptions.MP3Player | CarOptions.AirCon | CarOptions.Turbo;
    Console.WriteLine("Does car have MP3? {0}", myCar.HasFlag(CarOptions.MP3Player));
    Console.ReadKey();
}
```

String.Concat() and String.Join() support IEnumerable<T>

New overloads allow the concatenation and joining of `IEnumerable` elements without having to convert them to strings first, which can make LINQ queries cleaner.

String.IsNullOrWhiteSpace()

Detects if a string is null, empty, or consists of whitespace characters (avoiding a call to `Trim()`):

```
String.IsNullOrWhiteSpace(" ");
```

This is one of my favorite changes. It is such a common thing to do that it is great to have it baked into the framework.

StringBuilder.Clear

Removes content from the `StringBuilder` object (essentially the same as setting a string builder's length to 0, but with a more readable syntax):

```
StringBuilder sb = new StringBuilder("long string");
sb.Clear();
```

Note that calling `StringBuilder.Clear()` does not reset the `MaxCapacity` property.

Environment.SpecialFolder Enum Additions

The `SpecialFolder` enum has had a number of new options added to represent pretty much any type of folder on a Windows machine. For example, you can access the `CDBuring` folder:

```
Environment.SpecialFolder.CDBurning
```

Environment.Is64BitProcess and Environment.Is64BitOperatingSystem

64-bit is becoming mainstream now, so new methods have been added to return a Boolean value, indicating whether your application or process is running in a 64-bit process or on a 64-bit system:

```
Console.WriteLine(Environment.Is64BitOperatingSystem);
Console.WriteLine(Environment.Is64BitProcess);
```

Stopwatch.Restart()

Stops the recording of the current time period and starts a new one:

```
var sw = new Stopwatch();
sw.Start();
sw.Restart();
```

ServiceProcessInstaller.DelayedAutoStart

.NET services running on Vista or above can make use of the `ServiceProcessInstaller.DelayedAutoStart` feature to delay their start until other autostart services have already started. This can reduce the boot time for users.

Observable collection refactoring

`ObservableCollection<T>`, `ReadOnlyObservableCollection<T>`, and `System.Collections.Specialized.INotifyCollectionChanged` have been moved into `System.dll` because they were useful outside of WPF applications. This is great news because you no longer have to reference WPF assemblies.

IObservable<T>

An interface for implementation of the observer pattern.

Network Class Libraries (NCLs)

All classes in the `System.Net` namespace have improved stability and performance. Standards compliance has been improved for FTP, HTTP, SMTP, and URIs with better support for internationalization.

■**NOTE** At the time of writing, little information is available about these changes, so my apologies for the lack of detail.

IPv6 Support

Applications running on Vista onward can now handle multiple versions of the IP protocol (v4 & v6) by setting the `IPv6Only` option to `false` when creating the socket.

HttpWebRequest

`HttpWebRequest` has had two new properties added:

- Date for setting HTTP date header
- Host for setting HTTP host header (this can be useful for testing load balancing scenarios to test connection to a particular server)

Examples of these properties are as follows:

```
string loadbalancerIp = "http://127.0.0.1/";
string host = "mywebsite.com";
var request = WebRequest.Create("http://127.0.0.1/") as HttpWebRequest;
request.Date = System.DateTime.Now;
```

Support has also been added in `HttpWebRequest.AddRange()()` for int64 ranges.

DNS Endpoint

DnsEndPoint is a new class that allows you to create a socket connection by specifying a FQDN name without making a call to Dns.GetHostAddresses()() resulting in reduced and clearer code:

```
var socket = new System.Net.Sockets.Socket(new System.Net.Sockets.SocketInformation());
socket.Connect(new DnsEndPoint("www.microsoft.com", 80));
```

Default SSL policy

For interoperability, it is sometimes necessary to turn off SSL encryption (a null cipher). HttpWebRequest, FtpWebRequest, and SmtpClient now allow you to use a null cipher by specifying it using the System.Net.Security.EncryptionPolicy enum or in Web/machine.config:

SMTP Client

The SMTP client contains a number of useful enhancements:

- Enabling SSL mode in application config files
- Specifying heading encoding
- Multiple replying to addresses through MailMessage.ReplyToList()

TCPListener Support for NAT Transversal

Many applications are located behind a firewall, which can cause complications when communicating with them. One way around this is network address translation (NAT) transversal, which takes care of various complications. In .NET 4.0, NAT transversal support has been added to TcpListener and UdpClient.

WebRequest

New performance counters have been added for WebRequest:

- HttpWebRequests created/sec
- HttpWebRequests queued/sec
- HttpWebRequests aborted/sec
- HttpWebRequests failed/sec
- HttpWebRequest average lifetime
- HttpWebRequests' average queue time

You can review the diagram shown here to see where they occur in a request lifetime: http://blogs.msdn.com/blogfiles/ncl/WindowsLiveWriter/NewNCLFeaturesin.NET4.0Beta2_78A0/image_2.png.

Windows 7 Only

.NET 4.0 has some new features that are available only for Windows 7 machines.

System.Device.Location

.NET 4.0 contains a new API for querying Windows 7's location functionality. The Location class supports multiple devices such as GPS and wireless wide area network (WWAN—wireless by cellular phone technology). It returns the current latitude, longitude, altitude, horizontal and vertical accuracy, course, speed, and civic address (country/region, state/province, city, postal code, street, building, and floor level, if available). At the time of writing, the NCL team is refactoring these libraries.

ExtendedProtection

Windows 7 introduces enhanced security features to prevent replay network attacks. Classes in System.Net and related namespaces such as HttpWebListener, HttpWebRequest, NegotiateStream, SmtpClient, and SSLStream will now utilize these enhancements by default when Windows authentication is used. For the nitty-gritty full details of these changes, consult http://msdn. microsoft.com/en-us/library/dd582691(VS.100).aspx.

Deprecated APIs

A number of existing important APIs are now marked as deprecated. A full list is available at the following:

- http://msdn.microsoft.com/en-au/library/ee461503(VS.100).aspx (Types)
- http://msdn.microsoft.com/en-au/library/ee471421(VS.100).aspx (Members)

It is also worth noting two commonly used APIs that are now deprecated, as discussed in the next two sections.

System.Data.OracleClient

System.Data.OracleClient is available in .NET 4.0, but is marked as deprecated. Microsoft says this is because most developers use partner company Oracle providers. Microsoft will continue to issue hotfixes for critical OracleClient issues. For more info, refer to http://blogs.msdn.com/adonet/archive/2009/06/15/system-data-oracleclient-update.aspx.

Global Static Hosting Functions

Global static hosting functions have now been deprecated. For more info, please refer to http://msdn.microsoft.com/en-us/library/aa964945(VS.100).aspx.

Code Contracts

Code contracts are a method for expressing constraints and assumptions within your code. They allow specification of complex rules that can be validated at both compile time and runtime. Code contracts are also supported in VS2008.

NOTE Compile time or static verification is available only in the Premium/Ultimate editions of Visual Studio. This is a real shame because it will probably prevent widespread adoption of this great technology rather than encouraging users to purchase a more expensive edition of Visual Studio (similar to MSTest & VS2005?). Hopefully this is not permanent, and you will see static verification available in all future versions of Visual Studio.

In addition to providing validation, code contracts can assist with code documentation and aiding understanding of a problem. Functionality is available to automatically remove contracts from production code and separate them into a separate assembly if third parties want to use them. Code contracts are part of Microsoft's ongoing research project Spec #; Spec #'s developers say they have been influenced by the Eiffel, JML, and AsmL languages.

CAUTION Code contracts are still in active development, so this functionality might change.

Hello Code Contracts

To ensure that values are not null, you have probably written code similar to the following many times:

```
public void myFunction(string input)
{
    if(input==null) throw new System.NullReferenceException("Input cannot be null");
}
```

Or perhaps you utilized the debug or trace assert like so:

```
Debug.Assert(input != null);
```

Code contracts are superior to the previous methods because they do the following:

- Allow the creation of more complex rules
- Can help you write better code by getting you to think about constraints within your code
- Can reduce/prevent side effects

- Can be validated at both compile time and runtime

- Are easy to read

- Can be interpreted by automated tools such as PEX (http://research.microsoft.com/en-us/projects/Pex/)

- Work with XML documentation generation

- Unlike debug statements, can optionally be utilized in both debug and release builds

- Can be separated into separate assemblies for third-party use

Let's now create a simple code contract to ensure that an input value is not null or equal to 5.

Installing Code Contracts

Although VS2010 Professional edition contains some of the assemblies required for code contracts, the team didn't want to tie code contract development to the release of Visual Studio, so the Code Contract SDK is available as a separate download.

■**CAUTION** You can run the following code without downloading the SDK but the code contracts won't actually do anything. So make sure to download the SDK first.

There are two versions of the SDK available (currently named Standard edition and TFS edition). The TFS edition is for Premium/Ultimate and contains compile time verification and some additional features. The Standard edition does not contain this full static verification, but will offer warnings if contracts are breached (in my experiments with Invariants and Pure methods).

SDKs are available here: http://msdn.microsoft.com/en-us/devlabs/dd491992.aspx.

Example Code Contract

Once you have installed the Code Contract SDK, create a new console application and then add the following using directive:

```
using System.Diagnostics.Contracts;
```

Now add the following code:

```
static void Main(string[] args)
{
    DoSomething(5);
}
```

```
public static void DoSomething(int? Input)
{
    Contract.Requires(Input != null);
    Contract.Requires(Input != 5);
}
```

Before you run the application, go to the Properties page of your project and select the new Code Contracts tab (see Figure 4-4).

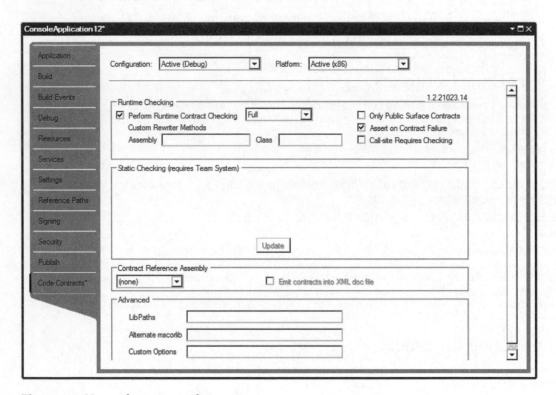

Figure 4-4. *New code contract tab*

Check the box marked Perform Runtime Contract Checking and run the code. You should receive an error message similar to that shown in Figure 4-5.

Figure 4-5. *Alert box showing failure of code contract assumption*

Enabling Code Contract Static Verification (Premium/Ultimate Edition Only)

To enable static verification, you need to go into the project Properties screen, select the Code Contract tab, and ensure that the static checking option is selected. When you compile your applications now, you should see the contracts are checked at compile time.

You might ask why static verification is not always on? One reason is that if you are writing unit tests, you might want to pass null values into your methods and ensure that your code handles them correctly. If static verification was always on, you could not run your unit tests.

Contract Inheritance

You should note that contracts are inherited between classes, but it is not possible to add additional preconditions.

Architecture

Behind the scenes, code contracts rewrite the generated IL. At a high level, you can divide code contract architecture into three main components:

- Static method (expresses assumptions and constraints; you will look at them shortly)
- Binary rewriter (performs runtime checks)
- Static checker (verifies assumptions at compile time; TFS edition only)

Let's now look at some of the different ways to declare assumptions in the code using the static methods available in code contracts.

Conditions

Code contracts allows you to create three types of conditions:

- Preconditions
- Postconditions
- Invariants

The following sections discuss some of the conditions you might want to utilize (this is by no means an exhaustive list and is being added to in each release).

Preconditions

Preconditions must be true at the start of a method.

Contract.Assert

In debug build, ensures that a condition is true.

```
Contract.Assert(Input != null);
```

Contract.Assume

Used for static verification and tells code analysis tools to assume that a condition is true (for example, if you are calling a method you have written and you are sure it will never return a null result):

```
Contract.Assume(Input!=null)
```

Contract.Requires

Ensures that a condition is true before subsequent code is run. The following will ensure that the input parameter is not null:

```
Contract.Requires(input != null);
```

Contract.Requires has an overload that allows you to specify and exception type and message to be thrown:

```
Contract.Requires<ArgumentNullException>(Input != null, "input");
```

Contract.EndContractBlock

The Contract.EndContractBlock statement tells the compiler to treat code as a precondition and allows you to utilize legacy code without converting it to code contracts format:

```
if (Input==null) throw new System.NullReferenceException("input is null");
Contract.EndContractBlock();
```

■**NOTE** You cannot use EndContractBlock in conjunction with any other preconditions.

Post Conditions

Post conditions are conditions that are true at the exit of your method calls.

Contract.Ensures

Ensures that a condition is true on exit of method:

```
Contract.Ensures(Output != 7);
```

Contract.EnsuresOnThrow

Ensures that a specific exception type is thrown for a condition:

```
Contract.EnsuresOnThrow<System.IO.IOException>(Input != null);
```

Contract.ForAll

Allows the iteration through a set to ensure that all members meet a specific condition:

```
Contract.ForAll(MySet, i=> i!=null);
```

Object Invariants

Object invariants allow you to specify conditions that must always be true for an object and are created by decorating a procedure with the [ContractInvariantMethod] attribute. The following code ensures that the ImportantData variable can never be null:

```
[ContractInvariantMethod]
void MyInvariant() {
    Contract.Invariant(ImportantData !=null);
}
```

Code Contract Values

Code contracts offer some useful pseudo variables that can be useful when writing your conditions.

Contract.Result

Contract.Result accesses a value in a condition that will be returned from a function without referring to it directly:

```
Contract.Ensures(Contract.Result<Int32?>() >= -1);
```

Contract.OldValue

Contract.OldValue represents the values state at the start of the method call. OldValue performs a shallow copy of the specified variable and can be used to see whether a value has changed:

```
Contract.Ensures(Input != Contract.OldValue(Input));
```

Pure

Methods that are called within a contract should be decorated with the attribute [Pure], which indicates that the method has no side effects (doesn't alter the state of any other objects). If you don't add this attribute, you will receive a warning similar to this:

```
Detected call to impure method
'ConsoleApplication6.Program.Multiply(System.Int32,System.Int32)' in a pure region
in method
```

To mark a method as pure, simply add the [Pure] attribute as follows:

```
[Pure]
public static double Multiply(int x, int y)
{
    return x * y;
}
```

Interface Contracts

Because interfaces cannot have method bodies, contracts must be declared in a slightly different way:

```
[ContractClass(typeof(ContractForInteface))]
interface IDoSomething
{
    int DoSomething(int value);
}

[ContractClassFor(typeof(IDoSomething))]
sealed class ContractForInteface : IDoSomething
{
    int IDoSomething.DoSomething(int value)
    {
        Contract.Requires( value != 0);

        //contracts require a dummy value
        return default(int);
    }
}
```

PEX

Developers interested in the code contracts features might also be interested in the PEX research project. PEX aims to automate testing by analyzing code. For more information, please refer to http://research.microsoft.com/en-us/projects/Pex/.

Conclusion

The changes to the CLR in this release have three main aims:

- Improve performance

- Offer better compatibility/control for applications built in previous versions of the .NET Framework

- Introduce functionality necessary for enhancements such as Dynamic Language Runtime (DLR) and parallelization (refer to Chapter 3)

The great news is that many of the low-level changes will make your applications run more quickly with no input required from you! A simplified security model is welcome, and it is good to see the addition of 64-bit support and APIs for working with some of the new Windows 7 features. A number of welcome tweaks have also been made to the BCL and NCL. Finally, you looked briefly at code contracts: a great method inspired outside of .NET to write safer and more reliable code. Great job, CLR and BCL team!

Further Reading

- http://blogs.msdn.com/bclteam/

- http://blogs.msdn.com/ncl/archive/2009/07/20/new-ncl-features-in-net-4-0-beta-2.aspx

- http://www.danielmoth.com/Blog/2008/11/new-and-improved-clr-4-thread-pool.html

- http://blogs.msdn.com/ericeil/archive/2009/04/23/clr-4-0-threadpool-improvements-part-1.aspx

- http://blogs.msdn.com/ukadc/archive/2009/10/13/background-and-foreground-gc-in-net-4.aspx

- http://blogs.msdn.com/shawnfa/

- http://msdn.microsoft.com/en-us/library/dd233103(VS.100).aspx

- http://download.microsoft.com/download/C/2/7/C2715F76-F56C-4D37-9231-EF8076B7EC13/userdoc.pdf

- http://msdn.microsoft.com/en-us/magazine/ee677170.aspx

CHAPTER 5

■ ■ ■

Parallelization and Threading Enhancements

Availability: Framework 4—Some Functionality in 3.5 with Parallel Extensions CTP

Until recently, CPU manufactures regularly released faster and faster processors. Speed increases, however, have all but ground to a halt due to various issues such as signal noise, power consumption, heat dissipation, and non-CPU bottlenecks.

No doubt these issues will be resolved in the future, but in the meantime manufacturers are instead concentrating on producing processors with multiple cores. Multicore processers can process sections of code in parallel, resulting in some calculations being performed quicker and thus increasing application performance. To take full advantage of multicore machines, however, code has to be designed to be run in parallel.

A number of years ago, Microsoft foresaw the importance that multicore processors would come to play and started developing the parallel extensions. In .NET 4.0, Microsoft built on this earlier work and integrated it into the core framework, enabling developers to parallelize their code in an easy and consistent way. Because this is the first mainstream release, it's probably wise to expect to see some minor tweaks and API changes in the future.

Although the parallelization enhancements make writing code to run in parallel much easier, don't underestimate the increasing complexity that parallelizing an application can bring. Parallelization shares many of the same issues you might have experienced when creating multithreaded applications. You must take care when developing parallel applications to isolate code that can be parallelized.

Parallelization Overview

Some of the parallelization enhancements might look familiar to a few readers because they were released previously as part of the parallel extensions. .NET 4.0 builds on this work but brings the extensions into the core CLR within mscorlib.dll.

The Microsoft parallel extensions and enhancements can be divided into five main areas:

- Task Parallel Library (TPL)) and Concurrency and Coordination Runtime (CCR)

- Parallel LINQ (PLINQ)

- New debugging and profiling tools

- Coordination data structures
- Parallel Pattern Library(PPL)—)—C++ only; not covered

Important Concepts

Parallelism and threading are confusing and there are a few questions many developers have (see the following questions).

Why Do I Need These Enhancements?

Can't you just create lots of separate threads? Well, you can, but there are a couple of issues with this approach. First, creating a thread is a resource-intensive process, so (depending on the type of work you do) it might be not the most efficient and quickest way to complete a task. Creating too many threads, for example, can slow task completion because each thread is never given time to complete as the operating system rapidly switches between them. And what happens if someone loads up two instances of your application?

To avoid these issues, .NET implements a thread pool that has a bunch of threads up and running, ready to do your bidding. The thread pool also can impose a limit on the number of threads created preventing thread starvation issues.

However the thread pool isn't so great at letting you know when work has been completed or cancelling running threads. The thread pool also doesn't have any information about the context in which the work is created, which means it can't schedule it as efficiently as it could have done. Enter the new parallelization functionality that provides additional cancellation and scheduling, and offers an intuitive way of programming.

Note that the parallelization functionality works on top of .NET's thread pool instead of replacing it. See Chapter 4 for details about improvements made to the thread pool in this release.

Concurrent!= Parallel

If your application is multithreaded is it running in parallel? Probably not—applications running on a single CPU machine can appear to run in parallel because the operating system allocates time with the CPU to each thread and then rapidly switches between them (known as time slicing). Threads might not ever be actually running at the same time (although they could be), whereas in a parallelized application work is actually being conducted at the same time (Figure 5-1). Processing work at the same time can introduce some complications in your application regarding access to resources.

Daniel Moth (from the Parallel computing team at Microsoft) puts it succinctly when he says the following (http://www.danielmoth.com/Blog/2008/11/threadingconcurrency-vs-parallelism.html):

> "On a single core you can use threads and you can have concurrency, but to achieve parallelism on a multi-core box you have to identify in your code the exploitable concurrency: the portions of your code that can truly run at the same time."

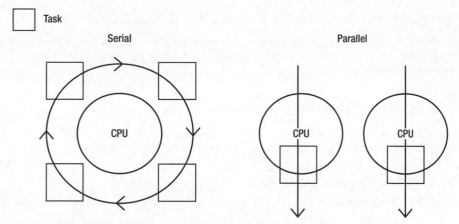

Figure 5-1. *Multithreaded!=parallelization*

Warning: Threading and Parallelism Will Increase Your Application's Complexity

Although the new parallelization enhancements greatly simplify writing parallelized applications, they do not negate a number of issues that you might have encountered in any application utilizing multiple threads:

- *Race conditions*: "Race conditions arise in software when separate processes or threads of execution depend on some shared state. Operations upon shared states are critical sections that must be atomic to avoid harmful collision between processes or threads that share those states."

  http://en.wikipedia.org/wiki/Race_condition.

- *Deadlocks*: "A deadlock is a situation in which two or more competing actions are waiting for the other to finish, and thus neither ever does. It is often seen in a paradox like the chicken or the egg." http://en.wikipedia.org/wiki/Deadlock.

  Also see http://en.wikipedia.org/wiki/Dining_philosophers_problem.

- *Thread starvation*: Thread starvation can be caused by creating too many threads (no one thread gets enough time to complete its work because of CPU time slicing) or a flawed locking mechanism that results in a deadlock.

- *Difficult to code and debug.*

- *Environmental*: Optimizing code for different machine environments (e.g., CPUs/cores, memory, storage media, and so on).

Crap Code Running in Parallel is Just Parallelized Crap Code

Perhaps this is an obvious point, but before you try to speed up any code by parallelizing it, ensure that it is written in the most efficient manner. Crap code running in parallel is now just parallelized crap code; it still won't perform as well as it could!

What Applications Benefit from Parallelism?

Many applications contain some segments of code that will benefit from parallelization; and some that will not. Code that is likely to benefit from being run in parallel will probably have the following characteristics:

- It can be broken down into self-encapsulated units.

- It has no dependencies or shared state.

A classic example of code that would benefit from being run in parallel is code that goes off to call an external service or perform a long-running calculation (for example, iterating through some stock quotes and performing a long-running calculation by iterating through historical data on each individual quote).

This type of problem is an ideal candidate for parallelization because each individual calculation is independent so can safely be run in parallel. Some people like to refer to such problems as "embarrassingly parallel" (although Stephen Toub of Microsoft suggests "delightfully parallel"!) in that they are very well-suited for the benefits of parallelization.

I Have Only a Single Core Machine; Can I Run These Examples?

Yes. The parallel runtime won't mind. This is a really important benefit of using parallel libraries because they will scale automatically, saving you from having to alter your code to target your applications for different environments.

Can the Parallelization Features Slow Me Down?

Maybe—although the difference is probably negligible. In some cases, using the new parallelization features (especially on a single core machine) could slow your application down due to the additional overhead involved. However, if you have written some custom scheduling mechanism, the chances are that Microsoft's implementation might perform more quickly and offer a number of other benefits, as you will see.

Performance

Of course, the main aim of parallelization is to increase an applications performance. But what sort of gains can you expect?

For the test application, I used some of the parallel code samples (http://code.msdn.microsoft.com/ParExtSamples). The code shown in Table 5-1 was run on a Dell XPS M1330 64bit Windows 7 Ultimate laptop with Visual Studio 2010 Professional Beta 2. The laptop has an Intel Duo Core CPU 2.5 MHz, 6 MB cache, and 4 GB of memory.

Table 5-1. *Comparison of parallelization effects*

Item	In Serial (seconds)	In Parallel (seconds)	Diff (seconds)	Percentage difference rounded to 0dp
Baby name PLINQ example (analyzes baby name popularity by state on 3 million randomly generated records)	5.92	3.47	-2.45	71%
Raytracing example	5.03	2.79	-2.24	80%

Interested? Thought you might be!

■**TIP** Want to know the sort of increase you can get from parallelization? Check out Amdahl's Law: `http://en.wikipedia.org/wiki/Amdahl%27s_law`.

Parallel Loops

One of the easiest ways to parallelize your application is by using the Parallel Loop construct. Two types of loop can be run in parallel:

- `Parallel.For()`
- `Parallel.ForEach()`

Let's take a look at these now.

Parallel.For()

In our example application, we will stick with the stock quote scenario described previously, create a list of stock quotes, and then iterate through them using a `Parallel.For()` loop construct, passing each quote into a function that will simulate a long running process.

To see the differences between running code in serial and parallel, we will also perform this task using a standard `for` loop. We will use a stopwatch instance to measure the time each loop takes to complete. It is worth stressing that you should always measure the performance impact that parallelization can have on your applications.

An Unrealistic Example?

Yes. To keep things very simple, we will just call `Thread.Sleep()` for two seconds and then return a random number to simulate performing a calculation. Most parallelization examples tend to calculate factorials or walk trees of data, but I think this distracts (at least initially) from understanding the basics. If you want to work with a more realistic example, take a look at the examples from the parallel team; you will find excellent ray tracing and other math related examples.

Note that calling the Thread.Sleep() method will involve a context switch (an expensive operation for the CPU), so it might slow the sample application down more than performing work might have.

1. Create a new console application called Chapter5.HelloParalleland add the following using directives:

```
using System.Diagnostics;
using System.Threading.Tasks;
```

2. Amend Program.cs to the following code:

```
class Program
{
    public static List<StockQuote> Stocks = new List<StockQuote>();

    static void Main(string[] args)
    {
        double serialSeconds = 0;
        double parallelSeconds = 0;

        Stopwatch sw = new Stopwatch();

        PopulateStockList();

        sw = Stopwatch.StartNew();
        RunInSerial();
        serialSeconds = sw.Elapsed.TotalSeconds;

        sw = Stopwatch.StartNew();
        RunInParallel();
        parallelSeconds = sw.Elapsed.TotalSeconds;

        Console.WriteLine(
         "Finished serial at {0} and took {1}", DateTime.Now, serialSeconds);
        Console.WriteLine(
         "Finished parallel at {0} and took {1}", DateTime.Now, parallelSeconds);

        Console.ReadLine();

    }


    private static void PopulateStockList()
    {
        Stocks.Add(new StockQuote { ID = 1, Company = "Microsoft", Price = 5.34m });
        Stocks.Add(new StockQuote { ID = 2, Company = "IBM", Price = 1.9m });
        Stocks.Add(new StockQuote { ID = 3, Company = "Yahoo", Price = 2.34m });
        Stocks.Add(new StockQuote { ID = 4, Company = "Google", Price = 1.54m });
        Stocks.Add(new StockQuote { ID = 5, Company = "Altavista", Price = 4.74m });
        Stocks.Add(new StockQuote { ID = 6, Company = "Ask", Price = 3.21m });
```

```
            Stocks.Add(new StockQuote { ID = 7, Company = "Amazon", Price = 20.8m });
            Stocks.Add(new StockQuote { ID = 8, Company = "HSBC", Price = 54.6m });
            Stocks.Add(new StockQuote { ID = 9, Company = "Barclays", Price = 23.2m });
            Stocks.Add(new StockQuote { ID = 10, Company = "Gilette", Price = 1.84m });
        }

        private static void RunInSerial()
        {
            for (int i = 0; i < Stocks.Count; i++)
            {
                Console.WriteLine("Serial processing stock: {0}",Stocks[i].Company);
                StockService.CallService(Stocks[i]);
                Console.WriteLine();
            }
        }

        private static void RunInParallel()
        {
            Parallel.For(0, Stocks.Count, i =>
            {
                Console.WriteLine("Parallel processing stock: {0}", Stocks[i].Company);
                StockService.CallService(Stocks[i]);
                Console.WriteLine();
            });
        }
    }
```

3. Create a new class called StockQuote and add the following code:

Listing 5-1. *Parallel For Loop*

```
public class StockQuote
{
    public int ID {get; set;}
    public string Company { get; set; }
    public decimal Price{get; set;}
}
```

4. Create a new class called StockService and enter the following code:

```
public class StockService
{
    public static decimal CallService(StockQuote Quote)
    {
        Console.WriteLine("Executing long task for {0}", Quote.Company);
        var rand = new Random(DateTime.Now.Millisecond);
        System.Threading.Thread.Sleep(1000);
        return Convert.ToDecimal(rand.NextDouble());
    }
}
```

Press F5 to run the code. When I run the code on my machine I receive the output shown in Figure 5-2.

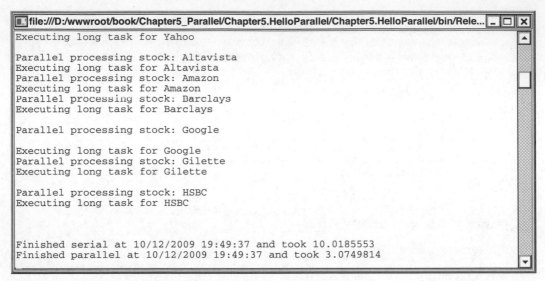

```
file:///D:/wwwroot/book/Chapter5_Parallel/Chapter5.HelloParallel/Chapter5.HelloParallel/bin/Rele...
Executing long task for Yahoo

Parallel processing stock: Altavista
Executing long task for Altavista
Parallel processing stock: Amazon
Executing long task for Amazon
Parallel processing stock: Barclays
Executing long task for Barclays

Parallel processing stock: Google

Executing long task for Google
Parallel processing stock: Gilette
Executing long task for Gilette

Parallel processing stock: HSBC
Executing long task for HSBC



Finished serial at 10/12/2009 19:49:37 and took 10.0185553
Finished parallel at 10/12/2009 19:49:37 and took 3.0749814
```

Figure 5-2. *Output of parallel for loop against serial processing*

Are the stock quotes processed incrementally or in a random order? You might have noted that your application did not necessarily process the stock quotes in the order in which they were added to the list when run in parallel. This is because work was divided between the cores on your machine, so it's important to remember that work might not (and probably won't) be processed sequentially. You will look at how the work is shared out in more detail when we look at the new task functionality.

Try running the code again. Do you get similar results? The quotes might be processed in a slightly different order, and speed increases might vary slightly depending on what other applications are doing on your machine. When measuring performance, be sure to perform a number of tests.

Let's now take a look at the syntax used in the Parallel.For() loop example:

```
System.Threading.Parallel.For(0, Stocks.Count, i =>
{
..
}
```

The Parallel.For() method actually has 12 different overloads, but this particular version accepts 3 parameters:

- 0 is the counter for the start of the loop.

- Stocks.Count lets the loop know when to stop.

- i=>: Our friendly lambda statement (or inline function) with the variable i representing the current iteration, which allows you to query the list of stocks.

ParallelOptions

Some of the various parallel overloads allow you to specify options such as the number of cores to use when running the loop in parallel by using the `ParallelOptions` class. The following code limits the number of cores to use for processing to two. You might want to do this to ensure cores are available for other applications.

```
ParallelOptions options = new ParallelOptions { MaxDegreeOfParallelism = 2 };

Parallel.For(0, 100, options, x=>
{
    //Do something
});
```

Parallel.ForEach()

Similar to the `Parallel.For()` loop, the `Parallel.ForEach()` method allows you to iterate through an object supporting the `IEnumerable` interface:

```
Parallel.ForEach(Stocks, stock  =>
{
    StockService.CallService(stock);
});
```

Warning: Parallelization Can Hurt Performance

Parallelizing code contains overhead and can actually slow down your code, including when there are loops that run a very small amounts of code in each iteration. Please refer to the following articles about why this occurs:

- http://msdn.microsoft.com/en-us/library/dd560853(VS.100).aspx
- http://en.wikipedia.org/wiki/Context_switch

Parallel.Invoke()

The `Parallel.Invoke()` method can be used to execute code in parallel. It has the following syntax:

```
Parallel.Invoke(()=>StockService.CallService(Stocks[0]),
    () => StockService.CallService(Stocks[1]),
    () => StockService.CallService(Stocks[2])
);
```

When you use `Parallel.Invoke()` or any of the parallel loops, the parallel extensions are behind the scenes using tasks. Let's take a look at tasks now.

Tasks

Task is a new class that represents the work you want completed. There are methods to create, schedule, and synchronize tasks in your application.

Task Scheduler

All the complexity of working with tasks is handled by the task scheduler, which in turn works with the main .NET thread pool. You can think of tasks as a wrapper for the thread pool and the preferred way of scheduling threads (although there is some additional overhead). The existing thread pool methods will continue to work, but tasks are much easier to use and have additional functionality.

So how does the task scheduler work?

1. When tasks are created, they are added to a global task queue.

2. The thread pool will create a number of "worker" threads. The exact number that are created depends on a number of factors such as the number of cores on the machine, current work load, type of work load, and so on. The thread pool utilizes a hill-climbing algorithm that dynamically adjusts the thread pool to use the optimum number of threads. For example, if the thread pool detects that many threads have an I/O bottleneck, it will create additional threads to complete the work more quickly. The thread pool contains a background thread that checks every 0.5 seconds to see whether any work has been completed. If no work has been done (and there is more work to do), a new thread will be created to perform this work.

3. Each worker thread picks up tasks from the global queue and moves it onto its local queue for execution.

4. Each worker thread processes the tasks on its queue.

5. If a thread finishes all the work in its local queue, it steals work from other queues to ensure that work is processed as quickly as possible. Note that tasks will steal work from the end of the other task's queues to minimize the chance that the task has started operating with the work already.

6. Figure 5-3 demonstrates this process.

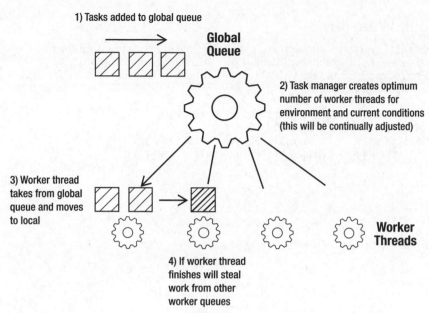

Figure 5-3. *Overview of task manager*

Creating a New Task

Tasks are very easy to schedule and I think more intuitive than working with traditional threading and the thread pool. There are a number of ways to create a new task, but before you see them, you need to add the following using directive because all the task functionality is found in the System.Threading.Tasks namespace:

```
using System.Threading.Tasks;
```

The easiest way to create a task is with the Task.Factory.StartNew() method. This method accepts an Action delegate and immediately starts the task when created.

```
Task task1 = Task.Factory.StartNew(() => Console.WriteLine("hello task 1"));
```

Another way to create a task is to pass the code you want run into the task's constructor. The main difference with this method is that you have to explicitly start the task when using this method. This method could be useful for scenarios in which you don't want the task to run as soon as it is declared:

```
Task task2 = new Task(() => Console.WriteLine("hello task 2"));
task2.Start();
```

Task.Wait() and Task.WaitAll()

The Task.Wait() and Task.WaitAll() methods allow you to pause the flow of execution until the tasks you specify have completed their work. The following listing shows an example of using the Wait() method to ensure that task1 has completed and the WaitAll() method to ensure that task2, task3, and task4 have finished before exiting the application:

```
Task task1 = Task.Factory.StartNew(() => Console.WriteLine("hello task 1"));
Task task2 = new Task(() => Console.WriteLine("hello task 2"));
Task task3 = Task.Factory.StartNew(() => Console.WriteLine("hello task 3"));
Task task4 = Task.Factory.StartNew(() => Console.WriteLine("hello task 4"));

task2.Start();

task1.Wait();
Task.WaitAll(task2, task3, task4);
```

Figure 5-4 illustrates the waiting process.

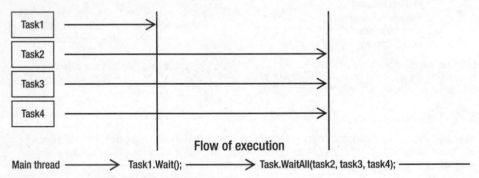

Figure 5-4. *Flow of execution for the Task.Wait() example*

Task.WaitAny()

You can wait for any task to complete with the Task.WaitAny() method. It could be used, for example, if many tasks were retrieving the same data (e.g., the latest Microsoft stock price) from a number of different sources and you didn't care which individual source you received the information from.

```
Task.WaitAny(task2, task3, task4);
```

IsCompleted

You can see whether a task is completed by querying the IsCompleted property. It returns a Boolean value indicating whether the task has completed its work.

```
while (task1.IsCompleted == false)
{
    Console.WriteLine("Waiting on task 1");
}
```

ContinueWith()

It is often necessary to specify that work should be performed in a specific order. This can be declared in a fluent manner with the ContinueWith() method. In previous examples, the tasks occurred out of the order in which they were created. If you want to enforce this order one way, you could use the ContinueWith() method as follows:

```
Task task3 = Task.Factory.StartNew(() => Console.WriteLine("hello task 1"))
    .ContinueWith((t)=>  Console.WriteLine("hello task 2") )
    .ContinueWith((t)=>  Console.WriteLine("hello task 3") )
    .ContinueWith((t)=>  Console.WriteLine("hello task 4") );
```

The ContinueWith() method also accepts a TaskContinuationOptions enumeration that allows you to specify what should occur if a task fails, as well as a number of other situations. The following code calls the stock service with Stocks[1] as a parameter if the previous task failed to run:

```
Task task3 = Task.Factory.StartNew(() => doSomethingBad())
    .ContinueWith((t) => System.Diagnostics.Trace.Write("I will be run"),
    TaskContinuationOptions.OnlyOnFaulted);
```

Do Parallel Loops Create a Thread for Each Iteration?

The answer is maybe but not necessarily. Tasks are created in order to perform the work as quick as possible but it is up to the task manager and scheduler to decide the optimum means to achieve this.

Returning Values from Tasks

You can retrieve a value that has been returned from a task by querying the result property:

```
var data = Task.Factory.StartNew(() => GetResult());
Console.WriteLine("Parallel task returned with value of {0}", data.Result);
```

An alternative method can be used if you are using Task<T> type:

```
Task<string> t = new Task<string>(()=>GetResult());
t.Start();
Console.WriteLine("Parallel task returned with value of {0}", t.Result);
```

What if the Task Does Not Yet Have a Result?

If you try and access the result of a task, and the task has completed its work, the value will be returned as you would expect. If, however, the task has not completed, execution will block until the task has completed. This could slow your application down as the common language runtime (CLR)) waits for a value to be returned. To minimize this, you probably want to run the task as soon as possible before you need access to the actual value.

Task Creation Options

When you create a task, you can specify hints to the scheduler about how the task should be scheduled using the TaskCreationOptions class:

- AttachedToParent: The task is not attached to the parent.

- LongRunning: Hints that the task will run for a long time for optimal scheduling.

- None: Default scheduling behavior.

- PreferFairness: The tasks should be scheduled in the order in which they are created.

Task Status

Tasks can have the following status:

- Cancelled: The task was cancelled before it reached running status or the cancellation acknowledged and completed with no exceptions.

- Created: The task was created but not initialized.

- Faulted: Completed due to an exception that was not handled.

- RanToCompletion: Completed successfully.

- Running: The task currently running.

- WaitingForActivation: The task waiting to be activated and scheduled.

- WaitingForChildrenToComplete: Waiting for child tasks to complete.

- WaitingToRun: Scheduled but not yet run.

Overriding TaskScheduler

When tasks are created, they are scheduled using the default implementation of the TaskScheduler class (TaskScheduler.Default). TaskScheduler is abstract and can be overridden if you want to provide your own implementation.

Scheduling on UI thread

TaskScheduler supports the ability to schedule items on the UI thread, saving you from writing some tedious marshalling code. For more info on this please refer to http://blogs.msdn.com/pfxteam/archive/2009/04/14/9549246.aspx.

Parallel Debugging Enhancements

Writing parallel and threaded applications is hard. To help, Microsoft has added additional debugging features to the Visual Studio IDE (premium versions include additional profiling features). To demonstrate these features, we will create a new simple console application.

Create a new project called Chapter5.Debugging and enter the following code:

```
using System.Threading.Tasks;

static void Main(string[] args)
{
    Task task1 = Task.Factory.StartNew(() => startAnotherTask());
    Task task2 = Task.Factory.StartNew(() => startAnotherTask());
    Task task3 = Task.Factory.StartNew(() => doSomething());
    Console.ReadKey();
}

static void startAnotherTask()
{
    Task task4 = Task.Factory.StartNew(() => doSomethingElse());
}

static void doSomething()
{
    System.Threading.Thread.Sleep(500000);
}

static void doSomethingElse()
{
    System.Threading.Thread.Sleep(500000);
}
```

Put a breakpoint on the line that reads as follows:

```
Task task3 = Task.Factory.StartNew(() => doSomething());
```

The first feature we will look at is the Parallel Task window.

Parallel Task Window

This window shows you all the tasks that are currently running and contains features for filtering and jumping directly to where the task is declared.

Run the application in debug mode, ensuring that you have added a breakpoint to the first line. When the breakpoint is hit on the main menu, go to Debug➤Windows➤Parallel Tasks (Ctrl+Shift+D+K) and you will see a window like the one shown in Figure 5-5 that allows you to review the current status of all your tasks.

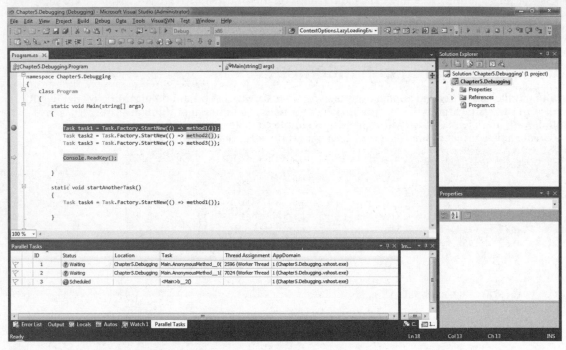

Figure 5-5. *Parallel Tasks debugging window*

The Parallel Tasks window offers the following functionality:

- You can order the view by clicking the column headings.

- You can group tasks by status by right-clicking the status column and selecting Group by status.

- To show more detail about a task, right-click any of the headings and check the options you want to view. Note that Parent is a useful option that displays the ID of the parent task that created it (if any).

- You can double-click the task to be taken into the code that task is running.

- Tasks can be flagged to help you identify them and filter views. To flag a task, simply click the flag icon on the left side.

- Tasks can have one of four statuses: running, scheduled, waiting, or waiting-deadlocked. If you have a task with waiting or deadlocked status, move the mouse over the task to display a tooltip of what it is currently waiting for.

- Tasks can be frozen by right-clicking them and selecting the Freeze Assigned Thread option. Select the Thaw Assigned thread option to unfreeze them.

■**TIP** When debugging parallelized applications, it is also useful to have the threads window open by going to Debug➤Windows➤Threads.

Parallel Stacks Window

The Parallel Stacks window enables you to visualize multiple call stacks within one window. It operates in two modes, Task or Thread, which can be changed in the drop-down menu in the left corner.

We will take a look at the Thread mode (the Task mode is very similar, but shows only tasks), so make sure that Threads is selected in the drop-down menu.

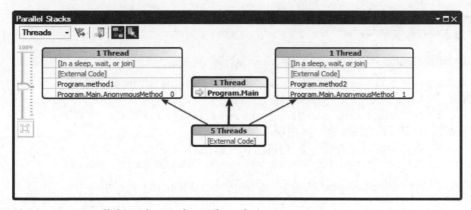

Figure 5-6. *Parallel Stacks window: Thread view*

At first the Parallel Stacks window can look a bit confusing:

- Threads are grouped together by the method (context) they are currently in, indicated by a box.

- The blue border around a box shows that the current thread belongs to that box.

- The yellow arrow indicates the active stack frame of the currently executing thread (in this case, the main method).

Figure 5-7 shows the Parallel Stacks window operating in Task mode.

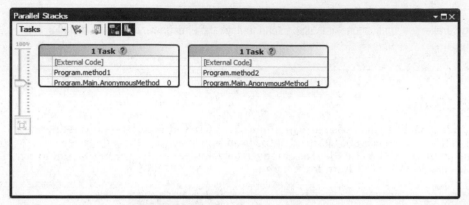

Figure 5-7. *Parallel Stack window: Task view*

The Parallel Stacks window offers the following functionality:

- If you hover the mouse over a box, the current associated thread ID will be shown in the tooltip.

- You can jump to the individual associated frames by right-clicking a box and selecting Switch To Frame on the context menu.

- If a box is associated to only one thread (indicated by 1 in the boxes header), you can double-click the box to be taken to the code associated with that stack frame.

There are a number of view options on the Parallel Stacks window. Reading from left to right, they are as follows:

- *Show only flagged*: Filters whether currently flagged tasks are displayed.

- *Toggle Method view*: Select a "box" on the diagram and then select this option. The current method then appears in the center of the view, showing the methods that call and are called from this method.

- *Toggle top down/bottom up display*: The default is that the initial thread is shown at the base of the view with subsequent calls above it. Select this option to invert the display.

- *AutoScroll option*: Moves the windows focus automatically as you step through the code to the currently executing frame.

- *Toggle Zoom Control option*: Controls whether to display zoom control to the left of the diagram. Note that you can zoom in and out by pressing Ctrl and moving the mouse scroll wheel.

- *Birds-eye view button*: On larger diagrams, when scroll bars are visible in the Parallel Stacks window, you can click between them to quickly move around the diagram

- *Individual threads:* Right-clicking on an individual thread brings up a context menu that allows you to switch to the task, frame, source code, setup symbols, and so on.

■**NOTE** Daniel Moth has recorded some great screen casts and written some excellent articles on parallel debugging at `http://www.danielmoth.com/Blog/2009/11/parallel-debugging.html`.

PLINQ (Parallel LINQ)

PLINQ is the parallelized version of LINQ to objects and supports all existing LINQ operators and functionality with a few new options for fine-grained control of parallelization functionality. The new functionality has been introduced through the interface `IParallelEnumerable<T>>` that inherits from `IEnumerable<T>>`.

At the time of writing, LINQ to SQL and LINQ to Entities will not benefit from parallelization because in these cases the query is executed on the database or the provider, so .NET cannot parallelize it.

Why Not Parallelize All LINQ Queries Automatically?

Parallelizing LINQ queries automatically is potentially the ultimate goal for LINQ, but it can introduce some issues (particularly around ordering), so at present you have to opt in to the parallel model.

A WORD OF WARNING

When using PLINQ, it is important to ensure that your query does not modify the result set because this might have unforeseen effects if values are utilized later in the query. PLINQ will do its best to work out best how to process the query (including not running it in parallel at all), but do you really want to take the chance of weird, scary, and hard-to-reproduce bugs?

Hello PLINQ

This example iterates through all the objects in the stock list, calls an external service, and processes the result.

Writing such a query in traditional LINQ might look something like this:

```
var query = from s in Stocks
                let result = StockService.CallService(s)
                select result;
```

To run the same query in parallel, simply use the `.AsParallel()` extension method to the `Stocks` object:

```
var query = from s in Stocks.AsParallel()
                let result = StockService.CallService(s)
                select result;
```

It really is as easy as that (well almost...).

Ordering Results

To order the results of your queries, use the AsOrdered() method to tell .NET to buffer the results before sorting them. This will slow the query down slightly because PLINQ now has to do additional work to preserve the ordering:

```
var query = from s in Stocks.AsParallel().AsOrdered()
                orderby s.Company
                let company = s.Company
                let result = StockService.CallService(s)
```

Note that the AsUnordered() operator can be used to tell PLINQ that you no longer care about ordering items.

ForAll Operator()

Iterating through the results of a LINQ query requires that all the output be merged together. If results ordering is not important, you should use the ForAll() operator, which avoids merging the results set, thus executing more quickly:

```
query.ForAll(result => Console.WriteLine(result));
```

■**TIP** Query performance can also be further increased by using the orderby clause in your LINQ query when combined with a filtering operation such as where because the ordering will then be applied only to the filtered results.

AsSequential()

The AsSequential() method forces PLINQ to process all operations sequentially, which can sometimes be required when you are working with user-defined query methods:

```
var query = from s in Stocks.AsParallel().AsSequential()
                let result = StockService.CallService(s)
                select result;
```

WithMergeOptions

The WithMergeOptions operator allows you to tell PLINQ how you want results to be merged when processing is complete. PLINQ is not guaranteed to do this, though. WithMergeOptions operates in three modes:

- NotBuffered: Results are returned sooner, but slower overall.

- FullyBuffered: Quickest option but results are returned slowest.

- AutoBuffered: Chunks items returned and offers a middle ground between the other two options.

PLINQ performance

Sometimes the overhead of parallelizing a query can actually make it perform more slowly than if it was run sequentially, so be sure to measure your queries' performance. LINQ queries are not actually executed until you enumerate through them (deferred execution), so measuring performance can be slightly harder. Thus if you want to measure the performance, be sure to iterate through the data in the result set or call a method such as ToList.

■**TIP** Visual Studio Premium edition onward also contains a parallel performance analyzer, which allows you to compare the performance of queries.

Cancelling a PLINQ Query

You can cancel a PLINQ query by passing in a CancellationTokenSource, which is discussed very shortly, into the WithCancellation() method.

Exceptions and Parallel LINQ

When a query is run in parallel, exceptions can occur in multiple threads. PLINQ aggregates these exceptions into an AggregateException class and returns them back to the caller. You can then iterate through each individual exception.

   If you run the following example, you need to modify a setting in the IDE to see it working. To do this, go to Tools➤Options➤Debugging➤General and uncheck the Enable Just my code option or run in Release mode.

```
//select stock that doesnt exist
var query =  from s in Stocks.AsParallel()
let result = StockService.CallService(Stocks[11])
select result;

try
{
    query.ForAll(result=>Console.WriteLine(result.ToString()));
}
catch (AggregateException e)
{
    foreach (var ex in e.InnerExceptions)
    {
        Console.WriteLine(ex.Message);
    }
}
```

Coordination Data Structures (CDS) and Threading Enhancements

In .NET 4.0, the thread pool has been enhanced, and a number of new synchronization classes have been introduced.

Thread Pool Enhancements

Creating many threads to perform small amounts of work can actually end up taking longer than performing the work on a single thread. This is due to time slicing and the overhead involved in locking, and adding and removing items to the thread pools queue.

Previously ,the queue of work in the thread pool was held in a linked list structure and utilized a monitor lock. Microsoft improved this by changing to a data structure that is lock-free and involves the garbage collector doing less work. Microsoft says that this new structure is very similar to ConcurrentQueue (discussed shortly).

The great news is that you should find that if your existing applications are using the thread pool and you upgrade them to .NET 4.0 then your applications performance should be improved with no changes to your code required.

Thread.Yield()

Calling the new Thread.Yield() method tells the thread to give its remaining time with the processor (time slice) to another thread. It is up to the operating system to select the thread that receives the additional time. The thread that yield is called on is then rescheduled in the future. Note that yield is restricted to the processor/core that the yielded thread is operating within.

Monitor.Enter()

The Monitor.Enter() method has a new overload that takes a Boolean parameter by reference and sets it to true if the monitor call is successful. For example:

```
bool gotLock = false;
object lockObject = new object();

try
{
   Monitor.Enter(lockObject, ref gotLock);
    //Do stuff
}
finally
{
   if (gotLock)
   {
       Monitor.Exit(lockObject);
   }
}
```

Concurrent Collections

The concurrent collection classes are thread-safe versions of many of the existing collection classes that should be used for multithreaded or parallelized applications. They can all be found lurking in the `System.Collections.Concurrent` namespace.

When you use any of these classes, it is not necessary to write any locking code because these classes will take care of locking for you. MSDN documentation states that these classes will also offer superior performance to `ArrayList` and generic list classes when accessed from multiple threads.

ConcurrentStack

Thread-safe version of stack (LIFO collection).

ConcurrentQueue

Thread-safe version of queue (FIFO collection).

ConcurrentDictionary

Thread-safe version of dictionary class.

ConcurrentBag

`ConcurrentBag` is a thread-safe, unordered, high-performance collection of items contained in `System.dll`. `ConcurrentBags` are used when it is not important to maintain the order of items in the collection. `ConcurrentBags` also allow the insertion of duplicates.

`ConcurrentBags` can be very useful in multithreaded environments because each thread that accesses the bag has its own dequeue. When the dequeue is empty for an individual thread, it will then access the bottom of another thread's dequeue reducing the chance of contention occurring. Note that this same technique is used within the thread pool for providing load balancing.

BlockingCollection

`BlockingCollection` is a collection that enforces upper and lower boundaries in a thread-safe manner. If you attempt to add an item when the upper or lower bounds have been reached, the operation will be blocked, and execution will pause. If on the other hand, you attempt to remove an item when the `BlockingCollection` is empty, this operation will also be blocked.

This is useful for a number of scenarios, such as the following:

- Increasing performance by allowing threads to both retrieve and add data from it. For example, it could read from disk or network while another processes items.

- Preventing additions to a collection until the existing items are processed.

The following example creates two threads: one that will read from the blocking collection and another to add items to it. Note that we can enumerate through the collection and add to it at the same time, which is not possible with previous collection types.

CAUTION It is important to note that the enumeration will continue indefinitely until the `CompleteAdding()` method is called.

```csharp
using System;
using System.Collections.Generic;
using System.Linq;
using System.Text;
using System.Dynamic;
using System.Threading.Tasks;
using System.Diagnostics;
using System.Threading;
using System.Collections.Concurrent;

namespace ConsoleApplication7
{
    class Program
    {
        public static BlockingCollection<string> blockingCol =
        new BlockingCollection<string>(5);
        public static string[] Alphabet = new string[5] { "a", "b", "c", "d", "e" };

        static void Main(string[] args)
        {
            ThreadPool.QueueUserWorkItem(new WaitCallback(ReadItems));
            Console.WriteLine("Created thread to read items");

            //Creating thread to read items note how we are already enumurating collection!
            ThreadPool.QueueUserWorkItem(new WaitCallback(AddItems));
            Console.WriteLine("Created thread that will add items");

            //Stop app closing
            Console.ReadKey();
        }

        public static void AddItems(object StateInfo)
        {
            int i = 0;
            while (i < 200)
            {
                blockingCol.Add(i++.ToString());
                Thread.Sleep(10);
            }
        }
    }
```

```
    public static void ReadItems(object StateInfo)
    {
        //Warning this will run forever unless blockingCol.CompleteAdding() is called
        foreach (object o in blockingCol.GetConsumingEnumerable())
        {
            Console.WriteLine("Read item: " + o.ToString());
        }
    }

  }
}
```

Synchronization Primitives

.NET 4.0 introduces a number of synchronization classes (discussed in the following sections).

Barrier

The Barrier class allows you to synchronize threads at a specific point. The MSDN documentation has a good analogy: the barrier class works a bit like a few friends driving from different cities and agreeing to meet up at a gas station (the barrier) before continuing their journey.

The following example creates two threads: one thread will take twice as long as the other to complete its work. When both threads have completed their work, execution will continue after the call to SignalAndWait()() has been made by both threads.

```
using System.Threading;

class Program
{
    static Barrier MyBarrier;
    static void Main(string[] args)
    {
        //There will be two participants in this barrier
        MyBarrier = new Barrier(2);

        Thread shortTask = new Thread(new ThreadStart(DoSomethingShort));
        shortTask.Start();

        Thread longTask = new Thread(new ThreadStart(DoSomethingLong));
        longTask.Start();

        Console.ReadKey();
    }

    static void DoSomethingShort()
    {
        Console.WriteLine("Doing a short task for 5 seconds");
        Thread.Sleep(5000);
        Console.WriteLine("Completed short task");
```

```
        MyBarrier.SignalAndWait();

        Console.WriteLine("Off we go from short task!");
    }

    static void DoSomethingLong()
    {
        Console.WriteLine("Doing a long task for 10 seconds");
        Thread.Sleep(10000);
        Console.WriteLine("Completed a long task");
        MyBarrier.SignalAndWait();
        Console.WriteLine("Off we go from long task!");
    }

}
```

The Barrier class also allows you to change participants at runtime through the AddParticipant()() and RemoveParticipant() methods.

Cancellation Tokens

Cancellation tokens are a struct that provide a consistent means of cancellation. You might want to use a cancellation token to cancel a function or task that is taking too long or using too much of a machine's resources. Support is provided in many of the Task and PLINQ methods for the use of cancellation tokens.

To use cancellation tokens, you first need to create a CancellationTokenSource. Then you can utilize it to pass a cancellation token into the target method by using the Token property.

Within your method, you can then check the token's IsCancellationRequested property and throw an operation cancelled exception if you find this to be true (e.g. a cancellation has occurred).

When you want to perform a cancellation, you simply need to call the Cancel() method on the cancellation source that will then set the token's IsCancellationRequested() method to true. This sounds more complex than it actually is; the following example demonstrates this process:

```
static CancellationTokenSource cts = new CancellationTokenSource();

static void Main(string[] args)
{
    Task t = Task.Factory.StartNew(() => DoSomething(), cts.Token);
    System.Threading.Thread.Sleep(2000);
    cts.Cancel();
    Console.ReadKey();
}

public static void DoSomething()
{
    try
    {
        while (true)
        {
            Console.WriteLine("doing stuff");
```

```
        if (cts.Token.IsCancellationRequested == true)
        {
            Console.WriteLine("cancelled");
            throw new OperationCanceledException(cts.Token);
        }
    }
}
catch (OperationCanceledException ex)
{
    //operation cancelled do any clean up here
    Console.WriteLine("Cancellation occurred");
}
}
```

CountDownEvent

The new CountDownEvent is initialized with an integer value and can block code until the value reaches 0
(the value is decremented by calling the signal method).

    CountDownEvent is particularly useful for keeping track of scenarios in which many threads have
been forked. The following example blocks until the count has been decremented twice:

```
using System.Collections.Concurrent;
using System.Threading;

namespace Chapter5
{

    static CountdownEvent CountDown = new CountdownEvent(2);

    static void Main(string[] args)
    {
        ThreadPool.QueueUserWorkItem(new WaitCallback(CountDownDeduct));
        ThreadPool.QueueUserWorkItem(new WaitCallback(CountDownDeduct));

        //Wait until countdown decremented by DecrementCountDown method
        CountDown.Wait();
        Console.WriteLine("Completed");
        Console.ReadKey();
    }

    static void CountDownDeduct(object StateInfo)
    {
        System.Threading.Thread.Sleep(5000);
        Console.WriteLine("Deducting 1 from countdown");
        CountDown.Signal();
    }
}
```

ManualResetEventSlim and SemaphoreSlim

ManualResetEventSlim and SemaphoreSlim are lightweight versions of the existing ManualResetEvent and Semaphore classes. The new classes do not use resource-expensive kernel features as their predecessors did.

SpinLock

SpinLock forces a program to loop until it can obtain and lock access to a particular resource. This should be used when you don't have to wait too long. Although looping (rather than handing control over to another thread) sounds like a wasteful thing to do, it can potentially be much more efficient than stopping to process other threads because it avoids a context switch (a resource-intensive process in which the current CPU state is stored, and a new state is loaded).

```
private static SpinLock MySpinLock = new SpinLock();

static void Main(string[] args)
{
    bool Locked = false;
    try
    {
        MySpinLock.Enter(ref Locked);
        //Work that requires lock would be done here
    }
    finally
    {
        if (Locked)
        {
            MySpinLock.Exit();
        }
    }
}
```

ThreadLocal<T>

ThreadLocal is a lazy initialized variable for each thread (see Chapter 4 for more info about lazy initialized variables).

Future Considerations

By parallelizing an application, you can greatly speed it up (or slow it down if you do it badly!). It is worth considering the following:

- It is a shame that the ability to utilize all available processing power on a machine (for example, dormant GPUs) was not included in this release.

- Many developers feel the Concurrency and Coordination Runtime (CCR) should have been included in this release. The CCR assists with creating loosely coupled asynchronous applications and was originally included with Microsoft Robotics Studio (it has since been separated out). At the time of writing, the CCR is not free for commercial usage. For more info on CCR, please refer to: http://msdn. microsoft.com/en-gb/library/bb648752.aspx.

- Looking toward the future, is it possible that a future version of Task Manager could allow you to distribute work across multiple machines paving the way for grid computing libraries within .NET?

- Multicore shift will mean that existing pricing/licensing models need to be reconsidered.

Danny Shih Interview

I talked to Danny Shih (Program Manager on parallel extensions for the .NET team) about his thoughts on the parallel extensions:

The underlying architecture of the Task Scheduler changed during development to use the thread pool; can you say a bit more about this decision?

Our managed scheduler (on which TPL was originally built) and the ThreadPool basically served the same purpose, and in Dev10, the two teams were working on different enhancements. The ThreadPool team was working on things like hill-climbing (an algorithm to determine and adjust to the optimal number of threads for a given workload), and we had added things like work-stealing queues to our managed scheduler. So to avoid duplicating code and to take advantage of all new enhancements, we wanted to either build the ThreadPool on TPL or build TPL on the ThreadPool. For various reasons, we took the latter approach.

What do you see as the potential pitfalls when using the new parallel enhancements?

I think the major one is adding parallelism to an application when it's unsafe to do so. New APIs like Parallel.For() make it extremely easy introduce concurrency, both correctly and incorrectly. A common scenario is parallelizing a serial loop that has iterations that depend on other iterations (possibly resulting in deadlock) or that has iterations that access shared state without synchronization (possible race conditions resulting in incorrect results).

Where do you see the .NET parallelization/threading APIs heading in the future?

In future versions, we're definitely trying to refine our APIs (adding stuff we think we missed, mainly). We're also discussing cluster and GPG support, but there's nothing to announce there yet.

Phil Whinstanley

http://weblogs.asp.net/plip/

I talked to Phil Whinstanley (ASP.NET MVP and author) about his experience of the parallel enhancements in .NET 4.

"Working on a very heavy IO (disk and network) project (zero configuration hosted build server) we parallelized the process in a matter of minutes changing a foreach to a Parallel.ForEach() giving us a performance increase which reduced the time taken to execute from one minute and thirty seconds down to fourteen seconds. We were gobsmacked"

Conclusion

In the future, the majority of machines will have multicore processors. The new parallelization improvements give the developer an easy-to-use and powerful way to take advantage of this resource.

Parallelization should enable the creation of applications that would currently run too slow to be viable. The applications that have the most to gain from parallelization are those in the fields of games, graphics, mathematical/scientific modeling, and artificial intelligence.

Parallelization will require us to make a major shift in the way we design and develop as we move from solving problems in serial to parallel. We currently have difficulty developing bug-free serial applications, and parallelization will undoubtedly increase the complexity of applications, so it is important not to underestimate the additional complexity running code in parallel will add to your application.

Further Reading

- Axum: a research project that aims to provide a "safe and productive parallel programming model for .NET"

- http://msdn.microsoft.com/en-us/devlabs/dd795202.aspx

- http://www.danielmoth.com/Blog/

- Fantastic free document on parallelization patterns: http://www.microsoft.com/downloads/details.aspx?FamilyID=86b3d32b-ad26-4bb8-a3ae-c1637026c3ee&displaylang=en

- A language aimed at making parallel applications "safer, more scalable and easier to write:" http://blogs.msdn.com/maestroteam/default.aspx –.

- http://managed-world.com/archive/2009/02/09/an-intro-to-barrier.aspx

- http://channel9.msdn.com/shows/Going+Deep/Erika-Parsons-and-Eric-Eilebrecht--CLR-4-Inside-the-new-Threadpool/

- Joe Duffy and Herb Stutter, *Concurrent Programming on Windows: Architecture, Principles, and Patterns* (Microsoft .Net Development). Addison Wesley, 2008

■ ■ ■

CHAPTER 6

Windows Workflow Foundation 4

Availability: Framework 4.0

Windows Workflow Foundation (WF) was first introduced in 2006 with .NET 3.0. It is probably fair to say that WF didn't receive the widespread adoption Microsoft was hoping for. This lack of uptake was probably due to a number of factors:

- Although the WF designer offers a natural way of working, it is a very different way of developing applications and contains a new API to master.

- Slow performance.

- Writing your own work flow activities was not as easy as it could be.

- Handling and passing data between activities was cumbersome

- Limited support for messaging scenarios and integration with WCF.

- Some developers were confused by the hosting model.

- A clunky designer interface made you want to poke your own eyes out (OK, it wasn't that bad but it wasn't that good either).

Microsoft has aimed to address these issues and also to integrate WCF and WF closer than ever before.

Why Use WF?

Before we look at how to use Microsoft WF you may be wondering why should I bother?

WF can greatly simplify the development of applications that deal with complex and long-running Processes as traditional coding methods are not ideal for solving this type of problem.

To understand why they are not, let's take the example of a visa approval system (loosely based on my experience of the UK/Australian emigration process) as shown in the flowchart in Figure 6-1.

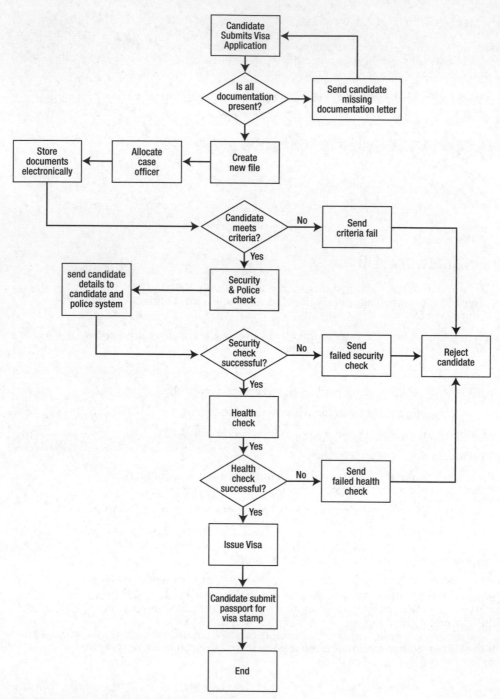

Figure 6-1. *Visa processing system workflow*

Even if you have no experience of the Australian emigration process you can probably gain an understanding from Figure 6-1. Windows Workflow enables you to design and develop your application in a similar visual manner. Consider how an application to handle such a process would be coded: it would probably be difficult to gain an understanding at a glance. Figure 6-2 shows a possible WF implementation of the process. As you can see it's not so different from Figure 6-1.

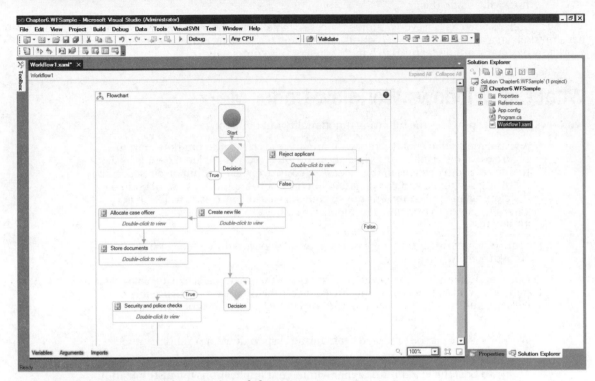

Figure 6-2. *Possible WF implementation of above process*

Now let's consider some of the issues we may encounter when developing this application:

- The client wants to process visa applications as quickly as possible, so he wants to alert staff when an application is ready for the next stage. How will you provide this functionality in an efficient and timely manner when processing hundreds of thousands of application?

- How will you pass data between different services and government departments, such as performing a police check on an applicant?

- Some tasks take a long time to complete or require human intervention before they can proceed. How will you handle this waiting?

- A typical visa will take weeks or months to process. How are you going to store the current state of a visa application?

- What will happen to an application in the event of system failure?

- How will you design your application so that it is flexible enough to accommodate future changes?

- Imagine you need to debug and monitor different stages of the approval process; how will you do this?

Agggrahh! As you can see even a simple process can get very complex quickly. Of course you can develop such an application very successfully (and many have) using current technologies, but Windows Workflow has many inbuilt features to handle some of this complexity.

What Can Windows Workflow Do for Me?

Windows Workflow provides the following functionality out of the box:

- A visual method of constructing your applications similar to our flowchart in Figure 6-1. This visual approach is more intuitive, can be easier to debug , is easier to unit test with changes in this release (a controversial idea, but discussed in the following sections), and can be understood by non-technical users. Of course developing an application entirely in code has its advantages as well — it is generally easier to test, and developers won't have to learn new ways of writing applications.

- More efficient use of server resources. Non-active workflows "sleep" and are "rehydrated" when needed.

- Coordination and synchronization. Workflows that make calls to external services may take weeks to receive a reply. By using correlation, we can ensure returned calls are automatically directed to the correct instance of a work flow that can then "wake up" and resume its work

- Workflow state can be persisted even during system down time and resumed automatically.

- Ability to host the workflow designer within your applications for customization and configuration by end users.

- Rich debugging and monitoring support.

- A common framework for workflow development on the Windows platform. WF is already utilized in flagship products such as Microsoft Sharepoint and Dynamics (note these use WF3 at time of writing). You can even host your workflows in Microsofts cloud computing platform Windows Azure (at the time of writing this is not available, but should be in the future).

- WF can assist you with versioning and updating issues (although for the forseeable future this is never going to be that easy).

Hopefully I have convinced you that Workflow is something that you should be interested in. Let's take a closer look.

What Is Windows Workflow Foundation?

WF is composed of three main components:

- Workflow instance/runtime
- Activities
- Workflow designer

Workflow Instance/Runtime

The workflow runtime takes care of instantiating individual workflows and handles persistence and synchronization. The workflow runtime does not exist on its own. It is created inside a host application. The host application can be anything from an ASP.NET web site to a windows service, or even the new "Dublin" or Windows Azure platforms.

This change makes it much easier to attach event handlers and delegates to individual workflows, but also arguably complicates tasks such as recording errors, as they now have to be dealt with on an individual workflow basis.

Activities

Workflows are made up of activities. Microsoft provides a number of building block activities providing basic logic and flow statements for you to use, called the Base Activity Library (BAL). You can of course (and should) create your very own activities. Figure 6-3 shows the WF activity hierarchy.

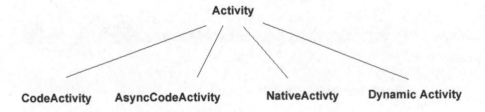

Figure 6-3. WF activity class hierarchy

Activities can be created as composites of existing activities, entirely in code or even just using XAML. Activities inherit from the class Activity (unlike WF3 that used SequentialWorkflowActivity or StateMachineWorkflowActivity). We will look at creating customized activities shortly.

Workflow Designer

The designer (Figure 6-4) is used to piece together your workflow, and contains tools for debugging and monitoring it.

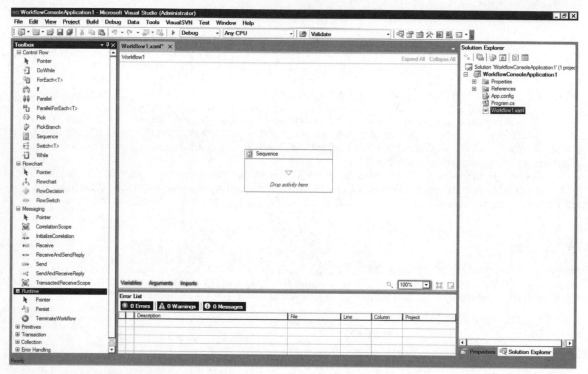

Figure 6-4. *Workflow designer*

It is even possible to host the workflow designer within your application. For more information on this please refer to the following links:

- `http://msdn.microsoft.com/en-us/library/dd489440(VS.100).aspx`

- `http://channel9.msdn.com/learn/courses/VS2010/WCFWF/IntroToWF/Exercise-10-Hosted-Designer/`

The trident project (a tool for customizing scientific workflows) used this facility extensively. Take a look at: `http://connect.microsoft.com/trident/`.

Existing WF3 Users

WF has undergone some radical changes from version 3.0, which unfortunately means that for those developers already utilizing WF3 are probably going to have to do some work to do to upgrade their applications.

Statemachine Workflow Has Gone

Probably the biggest problem you may encounter is in the initial release of WF there is no support for statemachine workflows. Microsoft seems undecided as to whether Statemachine will be introduced in future versions of WF but for now the answer is to utilize the new building blocks.

Upgrade White Papers

Microsoft has produced a number of excellent documents to assist you in upgrading to WF4, so your first step before you upgrade any applications should be to consult this link: http://go.microsoft.com/fwlink/?LinkID=153313.

WF3 Runtime

Version 3 of the WF runtime will be included with .NET 4.0 runtime, so your WF3 should continue to run on the .NET 4.0 framework.

Interop Activity

WF4 has a new activity called Interop (discussed later in this chapter) that can be used to run legacy WF code. This can serve as a halfway point until you are ready to upgrade your entire application.

Is It Worth the Upgrade?

Probably. WF4 lays the groundwork for future enhancements, and WF5 *should* not be such a radical upgrade. WF 4 offers superior performance (10 to 100 times quicker), a much improved designer, and many other changes that we will discuss in this chapter.

Kenny Wolf (architect on WCF and WF team) at PDC 08 noted that some customers in the early adopter program reduced their code by 80 percent by moving to WF4.

All Change

WF4 is a radical change, so even if you are an experienced WF developer please take the time to work your way through this example as the designer has changed completely and a number of new concepts have been introduced.

Hello WF 4

We will write a simple workflow that will handle a booking for a movie theatre. Our example workflow will do the following:

- Process a booking for a specific film

- Check if seating is available for the requested showing. In our example, to keep everything simple, if less than five tickets are requested, then the booking will succeed.

- Return a Boolean value indicating whether the booking was successful and a hardcoded alphanumeric ticket reference (blank if unsuccessful).

Hello WF

Open Visual Studio and create a new Workflow Console Application called Chapter6.HelloWF. You should now see a screen similar Figure 6-5.

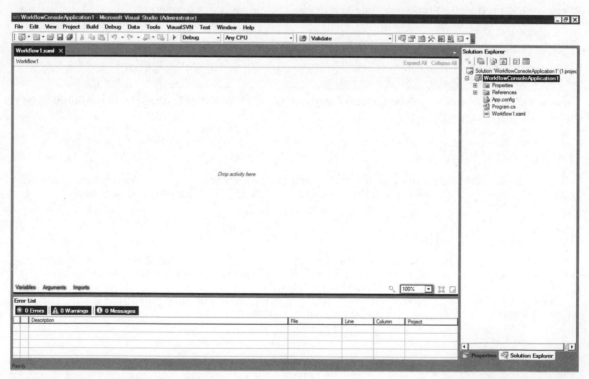

Figure 6-5. *New sequential workflow*

The first change that you will notice is that the WF designer like the IDE is rewritten in WPF and is much quicker than the previous version.

We are going to be creating a sequential workflow first, so open the toolbox and drag a Sequence activity from the Control Flow group to the designer.

Next we will need to supply our workflow with information about the customer's booking. In WF4 arguments and variables are used pass data between activities. This is much easier than in WF3 where dependency properties had to be used.

Arguments and Variables

Arguments and variables are unique to each running instance of a workflow and hold and return values.[1] They can be of any type and arguments can be used as inputs, outputs, or both input and outputs.

The visibility or scope of a variable is dependent on where it is declared. So if a variable is declared inside an activity, it will be visible to child activities, but not to parent activities. As per traditional coding practices you should minimize the exposure of your variables and arguments.

Creating an Argument

Let's create a new argument (no not the kind you have with your wife when she is trying to get you off the computer when you are trying to write a book), but a WF4 argument.

1. On the grey bar at the base of the designer window is an Arguments button. Click this. A new section will open on the designer (Figure 6-6).

2. Click where it says Create Argument and add three new arguments with the following settings:

    *   FilmName (type String, direction In).

    *   ShowingDate (type String, direction In). In reality we would pass in a FilmShowingID variable, but this reduces typing of pointless demo code.

    *   NumberOfTickets (type Int32, direction In).

---

1. Technically arguments and variables don't actually hold the values, but instead tell the individual workflow how to access the values.

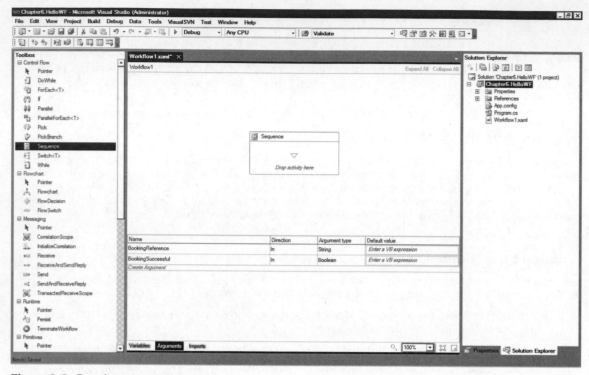

Figure 6-6. *Creating new arguments*

3. We will also need two variables to hold whether the booking was successful and the booking reference to return to the user. Click the Variables button at the base of the screen and create two new variables (Figure 6-7):

- BookingReference (type String, set the default to "")

- BookingSuccessful (type Boolean)

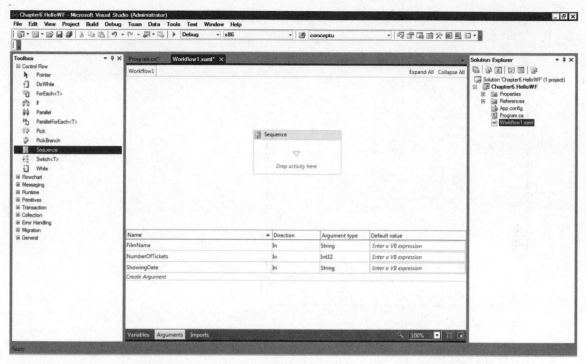

Figure 6-7. *Creating arguments for our workflow*

WriteLine

WriteLine is an inbuilt activity that allows us to write output to the console window or a text writer. We will use it to write a message to the console window to inform us that the workflow has started.

1. Drag a WriteLine activity from the toolbox (Primitives section) onto the Sequence activity, placing it on the grey arrow in the white box.

2. Click the WriteLine activity then in the Properties window change the Display Name to "Workflow started." Display Name is a property present on most activities, and is simply a label for the activity. Display Name is also used for constructing a breadcrumb trail in the IDE when we drill down into child activities, so it is good practice to set it to something useful. Finally, change the text property to "Workflow started" (include the quotes).

■**NOTE** When writing out values in expressions WF uses VB.NET expression syntax, and requires you to contain values such as text property within quotes. I use quotes in this tutorial to make the text easier to pick out, but you should not enter the quote characters when setting properties such as Display Name.

---

3. Click the Sequence activity and change the display name to "Book Film." Your workflow should be looking like Figure 6-8.

Figure 6-8. *Creating our workflow*

4. We want to see the output of our workflow before it closes, so open `Program.cs` and add the following code at the end of the `Main()` method:

```
Console.ReadLine();
```

5. Press F5 to run your workflow and you should see "Workflow started" outputted to the screen. Congratulations! You have created your first workflow application.

Creating Another Sequence Activity

The next step in our contrived example is to check if seating is available for a specific film showing. We will create a Sequence activity that contains a number of other activities to perform this check.

1. Drag a Sequence activity below the WriteLine activity.

2. Change the display name to "Check availability."

3. To drill down into an individual activity, you double-click on it. So double-click the "Check availability" sequential activity we have just created and you should see a screen similar to Figure 6-9.

Figure 6-9. *Drilled down view of Sequential activity*

As we are "inside" one of the activities you probably want to know how to get back to the level above. There are two ways of doing this:

- Right-click on the design surface and select the View Parent option.

- Use the breadcrumb trail that is automatically constructed at the top of the page. Note how the activity's display name is used to form the breadcrumb trail. This is a very good reason to set it to something descriptive.

Individual activities can be collapsed and expanded to improve your view of the workflow

Checking Number of Tickets with an If Activity

We now need to check if the number of tickets requested is more than five, and in our example we will prevent such a booking.

1. Drag an If activity onto the designer (in the "Check availability" activity).

2. Change the display name to "If NumberOfTickets>5."

3. Double click the If activity.

4. In the Properties window, select the Condition property and click the ellipsis button.

5. Enter the following in the Expression Editor window:

```
NumberOfTickets > 5
```

■**WARNING** Expressions are written in VB syntax. Expressions must be entered in VB syntax whether you are creating a VB or C# workflow project. The WF team claim that VB is more intuitive (ahem) and that some power users will be used to VBA syntax from a product such as Excel.

Booking Unsuccessful and Assign activity

The Assign activity allows us to assign values to variables. We will use it to update the BookingSuccessful variable.

1. Drag an Assign activity from the Primitives group into the Then box of the If activity.

2. Change the display name to "Booking unsuccessful."

3. Change the To property to the BookingSuccessful variable.

4. Change the Value property to False.

Booking Succssful and Parallel Activity

We want to set the BookingSuccessful property to True and also set a booking reference. The Parallel activity allows us to perform two activities at the same time (OK, this is unnecessary for this situation but I wanted to make you aware of this cool feature).

1. Drag a Parallel activity from the Control Flow group to the Else segment of the If activity.

2. Change the display name to "Booking successful." Your If activity should look like Figure 6-10.

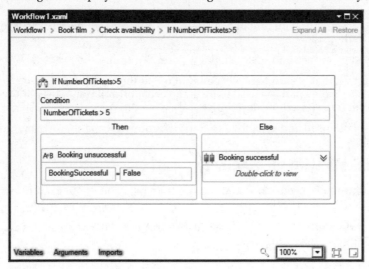

Figure 6-10. *If statement*

3. Double-click the "Booking successful" activity.

4. Drag an Assign activity onto the , and change its display name to "Assign Booking successful."

5. Change the To property to the BookingSuccessful variable.

6. Change the Value property to True.

7. Drag another Assign activity onto the arrows to the right of the original Assign activity and change the display name to "Get booking ref."

8. Change the To property to BookingReference.

9. Change the Value property to "abcde" (we will hard code this value in our example, and note that the quotes are needed). Your Parallel activity should look like Figure 6-11.

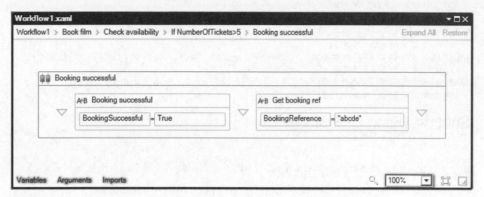

Figure 6-11. *Parallel activity allows you to specify that tasks should occur at the same time.*

Displaying the Output of the Booking

We will now use another WriteLine activity to display the output of our workflow.

1. Click Book Film in the breadcrumb trail to return to the top view.

2. Drag another WriteLine activity to the end of the workflow and change the display name to "Display output."

3. On the Text property click the ellipsis and enter the following:

```
"Booking result: " + BookingSuccessful.ToString() + " Reference: " +
BookingReference.ToString()
```

Supplying Arguments to a Workflow

The only thing left to do is supply our workflow with some initial arguments. As per previous versions of WF, arguments are supplied as a dictionary variable.

■**TIP** Names are case sensitive and magic strings are bad, so in real-world applications you will probably want to create a wrapper class instead of using the below approach. A common approach is to inherit from the Dictionary class and create properties to set values within it.

---

4. Open Program.cs and add the following using statement:

    ```
    using System.Collections.Generic;
    ```

5. Modify the Main() method to the following to create and pass in a dictionary of our initial variables:

    ```
    static void Main(string[] args)
    {
        Dictionary<string, object> Arguments = new Dictionary<string, object>();
        Arguments.Add("FilmName", "Terminator");
        Arguments.Add("ShowingDate", System.DateTime.Now.ToString());
        Arguments.Add("NumberOfTickets", 4);

        WorkflowInvoker.Invoke(new Workflow1(), Arguments);
        Console.ReadLine();
    }
    ```

6. That's it; you have just created your first workflow. Now press F5 to run it.

7. Try changing the NumberOfTickets to five. Do you get a different result?

Wow, we covered a lot in that short example. You discovered the new workflow designer, how to use arguments and variables, and some of the new activities in WF4.

Creating Your Own Activities

Microsoft supplies many activities out of the box, but you will want to and should create your own activities. Activities can be created in three main ways:

*   As a composition of other existing activities
*   In code
*   Pure XAML

Creating an Activity Composed of Other Activities

Let's create a simple activity to simulate writing a customer's ticket booking to a database.

1. Right-click on the project and add a new activity (from the Workflow section) called SaveBooking.xaml.

2. Open SaveBooking.xaml in the design view.

3. Create an argument for the SaveBooking activity (String, In) called BookingReference.

4. Drag a Sequence activity onto the design surface.

5. Drag a WriteLine activity onto this activity and change its display name to "Simulate booking storage."

6. We are not going to go to the bother of actually writing data access code, so change the Value property of the WriteLine activity to "Save booking " + BookingReference + "in database." Your workflow should look like Figure 6-12 (note the quotes).

7. Click Save.

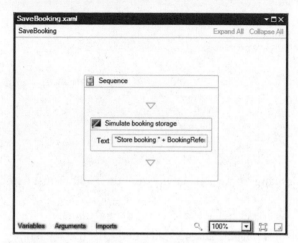

Figure 6-12. *Save booking activity*

Before this activity can be used, the project needs to be compiled.

1. Compile the project

2. Open Workflow1.xaml and in the Toolbox (Project section) you will now find the new SaveBooking activity should now be available. Drag it onto the Sequence activity just beneath the "Check availability" activity.

3. On the properties of the "Save Booking" activity, set the BookingReference argument to use the BookingReference variable defined in the main workflow.

4. Run your workflow. You should now see the output "Save booking" and whatever you have set the booking reference variable to.

Creating Activities Purely in Code

Anything that can be done in the WF designer can also be done programmatically. Let's say our client is running a new promotion that every theater booking has a 1 in 100 chance of being free. We will create a new code activity to simulate this.

1. Add a new Code activity to the project called FreeBookingPromotion.cs.

2. Ammend the code in FreeBookingPromotion.cs to the following:

```
public class FreeBookingPromotion : CodeActivity
{
    public InArgument<string> BookingReference { get; set; }
    public OutArgument<bool> FreeBooking { get; set; }
```

```
    protected override void Execute(CodeActivityContext context)
    {
        System.Random Random = new Random();

        if (Random.Next(0, 101) == 100)
        {
            //Customer has won free booking
            FreeBooking.Set(context, true);
        }
        else
        {
            FreeBooking.Set(context, false);
        }
    }
}
```

3. Save and build the project.

4. Open `Workflow1` and drag the FreeBookingPromotion activity from the Toolbox just before the "Display output" activity.

5. Create a new variable at `Workflow1.xaml` level called `FreeBooking` of type Boolean.

6. Drag a new If activity before the "Display output" activity and change the display name to "Check if booking free."

7. Modify the activity's `FreeBooking` argument to use the main workflow's `FreeBooking` variable.

8. Double-click on the If activity.

9. In the condition enter: `freebooking=true`.

10. In the Then block, drag a WriteLine activity and change the text to "Congratulations you have won a free booking."

11. In the Else block, drag a WriteLine activity and change the text to "Sorry try again next time."

12. Run your workflow.

Pure XAML Workflows

Activities can also be created purely in XAML, which is great news for third-party vendors and code generation. You could even hold your activities' XAML definition in a database and load them at run time. Let's take a look at the XAML of our SaveBooking activity.

1. In Solution Explorer, right-click `SaveBooking.xaml` and select Open with.

2. Select XML Editor and you can then see the XAML that makes up this activity:

```
<Activity mc:Ignorable="sap" x:Class="Chapter6.HelloWF.SaveBooking"
xmlns="http://schemas.microsoft.com/netfx/2009/xaml/activities"
xmlns:mc="http://schemas.openxmlformats.org/markup-compatibility/2006" xmlns:mv="clr-
namespace:Microsoft.VisualBasic;assembly=System" xmlns:mva="clr-
namespace:Microsoft.VisualBasic.Activities;assembly=System.Activities" xmlns:s="clr-
namespace:System;assembly=mscorlib, Version=4.0.0.0, Culture=neutral,
```

```
PublicKeyToken=b77a5c561934e089" xmlns:s1="clr-namespace:System;assembly=mscorlib"
xmlns:s2="clr-namespace:System;assembly=System" xmlns:s3="clr-
namespace:System;assembly=System.Xml" xmlns:s4="clr-
namespace:System;assembly=System.Core"
xmlns:sa="clr-namespace:System.Activities;assembly=System.Activities, Version=4.0.0.0,
Culture=neutral, PublicKeyToken=31bf3856ad364e35" xmlns:sad="clr-
namespace:System.Activities.Debugger;assembly=System.Activities"
xmlns:sap="http://schemas.microsoft.com/netfx/2009/xaml/activities/presentation"
xmlns:scg="clr-namespace:System.Collections.Generic;assembly=System" xmlns:scg1="clr-
namespace:System.Collections.Generic;assembly=System.ServiceModel" xmlns:scg2="clr-
namespace:System.Collections.Generic;assembly=System.Core" xmlns:scg3="clr-
namespace:System.Collections.Generic;assembly=mscorlib" xmlns:sd="clr-
namespace:System.Data;assembly=System.Data" xmlns:sd1="clr-
namespace:System.Data;assembly=System.Data.DataSetExtensions" xmlns:sl="clr-
namespace:System.Linq;assembly=System.Core" xmlns:st="clr-
namespace:System.Text;assembly=mscorlib"
xmlns:x="http://schemas.microsoft.com/winfx/2006/xaml">
  <x:Members>
    <x:Property Name="BookingReference" Type="InArgument(x:String)" />
  </x:Members>
  <mva:VisualBasic.Settings>Assembly references and imported namespaces serialized as
XML
namespaces</mva:VisualBasic.Settings>
  <Sequence sad:XamlDebuggerXmlReader.
FileName="D:\wwwroot\book\Chapter6_WF\Chapter6.HelloWF\Chapter6.
HelloWF\SaveBooking.xaml" sap:VirtualizedContainerService.HintSize="233,200">
    <sap:WorkflowViewStateService.ViewState>
      <scg3:Dictionary x:TypeArguments="x:String, x:Object">
        <x:Boolean x:Key="IsExpanded">True</x:Boolean>
      </scg3:Dictionary>
    </sap:WorkflowViewStateService.ViewState>
    <WriteLine DisplayName="Simulate booking storage"
sap:VirtualizedContainerService.HintSize="211,62" Text="[&quot;Store booking &quot; +
BookingReference + &quot;in database&quot;]" />
  </Sequence>
</Activity>
```

Yikes, probably not the sort of thing you want to be typing yourself.

Invoking Workflows

WF4 offers the ability to invoke individual activities without using the workflow run time. This could be used for scenarios such as unit testing. However, as many workflows will run for a long time, this won't be useful in all instances.

We will now invoke the workflow we created previously and check that requesting 10 tickets returns the variable BookingSuccessful set to false. Note in reality you would write this as a unit test but we are just covering the principles.

1. Add a new C# Console project to the solution called Chapter6.HelloWF.Tests.

2. Add a reference to System.Activities and Chapter6.HelloWF.

3. Enter the following using statements in Program.cs:

```
using System.Activities;
using System.Diagnostics;
```

4. Enter the following code in Program.cs:

```
static void Main(string[] args)
{
    Dictionary<string, object> Arguments = new Dictionary<string, object>();
    Arguments.Add("FilmName", "Terminator");
    Arguments.Add("ShowingDate", System.DateTime.Now.ToString());
    Arguments.Add("NumberOfTickets", 10);

    IDictionary<string, object> Output = new Dictionary<string, object>();

    Output = WorkflowInvoker.Invoke(new Chapter6.HelloWF.Workflow1(), Arguments);

    Debug.Assert((bool)Output["BookingSuccessful"] == false);
}
```

■**NOTE** When using the Invoke() method, the activity is guaranteed to be performed on the invoking thread and will time out after 60 seconds (unless you change this default — an overload in the Invoke() method).

Flowchart

Flowchart is a new type of workflow that makes it easier to model certain types of problems, particularly those that return back to previous activities. Prior to WF4 this could be achieved by using a while loop but flowchart workflows offer a more intuitive approach. We will create a flowchart workflow to simulate a customer's age being checked.

1. Open Visual Studio and create a new Workflow Console application called Chapter6.Flowchart.

2. Drag a Flowchart activity from the Flowchart group onto the designer surface. You should see something similar to Figure 6-13.

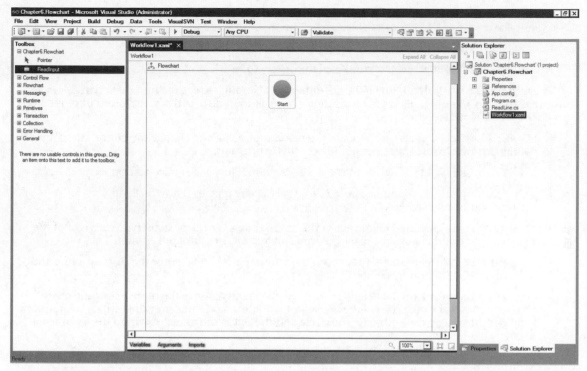

Figure 6-13. *New flowchart workflow*

3. The design view for flowcharts looks slightly different than sequential workflows. The green circle indicates where the workflow starts. We need to create a new activity to read input from the user. Create a new class called `ReadInput`.

4. Enter the following using statement:

   ```
   using System.Activities;
   ```

5. Now enter the following code:

   ```
   public class ReadInput : CodeActivity<Int32>
   {
       protected override Int32 Execute(CodeActivityContext context)
       {
           return Convert.ToInt32(Console.ReadLine());
       }
   }
   ```

6. Save the class and compile the application.

7. Open `Workflow1.xaml`.

8. Drag a WriteLine activity beneath the green circle and change the Display Name to "What is your age?" and set the Text to "What is your age?"

9. Drag the new ReadInput activity beneath the "What is your age?" activity and change the display name to "Read input."

10. Create a new variable called age of type `Int32`.

11. On the ReadInput activity, set the `Result` property to age.

The next thing to do is determine if the customer is old enough to see the film (which in this case will always have an 18 rating). Flow chart workflows have a new type of activity not found in sequential workflows, called FlowDecision.

1. Drag a FlowDecision activity beneath the read input block and change the condition to Age >= 18. There are obviously two possibilities to this expression:

   • Customer is old enough so they can see the film (FlowDecision condition = true).

   • Customer is too young, so shouldn't be seeing any movies (FlowDecision condition = false).

2. To simulate the customer failing age verification, drag a WriteLine activity to the right of the flow decision and change the display name and text to "Sorry not old enough."

3. Drag another WriteLine activity beneath the flow decision and change the display name and text to "Age validation successful."

4. We now need to link up the activities we have just created. Move the mouse over the green circle that indicates the start of the flow chart workflow, and three grey dots will appear around it. Click the one on the bottom of the circle and then drag the mouse down to the ReadInput activity.

5. When you near the WriteLine activity, three grey dots will appear around it. Drag the line to one of these dots and then release the mouse button to link up the start of the workflow with our read line activity.

6. Link up the "What is your age?" and ReadInput activities.

7. We need to join the FlowDecision up to the workflow. FlowDecision activities have two nodes, true or false, that surprisingly indicate the path to take when the condition specified is true or false. Drag the false node to the "Sorry not old enough" WriteLine activity and then drag another line from "Sorry not old enough" back round to the ReadInput activity.

8. Drag the true node on the FlowDecision activity to the "Age validation successful" activity.

9. Finally drag a line between the "What is your age?" and ReadInput activity. Your final work flow should look like Figure 6-14.

10. Open `Program.cs` and add a `Console.ReadKey();` beneath the invoke command so the application doesn't close immediately.

11. That's it; your workflow is ready to run. Press F5 to run it.

12. Try entering different ages and note that unless you enter at least 18 the workflow will write "Sorry not old enough."

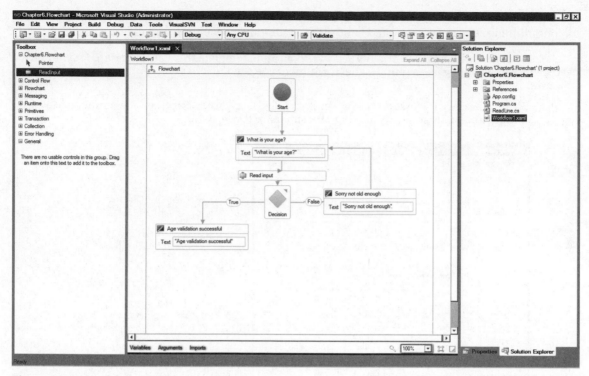

Figure 6-14. *Final age validation work flow*

WCF/Messaging Improvements

A number of enhancements have been introduced in WF4 to improve integration with WCF and to ease messaging scenarios.

Correlation

Correlation functionality first appeared in WF3.5 and allows you to route incoming messages to specific workflow instances based on their content or protocol used. For example if you have a very long running workflow where replies take weeks or months to return it is important that when a reply is received it is sent to the correct individual workflow.

ReceiveAndSendReply and SendAndReceiveReply are the new activities discussed in the following sections that provide a correlated send and receive activities with a number of new methods of correlation such as xpath and correlation scope.

WCF Workflow Service Applications

WCF Workflow Service applications are a new type of project in VS2010 that make it very easy to create workflows for sending and receiving data. They essentially provide a declarative WCF service defined using workflow activities. WCF Workflow Service applications have all the benefits of WF such as support for long-running services, GUI interface, and also the additional benefits that as they are declared declaratively so are easy to deploy and version.

VS2010 comes with a WCF Workflow Service Application template that you can adapt for your own needs. The sample application simply echoes a number you send to it back to you. Let's take this for a spin now.

1. Create a new WCF Workflow Service project called Chapter6.WFService. The template will contain a sequential activity looking very similar to Figure 6-15.

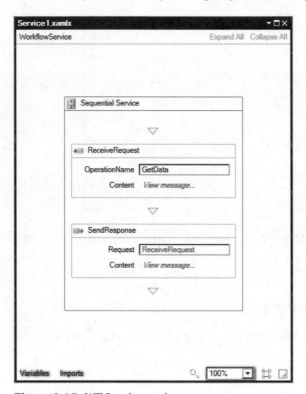

Figure 6-15. *WF Service project*

2. This sequential activity is defined in the file Service1.xamlx. If you open this up with the XML editor you will see the XAML that defines this service (boring bits removed as it's pretty long):

```
<p:Sequence DisplayName="Sequential Service"
sad:XamlDebuggerXmlReader.FileName="D:\wwwroot\book\Chapter6_WF\Chapter6.WFService\Cha
pter6.
WFService\Service1.xamlx">
    <p:Sequence.Variables>
      <p:Variable x:TypeArguments="CorrelationHandle" Name="handle" />
      <p:Variable x:TypeArguments="x:Int32" Name="data" />
    </p:Sequence.Variables>
```

150

```
    <Receive x:Name="__ReferenceID0" DisplayName="ReceiveRequest"
OperationName="GetData"
ServiceContractName="contract:IService" CanCreateInstance="True">
        <Receive.CorrelationInitializers>
          <RequestReplyCorrelationInitializer CorrelationHandle="[handle]" />
        </Receive.CorrelationInitializers>
        <ReceiveMessageContent>
          <p:OutArgument x:TypeArguments="x:Int32">[data]</p:OutArgument>
        </ReceiveMessageContent>
    </Receive>

    <SendReply Request="{x:Reference Name=__ReferenceID0}" DisplayName="SendResponse"
>
        <SendMessageContent>
          <p:InArgument x:TypeArguments="x:String">[data.ToString()]</p:InArgument>
        </SendMessageContent>
    </SendReply>

  </p:Sequence>

</WorkflowService>
```

3. As the template service doesn't do anything apart from echo a value back, we are going to modify it slightly so we can see a change. In the SendResponse box click the Content text box and amend the Message data property to the following:

    ```
    data.ToString() + " sent from WF service"
    ```

4. Click OK.

5. Save the project.

6. Now add a new console application to the solution called Chapter6.WFServiceClient.

7. Add a service reference to Chapter6.WFService (click Add Service Reference then Discover➤Services in Solution; it will be listed as Service1.xamlx).

8. Leave the namespace as ServiceReference1.

9. In Chapter6.WFServiceClient modify Program.cs to the following:

    ```
    ServiceReference1.ServiceClient client = new ServiceReference1.ServiceClient();
    Console.WriteLine(client.GetData(777));
    Console.ReadKey();
    ```

10. Set Chapter6.WFServiceClient as the startup project and press F5 to run. You should see the message "777 sent from WF Service" output to the console.

If you wanted to deploy this service, you could simply copy the the Service1.xamlx and Web.config file to a web server or even host it using "Dublin."

Activities

A number of new activities are introduced in WF4, and some activities from WF3 have been dropped. Note the Microsoft upgrade documents mentioned at the start of this chapter contain more detail on these changes and suggest an upgrade path.

WF3 Activity Replacements

Some existing WF3 activites have now been dropped. The suggested replacements are listed below:

- IfElse becomes If or Switch.
- Listen becomes Pick.
- Replicator becomes ForEach or ParallelForEach.
- CodeActivity is gone and you should use activity customization as described above.

New Activities

WF4 introduces a number of new activities.

AddToCollection, RemoveFromCollection, ExistsInCollection & ClearCollection

Activities for working with collections in your workflows.

Assign

Assign allows us to assign values to variables and arguments and has been used extensively in the previous examples.

CancellationScope

CancellationScope allows you to specify activities to be run should an activity be cancelled. The body section surrounds the code you may wish to cancel and the cancellation handler section specifies code to run if an activity is cancelled. See Figure 6-16.

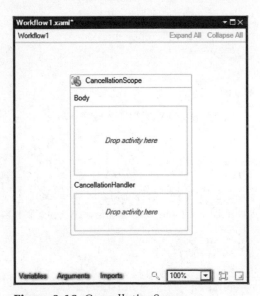

Figure 6-16. *CancellationScope*

CompensatableActivity

An advanced activity used for long running workflows that allows you to define compensation, confirmation, and cancellation handlers for an activity. This is used in conjunction with the compensate and confirm activities.

DoWhile

DoWhile continues to run code until the condition specified is true. The code inside it will be run at least once. See Figure 6-17.

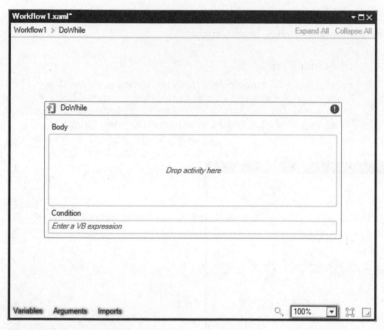

Figure 6-17. *DoWhile*

ForEach

An activity for looping round a collection.

Interop

Interop allows you to use your existing WF3 activities and workflow in a WF4 application. Interop can wrap any non-abstract types inherited from System.Workflow.ComponentModel.Activity. Any properties are exposed as arguments to WF4. Interop can help migration from WF3 or allow you to use existing WF3 workflows you don't possess the source to.

InvokeMethod

InvokeMethod allows the calling of an existing static method. You can pass generic types, pass parameters by reference and also call it asynchronously.

Parallel

Parallel activity was present in WF3, but didn't truly run activities in parallel (it used time slicing). In WF4 the Parallel activity and ParallelForEach the activities now run truly in parallel subject to suitable hardware.

Persist

Persist allows you to persist the workflow instance using the current workflow configuration settings. You can also specify areas where state should not be persisted with no-persist zones.

Pick

Provides functionality for using events and replaces WF3s listen activity.

ReceiveAndSendReply and SendAndReceiveReply

WF4 has improved support for messaging scenarios by introducing a number of new activities for sending and receiving data between applications and improved support for correlating messages. WF4 introduces the ReceiveAndSendReply (Figure 6-18) and SendAndReceiveReply (correlated versions of Send and Receive) activities that allow you to specify code to run in between the initial Send or receive.

Figure 6-18. *ReceiveAndSendReply*

These are advanced activities so please see the WF SDK for an example of their usage. The messaging activities can operate with the following types of data:

- Message
- MessageContracts
- DataContracts
- XmlSerializable

TryCatch

TryCatch allows you to specify activities to be performed should an exception occur and code that should always run in a Finally block similar to C# or VB.NET. See Figure 6-19.

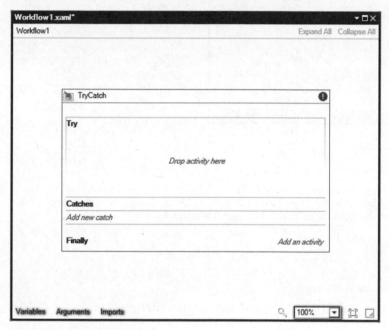

Figure 6-19. *TryCatch*

Switch<T> and FlowSwitch

Switch is similar to the switch statement in C# and contains an expression and a set of cases to process. FlowSwitch is the flowchart equivalent of the switch statement. See Figure 6-20.

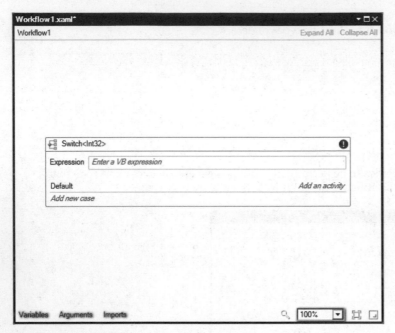

Figure 6-20. *Switch*

Powershell and Sharepoint Activities

In the preview versions of WF4, you may have seen Powershell, Sharepoint, and Data activities. These are now moved to the workflow SDK because Microsoft has a sensible rule for framework development that .NET should not have any dependencies on external n external technologies.

Misc Improvements

WF 4 also contains a number of other enhancements.

- WF version 4 is 10 to 100 times faster than WF3, and performance of the WF designer is much improved.

- Programming model has been simplified.

- Expressions now have intellisense (which can be utilized by activities you create as well).

- WF4 has support for running workflows in partial trust environments.

- Improved support for declarative (XAML only) workflows.

- Add breakpoints can be added to XAML directly. If breakpoints are added in design view and you switch to XAML view they will be shown (and vice versa). See Figure 6-21.

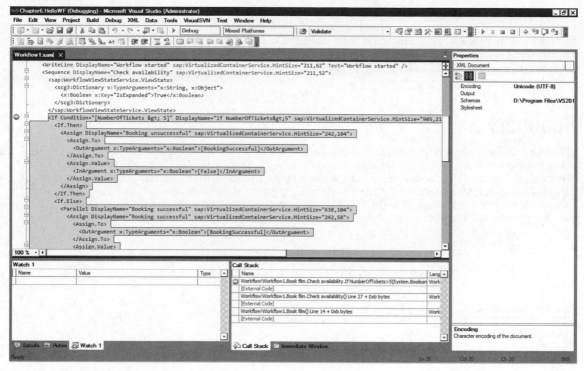

Figure 6-21. *Debugging XAML.*

- Support for ETW (Event Tracing for Windows) has been added.

- E2E (End to end) tracing with WF support ensures that traces are tied together to make debugging easier.

- Tracking profiles enable you to be notified when specific events occur in your workflows. Profiles can be created programmatically or through the configuration file and you have fine-grained control over the level of detail returned. For more information please refer to: http://blogs.msdn.com/endpoint/archive/2009/06/19/workflow-tracking-profiles-in-net-4-0-beta-1.aspx.

- Run your workflows on "Dublin" or Azure platform (see Chapters 7 and 16).

I talked to an experienced WF user John Mcloughlin, a freelance .NET consultant specializing in WF and coordinator of the user group Nxtgen Southampton.

John Mcloughlin

http://blog.batfishsolutions.com/

With .NET 3.0 Microsoft introduced the Windows Workflow Foundation to the .NET world as a new way of thinking about and modelling business processes and state machines. Version 3.5 expanded Windows Workflow Foundation to include support for the Windows Communcation Foundation, but otherwise the framework remained unchanged. Windows Workflow Foundation 4.0 is a major evolution of the framework, the entire library has been rewritten from the ground up to be a leaner, meaner and far more efficient beast. Not only has it been rewritten to be easily testable, it now uses the Windows Presentation Framework for all UI elements. Add in tighter integration with Windows Communication Foundation and the new "Dublin" functionality and it's a very exciting time for Windows Workflows Foundation users.

Summary

WF4 has many excellent features and is much easier to use in VS2010. The move to integrate WCF and WF more closely is a sensible given the overlap of the two technologies. The introduction of the flowchart model and new activity types will make it easier to model many scenarios. It is somewhat disappointing that Microsoft have chosen to drop support for state workflow, which could leave some users with a lot of work to upgrade their code base. In conclusion I suspect that despite its many excellent features WF will remain a "secondary" technology due to its learning curve.

CHAPTER 7

■ ■ ■

Windows Communication Foundation

Availability: Framework 4

Windows Communication Foundation (WCF) developers will be glad to know that this release of WCF shouldn't break any existing applications. The focus in WCF 4 has been to make it easier to use while also bringing in some new features, such as routing, support for WS-Discover protocol(a method for discovering services), and some enhancements from the WCF REST starter kit.

WCF and Workflow Foundation (WF) are more closely integrated than ever in .NET 4.0, so please refer to Chapter 6 for details of the new WF changes (in particular WF services). You should also be aware that there are some changes at the CLR level that may affect your WCF applications that were covered in Chapter 4.

■NOTE You can download many samples for WCF from `http://msdn.microsoft.com/en-us/netframework/cc896557.aspx`. I'll refer to a few in this chapter.

Configless WCF

One of the most frustrating aspects of WCF for me was the massive amount of configuration needed—it always seemed to be much harder to configure than it should be, especially when compared with the simplicity of creating an asmx services. With great flexibility and power comes great big XML configuration file.

WCF4 allows you to create a service with no configuration file at all in just a few lines of code. Let's do this now.

1. Create a new WCF Service Library project called `Chapter7.ConfiglessService`.

2. Add a console application to the solution called `Chapter7.ConfiglessHost`.

3. In `Chapter7.ConfiglessHost` add a reference to `Chapter7.ConfiglessService` and the `System.ServiceModel` assembly.

4. In the `Chapter7.ConfiglessHost Program.cs` add the following using directive:

    ```
    using System.ServiceModel;
    ```

5. Enter the following code in `Program.cs`'s `Main()` method to instantiate our service:

    ```
    ServiceHost MyServiceHost =
        new ServiceHost(typeof(Chapter7.ConfiglessService.Service1),
                        new Uri("http://localhost:8888/Chapter7"));
    MyServiceHost.Open();
    Console.WriteLine("Service running...");
    Console.ReadLine();
    MyServiceHost.Close();
    ```

6. Now right-click on `Chapter7.ConfiglessHost` in Solution Explorer and set it as the startup project, then press F5 to run the application. You should now have a running service without any configuration file.

You can verify this by browsing to `http://localhost:8888/Chapter7`, where you will find our running service(Figure 7-1):

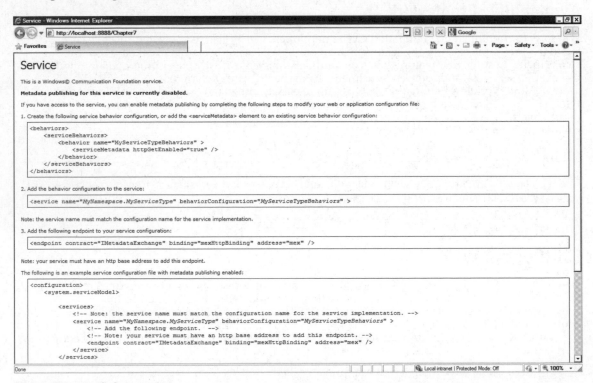

Figure 7-1. *Configless service*

WCF 4 defaults a number of settings to commonly used defaults, saving you time from having to configure them yourself. Of course should you not like the defaults, then you have the flexibility to override them or not use them at all. Let's look at this default configuration now.

Default Binding, behavior, and Endpoints

In our previous example we set a base address for our service to listen to (http://localhost:8888/Chapter7) with the following code, but we didn't actually create any endpoints:

```
ServiceHost MyServiceHost =
  new ServiceHost(typeof(Chapter7.ConfiglessService.Service1),
                  new Uri("http://localhost:8888/Chapter7"));
```

In WCF 4, if you don't specify any endpoints in code or by configuration, then WCF will automatically create a default endpoint for your service (one for each interface your service implements).

The type of endpoint that gets created is dependent on what you use as the base address. In this case a basicHttpBinding was created as we used an address starting with http://. However if the address specified began net.tcp://localhost:8081/greeting a netTcpBinding would be used. This is a huge step forward from WCF 3.5 that made you create endpoints and would throw an exception if you didn't. Table 7-1 shows the bindings that are used for different addresses.

Table 7-1. *Default Protocol Mappings for Different Types of Addresess*

Address	Binding
http	basicHttpBinding
net.pipe	netNamedPipeBinding
net.msmq	netMsmqBinding
net.tcp	netTcpBinding

■**TIP** If you are using a configuration file or creating an endpoint in code and still want default endpoints to be created, then you can call the AddDefaultEndpoints method on your ServiceHost class (MyServiceHost in this example).

Default Binding and Behaviors

WCF allows you to create bindings and behaviors to be used by all endpoints by simply not specifying a configuration or behavior configuration name. This technique could, for example, be used to enable the Metadata Exchange (MEX) endpoint on all services, to offer a metadata description for each service:

```
<behaviors>
    <serviceBehaviors>
      <behavior>
        <serviceMetadata httpGetEnabled="True"/>
      </behavior>
    </serviceBehaviors>
</behaviors>
```

Standard Endpoints

WCF4 comes packaged with a number of standard or preconfigured endpoints. These endpoints are configured in a manner that Microsoft believes will be suitable for most developers. To use a standard endpoint configuration, simply specify the endpoint name by using the new kind attribute. For example, the following configures and endpoint to use the mexEndpoint:

```
<endpoint kind="mexEndpoint" />
```

If you want to override the settings of standard endpoints, you can do this in the new <standardEndpoints> section. The WCF4 samples also have an example of creating your own standard endpoint (WCF\Basic\Services\StandardEndpoints\CS\Service).

Table 7-2 lists the standard endpoints contained within WCF4.

Table 7-2. *Standard Endpoint Types*

Name	Description
announcementEndpoint	Used to send announcments.
discoveryEndpoint	Used for service discovery.
dynamicEndpoint	No info at time of writing.
mexEndpoint	Metadata information.
udpAnnouncementEndpoint	Used to send announcement messages over UDP multicast binding.
udpDiscoveryEndpoint	Discovery operations over UDP multicast binding.
webHttpEndpoint	Standard endpoint with WebHttpBinding binding.
webScriptEndpoint	WebHttpBinding binding with WebScriptEnablingBehavior behavior.
workflowControlEndpoint	Endpoint for calling control methods on WF instances.

No svc File

WCF 4 gives you control over the endpoint exposed for web-based services, allowing you to hide the internal representation of your services, do away with the pesky .svc extension in the service address, and create REST friendly URLs (note WCF probably isn't the best framework for REST services—you would probably be better off using ASP.net MVC).

To see this great new feature, create a new WCF service application (under the web templates section) called Chapter7.Fileless, open web.config, and add the following section inside the system.serviceModel section:

```
<serviceHostingEnvironment>
    <serviceActivations>
        <add relativeAddress="ICouldBeAnything.svc" service="Chapter7.Fileless.Service1"/>
    </serviceActivations>
</serviceHostingEnvironment>
```

This configuration will route requests to ICouldBeAnything.svc through to your service. Press F5 to run your application and change the URL to ICouldBeAnything.svc (for example, http://localhost:52458/ICouldBeAnything.svc) and you should see the service metadata appear.

Router Service

WCF4 has great new routing capabilities that save you from writing your own message routing solution. A routing solution can be very useful for many scenarios such as:

- Crossing network boundaries
- Redundancy—providing alternative endpoints in case of failure
- Load balancing
- Bridging of different protocols
- Versioning
- Providing an additional layer of security

WCF 4's routing capabilities support all of these scenarios and allow you to listen for incoming WCF communications and route them, depending on customizable criteria. Let's create a simple routing example now to route messages from one endpoint to another.

Routing Example

We will create a very simple routing service that will listen for all calls to the endpoint http://localhost:1000/Router and route them through to a service at http://localhost:1111/TestService.

1. Open Visual Studio and create a new console application called Chapter7.Router.

2. Add a WCF service library project called Chapter7.RouterTestService to the solution.

3. Add a project reference in Chapter7.Router to Chapter7Router.TestService.

4. In Chapter7.Router add a reference to the following assemblies System.ServiceModel and System.ServiceModel.Routing.

5. In Chapter7.Router open Program.cs and replace the existing code with the following:

```
using System;
using System.Collections.Generic;
using System.Linq;
using System.Text;
using System.ServiceModel;
using System.ServiceModel.Routing;

namespace Chapter7.Router
{
    class Program
    {
        static void Main(string[] args)
        {
            //Open client service
            ServiceHost ClientService =
```

```
            new ServiceHost(typeof(Chapter7.RouterTestService.Service1),
        new Uri("http://localhost:1111/TestService"));
    ClientService.Open();
    Console.WriteLine("Service running...");

    //Open routing service
    ServiceHost RouterService = new ServiceHost(typeof(RoutingService));
    RouterService.Open();
    Console.WriteLine("Routing service running");

    Console.ReadLine();
    ClientService.Close();
    RouterService.Close();

        }
    }
}
```

6. We now need to define our routing rules. Add an App.config file to the Chapter7.Router project and enter the following configuration:

```xml
<configuration>
  <system.serviceModel>
    <services>
      <service behaviorConfiguration="routingData"
          name="System.ServiceModel.Routing.RoutingService">
        <host>
          <baseAddresses>
            <add baseAddress="http://localhost:1000/Router"/>
          </baseAddresses>
        </host>

        <endpoint address=""
                  binding="basicHttpBinding"
                  name="requestReplyEndpoint"
                  contract="System.ServiceModel.Routing.IRequestReplyRouter" />
      </service>
    </services>

    <behaviors>
      <serviceBehaviors>
        <behavior name="routingData">
          <serviceMetadata httpGetEnabled="True"/>
          <routing filterTableName="MyRoutingTable" />
        </behavior>
      </serviceBehaviors>
    </behaviors>

    <client>
      <endpoint name="ServiceInstance"  address="http://localhost:1111/TestService"
              binding="basicHttpBinding"  contract="*">
      </endpoint>
    </client>
```

```
    <routing>
      <filters>
        <filter name="MatchAllFilter" filterType="MatchAll" />
      </filters>
      <filterTables>
        <filterTable name="MyRoutingTable">
          <add filterName="MatchAllFilter" endpointName="ServiceInstance" />
        </filterTable>
      </filterTables>
    </routing>
  </system.serviceModel>
</configuration>
```

Now open a browser and go to http://localhost:1000/Router. If everything is working properly, then you should find your request is routed through to the service at: http://localhost:1111/TestService.

Note how configuring the router was very similar to configuring any other service. Routing services support any endpoint that WCF does.

Routing Filters

In the last example we created a simple filter that would route any type of communication. Of course, normally you will want to route messages depending on specific conditions. WCF provides a number of options for defining more complex filters, including:

- XPathMessageFilter (XPath queries against incoming messages)

- ActionMessageFilter (WS-Addressing "action" parameters)

- EndpointAddressMessageFilter and PrefixEndpointAddressMessageFilter (match against endpoint address)

- Your own filters

This example shows the creation of an ActionMessage filter that would be added to the entries section:

```
<filter name="addFilter" filterType="Action"  filterData="http://www.apress.com/Book"/>
```

Multicast Support

You can use the new routing functionality to multicast messages by creating filters that will be matched multiple times with different endpoints. For example, we could route messages to 3 different endpoints using the following configuration:

```
<add filterName="MatchAllFilter" endpointName="ServiceInstance1" />
<add filterName="MatchAllFilter" endpointName="ServiceInstance2" />
<add filterName="MatchAllFilter" endpointName="ServiceInstance3" />
```

Bridging Protocols

The router service can also be used to bridge between the bindings that are used. For example, on an internal trusted network, you could use an unsecured connection for better performance that is then bridged to a secure connection for external communication.

Redundancy

You can also use the new routing functionality to define a list of backup endpoints that will be used if WCF encounters a `CommunicationException` or `TimeoutException` on the main endpoints. To define a list of backup endpoints create a new `backupLists` section inside the `routing` block like so:

```
<backupLists>
  <backupList name="backupList">
    <add endpointName="fallover1" />
    <add endpointName="fallover2" />
  </backupList>
</backupLists>
```

WS-Discovery

WCF4 contains support for the WS-Discovery protocol that allows the discovery of services on a network. WS-Discovery was originally developed as joint venture between BEA Systems, Canon, Intel, Microsoft, and WebMethods, and is famously used in Windows Vista to provide the "people near me" functionality. For more information on WS-Discovery please refer to `http://schemas.xmlsoap.org/ws/2004/10/discovery/ws-discovery.pdf`.

WS-Discovery is a great way of easing deployment of your applications, and perhaps even making them more robust by discovering alternative endpoints to use in the event of failure.

WCF4 implements WS-Discovery via a new behavior called `ServiceDiscoveryBehaviour` that tells WCF to make a service discoverable. WCF then creates an `UdpAnnouncementEndpoint` to listen for discovery requests. WS-Discovery can operate in two different modes: managed and adhoc.

Managed Mode

In managed mode, a list of services is held in a central location (called the discovery proxy). When services start up, they inform the discovery proxy of their location. Managed mode is more complex to implement than adhoc, but it creates much less network traffic and is more suitable for use in larger networks. It does, however, have the drawback that if your discovery proxy goes down there will be no more service discovery (single point of failure).

Adhoc Mode

Services operating in adhoc mode broadcast their location over the network, which generates much more network traffic but has no central point of failure. Adhoc mode is also restricted to the current subnet. Let's look into how to use WS-Discovery Adhoc mode now (note the WCF samples contain an example of managed mode).

We will create a simple service that capitalizes a string, make it discoverable, and then find and invoke it.

1. Open Visual Studio and create a new C# console project called `Chapter7.WCFDiscovery`. This will be the new service that we will discover.

2. Now add references to `System.ServiceModel` and `System.ServiceModel.Discovery` assemblies and replace `Program.cs` with the following code:

```csharp
using System;
using System.Collections.Generic;
using System.Linq;
using System.Text;
using System.ServiceModel;
using System.ServiceModel.Discovery;
using System.ServiceModel.Description;

namespace Chapter7.WCFDiscovery
{
    public class Program
    {
        static void Main(string[] args)
        {
            ServiceHost host =
              new ServiceHost(typeof(ToUpperService),
                          new Uri("http://localhost:8081/DiscoverMe"));
            host.AddServiceEndpoint(typeof(IToUpper), new BasicHttpBinding(),
"ToUpper");
            host.AddServiceEndpoint(typeof(IToUpper), new WS2007HttpBinding(),
"ToUpper2");
            host.Description.Behaviors.Add(
              new ServiceMetadataBehavior() { HttpGetEnabled = true }
            );

            ServiceDiscoveryBehavior discoveryBehavior = new
ServiceDiscoveryBehavior();
            host.Description.Behaviors.Add(discoveryBehavior);

            host.AddServiceEndpoint(new UdpDiscoveryEndpoint());
            discoveryBehavior.AnnouncementEndpoints.Add(new
UdpAnnouncementEndpoint());

            host.Open();

            Console.WriteLine("Service running");
            Console.ReadKey();

        }

        public class ToUpperService : IToUpper
        {
            public string ToUpper(string Input)
            {
                return Input.ToUpper();
            }
        }
    }
}
```

```
[ServiceContract]
public interface IToUpper
{
    [OperationContract]
    string ToUpper(string Input);
}
}
```

3. Now add another console project to the solution called Chapter7.WCFFindServices. Add references to the System.ServiceModel and System.ServiceModel.Discovery assemblies.

4. We now need to generate a proxy to enable us to call the service in the Chapter7.WCFDiscovery project. To create the proxy we need to have Chapter7.WCFDiscovery running so right click on the Chapter7.WCFDiscovery project, select Debug➤Start new instance (click allow to the security warning if you get one).

5. You can check the service is running correctly by opening a web browser and going to http://localhost:8081/DiscoverMe, where you should be presented with the service metadata page.

6. Open a Visual Studio command prompt and enter the following command to generate a proxy class for this service:

    svcutil.exe http://localhost:8081/DiscoverMe?wsdl

7. Copy the generated proxy class (which will be at the Visual Studio command prompt location) to the Chapter7.WCFFindServices project.

8. In Chapter7.WCFFindServices amend Program.cs to the following:

```
using System;
using System.Collections.Generic;
using System.Linq;
using System.Text;
using System.ServiceModel.Discovery;
using System.ServiceModel;

namespace Chapter7.WCFFindServices
{
    class Program
    {
        static void Main(string[] args)
        {
            DiscoveryClient discoveryClient =
              new DiscoveryClient(new UdpDiscoveryEndpoint());
            Console.WriteLine("Finding end points please wait this may take some
time..");

            FindResponse discoveryResponse =
              discoveryClient.Find(new FindCriteria(typeof(ToUpperClient)));

            for (int Index = 0; Index < discoveryResponse.Endpoints.Count; Index++)
            {
                Console.WriteLine("Found end point at: " +
                  discoveryResponse.Endpoints[Index].Address.ToString());
            }
```

```
            Console.WriteLine("Using end point: " +
              discoveryResponse.Endpoints[0].Address.ToString());

            EndpointAddress address = discoveryResponse.Endpoints[0].Address;

            ToUpperClient service = new ToUpperClient(new BasicHttpBinding(),
    address);
            Console.WriteLine(service.ToUpper("make me uppercase!"));
            Console.ReadKey();
        }
    }
}
```

9. Okay we're ready to go so start up Chapter7.WCFDiscovery project first (otherwise we are not going to find anything) by right clicking on it select Debug➤Start new instance. Once Chapter7.WCFDiscovery is running then start up the Chapter7.WCFFindServices project in the same manner then after a few minutes you should find that the service is discovered and invoked as shown in Figure 7-2.

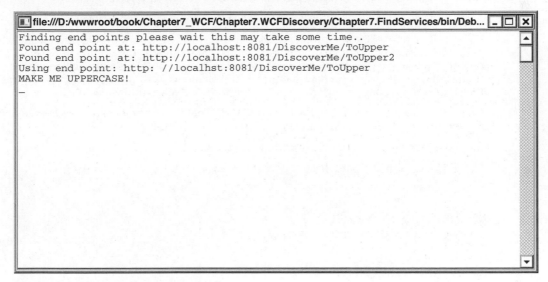

Figure 7-2. *WCF discovery example*

Service Announcement Events

WS-Discovery is also used when services go on and offline. WCF4 allows you to hook into this capability by subscribing to the AnnouncementService's OnlineAnnouncementReceived and OfflineAnnouncementReceived events.

WCF Starter Kit Integration

Two great features previously seen in the WCF REST starter kit (http://www.asp.net/downloads/starter-kits/wcf-rest/) have been brought into WCF4:

- Help pages
- HTTP caching

Help Pages

Help pages are automatically generated HTML pages that describe how to call your service and the type of response it will return, and can be very helpful for working out how to call the darn thing. Help pages are created automatically when you use the WebServiceHost class (although at the time of writing this doesn't seem to be the case) and using the HelpEnabled property on WebHttpBehaviour.

Let's take a look at this now with a contrived example:

1. Create a new WCF service library project called Chapter7.WCFWebService.

2. Add a console application to the solution called Chapter7.WCFWebServiceHost.

3. By default in .NET 4.0, some project types reference the .NET client profile framework, which is a smaller subsection of the main framework aimed at reducing your applications size. To demonstrate help pages, we need to use functionality not contained in the client profile framework, so right-click on the Chapter7.WCFWebServiceHost project, select Properties on the context menu, and change the target framework to .NET Framework 4.0.

4. Now add a project reference to the Chapter7.WCFWebService project and a reference to the System.ServiceModel and System.ServiceModel.Web assemblies.

5. Enter the following code in Program.cs (main method):

```
using System.ServiceModel.Web;

...

WebServiceHost MyServiceHost =
    new WebServiceHost(typeof(Chapter7.WCFWebService.Service1),
                       new Uri("http://localhost:8888/Test"));
MyServiceHost.Open();
Console.WriteLine("Service running...");
Console.ReadLine();
MyServiceHost.Close();
```

6. Now open a browser and go to http://localhost:8888/Test/help and you should see something similar to Figure 7-3 and 7-4.

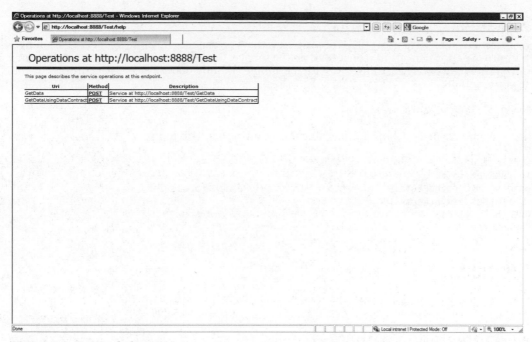

Figure 7-3. *Service help page*

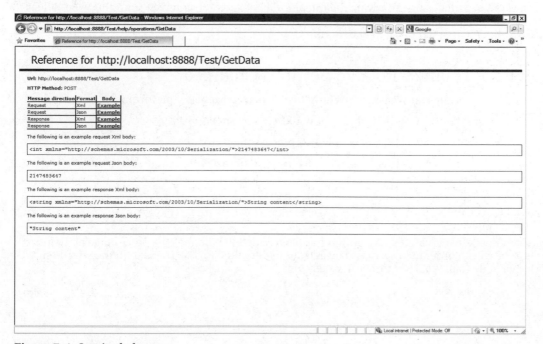

Figure 7-4. *Service help page*

HTTP Caching

One of the biggest advantages to using RESTful services is that you can take advantage of HTTP caching features to improve performance and reduce load on the service. Caching wasn't too easy to implement prior to WCF4 however it is very easy in WCF4 with the simple addition of the AspNetCache profile attribute to your methods:

```
[AspNetCacheProfile("MyCachingProfile")]
```

You then need to create a caching profile using the following configuration:

```
<outputCacheSettings>
  <outputCacheProfiles>
    <add name=" MyCachingProfile " duration="30" varyByParam="format"
        varyByHeader="Accept" />
  </outputCacheProfiles>
</outputCacheSettings>
```

Misc Changes

What follows are a number of other enhancements that have been introduced in WCF4.

Improved Integration with WF

Microsoft has put a big focus on improving the integration between WF and WCF, and this release sees the introduction of a new project type called WF Service (a combined WCF and WF service represented entirely in XAML). Please refer to Chapter 6 for full details.

Default Performance-Related Settings Changed

A number of default settings for WCF services have been tweaked for better performance:

- MaxConcurrentSessions was 10, and is now 100 x processor count.

- MaxConcurrentCalls was 16, and is now 16 x processor count.

- MaxConcurrentInstances was 26, and is now the total of MaxConcurrentSettions and MaxConcurrentCalls.

Low Memory

A new minFreeMemoryToActivateService option has been added that defines the percentage of memory that needs to be free in order for a service to be activated (defaulted to 5%). If less than the specified memory is available then WCF will throw an exception.

Other changes

The following lists some other changes that have been made.

- Event Tracing for Windows is now used for tracing offering better performance.

- There's a new `DataContractResolver` class that allows control over the serialization process of types (`http://msdn.microsoft.com/en-us/library/system.runtime.serialization.datacontractresolver(VS.100).aspx`).

- There's a new byte stream encoder (a new encoder for sending binary content over WCF—see samples again).

- Automatic decompression over HTTP for client has been added (server not currently supported).

- Extended protection of secure channels has been added (a new Windows feature that binds one security system to another making attacks harder).

- The addition of non-destructive queue receive (an alternative way of processing messages that makes a queue item invisible to other consumers and creates a transaction for performing work on it that if rolled back will return the item to its place on the queue – for more info please refer to: `http://blogs.msdn.com/drnick/archive/2008/12/04/an-alternative-queuing-model.aspx`).

Dublin/Windows Application Server

It is important to note that Microsoft are working on a new technology code named Dublin (which will probably become Windows Application Server when the marketing guys get their way) that aims to make it easy to deploy and manage your WCF and WF applications and services and will probably become the preferred means of hosting services.

At the time of writing Dublin will ship as an add-in to Windows Server 2008 and will be contained in future versions of Windows as part of the application server role.

Dublin is an extension to IIS and Microsoft say will provide the following functionality:

- Allows easier deployment of workflow and services.

- Provides an overview of service health and dashboard for monitoring services.

- Has tools for easier management of services.

- Comes with forwarding/routing functionality.

- Has built-in tracking profiles for monitoring common events.

Further reading

- `http://msdn.microsoft.com/en-gb/library/dd456789(VS.100).aspx`
- `http://blogs.thinktecture.com/cweyer/default.aspx`
- `http://msdn.microsoft.com/en-us/library/ee354381.aspx`
- `http://blogs.msdn.com/drnick/`
- `http://blogs.msdn.com/endpoint/`
- `http://msdn.microsoft.com/en-us/netframework/aa663324.aspx`

■ ■ ■

CHAPTER 8

Entity Framework

Entity Framework (EF) is Microsoft's Object Relational Mapping (ORM) solution and was first released with .NET 3.5SP1. Entity Framework received much criticism when it was first released and the team at Microsoft has been hard at work to address some of these criticisms in the latest version.

■**WARNING** This chapter is written using a preview version of EF4, so final functionality may differ. It is also worth noting that EF is likely to have releases out of band. For the examples in this chapter you will need to install the EF CTP 2.

EF and LINQ to SQL

Some developers are understandably confused by the overlap between EF and LINQ to SQL. EF and LINQ to SQL were developed by two different teams—hence the overlap. LINQ to SQL is a great piece of technology and very suitable as a simple, light-weight wrapper to SQL. It is pretty clear, however, that Microsoft is pushing developers to use EF. This is a sensible (although no doubt irritating) move as LINQ to SQL is fundamentally flawed as a generic ORM solution in that

- It only works with SQL Server.

- Generated classes must have a 1 to 1 relationship with database objects.

EF provides an abstraction above the database layer and a number of enhancements that make it superior to LINQ to SQL.

Is LINQ to SQL Dead?

Er, probably not.

In October 2008 Microsoft's Tim Mallalieu (Program Manager, LINQ to SQL and LINQ to Entities) stated:

> *"We're making significant investments in the Entity Framework such that as of .NET 4.0 the Entity Framework will be our recommended data access solution for LINQ to relational scenarios."*

> http://blogs.msdn.com/adonet/archive/2008/10/29/update-on-linq-to-sql-and-linq-to-entities-roadmap.aspx

However, after feedback from a large number of LINQ to SQL customers, Microsoft seemed to back off on this a bit, when Tim said:

> "*We will continue make some investments in LINQ to SQL based on customer feedback. This post was about making our intentions for future innovation clear and to call out the fact that as of .NET 4.0, LINQ to Entities will be the recommended data access solution for LINQ to relational scenarios* "

http://blogs.msdn.com/adonet/archive/2008/10/31/clarifying-the-message-on-l2s-futures.aspx

LINQ to SQL changes

In VS2010/.NET 4.0 LINQ to SQL has a number of welcome performance enhancements and bug fixes. It is slightly troublesome that there is very little information on this at the time of writing, but for a full list please see the blog post by Damien Guard (who works at Microsoft within the data programmability team) at http://damieng.com/blog/2009/06/01/linq-to-sql-changes-in-net-40.

Why Use EF?

The sections below cover the benefits of using an ORM solution, although please note that some of these advantages are not EF specific—excellent (and more mature) alternatives do exist. Probably the best-known and one of the most mature ORM in the .NET world is NHibernate. You can, however, view an extensive list at http://en.wikipedia.org/wiki/List_of_object-relational_mapping_software.

Abstraction

Data is generally held in a relational manner that is optimized for storage and quick retrieval (well, in most cases it should be). However, this format tends to not map that easily to how we want to work with objects. ORMs can provide a conceptual mapping that allows you to organize your entities and their properties in a manner that is different than how they are physically stored.

For example, I worked on an application for a hospital that stored data about patients in two tables: Person and Patient. These tables had a one-to-one relationship. Person held demographic details and Patient held clinical-specific information. Whether this is the best database design is not important, but you can probably see that when you want to work with a "patient," it is tedious to have to work with two separate objects. EF allows you to create an object that is spread across two tables, allowing you to write more intuitive code, such as the following:

```
Patient.Firstname
Patient.BloodType
```

Code Generation

A great advantage of using an ORM solution is that it provides basic CRUD (created, read, update, delete) functionality saving you from having to write this part. As code is automatically generated, the potential for errors is also reduced. Using an ORM can also make it easier to adhere to naming conventions as classes and methods are automatically generated.

It is worth noting that by utilizing an ORM framework for data access, you are introducing additional overhead to data access, and that for high performance applications, you may be better off working with the database directly. Generally, however, the performance implications will probably be pretty minimal and outweighed by the other advantages an ORM solution can bring.

Support for Different Databases

EF provides support for a number of different databases in addition to SQL Server, such as Oracle, MySQL, SQLAnywhere, and, recently, Synergex's Synergy and a few more.

EF contains its own query language and mechanisms that provide you with a consistent query mechanism that can be used across many different data sources. EF doesn't care whether your database uses T-SQL or PL/SQL—querying is the same.

Design Time Support

EF has excellent design-time support that developers will quickly get to grips with. Yes, it was a bit ropey in the original version, but this is much improved in VS2010. I don't think the majority of ORMs provide this level of GUI functionality, so this is definitely one of EF's strengths.

Utilize LINQ

LINQ to Entities allows you to construct some very complex queries utilizing the .NET Framework that would not be possible with standard SQL.

N-Tier Application Development

EF has a number of features (particularly in the latest release), such as support for POCO (Plain old CLR object e.g.net classes!) and self-tracking of change templates, that make it a great solution for the development of n-tier applications.

Where is EF Used?

Several areas of .NET 4.0 and VS2010 support or are dependent on EF:

- WCF Data Services
- Windows Azure
- Dynamic data framework
- Microsoft Ajax libraries

You can, of course, use EF anywhere in your application, but you may find it is particularly suitable to some areas, such as:

- ASP.NET MVC
- Silverlight/WPF (many controls have inbuilt EF support)
- ASP.NET (many controls have built-in support for binding to EF objects)

EF 101

Many developers may be unfamiliar with EF as it was released in between VS2008 and VS2010, or others may have heard bad things about it (not all of which are true). Let's take a quick look at how to work with EF before looking at the new features in EF4.

Entity Data Model

All EF applications contain an entity data model (EDM) that describes the objects in the underlying data source. The EDM can be further divided into three layers:

- Conceptual model (the view your users see)
- Storage model (how data is actually stored)
- Mapping model (links the conceptual and storage models)

EDMs are stored as XML and are composed of three main sections (which link to the three conceptual layers already described):

- CSDL (Conceptual Schema Definition Language)
- SSDL (Store Schema Definition Language)
- MSL (Mapping Specification Language)

It is important to understand the format of the EDM file. EF contains good GUI support, but for more advanced customizations it is necessary to modify the XML file directly. The exact format of your EDM file is also dependent on how it is generated (described next).

If you generate your model using the wizard in Visual Studio, the EDM will be held in one file with the extension .edmx with the conceptual, storage, and mapping sections split under the following nodes:

- edmx:StorageModels
- edmx:ConceptualModels
- edmx:Mappings

If, however, you generate your model using EDMGen.exe (discussed next) then the model will be split into three separate files: .SSDL, .CSDL, and .MSL.

Creating an EDM

You can create an EDM in three different ways:

- The EDMGen command-line tool
- By using the ADO.NET data model wizard in Visual Studio
- By creating the model in Visual Studio and then having VS generate your database structure from this model (new to EF4)

EdmGen.exe

EdmGen.exe is a command-line tool primarily used for generating an EDM, but it also performs a number of other tasks, such as verification of models and splitting generated files. You may want to utilize EdmGen as part of your application's build process.

Creating an Entity Data Model in Visual Studio

The easiest way to create an EDM is by using the ADO.NET data model wizard in Visual Studio.

1. Open up Visual Studio.

2. Create a New C# Console application and call it Chapter8.HelloEF.

3. Right-click on the project and select Add➤New Item.

4. Select ADO.NET Entity Data Model, and name it Chapter8Model.edmx (Figure 8-1).

5. Click Add.

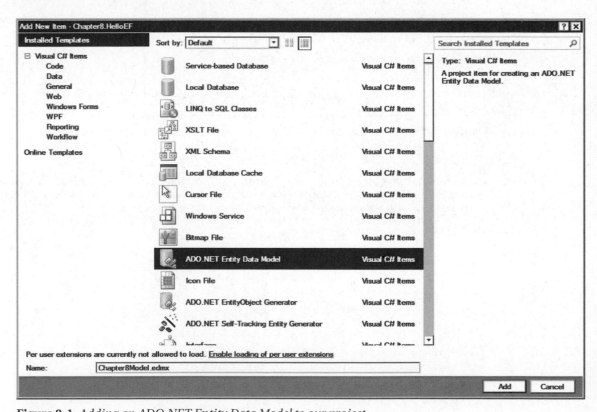

Figure 8-1. *Adding an ADO.NET Entity Data Model to our project*

6. The Choose Model Contents wizard screen will now appear (Figure 8-2). Select the "Generate from database" option.

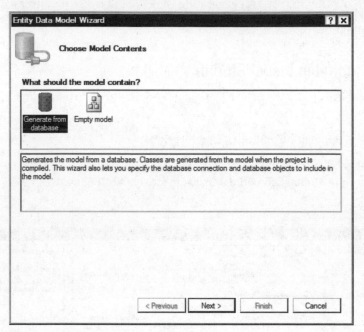

Figure 8-2. *Generate from database*

7. Click Next.

8. VS will now ask you for a connection (Figure 8-3). If you haven't done this already, create a new connection to the example database. Note that my database is called Book, so EF will prefix many settings with the name of the database (you may wish to change this).

9. Click Next.

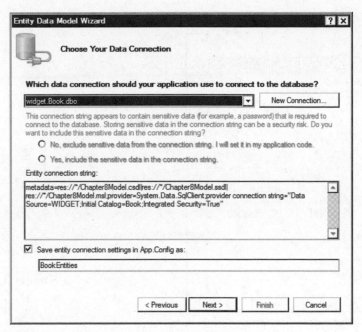

Figure 8-3. *Connection string properties*

10. We now need to select the items in the database that we want EF to create entities for. Expand the Tables node and select the following tables (Figure 8-4):

- `Film`
- `FilmShowing`
- `Order`
- `OrderItem`

■**NOTE** The wizard also allows you to create entities for views and stored procedures.

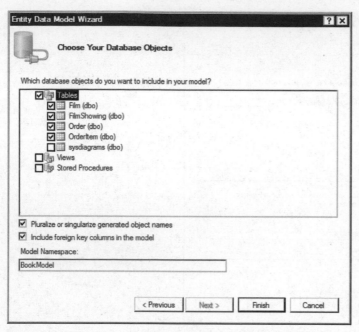

Figure 8-4. *Selecting items to generate EF classes for*

11. Ensure that you have checked the "Pluralize or singularize generate object names" and "Include foreign key columns in the model" (these are new options in EF—for more information please refer to the following Pluralization section).

12. Set the model namespace as `BookModel`.

13. Click Finish. EF will then generate entities for the classes we have created and you will be taken to the design view of the generated EF model (Figure 8-5).

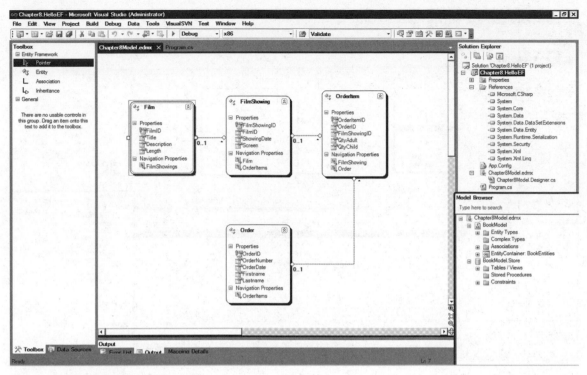

Figure 8-5. *Design view of EF model*

Notice how relationships between the entities have been automatically created. This is because our database contained a number of constraints and relationships that were automatically imported into our model. You can also create relationships yourself in the design view.

Navigating the EF model

When your EF model contains many entities then the designer window can get pretty crowded. You can zoom in and out of the model view by clicking the magnifying icons in the corner of the scroll bars or by right-clicking and selecting the zoom level.

Viewing How Entities Are Mapped

If you select one of the entities, then view the Mapping Details window, you will see how the individual properties on the entity are mapped to the underlying database fields (Figure 8-6).

Now select one of the individual entity properties and Visual Studio will display information in the Properties window, such as the type of field, length, and so on. Notice how you can also change the name of the field and the getter and setter properties' access levels (Figure 8-7).

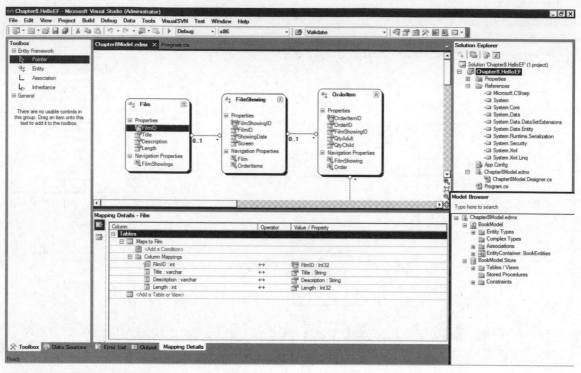

Figure 8-6. *EF Mapping window*

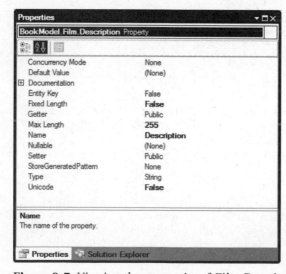

Figure 8-7. *Viewing the properties of Film.Description*

What Happens If My Database Structure Changes?

When you make changes to your database then you will also need to update your EDM. To update the model simply right-click on the design surface and select Update Model from Database. Visual Studio will then bring up a dialog box allowing you to add additional tables and fields (Figure 8-8). Note that this release of EF improves the resolution of conflicts/orphaned model elements in the model browser window:

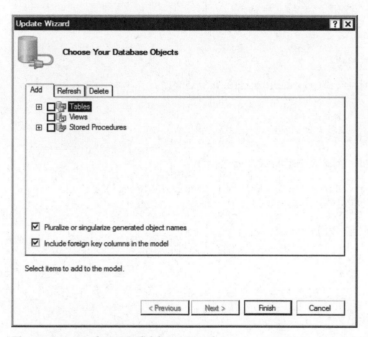

Figure 8-8. *Update Model from Database*

Querying Data

EF allows you to query objects in a number of different ways:

- LINQ to Entities (L2E)
- ObjectQuery methods
- Entity SQL

Whichever query method you use, the query gets transformed into the same query tree structure that is then processed by your model's data source provider.

LINQ to Entities

LINQ to Entities (L2E) is probably the easiest query method. L2E gives you rich query functionality and Intellisense support, and it is very easy to use. Lets write some code to iterate through our Orders and OrderItem tables displaying information about these entries.

1. Open Program.cs.

2. Modify the Main() method to the following (note your entity set will, by default, be prefixed with the same name as the database—in the following example, mine is Book).

```
static void Main(string[] args)
{
    BookEntities ctx = new BookEntities();

    var query = from o in ctx.Orders
                        select o;

    foreach (Order order in query)
    {
        Console.WriteLine("Order: " + order.OrderID.ToString() + " " + order.Firstname
+ " "
          + order.Lastname);

        order.OrderItems.Load();

        foreach(OrderItem orderItem in order.OrderItems)
        {
            Console.WriteLine("Adult: " + orderItem.QtyAdult.ToString() + " Child:"
              + orderItem.QtyChild.ToString());
        }

        Console.WriteLine("");

    }

    Console.ReadKey();
}
```

The results are shown in Figure 8-9.

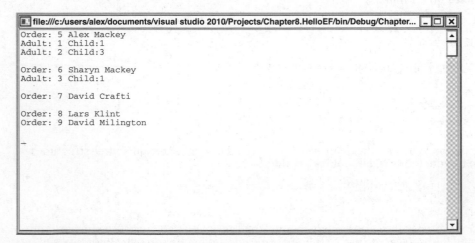

Figure 8-9. *Output of LINQ to Entities query*

ObjectQuery

You can also query EF objects with the `ObjectQuery` class. Let's take a look at this now.

1. Add the following using directive to `Program.cs`:

   ```
   using System.Data.Objects;
   ```

2. Replace the LINQ query with the following line of code (Note that `it` refers to the current entity, which in this case is `Order`):

   ```
   ObjectQuery<Order> query = ctx.Orders.OrderBy("it.OrderID");
   ```

Entity SQL

Entity SQL is similar to T-SQL (but has its own EF-specific features and intricacies); the following is an example Entity SQL query:

```
string queryString = @"SELECT VALUE o FROM BookEntities.Orders AS o";
ObjectQuery<Order> query = new ObjectQuery<Order>(queryString, ctx, MergeOption.NoTracking);
```

We have barely touched what Entity SQL is capable of, so for more information (on anything EF related) please refer to Julia Lerman's book *Programming Entity Framework*, published by O'Reilly.

CRUD Operations in EF

When you utilize EF, a connection to a database called an object context is created. When new entities are created or properties changed they are not written back to the database immediately; rather a flag is set on the entity to indicate that it has changed, but not saved to the database (a dirty state). Changes are then saved back to the database when the `SaveChanges()` method is called on the object context.

Creating

The following example shows how to create a new `Film` entity with a related `FilmShowing` entity and save the new items back to the database:

```
BookEntities ctx = new BookEntities();

Film NewFilm = new Film();
NewFilm.Title = "New film";
NewFilm.Description = "New film";
NewFilm.Length = 300;

FilmShowing NewFilmShowing = new FilmShowing();
NewFilmShowing.Screen = 5;
NewFilmShowing.ShowingDate = System.DateTime.Now;
NewFilm.FilmShowings.Add(NewFilmShowing);

ctx.AddObject("Films", NewFilm);
ctx.SaveChanges();
```

You can also use the CreateFilm() method on the Film class itself to perform the same action:

```
BookEntities ctx = new BookEntities();
Film NewFilm = Film.CreateFilm(0);
NewFilm.Title = "New film2";
NewFilm.Description = "New film";
NewFilm.Length = 300;

ctx.AddToFilms(NewFilm);
ctx.SaveChanges();
```

Notice how in the previous example we created a film with ID 0 that EF automatically incremented when we saved it back to the database.

Entities can be customized by using partial classes. So in the previous example you might want to add some new methods to your Film entity. This could be achieved as follows:

```
public partial class Film : EntityObject
{
    public void CheckAvailability()
    { }

    public void PrintTicket()
    { }
}
```

Updating

To update an EF object, simply retrieve an entity, make your changes, and then call the SaveChanges() method on the DataContext:

```
BookEntities ctx = new BookEntities();

Film FilmToUpdate = ctx.Films.Where("it.FilmID = 3").First();
FilmToUpdate.Title = "New updated title";
ctx.SaveChanges();
```

CONCURRENCY

EF supports a number of different concurrency options. The default is optimistic concurrency (last write wins). Other advanced concurrency options enable EF to check if underlying data has changed before writing it back.

Deleting

Deleting entities is very easy. You must remember however to delete related child objects if referential integrity is enforced in your database (note the example database doesn't enforce referential integrity to make it easier to play with).

```
BookEntities ctx = new BookEntities();

ctx.Films.DeleteObject(ctx.Films.Where("it.FilmID = 5").First());

foreach (FilmShowing fs in ctx.FilmShowings.Where("it.FilmID = 5"))
{
    ctx.FilmShowings.DeleteObject(fs);
}
```

I hope you now have a basic idea of what EF can provide for you:

ctx.SaveChanges();

EFv1 Criticisms

ORM frameworks are a subject many people feel strongly about and EF received a huge amount of criticism when it was first released. A number of developers even set up a petition website entitled "ADO.NET Entity Framework vote of no confidence" to highlight to Microsoft their concerns about Entity Framework's design. The criticisms are well worth a read and can still be viewed at http://efvote.wufoo.com/forms/ado-net-entity-framework-vote-of-no-confidence/.

The main criticisms most have of EFv1 are that

- EF is too focused on the data aspects of an ORM framework and neglects other areas, for example, validation and transactions

- No support for persistence ignorance (EF is too tightly coupled to the underlying data store)

- EF has too many dependencies and lacks the ability to create entities as standard .NET classes (you will hear this referred to as POCO or plain old CLR objects)

- Lack of support for lazy loading

- Difficult/unsatisfactory methods to add domain logic to entities (currently this has to be carried out by creating partial classes)

- The EDM is held in a single file, which creates a bottle-neck for source control in multi-user environments

- Immature tooling support, which sometimes mangles model files or will not open when customizations to raw models are made

While there are workarounds to some of these issues, such as lazy loading and persistence ignorance, it was evident that these areas would need to be addressed for EF to gain the acceptance Microsoft hoped for.

Entity Framework 4

The EF team was determined to make the next version of EF an excellent ORM solution, so it formed an advisory panel that included well-known experts, such as Martin Fowler (patterns) and Eric Evans (domain-driven design). I believe this release has resolved a number of the original concerns and introduced some great new features. Let's see what they changed.

EDM Designer Changes

VS2010 contains a new Model Browser window that allows you to easily navigate your EDM (Figure 8-10). It is worth noting that previously in EF if an entity was removed from the model and subsequently brought back by using the wizard's update model functionality, then it would not be recreated. This was because a reference to the original object was still held in the CSDL file, so EF believed it still existed.

In VS2010 the Model Browser window now contains a new facility that allows you to remove the CSDL entries as well. To do this, simply right-click on the item you want to remove under the Store node and select Delete. This will then remove the entity from the storage model.

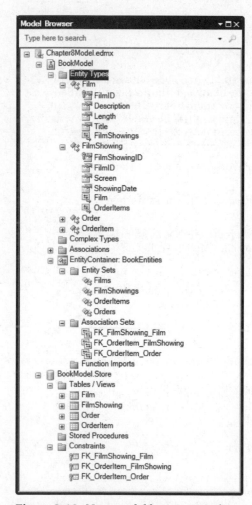

Figure 8-10. *New model browser window*

Performance

The EF team has fine-tuned the performance of EF. One area that was improved is query generation. Previously parameter length was passed into queries. This was a bad decision; parameters could vary in length, which would prevent SQL Server from utilizing the query cache. In EF4 parameter length is no longer passed so the query cache can be utilized. The team has also tweaked how joins are made and removed unnecessary IsNull() calls.

Pluralization

Pluralization is a new feature in EF4 that generates more readable entity names. In EFv1 if you had a table called Film, then your entities would be called Film, and entity sets of Film would also be called Film, which made querying not as readable as it could be. Thus many developers would manually rename entity sets of Film to be called Films, which could be pretty boring.

In EF4 if you select to use the pluralization option when creating the model, then Film's entity set will be automatically named as Films.

Note that the new pluralization feature doesn't just stick an -s on the end of the table name. It is cleverer than that; for example, it knows when to append or remove -s, or when to modify the ending of a word to -ies (e.g., Category becomes Categories). Pluralization currently only works with U.S. English, although there is an option to override this and provide your own pluralization provider.

The pluralization service is contained in System.Data.Entity.Design.dll (which is a shame as this would be useful elsewhere) and has a static method called CreateService(). For more information please see http://www.danrigsby.com/blog/index.php/2009/05/19/entity-framework-40-pluralization/.

Deferred/Lazy Loading

Lazy loading is a coding technique that minimizes resource usage and database access by not loading an entity until it is actually accessed. In EF4 lazy loading is switched on by default. If you want to turn lazy loading off, then set the ContextOptions.LazyLoadingEnabled option to false in the context class:

```
ctx.ContextOptions.LazyLoadingEnabled = false;
```

Eager Loading

While we are looking at lazy loading it's worth mentioning its evil twin, eager loading. Eager loading is the exact opposite to lazy loading and means pre-loading an entity before you need it. This can increase the responsiveness of your application if the initialization is spread out over your application's lifetime. Julia Lerman has a great post that describes a number of ways to implement eager loading and measures the effect it has on performance: http://thedatafarm.com/blog/data-access/the-cost-of-eager-loading-in-entity-framework/.

Complex Type Designer Support

If your entities contain many fields then it can be useful to subdivide them into types. For example, a Patient entity in a medical system may have a huge amount of properties, but using complex types we could divide this information up like so:

```
Patient.Demographic.FirstName
Patient.Demographic.Age
Patient.Demographic.LastName

Patient.Clinical.BloodType

Patient.Financial.InsurerName
```

Previously, if you wanted to accomplish this it was necessary to manually edit the CSDL, but as of EF4 you can accomplish this in the designer. Let's see how to work with this feature with our Film entity.

1. Select the Film entity.

2. Hold down the Ctrl key and select the Description and Length properties (Figure 8-11).

3. Right-click and select the Refactor into New Complex Type option on the context menu.

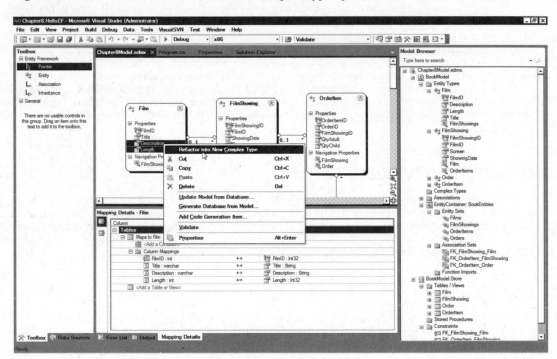

Figure 8-11. *Refactoring description and Length into a complex type*

4. VS will create a new property called ComplexProperty: rename this property to Detail.

5. If you open Program.cs you will now be able to access these properties using code similar to the following:

```
Film Film = new Film();
Film.Detail.Description = "New film";
Film.Detail.Length = 200;
```

■TIP To undo this change, remove the `Film` table from the model designer and then add it in again by right-clicking and selecting Update Model from Database.

Complex Types from Stored Procedures

The function import wizard will now create complex types from stored procedures. For example, let's imagine we wanted to add a method to our `Film` entity to return information about some of the crew, which is retrieved using the following stored procedure (mocked up for ease of use):

```
CREATE PROCEDURE FilmGetCrewInfo

@filmID int

AS

SELECT
'James Cameron' as Director,
'Arnold Schwarzenegger' as LeadActor1,
'Linda Hamilton' as LeadActor2
```

1. Go to the Model Browser window (tab next to Solution Explorer).

2. Right-click on the Complex Types folder and add a new complex type called `FilmCrew`.

3. Right-click on the newly created complex type and add three new string scalar properties called `Director`, `LeadActor1`, and `LeadActor2` (Figure 8-12).

Figure 8-12. *Creating a new complex type*

4. Open `Chapter8.Model.edmx` and on the designer surface right-click and select the Update Model from Database option.

5. Under the Stored Procedures node select the `FilmGetCrewInfo` stored procedure and click Finish.

6. Right-click on the designer surface and select Add➤Function Import to bring up the screen shown in Figure 8-13. (I also clicked Get Column Information button when completed the other information to populate the stored procedure column information section).

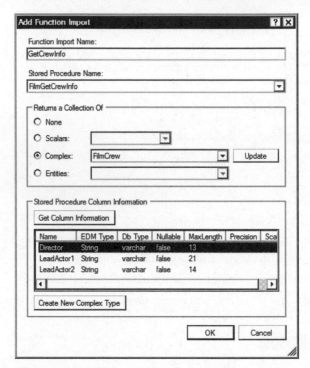

Figure 8-13. *Add function import screen*

7. Enter the function import name `GetCrewInfo`.

8. Select the stored procedure name `FilmGetCrewInfo`.

9. Select Complex in the Returns a Collection Of radio button options and then `FilmCrew` on the dropdown (notice how you have the option to create a complex type from the results of the stored procedure).

10. Click OK. The EF designer will now have added this function to the context where it can be accessed as follows (note you could then move this into your entity using partial classes):

```
var crew = ctx.GetCrewInfo(1);
```

Model Defined Functions

Model defined functions allow you to define reusable functions at a model level. To create them at present you must modify the `.edmx` file directly, although this will probably change in future versions of

EF. In our convoluted example we will create a new property for our `Film` entity that will return the `Film` title and description separated by a space.

1. Right-click on the `Chapter8Model.edmx` file and select Open With.

2. Select XML Editor.

3. Find the following section:

```
<edmx:ConceptualModels>
    <Schema Namespace="BookModel" Alias="Self"
xmlns:annotation="http://schemas.microsoft.com/ado/2009/02/edm/annotation"
xmlns="http://schemas.microsoft.com/ado/2008/09/edm">
```

4. Add the following inside the previous section:

```
<Function Name="LongFilmDescription" ReturnType="Edm.String">
    <Parameter Name="Film" Type="BookModel.Film">
    </Parameter>
    <DefiningExpression>
      Trim(Film.Title) + " " + Film.Description
    </DefiningExpression>
</Function>
```

5. Open `Program.cs` and add the following using directive:

```
using System.Data.Objects.DataClasses;
```

6. Unfortunately LINQ to Entities doesn't yet know about the `LongFilmDescription` function, so we have to tell it by creating a static class decorated with the `[EdmFunction]` attribute to allow us to access it. Add the following code in `Program.cs`.

```
public static class MDF
{
    [EdmFunction("BookModel", "LongFilmDescription")]
    public static string LongFilmDescription(Film f)
    {
        throw new NotSupportedException("This function can only be used in a query");
    }
}
```

7. Once this is done we can now utilize our function in L2E queries as follows:

```
var query = from f in ctx.Films
select new { FullName = MDF.LongFilmDescription(f) };
```

Model First Generation

EF4 allows you to create your entity model in Visual Studio and use it to generate and update database structure. At the time of writing this works only with SQL Server. This facility is great for users unfamiliar with SQL or in situations where you do not have access to the database.

1. Create a new C# console project called `Chapter8.ModelFirst`.

2. Add a new ADO.NET Entity Data Model called `CustomerModel`.

3. Click Next.

4. Select Empty model (Figure 8-14) on the next step and click Finish.

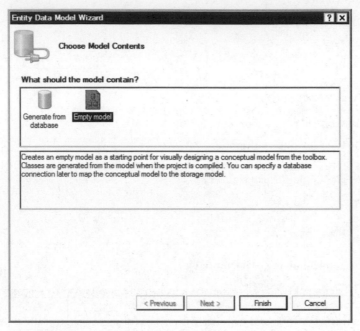

Figure 8-14. *Select empty model option*

5. Open the newly created empty CustomerModel.edmx.

6. Right-click on the design surface and select Add➤Entity.

7. Call the entity Customer.

8. Change the key property name to CustomerID (Figure 8-15).

9. Right-click on Customer and select Add➤Scalar Property. Call it Firstname.

10. Add three more properties: Lastname, Company, Phone.

11. Add another entity called Address.

12. Change the key property name to AddressID .

13. Add five scalar properties to Address called Address1, Address2, Address3, City, and PostalCode (Figure 8-16).

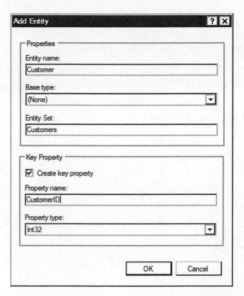

Figure 8-15. *Adding an entity to our blank model*

Figure 8-16. *Our manually created Customer and Address entities*

14. We need to give Visual Studio a bit more information about the fields for this entity; otherwise, when it creates the database structure all fields will be created in the format `varchar(max)`. Select the `Firstname` field; then in the Properties window set the `MaxLength` property to 100.

15. Repeat this for the other fields (Figure 8-17).

Figure 8-17. *Setting field length properties*

16. We now need to link our `Customer` and `Address` entities. Right-click on the design surface and select the Add➤Association option. You'll see the screen in Figure 8-18.

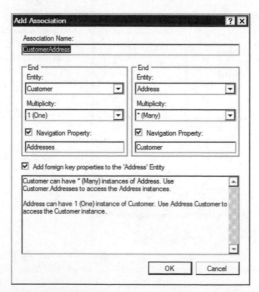

Figure 8-18. *Adding an association*

17. Accept the association defaults and then click OK.

18. Select the Model Browser tab next to the Solution Explorer tab.

19. Right-click on CustomerModel node and select Generate Database from Model (Figure 8-19).

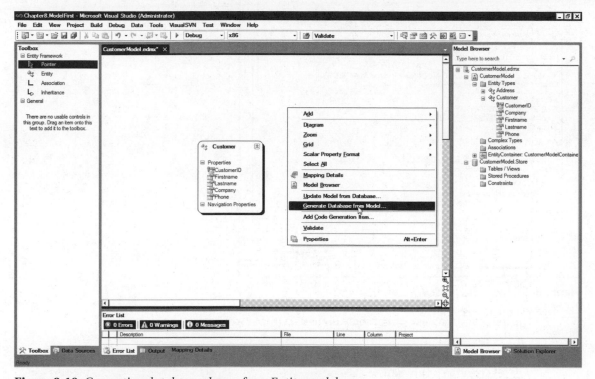

Figure 8-19. *Generating database schema from Entity model*

20. The Choose Your Data Connection dialog will now pop up.

21. Select the connection we used earlier and select "Yes, include the sensitive data in the connection string" option and click Next. Visual Studio will then generate the necessary SQL to create a structure to hold these entities (Figure 8-20).

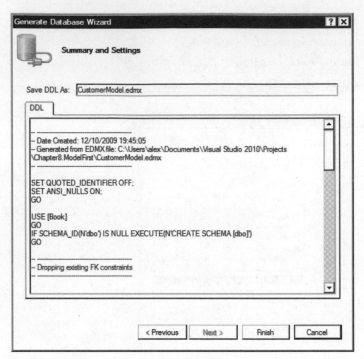

Figure 8-20. *Generated T-SQL for our EDM*

The following is an excerpt of some of the T-SQL that will be generated:

```
-- Creating table 'Customers'
CREATE TABLE [dbo].[Customers] (
    [CustomerID] int  NOT NULL,
    [Firstname] nvarchar(100)  NOT NULL,
    [Lastname] nvarchar(100)  NOT NULL,
    [Company] nvarchar(100)  NOT NULL,
    [Phone] nvarchar(100)  NOT NULL
);
GO
-- Creating table 'Addresses'
CREATE TABLE [dbo].[Addresses] (
    [AddressID] int  NOT NULL,
    [Address1] nvarchar(100)  NOT NULL,
    [Address2] nvarchar(100)  NOT NULL,
    [Address3] nvarchar(100)  NOT NULL,
    [City] nvarchar(100)  NOT NULL,
    [PostalCode] nvarchar(100)  NOT NULL
);
GO
```

```
-- ----------------------------------------------------
-- Creating all Primary Key Constraints
-- ----------------------------------------------------

-- Creating primary key on [CustomerID] in table 'Customers'
ALTER TABLE [dbo].[Customers] WITH NOCHECK
ADD CONSTRAINT [PK_Customers]
    PRIMARY KEY CLUSTERED ([CustomerID] ASC)
    ON [PRIMARY]
GO
-- Creating primary key on [AddressID] in table 'Addresses'
ALTER TABLE [dbo].[Addresses] WITH NOCHECK
ADD CONSTRAINT [PK_Addresses]
    PRIMARY KEY CLUSTERED ([AddressID] ASC)
    ON [PRIMARY]
GO


-- ----------------------------------------------------
-- Creating all Foreign Key Constraints
-- ----------------------------------------------------

-- Creating foreign key on [CustomerCustomerID] in table 'Addresses'
ALTER TABLE [dbo].[Addresses] WITH NOCHECK
ADD CONSTRAINT [FK_CustomerAddress]
    FOREIGN KEY ([CustomerCustomerID])
    REFERENCES [dbo].[Customers]
        ([CustomerID])
    ON DELETE NO ACTION ON UPDATE NO ACTION
GO
```

22. Click Finish.

23. You will receive a warning (Figure 8-21)—click Yes.

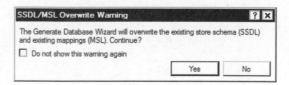

Figure 8-21. *Warning displayed on generated T-SQL*

That's it—you can now run this SQL on your database and use the EDM in the standard way.

Foreign Keys

In previous versions of EF, foreign key fields on entities were hidden from the developer in the generated model. Developers were expected to access the related entity directly instead of querying foreign key fields. This could mean making some additional database queries to join entities and writing some tedious code.

For example, in our code we might be creating a UI for managing FilmShowings. It would be a lot easier if when creating a new film showing we could just set the related FilmID property:

```
NewFilmShowing.FilmID = FilmID;
```

In EF4, you can. It may be worth questioning whether you should be working this way but I think on the whole it avoids additional database queries.

Code Only/POCO

One of the biggest complaints about Entity Framework v1 was that, unless you wanted to write some complex code, you had to work with the generated classes and associated data context. This dependence on Entity Framework made it harder to perform unit testing, create n-tier applications, and work with third-party systems.

A number of methods (loosely referred to as IPOCO) were developed involving inheritance and implementing a number of interfaces to try and achieve this, but for many these were unsatisfactory solutions. EF4 will, however, allow you to create classes that have no dependency on EF whatsoever.

STILL USING EFV1 AND WANT POCO?

Jaroslaw Kowalski describes a possible method for implementing POCO classes in EFv1:

```
http://code.msdn.microsoft.com/EFPocoAdapter
```

POCO in EF4

Creating POCO classes in EF4 is very easy:

1. Create a new Console project called Chapter8.CodeOnly.

2. Add a new class called Film.cs and enter the following code:

    ```
    public class Film
    {
        public int FilmID { get; set; }
        public string Title { get; set; }
        public string Description { get; set; }
        public int Length { get; set; }
    }
    ```

3. Add a reference to the System.Data.Entity and Microsoft.Data.Entity.CTP assemblies.

4. Add a new class called FilmModel.

5. Now add the following using directives to the FilmModel class:

    ```
    using System.Data.Objects;
    using System.Data.EntityClient;
    ```

6. Add the following code to FilmModel.cs:

```
public class FilmModel : ObjectContext
{
    public FilmModel(EntityConnection connection)
      : base(connection)
    {
        DefaultContainerName = "FilmModel";
    }

    public IObjectSet<Film> Film { get { return base.CreateObjectSet<Film>(); } }
}
```

7. In Program.cs add the following using statements:

```
using Microsoft.Data.Objects;
using System.Data.SqlClient;
```

8. Now add the following code to Program.cs (ensuring you amend the connection string to reflect the location of your example database):

```
static void Main(string[] args)
{
    var ctxBuilder = new ContextBuilder<FilmModel>();
    ctxBuilder.Configurations.Add(new FilmConfiguration());

    var ctx =
      ctxBuilder.Create(new SqlConnection(
        "server=localhost;UID=USERNAME;PWD=PASSWORD; database=book;Pooling=true")
      );
    var NewFilm =
      new Film { Description = "Code only", Length = 200, Title = "Total Recall" };

    ctx.Film.AddObject(NewFilm);
    ctx.SaveChanges();
    ctx.Dispose();
}

class FilmConfiguration : EntityConfiguration<Film>
{
    public FilmConfiguration()
    {
        Property(f => f.FilmID).IsIdentity();
        Property(f => f.Title).HasMaxLength(100).IsRequired();
    }
}
```

9. That's it; run the application and you will find a new entry is added to the Film table. Notice how our configuration class allows us to define mappings and property attributes.

Code Generation Templates

VS2010 contains a number of T4 templates. At the time of writing there are two templates available: ADO.NET EntityObject Generator and ADO.NET Self-Tracking Entity Generator. To use the templates, simply right-click on the designer surface and select Add Code Generation Item.

1. Select the template you want to use (Figure 8-22).

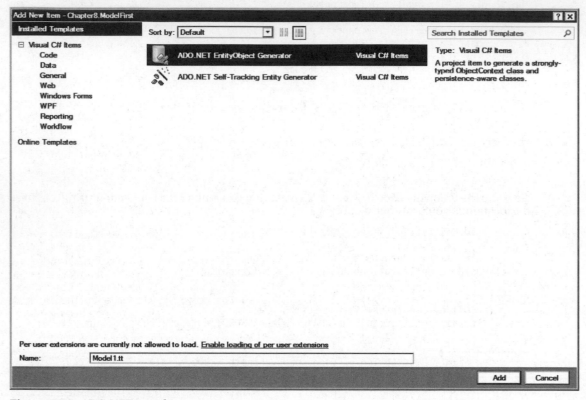

Figure 8-22. *ADO.NET templates*

2. The template will then be added to your project (default name `Model.tt`).

3. You will receive a security warning; click OK to this.

4. To run the template, simply right-click on it and select the Run Custom Tool option.

5. The template will then run and generate code contained beneath the `Model` class (the default generated code is `Model.cs` if you don't rename anything). You can then utilize the generated code within your solution.

Julie Lerman (Author of Programming Entity Framework and MVP)

http://thedatafarm.com/blog/

There is so much to write home about in Entity Framework 4, from myriad designer improvements to API changes. If I had to pick a shortened list it would include the greatly improved stored procedure support, added support for n-tier development, support for POCO classes, which leads to agile development and unit testing, the use of T4 to generate code from an EDM, foreign key support, model first design and Code-Only, which provides the ability to use Entity Framework without a model. Code-Only support elicits joy from domain-driven developers.

Dane Morgridge

http://geekswithblogs.NET/danemorgridge

I have been using ORM tools for several years and decided to take a look at the Entity Framework when it was released with .NET 3.5SP1. Previously, I had been using LINQ to SQL and given their similarities, moving to Entity Framework wasn't difficult. The first version of Entity Framework was missing quite a few features that were present in most ORM tools, mainly lazy loading. I tend to personally prefer to preload as much data as I can, so not having lazy loading wasn't a huge problem for me. One of the biggest problems I ran into was the fact that you didn't have direct easy access to foreign keys, which required you to pull back additional data to get basic relationship data. Other than a few API differences, this was the biggest pain point in moving from LINQ to SQL to Entity Framework. Despite these issues and its critics, I have grown to love the Entity Framework and have been using it in production since its initial release.

There are really two paths into working with the Entity Framework, those who have used ORM tools before and those that haven't. Those that have used ORM tools before will quickly notice the features that are missing and may be a barrier to adoption. Those coming from normal ADO.NET development will likely not miss the features that aren't included, since you can't do things like lazy loading with ADO.NET datasets or inline SQL. Version 4 of the Entity Framework will be a game changer. I have been working with Visual Studio 2010 since the first public beta and I am very happy to see where the Entity Framework is going. The product team has been listening to users and a majority of the issues with the first version of Entity Framework have been addressed with version 4.

I am personally very excited about the features that allow for persistence ignorance, like POCO classes and self-tracking entities. When building services and web applications, I like to have a data layer that is ignorant of the database. This is for multiple reasons like reducing the amount of data that goes over the wire and being able to use the same classes on both sides of the service. With version 1, I have to write my own additional layer to achieve this. The way POCO classes are implemented, I can use persistent ignorant classes that can also directly be used with the Entity Framework data context. The added ability of T4 code generation allows me to generate those classes as well, so I don't have to code them by hand.

I am also very impressed with the implementation of model first development in Visual Studio 2010. Visual Studio 2010 now has a model designer that you can use to create a database from. This allows you to use Visual Studio as a database modeling tool instead of relying on third party modeling tools, which can be very expensive. While modeling in Visual Studio 2010 doesn't cover every single option you can use when creating a database, combined with a good schema compare tool, it will allow you to simply create and maintain data models.

Out of all the ORM tools I have used in the past, I always find myself using the Entity Framework above all others. While version 1 had its shortcomings, it was still a good tool for interacting with databases. I have done several presentations on the Entity Framework and every session has been packed, which tells me there is great interest in the Entity Framework by the development community. I believe that Entity Framework 4, with its new features, will be a first-class ORM and will continue to see greater use. If you haven't taken a good long look at the Entity Framework, now is the time.

Conclusion

I have to admit I had heard nothing but bad things about Entity Framework before I starting writing this chapter so I wasn't looking forward to it. However, after working with EF for some time I have to admit I really quite like it.

I am cautious, however, with recommending its use, since Microsoft can be fickle with their data access strategies. I would consider that a mature open-source solution such as NHibernate probably has less chance of being dropped and has a large community around to support and offer advice. Thus it could be said that NHibernate is potentially a safer option from a future proofing point of view.

In conclusion, while EF is not as feature-rich as some of its competitors, it is arguably easier to use, integrates well with other Microsoft technologies, performs well (`http://gregdoesit.com/2009/08/nhibernate-vs-entity-framework-a-performance-test/`) and I heartily recommend you investigate it further.

References/Further reading

- *Programming Entity Framework* by Julia Lerman (O'Reilly, 2009); a fantastic book—can't recommend enough)

- `http://thedatafarm.com/blog/`

- `http://en.wikipedia.org/wiki/ADO.NET_Entity_Framework`

- `http://blogs.msdn.com/efdesign/`

- `http://blogs.msdn.com/adonet/`

- `http://codebetter.com/blogs/ian_cooper/archive/2008/06/26/the-criticism-of-the-entity-framework-is-not-just-around-domain-driven-design.aspx`

- `http://efvote.wufoo.com/forms/ado-net-entity-framework-vote-of-no-confidence/`

- `http://ormbattle.NET/`

- `http://ayende.com/blog/`

CHAPTER 9

■ ■ ■

WCF Data Services

Availability: .NET 3.5SP1 (limited functionality) onwards

WCF Data Services (previously "Astoria" and ADO.NET Data Services) allows data to be modified and exposed over an HTTP RESTful interface. WCF Data Services (WDS) contains a rich query language and can be accessed easily with automatically generated proxy classes or crafting raw HTTP requests.

WCF Data Services supports returning data in a number of popular data formats such as XML, AtomPub, and JSON and is potentially very useful for integration scenarios and applications that don't maintain a direct connection to the database such as Silverlight.

■**NOTE** During the course of writing this chapter, Microsoft changed the name of ADO.NET Data Services to WCF Data Services. However, the VS template names have not changed yet, so the examples in this chapter use the ADO.NET Data Services template names.

Hello WCF Data Services

Before we can get started with WDS we are going to need some data to play with. If you haven't already done so, please refer to the introduction and set up the example database. In this chapter we will be using SQL Server 2008, but don't think that you are limited to using just SQL Server since WDS will work with anything supported by Entity Framework (Chapter 8).

To expose our data we have to perform four steps:

1. Create Entity Framework classes for the data we want to expose

2. Create a host ASP.NET application for the WDS service

3. Create the WDS service

4. Configure access rules for the service

Let's get started. Open Visual Studio and create a new ASP.NET web site; change the Web location dropdown to HTTP and enter the location as `http://localhost/Chapter9/`.

■**WARNING** Hosting WCF Data Services in IIS on one machine gave me HTTP 500 whenever I tried to query data. I never got to the bottom of why this was, so all I can say is if you experience this try working with the local web server instead.

Entity Framework

WDS needs to know how the data we want to expose is structured and related. We will utilize the Entity Framework to provide this information:

1. Add a new ADO.NET entity data model to the project.

2. Call the ADO.NET entity data model Chapter9Model.edmx.

3. Click Add.

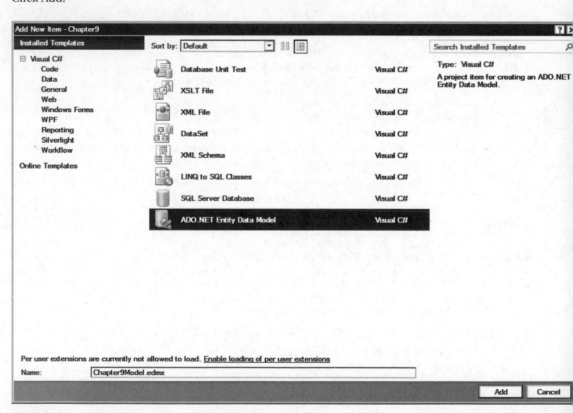

Figure 9-1. *Adding ADO.NET entity data model*

4. Visual Studio will ask you about placing these files in the App_Code directory. Agree to this.

5. Visual Studio will now ask you how you want it to generate the model. Select the "Generate from database model" option and then click Next.

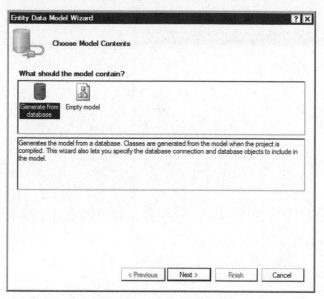

Figure 9-2. *Generate model from database*

6. If you don't have a connection already to the example database, then create one by clicking New Connection and enter the connection details for the example database.

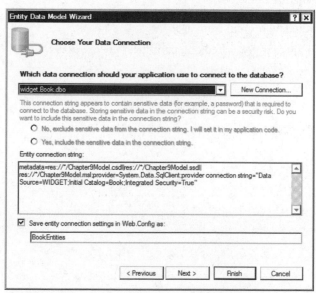

Figure 9-3. *Creating a new database connection*

7. Visual Studio will now examine the database structure and present you with a screen similar to Figure 9-4, where you select the items to generate EF classes for. Expand the Tables node to show all the available tables.

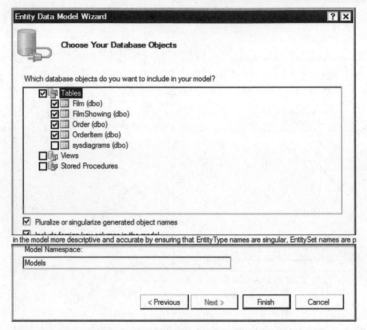

Figure 9-4. *Selecting items to generate EF classes for*

8. Put a check against each individual table apart from sysdiagrams.

9. Ensure that the "Pluralize or singularize generated object names" checkbox is checked.

10. Ensure the Model Namespace box is set to Models.

11. Click Finish.

12. Click OK.

VS2010 will then generate EF classes for the database and display the design surface (Figure 9-5):

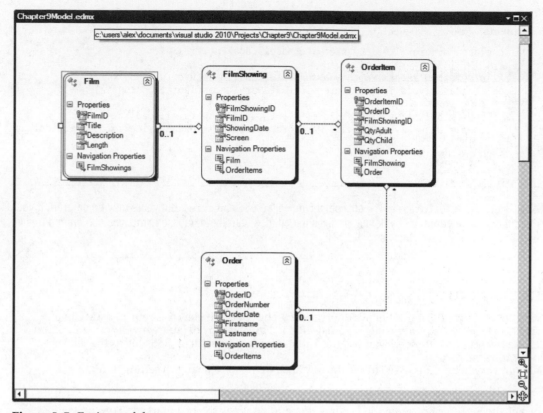

Figure 9-5. *Entity model*

Creating a Data Service

All that is left to do now is to expose the EF classes by adding a new data service and configuring the rules to access it.

1. Add a new ADO.NET data service to your project called MovieService.svc.

2. Click OK.

3. Open ~/MovieService.cs.

4. You now need to tell WDS what type of class your service will expose. Amend the code to the following:

```
public class MovieService : DataService<Models.BookEntities>
{
    // This method is called only once to initialize service-wide policies.
    public static void InitializeService(DataServiceConfiguration config)
    {
        config.SetEntitySetAccessRule("*", EntitySetRights.AllRead);
        config.DataServiceBehavior.MaxProtocolVersion = DataServiceProtocolVersion.V2;
    }
}
```

■**WARNING** In my example, DataService accepts a type called BookEntities, but yours may be different if you have a different database name. VS by default prefixes the entities with the database name (you can amend this in Chapter9Model.Designer.cs if you wish).

IE Content Settings

By default, WDS will return XML when we query it. It can be useful to view this returned XML in a browser such as Internet Explorer while we are testing it. However, by default when Internet Explorer processes the results of a data service, it will think that it is working with an RSS feed as the data is returned in AtomPub form.

This is not very helpful for us, so to see the raw XML we need to change a setting in IE:

1. Open IE and go to the Tools➤Internet Options➤Content tab.

2. Click the Settings button in the Feed section and uncheck the box marked "Turn on feed reading view" (Figure 9-6).

Figure 9-6. *Altering content view setting in IE8*

Hello WDS

OK, we are now ready to work with our data service.

1. Right click on `MovieService.svc` and select Set As Start Page.

2. Press F5 to run your application. If all is well then you will see a screen similar to Figure 9-7 showing an XML representation of our EF classes:

Figure 9-7. *Output from accessing our test service*

Querying WCF Data Services

WCF Data Services uses the URL to pass query parameters. For example, to retrieve the film entities, add `/Films` to the end of the existing URL (for example, `http://localhost/Chapter9/MovieService.svc/Films`).

You should then be returned a list of all the films in AtomPub format (Figure 9-8):

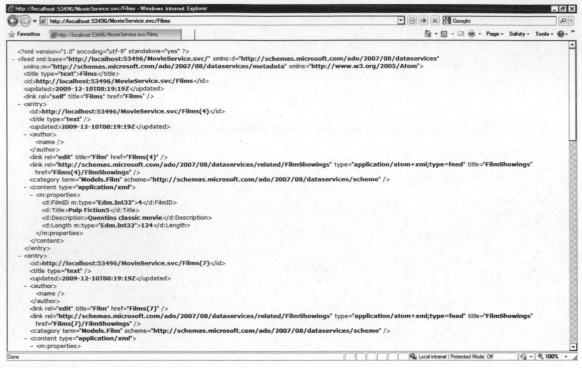

Figure 9-8. *Returning all the films from the database*

Having all the data returned at once isn't too useful, so WDS supports a number of different query operators that all work with the URL.

I have listed some commonly used methods in Table 9-1, but for a full list please refer to `http://msdn.microsoft.com/en-us/library/cc907912.aspx`.

Table 9-1. *List of Common Query Operators*

Action	Operator
Get film with ID 3	`Films(3)`
Select Film where FilmID is equal to 3	`Films?$filter=FilmID%20eq%203`
Get FilmName field from first FilmShowing	`FilmShowings(1)/Film/Title`
Get film showings for first film	`Films(1)/FilmShowings`
Display orders by order date	`Orders?$orderby=OrderDate`
Order list of films in descending order	`Orders?$orderby=OrderDate%20desc`
Select top two orders	`Orders?$top=2`
Skip first orders and select next two	`Orders?$skip=1&top=2`

When working with WCF Data Services you should note the following:

- Objects are case sensitive. `Film` is not the same as `film` (grrrrr!).
- The query needs to be URL-encoded, so spaces must be encoded as %20.
- Note the use of the ? query string character and $ to specify options.

IS THERE A WAY TO LIMIT THE AMOUNT OF RECORDS RETURNED?

Yes—when you are using WCF Data Services version 1.5. Please refer to the VS2010/.NET 4.0 changes section below.

Security in WCF Data Services

WDS allows you to fine-tune access to individual entities. For example, open `MovieService.cs` and find the line that reads:

```
config.SetEntitySetAccessRule("*", EntitySetRights.AllRead);
```

This code allows read-only access to all entities (defined by the *). If you wanted to enable full access to everything (generally a very bad idea, but useful for testing) then you can change this to:

```
config.SetEntitySetAccessRule("*", EntitySetRights.All);
```

■**WARNING** If you do this anyone who can access the data service will have full access.

Permissions can be applied to individual objects by specifying them by name. The following line of code will enable full access to the Film entity.

```
config.SetEntitySetAccessRule("Films", EntitySetRights.All);
```

We will need full access to the Film entity in a few minutes, so add the previous line to MovieService.cs.

Query Interceptors

Sometimes you might want to intercept the user's query to apply additional logic to it (for example, to filter depending on the current user). WDS allows you to do this through query interceptors.

The following example demonstrates applying this technique to any films requests to only allow those where FilmID equals 1. Add the following code to MovieService.svc:

```
using System.Linq.Expressions;

[QueryInterceptor("Films")]
public Expression<Func<Film, bool>> FilterOnlyShowFilmID1()
{
    return f => f.FilmID==1;
}
```

Returning Results in Different Formats

WDS services can return data in the following formats:

- AtomPub
- JSON
- XML

AtomPub is the default format that is returned, and from WDS 1.5 you have control over how elements are mapped to AtomPub elements.

Let's look at how to return results in JSON format using jQuery and then how to access an WDS service from a console application.

Using JSON with JavaScript

JSON is a format commonly used by web applications since it is much less verbose than XML. JSON is also understood by many JavaScript frameworks and libraries. If you want to have WCF Data Services format your results as JSON, simply set the Accept header to application/json when making a request.

The following example shows how to use jQuery to retrieve the title of the first film in the set (for more information on jQuery please refer to Chapter 12):

```
<script>
    function getMovieTitle() {
        $.ajax({
            type: "GET",
            dataType: "json",
```

```
            url: "MovieService.svc/Films(1)",
            success: function (result) {
                alert(result.d.Title);
            },
            error: function (error) {
                alert('error ');
            }
        });
    }
</script>
<input type="button" Value="Get Movie Title"
        onclick="javascript:getMovieTitle();" />
```

But what JSON data will be returned by making the previous call? By using a web debugging proxy called Fiddler (www.fiddlertool.com) you can see what is returned. The following code shows the raw JSON:

```
{ "d" : {
"__metadata": {
"uri": "http://localhost/Chapter9/MovieService.svc/Films(1)", "type": "Models.Film"
}, "FilmID": 1, "Title": "Kung Fu Panda", "Description": "Classic martial arts tale",
"Length": 120, "FilmShowings": {
"__deferred": {
"uri": " http://localhost/Chapter9/MovieService.svc/Films(1)/FilmShowings"
}
}
} }
```

Notice how the results were wrapped by an object called d. This is to prevent Cross Site Request Forgery (CSRF) (see Chapter 11 for more details on this).

Using JSON with C#

The following code shows how to retrieve results formatted as JSON using the HttpWebRequest class in C#:

```
System.Net.HttpWebRequest Request =
    (System.Net.HttpWebRequest)System.Net.HttpWebRequest.Create(
      "http://localhost/Chapter9/MovieService.svc/Films(1)"
    );

Request.Method = "GET";

Request.Accept = "application/json";

System.Net.HttpWebResponse Response = (System.Net.HttpWebResponse)Request.GetResponse();

using (System.IO.StreamReader sr = new System.IO.StreamReader(Response.GetResponseStream()))
{
    Console.WriteLine(sr.ReadToEnd());
}

Console.ReadKey();
```

WDS Proxy Classes

Although in many cases you will want to work with the raw XML or JSON returned from an WDS service, it is easier to work with generated proxy classes. The generated proxy classes make it very easy to perform simple CRUD and query operations. Of course, behind the scenes they use HTTP.

Retrieving Items with Proxy Classes

We will create an application to iterate through the Order objects using LINQ and the DataServiceContext class.

1. Add a new console application to the solution called Chapter9.ADOProxy.

2. Right click the References folder.

3. Select Add Service Reference to add the URL your WDS is set up at (for example, http://localhost/Chapter9/MovieService.svc).

4. Select the BookEntities node in the Services box.

5. Enter the namespace MovieService.

6. Click OK. Visual Studio will generate classes representing the entities in our console application.

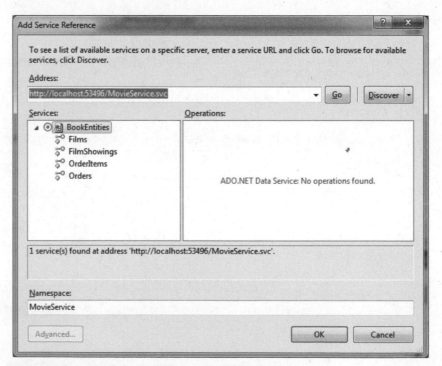

Figure 9-9. *Adding service reference to WDS service*

7. Open `Program.cs` and add the following using statement:

```
using System.Data.Services.Client;
```

8. Enter the following code to iterate through a list of `Orders`, printing the first name to the output window:

```
static void Main(string[] args)
{
    DataServiceContext ctx =
      new DataServiceContext(new Uri("http://localhost/Chapter9/MovieService.svc"));
    var Orders =
      ctx.Execute<MovieService.Models.Order>(new Uri("Orders", UriKind.Relative));

    foreach (MovieService.Models.Order Order in Orders)
    {
        Console.WriteLine(Order.Firstname);
    }

    Console.ReadKey();
}
```

9. Press F5 to run the application and you should see a list of first names from the `Orders` table printed out.

Adding a New Item with Proxy Classes

To create a new item using WCF Data Services is very easy and just requires using the `DataServiceContext`'s `AddObject()` and `SaveChanges()` methods:

```
static void Main(string[] args)
{
    DataServiceContext ctx =
      new DataServiceContext(new Uri("http://localhost/Chapter9/MovieService.svc"));

    MovieService.Models.Film NewFilm = new MovieService.Models.Film();
    NewFilm.Title = "Pulp Fiction";
    NewFilm.Length = 124;
    NewFilm.Description = "Quentins classic movie";
    ctx.AddObject("Films", NewFilm);
    ctx.SaveChanges();
}
```

Update an Item

To update an existing item, load an object then use the `UpdateObject()` and `SaveChanges()` methods of the `DataServiceContext`:

```
static void Main(string[] args)
{
    DataServiceContext ctx =
      new DataServiceContext(new Uri("http://localhost/Chapter9/MovieService.svc"));
```

```
MovieService.Models.Film FilmToUpdate =
    ctx.Execute<MovieService.Models.Film>(new Uri("Films(1)", UriKind.Relative)).First();
FilmToUpdate.Title = "Updated title";
ctx.UpdateObject(FilmToUpdate);
ctx.SaveChanges();
}
```

Delete an Item

To delete an item, use the `DataServiceContext` `DeleteObject()` method with the `SaveChanges()` method (if you have defined any table constraints or rules you will need to ensure you fulfill them; otherwise this call will fail):

```
static void Main(string[] args)
{
    DataServiceContext ctx =
      new DataServiceContext(new Uri("http://localhost/Chapter9/MovieService.svc"));

    MovieService.Models.Film FilmToDelete =
      ctx.Execute<MovieService.Models.Film>(new Uri("Films(1)", UriKind.Relative)).First();
    ctx.DeleteObject(FilmToDelete);
    ctx.SaveChanges();
}
```

WDS 1.5

WDS version 1.5 is included with VS2010 and adds a number of features, such as the ability to limit the number of data items returned and produce web-friendly feeds (mapping of AtomPub items).

■**NOTE** The team even says in the future that they are looking at implementing an offline mode for WDS.

RowCount and Server-Driven Paging

One of the main issues when working with WDS previously was that there was no way of knowing how many results would be returned. This made it impossible to page through data and work with WDS efficiently. WDS 1.5 now offers the ability to query how many results are returned through the $count and $inlinecount operators.

$count

$count will return just a single text value indicating the number of rows for a specific query. The following URL shows how to return a count of the orders:

```
http://localhost/Chapter9/MovieService.svc/Orders/$count
```

Note that if the count was applied to a set of 100 and the $skip, $top, or $take operators are also applied, then the number returned is the count *after* the $skip or $take operator is applied.

$inlinecount=allpages

$inlinecount=allpages returns a count of the number of items along with the current query results. It will return the count of items ignoring any $skip or $take operators (the opposite to $count). The count is contained in a new m:count element (m stands for metadata). The following example demonstrates using this feature on the Orders table:

http://localhost/Chapter9/MovieService.svc/Orders?$inlinecount=allpages

If you examine the XML you will find the following new element that indicates the inline count:

<m:count>4</m:count>

Limiting Number of Results Returned

You can limit the number of results returned from a call to WDS with the new Config.SetResourcePageSize() method. The following method limits queries to the Orders table to return just two results:

config.SetEntitySetPageSize("Orders", 2);

If more results are available than the page size then WDS will also supply a next link, which can be accessed to retrieve subsequent pages:

<link rel="next" href="http://localhost/Chapter9/MovieService.svc/Orders?$skiptoken=2" />

Currently there is no client-side support for this functionality, although the WDS team says they intend to add it to a future release.

Projections

Projections allow you to tell WDS to only return certain item types and are created by adding the $select operator to your query, e.g.,

http://localhost/Chapter9/MovieService.svc/Orders?$select=Firstname,Lastname

Note that version 2 of WDS must be enabled for this feature to be used:

config.DataServiceBehavior.MaxProtocolVersion = DataServiceProtocolVersion.V2;

You can also use complex types and navigation properties when using projections:

http://localhost/Chapter9/MovieService.svc/Orders?$select=Firstname,Lastname,OrderItems

The previous query returns a link to the complex type or navigation property, but you can also use the $expand operator to return the details from the related item as well. The following query returns the Firstname and Lastname, along with OrderItems details:

```
http://localhost/Chapter9/MovieService.svc/Orders?$select=Firstname,Lastname,OrderItems&
$expand=OrderItems
```

Friendly Feeds

It is now possible to map EF model properties to individual AtomPub elements. In our film example you could map a director's name to AtomPub's author element. It is also possible to create custom classes and control how these are formatted in the output.

For more information on these features please refer to http://blogs.msdn.com/phaniraj/archive/2009/03/21/ado-net-data-services-friendly-feeds-mapping-clr-types.aspx.

Miscellaneous Improvements

The WDS team has made a number of other improvements:

- WDS 1.5 supports two-way data binding (DataServiceCollection), which is great for WPF/Silverlight scenarios. For more information, please see Chapter 15 and this blog entry:

  http://blogs.msdn.com/astoriateam/archive/2009/09/17/introduction-to-data-binding-in-silverlight-3-with-ctp2.aspx

- Improved support for streaming large sets of binary data

What's the Relationship Between WDS and WCF RIA Services?

Scott Guthrie spoke to RedDevNews.com regarding this (before the name changes):

"Is .NET RIA Services going to be preferred over ADO.NET DataServices for Silverlight Data Access?

No. The bits that are being released today for RIA Services actually build on top of ADO.NET DataServices. So you can think of ADO.NET DataServices as providing a kind of lower layer RAW/REST API, and then RIA Services as a layer on top. We definitely think that there are scenarios where you would want to have a pure REST service model. And then the .NET RIA Services gives you things like the validation, cross-tiering, and higher-level services on top. We've worked hard to layer them nicely, so that RIA Services isn't a competitive technology, but actually just builds on top of ADO.NET DataServices."

http://reddevnews.com/articles/2009/07/13/interview-with-scott-guthrie-on-silverlight-3.aspx

Conclusion

WCF Data Services makes it very easy to expose your data for integration scenarios or to third parties. WDS could also be employed as an integration layer for web and Silverlight projects. The latest release of WCF Data Services contains much-needed paging and projection features and seems to be a very useful technology. Interested developers should also take a look at WCF RIA Services, which builds on top of WDS, adding many additional features.

Further Reading

- `http://blogs.msdn.com/astoriateam/`
- `http://msdn.microsoft.com/en-us/library/cc907912.aspx`

CHAPTER 10

■ ■ ■

ASP.NET

ASP.NET is a mature platform on which to build web applications, and it is probably fair to say that most of the changes in this release are enhancements and tweaks. However, don't skip this chapter, because Microsoft has fixed a number of long-term omissions and introduced some very welcome changes.

Project Templates

VS2010 contains a number of new types of ASP.net project and some modifications to existing types:

- New Empty ASP.NET Web Application (just the bare minimum)
- New Silverlight 1.0 Web Site (erm, time to move on)
- New ASP.NET AJAX Server Control and Server Control Extender
- New ASP.NET MVC 2 Web Application
- Modified ASP.NET Web Site and a modified ASP.NET Web Application (like VS2008's ASP.NET Web Site project but with new changes in ASP.NET Web Application as discussed below)

The ASP.NET Web projects now contain common authentication and profile functionality, a master page with a simple layout and jQuery scripts (see Figure 10-1).

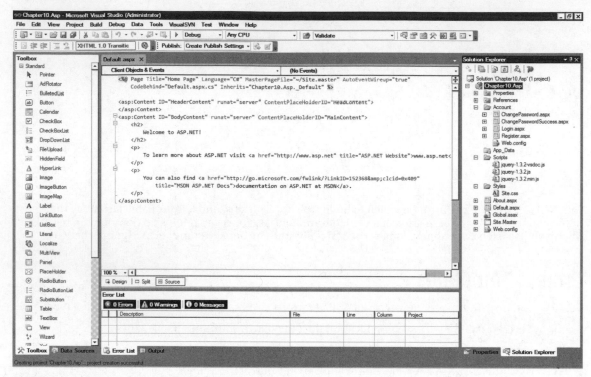

Figure 10-1. *New Web Application Project template*

Web.config

One of the aspects of ASP.NET that irritated me was how bloated `Web.config` files have become. To some extent, this bloat was due to ASP.NET 3.0 and 3.5 using version 2 of the CLR and, in order to introduce additional functionality, Microsoft had to override default settings, as well as cope with different versions of IIS (that is, settings for IIS 7.0 and settings for earlier versions).

.NET 4.0, however, has a new version of the CLR, so this is no longer a problem. A number of settings have been moved to `machine.config`, which drastically reduces the size of `Web.config`. Functionality such as ASP.NET charting, dynamic data, Ajax, and routing is now also automatically registered for you, and so no longer has to be added to the `Web.config` file. Some developers may not like this addition of functionality that they may not use, but for the majority it will save a bit of configuration and can be overridden in `machine.config`.

What follows is the default `Web.config` file that is generated for an ASP.NET 4.0 empty web project (the standard ASP.NET project has a larger `Web.config` as contains authentication and membership stuff as well).

```xml
<?xml version="1.0"?>
<configuration>
    <system.web>
        <compilation debug="true" targetFramework="4.0" />
    </system.web>
    <system.webServer>
      <modules runAllManagedModulesForAllRequests="true"/>
    </system.webServer>
</configuration>
```

Much better.

MULTITARGETING SUPPORT

Please refer to Chapter 2 for details of multitargeting changes that will affect ASP.NET developers. ASP.NET developers should be aware that VS2010 has two different versions of the development web server: one for .NET 2.0 and the other for .NET 4.0 applications.

IDE Changes

Several enhancements have been made to the IDE and designer that will interest ASP.NET developers.

- CSS 2.1 compliance has been improved.

- Designer is now more robust and less likely to rewrite HTML (front page syndrome).

- There is improved support for third-party libraries (in particular, jQuery).

- There is better performance when working with large JavaScript files.

- Intellisense support for different styles of JavaScript coding has been improved.

- JavaScript documentation comments are parsed as you code.

- There is Intellisense support for ASP.NET AJAX register namespaces calls.

- Refactored IDE designer code will make it easier for Microsoft to improve the designer in the future

jQuery

I cover this in more detail in Chapter 12, but it is worth noting here that VS2010 comes bundled with the open source jQuery libraries and provides Intellisense support. When you create a new ASP.NET or ASP.NET MVC project, you will find many of the project templates include these libraries.

Code Snippets

Web development can sometimes be pretty repetitive. No, I am not talking about creating a lengthy online questionnaire that no sane person will ever fill out, but rather in terms of the markup you have to write. To ease this pain, Microsoft has introduced a number of prewritten HTML and ASP.NET snippets (blocks of code) that will substantially reduce the amount of typing you have to do and minimize typos (and possibly reduce RSI in the web development community). I am a big believer in saving time spent on tedious tasks, so let's take a look into these snippets now.

ASP.NET Code Snippets

Let's look at an example by following these steps.

1. Create a new ASP.NET project.

2. In `Default.aspx`, type "textbox" and then quickly press Tab. Visual Studio will insert the following code:

   ```
   <asp:TextBox runat="server" />
   ```

3. But wait it gets better. Give your `TextBox` an ID of "txtTest "and press Enter to add a new line.

4. Type "requiredfieldvalidator" and press tab.

5. Visual Studio will then insert the markup below. Note how the `ControlToValidate` property was set to the nearest textbox automatically (if you add another textbox to the page you should still find this is the case), and how the cursor was focused on the `ErrorMessage` property . VS2010 will attempt to guess any properties it can (in this case due to the textbox's proximity), and intelligently set the focus on any other fields that need to be filled in.

   ```
   <asp:RequiredFieldValidator ErrorMessage="errormessage" ControlToValidate="txtTest"
   runat="server" />
   ```

6. The focus is currently set to the `ErrorMessage` property, so change it to "You must fill in this field" and then press Tab to move the focus to the next field.

■**NOTE** Refer to Chapter 2 for details about how to create your own snippets.

Using Snippets

Web development snippets are divided into two types: ASP.NET and HTML. Most of the snippets are pretty much self explanatory, but in Table 10-1, I have described some of the more cryptic ones.

Table 10-1. *ASP.NET Code Snippets*

Shortcut/trigger key	Notes
Checkbox	
Formr	Server-side form
hyperlink	
Image	
Label	
listbox	
listitem	
listview	
loginname	
loginstatus	
loginview	
multiview	
panel	
placeholder	
radiobutton	
register	Custom control register directive
registerascx	User control register directive
repeater	
requiredfieldvalidator	
runat	
scriptreference	
scripts	
servicereference	
sitemappath	
sm	ScriptManager

(Continued)

Table 10-1. *Continued*

Shortcut/trigger key	Notes
smp	ScriptManagerProxy
sqldatasource	
textbox	TextBox
updatepanel	
updateprogress	
validationsummary	
view	

There are also a number of HTML snippets available. I would like to draw your attention to the XHTML doctype snippets as I believe these are particularly useful, shown Table 10-2.

Table 10-2. *HTML Snippets*

Shortcut	Notes
a	
br	
class	
div	
form	
hr	
html	
html4f	HTML 4.01 frameset doctype declaration
html4s	HTML 4.01 strict doctype declaration
html4t	HTML 4.01 transitional doctype declaration
img	
input	
link	
metaie8	IE compatibility flag: `<meta http-equiv="X-UA-Compatible" content="IE=8" />`

(Continued)

Table 10-2. *Continued*

Shortcut	Notes
script	Client script block
scriptr	Server script block
scriptref	Client script reference
select	
span	
style	
table	
ul	
xhtml10f	XHTML 1 frameset declaration
xhtml10s	XHTML 1.0 Strict document declaration
xhtml10t	XHTML 1.0 Transitional document declaration
xhtml11	XHTML 1.1 doctype

Deployment

I think one of the biggest and most valuable changes in ASP.NET 4.0 is the new deployment functionality. VS2010 makes it easier than ever before deploy your ASP.NET application.

VS2010 allows you to

- Perform transformations on Web.config for different build configurations.

- Create web packages (zip files that contain your application, database, and settings in a single file).

- Install your application and all its settings with just one click (one-click publishing).

Automating your deployment processes is a smart move, because it reduces mistakes, saves you time, and creates a repeatable and self-documented process.

Web.config Transformation

Many developers use Web.config file to hold application specific settings, such as database connection strings. The trouble with Web.config is that when you deploy your applications, you normally have to change these settings. VS2010 offers the ability to create a build configuration that allows you to modify the contents of the Web.config file for different build configurations. Note you can also use this feature on Web.config files in sub folders.

VS2010 actually uses this functionality already when you switch between debug/release mode, let's take a look at this now.

1. Create a new ASP.NET web application called `Chapter10.WebConfigTransformation`.

2. Click the Show All Files option in Solution Explorer.

3. Expand `Web.config`. Note how `Web.config` has two files nested beneath it: `Web.Debug.config` and `Web.Release.config`.

4. Open `Web.Release.config`. It will have code similar to the following (shortened for brevity):

```
<configuration xmlns:xdt="http://schemas.microsoft.com/XML-Document-Transform">
  <system.web>
    <compilation xdt:Transform="RemoveAttributes(debug)" />
  </system.web>
</configuration>
```

This is a simple transformation that is used to remove debug attributes when the application is built in release mode.

Creating a New Deployment Configuration

I will now walk you through creating your own transformation. Let's imagine we have a server allocated for user acceptance testing (UAT) and we need to change an individual setting when our application is moved from our development machine to the user-acceptance machine.

1. The first thing we need to do is create a new build configuration, so go to the build configuration manager. On the main menu, go to Build➤Configuration Manager.

2. Click the drop-down menu labeled Active solution configuration and select <New>.

3. Enter the name UAT.

4. Select the "Copy settings from Release" drop-down menu option.

5. Make sure the "Create new project configurations" checkbox is ticked and click OK.

6. Close the Configuration window.

7. Right-click on Web.config in Solution Explorer and select the Add Config Transforms option. Visual Studio will create a new Web.UAT.config file.

8. Open `Web.config` and add a new appsetting key called `RunMode`:

```
<?xml version="1.0"?>
<appSettings>
  <add key="RunMode" value="Default" />
</appSettings>
```

5. Now open `Web.UAC.config` and replace the code with the following:

```
<?xml version="1.0"?>
<configuration xmlns:xdt="http://schemas.microsoft.com/XML-Document-Transform">

  <appSettings>
    <add key="RunMode" xdt:Transform="Replace" xdt:Locator="Match(key)"
        value="User acceptance testing" />
  </appSettings>
```

```
<system.web>
  <compilation xdt:Transform="RemoveAttributes(debug)" />

</system.web>
</configuration>
```

6. If you want to run your app to see if the changes have occurred, open `Default.aspx.cs` and add the following code to `Page_Load`:

```
Response.Write(System.Configuration.ConfigurationManager.AppSettings.Get("RunMode"));
```

If you run your project now you will not see the results of this transformation. This is because transformations are part of your build process and will only occur when you publish your application or use the MSBuild utility with certain options. This does seem a bit of shame, as it would have been nice to easily test transformations by changing the build mode.

The easiest way to see the transformations is to publish the project.

1. Right-click on the project and select Publish.

2. Change the Publish Method in the drop-down menu to File System, enter a path where the project should be built, and click the Publish button. If you now open the `Web.config` in your published application you will find the `RunMode` setting has been changed.

Transforming Web.config from the Command Line

You can also transform Web.config from the command line.

1. Open Visual Studio command prompt.

2. Change the path to your current project directory and enter the following command:

```
MSBuild Chapter10.WebConfigTransformation.csproj /t:TransformWebConfig
/p:Configuration=UAC
```

3. If you now take a look at the `~/obj/UAC/TransformWebConfig` folder of your application, you will find the default `Web.config` file has had the transformation applied to it.

Web.config Transformation Options

I have just demonstrated a very simple replace, but VS2010 allows you to carry out much more complex changes. VS2010 offers 3 options to locate the item you want to change (full details at http://msdn. microsoft.com/en-us/library/dd465326%28VS.100%29.aspx):

*   Match on a node attribute value

    `xdt:Transform="Replace" xdt:Locator="Match(name)"`

*   Match on XPath expression

    `xdt:Locator="XPath(//system.web)"`

*   Match on value

    `xdt:Locator="Condition(@name='MyDb')"`

The following actions can be performed on `Web.config` settings:

- Replacement

  `xdt:Transform="Replace"`

- Insertion

  ```
  xdt:Transform="Insert"
  xdt:Transform="InsertAfter(/configuration/system.web/authorization/
  allow[@roles=Authors])"
  xdt:Transform="InsertBefore(/configuration/system.web/authorization/
  deny[@users='Alex'])"
  ```

- Deletion

  `xdt:Transform="RemoveAll"`

- Removal

  `xdt:Transform="RemoveAttributes(debug,batch)"`

- Setting individual attributes

  `xdt:Transform="SetAttributes(batch)"`

Web Packages

Deploying an ASP.NET application is often more complex than simply copying files to a remote server. Applications often need specific IIS settings, GAC components, COM DLLs, and so on. VS2010 allows you to wrap your application up in a package that contains all this functionality. The following can be included in a web package:

- The application's pages, controls, images, CSS, media, and so on (duh!)

- GAC assemblies

- COM components

- IIS settings

- SQL databases

- Security certificates

Web packages are created by the `MsDeploy` tool and contain your application's content and additional information that describes its setup requirements.

Once you have created your web package, it can be deployed in three main ways:

- Manually, by using IIS's management features and selecting Import Application

- By entering the following in the command line

  `MSBuild "MyProjectname.csproj" /T:Package /P:Configuration=UAC`

- Using the deployment API

Let's look at how we specify the items our web package should include. Either right-click on your project and select the Package/Publish Settings, or open up the project Properties window and select the Package/Publish tab (Figure 10-2).

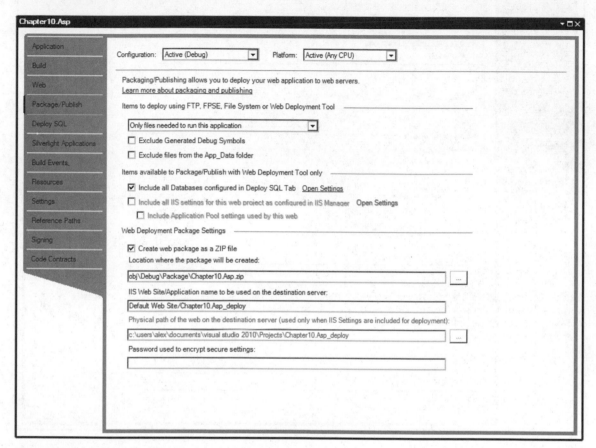

Figure 10-2. *Package/Publish settings*

I would like to bring your attention to the IIS settings option (disabled at the time of writing) that allows you to specify IIS settings should you require. VS2010 also contains support for deploying SQL databases and running SQL scripts which are configured on the Deploy SQL tab (Figure 10-3).

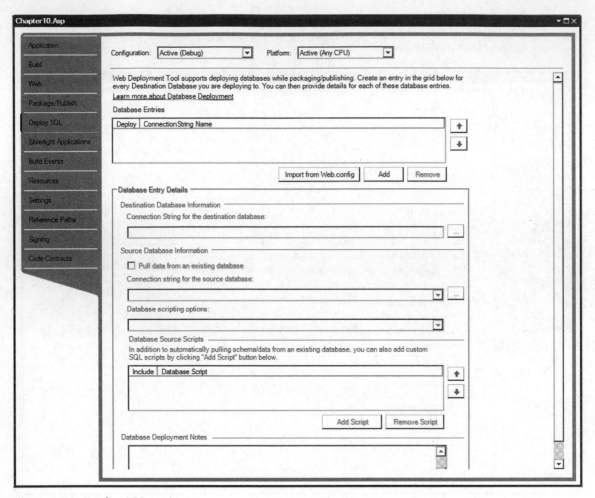

Figure 10-3. *Deploy SQL settings*

When you have configured these settings to your liking, right-click on your project and select the Package option. VS2010 will then create your package at ~/obj/YOURBUILDCONFIGNAME/Package. Note that MSDeploy is even nice enough to create a command script that will deploy your application.

One-Click Publishing

One-click publishing uses IIS remote management services to allow you to publish your application to a remote server with one click. One-click publishing only deploys files that have changed, so is very efficient. To use one-click publishing, you will need a hoster that supports One Click (at the time of writing Discount ASP or OrcsWeb) or, if deploying to your own server, to have IIS remote management services enabled (`http://technet.microsoft.com/en-us/library/cc731771(WS.10).aspx`). One Click is also only available for projects in the VS2010 format.

Before we can use one-click publishing we need to configure a number of settings. Right-click on your project and select the Publish option. You will see a screen similar to Figure 10.4.

Figure 10-4. *One-click publishing profile settings*

Fill in the details as shown (using MSDeploy Publish as the Publish Method) and click Close. Once these details are completed, you can publish your application by selecting the Publish Profile you want to use from the drop-down menu (top left-hand side of the VS2010 screen) and clicking the Publish button (Figure 10-5). Note if this tool bar is not showing, right-click on the toolbar and select Web One Click Publish. VS2010 allows a single project to contain up to 50 different one click publishing profiles.

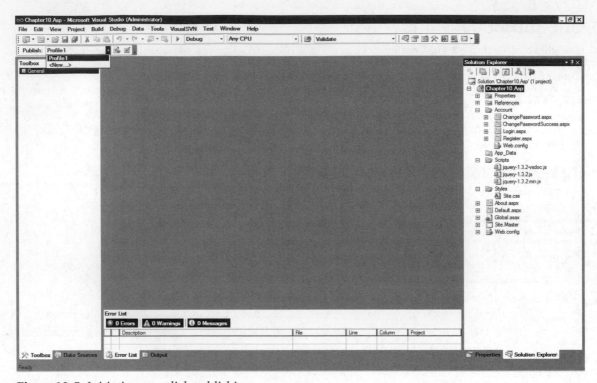

Figure 10-5. *Initiating one-click publishing*

ViewState

ViewState is the mechanism by which ASP.NET stores the state of controls on a web form. This information is held in a hidden form value called __VIEWSTATE. Depending on the page's content, ViewState can get pretty large, and is often unnecessary for controls that don't change such as labels.

ASP.NET 4.0 gives you the ability for controls to inherit ViewState settings from parent controls by using the new ViewStateMode property. This makes it very easy to efficiently set ViewStateMode on a large number of controls.

ViewStateMode has three settings

- Enabled (ViewState used)

- Disabled (ViewState not used)

- Inherit (ViewStateMode is inherited from parent control)

The following example shows how to make lbl1 Label inherit pnlParent's ViewStateMode.

```
<asp:Panel ID="pnlParent" runat=server ViewStateMode=Disabled>
  <asp:Label ID="lbl1" Text="text" ViewStateMode=Inherit runat="server" />
</asp:Panel>
```

238

ClientIDMode

A long-term irritation in ASP.NET is the lack of control you have over the ID property of rendered controls. For example, take the following HTML that is rendered from a few simple controls that are nested inside a Master page:

```
<span id="MainContent_label1"></span>
<div id="MainContent_panel1">
  <span id="MainContent_label2"></span>
</div>
```

Most of the time, ASP.NET's automatic ID generation features work pretty well, but in some situations, say, when working with Master pages or writing client script, you need a finer level of control. ASP.NET 4.0 gives you this control with the new ClientIDMode.

ClientIDMode has four settings

- *AutoID:* Works as per previous ASP.NET releases.

- *Static:* Allows you to specify the ID that is used. Warning: you can obviously generate duplicate client IDs, so it is up to you to ensure your ID is unique or face client-side script hell (well, probably an annoying JavaScript error, anyway).

- *Predictable:* Used in conjunction with RowClientIdSuffix property to generate incrementing IDs for repeating controls such as DataGrid and Repeater, for example, myrow1, myrow2, myrow3.

- *Inherit:* Controls uses the same ClientIDMode as its parent control (default).

ClientIdMode can be set at control, page, and application level.

- To set on an individual control:

    ```
    <asp:Label ID="lblTest" runat="server" Text="Test" ClientIdMode="Inherit"></asp:Label>
    ```

- At page level:

    ```
    <%@ Page Language="C#" AutoEventWireup="true" CodeFile="Default.aspx.cs"
    Inherits="_Default" ClientIdMode="Predictable" %>
    ```

- Or application wide in Web.config:

    ```
    <system.web>
      <pages clientIdMode="Inherit"></pages>
    </system.web>
    ```

Response.RedirectPermanent()

Response.Redirect() is a frequently used method that redirects the current request to another URL. At an HTTP level Response.Redirect() issues a temporary redirect (HTTP 302) message to the user's browser. ASP.NET 4.0 now offers a new Response.RedirectPermanent() method that issues a permanently moved (HTTP 301) message (http://www.w3.org/Protocols/rfc2616/rfc2616-sec10.html).

Why bother? HTTP 301 is mainly used to tell search engines that they should save the new page location in their indexes rather than the old location. This saves an unnecessary trip to the server. Response.RedirectPermanent() usage is very similar to Response.Redirect():

```
Response.RedirectPermanent("/newpath/foroldcontent.aspx");
```

Meta-tags

ASP.NET 4.0's Page class has two new properties that allow you to set the keyword and description Meta-tags that are generated: MetaKeywords and MetaDescription properties. It is worth noting that most search engines (or certainly the big one beginning with G) probably ignore meta-tags (due to previous abuse), and that if you have already specified meta-tags on your page then MetaKeywords and MetaDescription will act as properties so make sure you append rather than overwrite when using them.

URL Routing

Routing was first introduced in ASP.net in .net 3.5sp1 and further enhanced in ASP.NET MVC (see Chapter 13). Routing allows you to map a URL to a physical file, which may or may not exist. To implement this functionality in previous versions of ASP.NET complex hacks or ISAPI filters were needed.

Why use this feature? Well let's say you are working for an online shop that has a new product they are advertising on TV and it is located at the following URL:

www.myshop.com/productDetail.aspx?id=34534

Routing allows you to create a more readable URI mapped through to the page, such as:

www.myshop.com/PopularProduct/

URL routing also allows you to create more memorable and search engine-friendly URIs, hiding the internal structure of your application.

Routes are created in the Global.asax file. The code below maps the URL ~/PopularProduct to the page ~/default.aspx?id=34534:

```
protected void Application_Start(object sender, EventArgs e)
{
    System.Web.Routing.RouteTable.Routes.MapPageRoute(
      "myPopularRoute", "PopularProduct", "~/default.aspx?id=34534"
    );

}
```

Routing has implications for security policies that you may have defined in Web.config, because ASP.NET will check policies for the route rather than mapped page. To remedy this, MapPageRoute supports an overloaded method that allows you to check that the user has access to the physical file (~/default.aspx?id=34534) as well. Access for defined routes is *always* checked.

As well as creating simple one-to-one mapping URLs, it is useful to be able to pass in parameters to routes. For example most shops sell a number of different types of products so you could create URLs such as myshop.com/cats or myshop.com/dogs (note selling cats and dogs online is probably a bad idea). To create these type of routes enclose the value that will change inside curly brackets:

```
System.Web.Routing.RouteTable.Routes.MapPageRoute(
  "myProductGroupRoute", "{groups}", "~/default.aspx?id=123"
);
```

Routing parameters can then be retrieved with the following syntax:

```
string searchTerm=Page.RouteData.Values["group"];
```

Sometimes it can also be useful to retrieve the URL that will be generated for a specific route to create hyperlinks or redirect the user; this can be done with the GetRouteUrl() method:

```
Page.GetRouteUrl("myProductGroupRoute", new { group = "brandNew" })
```

HTML Encoding

All web developers should be aware that it is important to HTML encode values that are output to prevent XSS attacks (particularly if you have received them from the user). ASP.NET 4.0 offers a new markup syntax that uses the colon character to tell ASP.NET to HTML encode the expression:

```
<%: "<script>alert('I wont be run');</script>" %>
```

When ASP.NET parses this it does the following:

```
<%= HttpUtility.HtmlEncode(YourVariableHere) %>
```

It is important to bear in mind that the use of this syntax may not negate all XSS attacks if you have complex nested HTML or JavaScript.

HtmlString

ASP.NET 4.0 includes the new HtmlString class that indicates an expression is already properly encoded and should not be re-examined. This prevents "safe" values from potentially firing dangerous request validation rules:

```
<%: new HtmlString("<script>alert('I will now be run');</script>") %>
```

Custom Request Validation

It is now possible to override the default request validators by inheriting from the System.Web.Util.RequestValidator class and overriding the method IsValidRequestString(). You must then specify the custom validator in the httpRuntime section in Web.config:

```
<httpRuntime requestValidationType="Apress.MyValidator, Samples" />
```

Custom Encoders

If you feel that ASP.NET's existing page encoders are insufficient then you can now create your own by inheriting from System.Web.Util.HttpEncoder class and specifying the new encoder in the encoderType attribute of httpRuntime, for example:

```
<httpRuntime encoderType="Apress.MyEncoder, Samples"  />
```

URL and Query String Length

Previously ASP.NET limited accepted URLs to a maximum of 260 characters (an NTFS constraint). ASP.NET 4.0 allows you to extend (or limit) the URL and query string maximum length. To modify these settings change the maxRequestPathLength and maxQueryStringLength properties (in the httpRuntime section) in Web.config:

```
<httpRuntime maxQueryStringLength="260" maxRequestLength="2048"/>
```

Valid URL Characters

Previous versions of ASP.NET limit accepted URLs to a specific set of characters. The following characters were considered invalid in a URL: <, >, &. You can use the new requestPathInvalidChars property to specify invalid characters (such as the above). The below example makes a,b,c invalid in requests (which isn't too useful but demonstrates the feature):

```
<httpRuntime requestPathInvalidCharacters="a,b,c">
```

■**NOTE** The Microsoft documentation states that ASP.NET 4.0 will reject paths with characters in ASCII range 0x00 to 0x1F (RFC 2396).

Accessibility and Standards

Accessibility and standards, whether you like it or not, are becoming increasingly important. Microsoft is aware of this and has introduced a number of changes.

controlRenderingCompatibilityVersion

The pages section in Web.config contains a new controlRenderingCompatibilityVersion property that determines how controls are rendered by default. The controlRenderingCompatibilityVersion property can be set to 3.5 or 4.0.

```
<system.web>
  <pages controlRenderingCompatibilityVersion="4.0"/>
</system.web>
```

Setting controlRenderingCompatibilityVersion to 3.5 will ensure ASP.NET renders as in ASP.NET 3.5. If however you set controlRenderingCompatibilityVersion to 4.0 then Microsoft say that the following will occur:

- The xhtmlConformance property will be set to Strict and controls will be rendered according to XHTML 1.0 Strict markup.

- Disabled controls will not have invalid styles rendered.

- Hidden fields that have div elements around them will now be styled in a manner that will not interfere with user-defined CSS rules.

- Menu controls are now rendered using unordered list (UL) tags (fantastic).

- Validation controls will not use inline styles.

- Previously some controls such as Image rendered the property border="0"; this will no longer occur.

RenderOuterTable

Previous versions of ASP.NET used a Table tag to wrap the following controls:

- ChangePassword
- FormView
- Login
- PasswordRecovery

In ASP.NET 4.0, however, all these controls support a new RenderOuterTable property that if set to false will use a div instead.

CheckBoxList and RadioButtonList

CheckBoxList and RadioButtonList benefit from a the new property RepeatLayout. RepeatLayout has four modes: UnorderedList, OrderedList, Flow, and Table, allowing you fine control over how they are rendered.

ASP.NET Menu control

The ASP.NET Menu control now renders menu items using unordered list elements. Keyboard support for the menu has also been improved so once an ASP.NET menu receives focus the user can navigate through menu items using the arrow keys.

Browser Capability Files

Browser capability files are used to determine how best to render content for individual browsers and are held in XML format. If you feel the need you can create your own browser provider by deriving from the HttpCapabilitiesProvider class.

Further Control Enhancements

There are a number of control enhancements, and a couple of miscellaneous new controls as well.

Wizard Control

The Wizard control now contains new templating functionality (LayoutTemplate).

ListView Enhancements

In previous versions of ASP.NET, when a row was selected within a ListView (or GridView) and the user moved to another page, the selection was maintained on the next page. This can be bad news if you then use this selection to perform an action on the selected record.

ASP.NET 4.0 resolves this problem with the new EnablePersistedSelection property. If EnablePersistedSelection is set to True, then row selection is maintained using the datakey of each item.

Another welcome change is that the declaration of ListViews has been much simplified. The following code shows how a ListView control had to be declared previously:

```
<asp:ListView ID="lstView" runat="server">
    <LayoutTemplate>
        <asp:PlaceHolder ID="itemPlaceholder" runat="server"></asp:PlaceHolder>
    </LayoutTemplate>

    <ItemTemplate>
        <%# Eval("firstname")%>
    </ItemTemplate>
</asp:ListView>
```

ASP.NET 4.0 allows you to do the following:

```
<asp:ListView ID="ListView1" runat="server">
    <ItemTemplate>
        <%# Eval("firstname") %>
    </ItemTemplate>
</asp:ListView>
```

GridView

The GridView control now supports persisted selection (see previous example) and offers the ability to style header columns when they are sorted and contains improved support for working with ViewState disabled.

CompareValidator

The CompareValidator now supports the comparison of Time and DateTime values.

Query Extender

Query extender is a new control that aims to make the filtering of data easier by providing a declarative query syntax that you can link to the Entity or LinqDataSource controls.

Browser capability files

Browser capability files are to determine how best to render content for individual browsers and are held in XML format. If you feel the need (perhaps to override the rendering capabilities for iPhones, for example) you can create your own browser provider by deriving from the HttpCapabilitiesProvider class.

Auto-Start Web Applications

Some ASP.NET applications perform a lot of startup work (usually in Global.asax's Application_Load() method). For example, preloading or caching data. ASP.NET 4.0 introduces a new feature called auto-start that enables you to define code to be run as soon as your application is installed (or the app pool is recycled). Until this startup work has completed ASP.NET will prevent access to the application.

Not all applications will be able to benefit from this facility through as they must

- Be running on Windows Server 2008 R2 and IIS 7.5.

- Be written in ASP.NET 4.0.

- To use add the setting below to the applicationHost.config file (held at C:\Windows\System32\inetsrv\config\):

```
<applicationPools>
    <add name="ApressAppPool" startMode="AlwaysRunning"" />
</applicationPools>
```

You must now specify the sites to be automatically started and the serviceAutoStartProvider they should use:

```
<sites>
  <site name="ApressSite" id="5">
    <application path="/"
        serviceAutoStartEnabled ="true"
        serviceAutoStartProvider ="PrewarmMyCache" >
            </application>
  </site>
</sites>
```

An auto start class is created by implementing the IProcessHostPreloadClient interface and added as a provider in applicationHost.config:

```
<serviceAutoStartProviders >
    <add name="StartmeUp"
        type="Apress.CustomInitialization, ASPStartup" />
</serviceAutoStartProviders >
```

Compress Session State

It is generally a good rule to avoid storing anything in session unless absolutely necessary but if you must ASP.NET 4.0 allows you to compress session state. Session state compression cannot be used by an in-process session so is only applicable if your application is using state or SQL Server. To compress session simply set the compressionEnabled property to true in Web.config:

```
<sessionState compressionEnabled="true"></sessionState>
```

Session state is compressed using the GZip algorithm. It is important to note that compressing session requires a server to do more work so *could* adversely impact on the performance of your application.

Caching

ASP.NET 4.0 gives you the option to create and utilize custom cache providers. The cache provider can be set at an application, control, and even individual request level (by overriding the GetOutputCacheProviderName() method) offering very fine grained control.

To create your own cache provider you must inherit from System.Web.Caching.OutputCacheProvider.

Velocity

Before you create your own caching system (you crazy fool), you would be wise to take a look into Microsoft's new free distributed caching system, Velocity. Velocity provides a huge amount of functionality and is easily utilized by both web and Windows applications. Velocity presents a view of the cache that can be spread out amongst many machines and accessed by any type of application. For more information please refer to: http://msdn.microsoft.com/en-au/library/cc645013.aspx.

System.Runtime.Caching

In previous versions of .NET, caching functionality was contained in the System.Web assembly. To enable easier integration for non-web clients, Microsoft has created the new System.Runtime.Caching assembly. System.Runtime.Caching contains abstract classes for creating your own cache provider, and a new class called MemoryCache. MemoryCache can be used by non-web clients and offers simple in memory caching functionality. Microsoft say that the internal implementation of MemoryCache is very similar to ASP.NET's cache.

The following example shows how to utilize MemoryCache to store a string for an hour (note you can also create watchers to invalidate the cache if an item changes and add them to the policy.ChangeMonitors property):

```
ObjectCache cache = MemoryCache.Default;
string testData = cache["someData"] as string;

if (testData == null)
{
    CacheItemPolicy policy = new CacheItemPolicy();
    policy.AbsoluteExpiration = new DateTimeOffset(DateTime.Now.AddHours(1));
    cache.Set("someData", "some test data", policy);
}
```

Resource Monitoring

Some web servers run many applications within one app pool. If issues occur on an individual site, it can be difficult for an administrator to determine which particular application is having difficulties. ASP.NET 4.0 introduces additional performance counters allowing you to monitor individual applications CPU and memory usage.

To utilize this, you must add the appDomainResourceMonitoring setting to Aspnet.config (Aspnet.config is located where the .NET framework is installed: C:\Windows\Microsoft.NET\ Framework\v4.0.21006):

```
<runtime>
  <appDomainResourceMonitoring enabled="true"/>
</runtime>
```

When you have added this line go into perfmon and you should find that you will have access to two new performance counters in the ASP.NET applications performance category section (Figure 10.6):

- Managed Processor Time

- Managed Memory Used

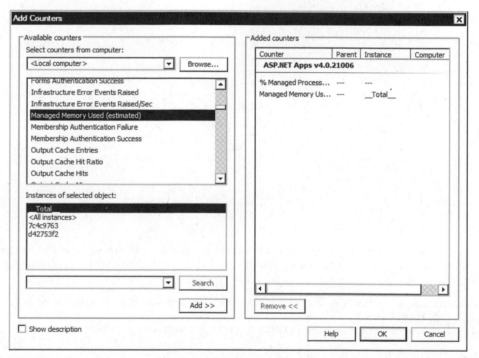

Figure 10-6. *New perf counters for ASP.NET*

Charting Controls

Microsoft purchased and integrated the Dundas ASP.NET charting controls in early 2008. This set contains over 35 different types of charts and a huge amount of functionality, some of which is shown in Figure 10-7. Previously these controls had to be installed as an add-on and a number of settings added to Web.config. ASP.NET 4.0, however, includes these controls, and it is no longer necessary to make changes to Web.config to include them.

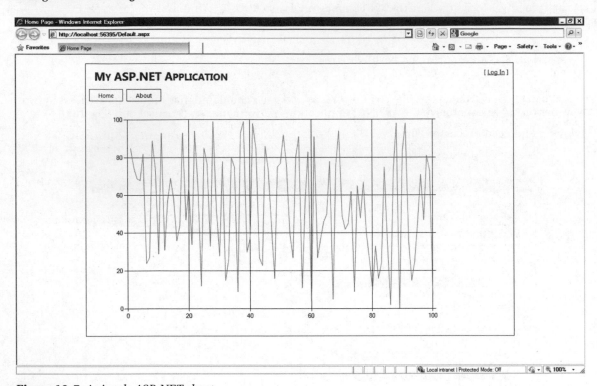

Figure 10-7. *A simple ASP.NET chart*

To add a chart to your web page simply drag the Chart control from the toolbox or add a reference to System.Web.DataVisualization and the Register directive below (note this may be slightly different for the final release of VS2010):

```
<%@ Register Assembly="System.Web.DataVisualization, Version=4.0.0.0, Culture=neutral,
            PublicKeyToken=31bf3856ad364e35"
            Namespace="System.Web.UI.DataVisualization.Charting" TagPrefix="asp" %>
```

Charts are then added to the page with the following code:

```
<asp:Chart runat="server">
    <series><asp:Series Name="Series1"></asp:Series></series>
    <chartareas><asp:ChartArea Name="ChartArea1"></asp:ChartArea></chartareas>
</asp:Chart>
```

The following code binds a series of random points to the chart:

```
Random r = new Random();
Series series = new Series("Line");
series.ChartType = SeriesChartType.Line;

for (int i = 0; i < 100; i++)
{
    series.Points.AddY(r.Next(0,100));
}

chart1.Series.Add(series);
```

Dynamic Data Framework

It is worth noting that the Dynamic Data Framework has a number of additions in VS2010/ASP.NET 4.0. I will not be covering these but for interested readers please refer to: http://www.asp.net/dynamicdata.

Conclusion

ASP.NET 4.0 fixes some long-term omissions and bugs and looks likely to continue to be a popular method of developing web applications. Alternative approaches such as ASP.NET MVC (Chapter 13) are gaining ground (due in part to their easy testability), so it will be interesting to see if this remains the case in years to come.

Further Reading

- http://www.asp.net/LEARN/whitepapers/aspnet4/default.aspx

CHAPTER 11

■ ■ ■

Microsoft AJAX Library

Visual Studio 2010 includes a new version of the Microsoft AJAX libraries that can be used in any web application. When working with the Microsoft AJAX library, many developers believe that it consists of little more than the UpdatePanel, which is a shame because it offers so much more. Many developers also believe that the Microsoft AJAX libraries can be utilized only in ASP.NET applications. They would be wrong; the Microsoft AJAX library is (mostly) just plain ol' JavaScript files and can be utilized in any web application—ASP.NET, PHP, Ruby, or anything else you can think of. Although some functionality doesn't make much sense outside of the ASP.NET platform, it's a tiny part of the libraries.

This release introduces a new mechanism for loading scripts, easy-to-use client side data binding, and integration with jQuery. Existing users also benefit from refactoring and performance enhancements. The libraries will soon be put to the test in the upcoming NASA community web site and MSN Messenger web toolkit.

■**CAUTION** This chapter was written with the beta version of Microsoft AJAX library, so functionality might differ come final release. You have been warned.

Architecture Changes

One of the biggest changes in this release is that the AJAX control toolkit and AJAX libraries have now been combined. The libraries have also been open sourced (New BSD License) and donated to the codeplex foundation as its first project. Microsoft is keen to point out that the decision to open source the libraries won't affect its support and it is also encouraging community contributions.

Compatibility

The libraries have been tested with the following browsers (and might work with others, but no guarantees):

- Microsoft Internet Explorer 6, 7, and 8
- Mozilla Firefox 3 and 3.5
- Apple Safari 4
- Opera 10
- Chrome 3

A pageLoad Problem Fixed

Microsoft has fixed a bug present in previous releases, so you will no longer have to manually call the `sys.application.initialize()` method to ensure that the `pageLoad()` method is called before the `window.onload` event occurs (see `http://seejoelprogram.wordpress.com/2008/10/03/fixing-sysapplicationinitialize-again/`).

Installation

A number of Visual Studio 2010 project templates such as ASP.NET MVC 2 and ASP.NET web application projects include the Microsoft AJAX libraries out of the box. The libraries will, however, be maintained separately from Visual Studio/.NET 4.0, so to obtain the latest release you will need to download it from `http://ajax.codeplex.com/`.

Adding Microsoft AJAX Libraries to Your Project

The easiest (but not necessarily best) way to include the Microsoft AJAX libraries in your project is to use the ASP.NET `ScriptManager` control on your page:

```
<asp:ScriptManager runat="Server" />
```

`ScriptManager` is a great little control that takes care of referencing Microsoft script files and helps you manage your own scripts. In previous versions, `ScriptManager` had a dark and not so secret flaw—it loaded all the Microsoft AJAX libraries, whether you needed them or not.

Downloading unnecessary stuff is always bad, so the latest version of `ScriptManager` included with VS2010 offers you finer control over which scripts are included by using the new `MicrosoftAjaxMode` setting.

`MicrosoftAjaxMode` has three different settings:

- `Enabled` (includes all Microsoft AJAX scripts—default setting and mimics the behavior of previous releases)

- `Explicit` (you specify the script files to be imported)

- `Disabled` (Microsoft AJAX script features disabled and no script references added)

The following code shows how to use the `ScriptManager` control to import just the `MicrosoftAjaxCore.js` script:

```
<asp:ScriptManager ID="NewScriptManager"
    MicrosoftAjaxMode="Explicit"
    runat="server">
  <CompositeScript>
    <Scripts>
      <asp:ScriptReference Name="MicrosoftAjaxCore.js" />
    </Scripts>
  </CompositeScript>
</asp:ScriptManager>
```

It is important to remember that some scripts depend on other scripts when you use the `Explicit` mode, so you need to also include the dependent scripts. The dependencies between the script files are shown in the following link: `http://www.asp.net/ajaxlibrary/Ajax%20Script%20Loader.ashx`.

The client script loader is an alternative to the `ScriptManager` control, and I think it's a better and cleaner platform-independent method. You'll use the client script loader in the rest of this chapter, so let's take a look at it now.

Client Script Loader

Using the client script loader is very easy. Once you have downloaded the libraries and included them in your project you need to reference the JavaScript file `Start.js`. `Start.js` contains the client script loader functionality that can reference all the other script files:

```
<script src="../Scripts/Start.js" type="text/javascript"></script>
```

Once you have referenced the client script loader, you can then use its methods to load other scripts with the `Sys.require()` method (the following code references the new `dataView` component that you will look at shortly):

```
Sys.require(Sys.components.dataView);
```

The client script loader loads scripts in a very efficient and parallelized manner, taking care of resolving dependencies and ensuring that scripts are loaded only once. It even supports lazy loading and working with third-party libraries.

Referencing jQuery Scripts

You can even use the client script loader to load the jQuery or jQuery validation scripts:

```
Sys.require(Sys.scripts.jQuery);
```

Table 11-1 shows some of the scripts/components you can load with the client script loader.

Table 11-1. *Client Script Loader*

Script Alias and Purpose	Script/Functionality
`Sys.scripts.AdoNet` WCF Data Services	`MicrosoftAjaxAdoNet.js`
`Sys.scripts.ApplicationServices` ASP.NET profile and security services	`MicrosoftAjaxApplicationServices.js`
`Sys.scripts.ComponentModel` behavior	`MicrosoftAjaxComponentModel.js`
`Sys.scripts.Core`	`MicrosoftAjaxCore.js`
`Sys.scripts.DataContext` (new `DataContext` and `AdoNetDataContext` functionality)	`MicrosoftAjaxDataContext.js`

(Continued)

Table 11-1. *Continued*

Script Alias and Purpose	Script/Functionality
Sys.scripts.Globalization	MicrosoftAjaxGlobalization.js
Sys.scripts.History (browser history)	MicrosoftAjaxHistory.js
Sys.scripts.jQuery	jquery-1.3.2.min.js
Sys.scripts.jQueryValidate	jquery.validate.min.js
Sys.scripts.Network	MicrosoftAjaxNetwork.js
Sys.scripts.Serialization	MicrosoftAjaxSerialization.js
Sys.scripts.Templates (client-side templates)	MicrosoftAjaxTemplates.js
Sys.scripts.WebServices (proxy calls)	MicrosoftAjaxWebServices.js
Sys.components.colorPicker	Note this is the format to load various controls from the AJAX toolkit

Note that each of these scripts has a .debug.js version and that the AJAX control toolkit now lives in the scripts/extended directory.

Specifying Script Directories

By default, the client script loader will load scripts from the same directory in which it is located, although you can modify it by specifying a new basePath property:

```
Sys.loader.basePath = "../MyLocation/";
```

You can also specify a separate directory for jQuery scripts to be loaded from:

```
Sys.scripts.jQuery.releaseUrl = "../jQuery/jquery-1.3.2.js";
Sys.scripts.jQuery.debugUrl = "../ jQuery /jquery-1.3.2.js ";
```

Loading Custom Scripts

You can also make use of the parallelization capabilities of the client script loader to load your own scripts with the loadScripts() method that accepts an array of script files to load:

```
Sys.loadScripts(["../AnnoyingTrailingCursor.js", "../Scripts/HorribleFlashingDiv.js"]);
```

Lazy Loading

A good use of the loadScripts() method is to load scripts only when they are needed (lazy loading). For example, you might have a function that is rarely called and instead of forcing all users to have to download it you can load it only when you need to:

```
function btnHardlyEverClicked_click()
{
  Sys.loadScripts(["../Scripts/myFunction.js"], function() {
    myFunction();
  });
}
```

AJAX Libraries Now Hosted by Microsoft

The Microsoft AJAX and jQuery libraries are now hosted by Microsoft's content delivery network (CDN). By using DNS trickery, script files can be served from a server local to the user, thus reducing download time and load on your server (not to mention your bandwidth bill).

The following code shows how to reference the CDN version of the scripts. (The URL, version 0911, will probably change by release, so for the most up-to-date information, please refer to http://www.asp.net/ajax/cdn/.)

```
<script src="ajax.microsoft.com/ajax/0911/start.js"></script>
```

ScriptManager EnableCDN

The ASP.NET ScriptManager control has a new Boolean property called EnableCdn that if set to true will serve scripts from the Microsoft CDN.

AJAX Toolkit Integration

The AJAX toolkit controls are now combined into the AJAX libraries. Apart from easier deployment, this feature also allows you to programmatically create them. The following example shows how to add the color picker control from the toolkit to a textbox programmatically (note that it wasn't necessary to reference any toolkit assemblies):

```
<script src="./Scripts/Start.js" type="text/javascript"></script>
<script src="./Scripts/Extended/ExtendedControls.js" type="text/javascript"
type="text/javascript"></script>

<script>
  Sys.require(Sys.components.colorPicker, function() {
  Sys.create.colorPicker("#txtChooseColor");
  });
</script>

<input id="txtChooseColor" />
```

Controls Now Exposed as jQuery Plug-ins

In this release, all the ASP.NET AJAX controls are exposed as jQuery plug-ins. So you can instantiate them using jQuery syntax, even making use of jQuery's chaining capabilities. The following code attaches an ASP.NET AJAX watermark control to a text box and an ASP.NET AJAX color picker:

```
Sys.require([Sys.scripts.jQuery, Sys.components.watermark, Sys.components.colorPicker]);
    Sys.onReady(function () {
    $("#txtChooseColor").watermark("Choose a color", "watermarked").colorPicker();
});
```

DataView

One of the coolest controls in this release is the new DataView control. DataView allows you to easily define a template that can be bound to various types of data or services. WPF/Silverlight developers might notice some similarity with the binding syntax.

XHTML-Compliant?

Microsoft wants you to know that it has made great efforts to ensure that declarative binding is XHTML-compliant. I'm not sure this is strictly true, but you will see a very clean way of performing it. Sebastian Lambla has a lengthy post on this subject (note that Sebastian would have been using a previous version of the AJAX libraries when this post was written): http://serialseb.blogspot.com/2009/06/in-how-many-ways-can-microsoft-ajax-4.html.

Hello, Microsoft AJAX

It's time to look at the new DataView functionality, so let's create a new empty ASP.NET web project called Chapter11.HelloAjax.

1. Create a directory called Scripts within your project.

2. Download the latest AJAX libraries from http://ajax.codeplex.com/.

3. Unzip the downloaded file and copy the contents of the Scripts directory to the new project's root directory.

4. You don't want any of the master page stuff, so delete the Default.aspx file.

5. To show the libraries are platform-independent, add a new HTML file called dataviewDeclarative.htm.

6. Drag Start.js to the default.htm head HTML section to create the following script reference to the client script loader:

    ```
    <script src="Scripts/start.js" type="text/javascript"></script>
    ```

sys-template CSS rule

When you retrieve data from a remote source, you don't want to display anything to the user until you have the results back because otherwise the template could flicker, which would look poor. You will thus create a new CSS rule to hide the element until you have finished retrieving data and binding it. Because you are being lazy, simply add an inline style rule to the header as follows (obviously, external CSS files are a better way to go):

```
<style>
.sys-template { display: none; }
</style>
```

The name of the class selector (`.sys-template`) is a convention suggested by Microsoft for this purpose, which doesn't seem a bad idea so you might want to stick with it.

Let's also add a couple of other styles to make the examples clearer:

```
.dataItem
{
    font-family:Arial;
    font-size:20px;
}

#staticBind
{
    width:700px;
}
```

OK, you have everything set up now. It's time for some client-side–binding fun.

DataView Binding

`DataView` binding can be carried out declaratively, programmatically, or a mixture of the two. Let's look at declarative binding first of all.

Declarative Binding

In the first example, you will create an array of people consisting of a person's name and age, and then bind it declaratively.

1. Add the following `script` block in the header of your page:

    ```
    <script type="text/javascript">
    Sys.require(Sys.components.dataView);

    var people = [
        { Name: "Alex Mackey", Age: "28" },
        { Name: "Sharyn Mackey", Age: "35" },
        { Name: "Brett Chaney", Age: "33" },
        { Name: "Jenny Chai", Age: "24"}];
     </script>
    ```

2. Now replace the body tag with the following HTML:

```
<body xmlns:dataview="javascript:Sys.UI.DataView">
<div id="peopleView" class="sys-template"
sys:attach="dataview"
dataview:data="{{people}}"
>
 <div class="dataItem">
        {{ $index }},
        {{ Name }},
        aged: {{ Age }}
         <hr />
    </div>
</div>
</body>
```

3. Press F5 to run your application and you should see a screen similar to Figure 11-1.

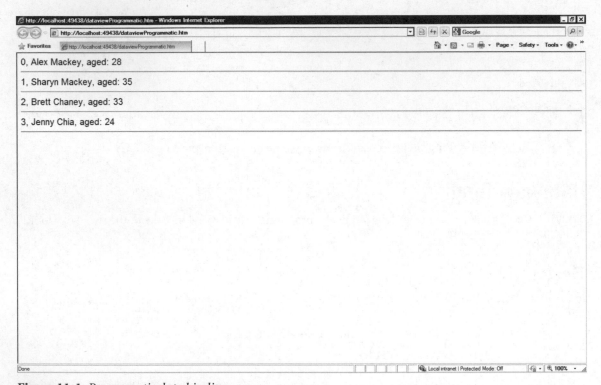

Figure 11-1. *Programatic data binding*

The preceding example created an array called people, imported the namespaces that DataView uses in the document's body tag, and then bound the items in the peopleView with dataview:data="{{people}}" and specified where items should appear with the {{Property}} syntax.

This approach is very open to corruption by meddling designers. It certainly isn't XHTML-compliant and is a bit fiddly to debug. A better, more flexible approach is to use programmatic binding.

Programmatic Binding

You will now see how to produce the same result programmatically:

1. Copy the dataviewDeclarative.htm file and rename the new copy as dataviewProgrammatic.htm.

2. Replace the script tag with the following:

```
<script type="text/javascript">

Sys.require([Sys.components.dataView], function() {
var people = [
    { Name: "Alex Mackey", Age: "28" },
    { Name: "Sharyn Mackey", Age: "35" },
    { Name: "Brett Chaney", Age: "33" },
    { Name: "Jenny Chai", Age: "24" }
];

Sys.create.dataView('#peopleView',
{
    data: people
});
});

</script>
```

3. Now replace the body tag with the following:

```
<body>
    <div id="peopleView" class="sys-template">
    <div class="dataItem">
    {{ $index }},
    {{ Name }},
    aged: {{ Age }}
    <hr />
    </div>
    </div>
</body>
```

Simple, huh? First, you told the AJAX libraries that you will need the DataView scripts with the Sys.Require call. You then created an array of people. You then used the new functionality in the AJAX libraries to create a DataView and set the people array to the data property. Finally in the HTML you defined where data items should be bound to.

A Cleaner Programmatic Binding

The previous example still utilizes custom tags to perform the binding. The AJAX libraries offer an even better method by handling the itemRendered event that allows no binding tags at all. To accomplish this task, you will intercept the itemRendered event and then target the spans you want to change with the innerHTML property:

1. Copy the file dataviewProgrammatic.htm and rename it as dataviewOnRendered.htm.

2. Replace the existing script block with the following:

```
<script type="text/javascript">

Sys.require([Sys.components.dataView], function() {
var people = [
  { Name: "Alex Mackey", Age: "28" },
  { Name: "Sharyn Mackey", Age: "35" },
  { Name: "Brett Chaney", Age: "33" },
  { Name: "Mark Clugston", Age: "28" }
];

Sys.create.dataView('#peopleView',
{
  data: people,
  itemRendered: onRendered
});
});

function onRendered(dataview, ctx) {
  Sys.bind(Sys.get(".name", ctx), "innerHTML", ctx.dataItem, "Name");
  Sys.bind(Sys.get(".age", ctx), "innerHTML", ctx.dataItem, "Age");
}
</script>
```

3. Now replace the body tag with the following HTML, noting the lack of binding attributes and just nice good ol' HTML:

```
<body>
    <div id="peopleView" class="sys-template">

    <div class="dataItem">

     <span class="name"></span>
       
       aged:
     <span class="age"></span>
       <hr />

    </div>
  </div>

  </body>
```

This code creates a DataView, setting the newly created people array to the data property. Because you don't want to meddle with the HTML, you create a function called onRendered()() to handle the itemRendered event. In this function, you then access the HTML elements with class name and age and set their innerHTML property to the bound item's name and age properties.

Master Detail Binding

A common scenario in line of business applications is the need to create master detail forms. The DataView control makes this very easy; let's see how:

1. Copy the existing dataviewProgrammatic.htm and rename the new file as dataviewMasterDetail.htm.

2. Replace the existing script block with the following:

```
<script type="text/javascript">

Sys.require([Sys.components.dataView], function() {
var people = [
    { Name: "Alex Mackey", Age: "28", Address: "20 Tree road", Telephone: "888888" },
    { Name: "Sharyn Mackey", Age: "35", Address: "10 Oak ave", Telephone: "777777" },
    { Name: "Brett Chaney", Age: "33", Address: "5 Riversadale Road", Telephone:
"6666666" },
    { Name: "Jenny Chai", Age: "24", Address: "88 Burleigh Gardens", Telephone:
"5555555" }
];

var master = Sys.create.dataView('#peoplesNames',
{
    data: people
});

var detail = Sys.create.dataView("#peopleDetail");
Sys.bind(detail, "data", master, "selectedData");

});
</script>
```

3. Now replace the body section with the following code:

```
<body>
<div id="peoplesNames" class="sys-template">
<div class="dataItem" sys:command="select">
    {{ Name }}
    <hr />
    </div>
</div>

<!--Detail View-->
<div id="peopleDetail" class="sys-template">
<span class="nameddetailitem">
    Age: {{ Age }}  <br />
    Address: {{ Address }}   <br />
    Telephone: {{ Telephone }}
</span>
</div>

</body>
```

4. That's it. Run the code up, click a name, and see that the individual's details are retrieved. Note the line Sys.bind(detail, "data", master, "selectedData") that links the master and detail DataViews together.

Binding to External Services

Of course, when you are binding to data, you usually want to retrieve it from an external source. The DataView control allows you to very easily accomplish this and bind to many different types of services, for example:

- ASMX web service

- WCF web services

- WCF Data Services

- ASP.NET MVC controller actions

- JSONP service

- Basically anything that returns JSON-formatted data

You will now use client templates to bind to both an ASMX and WCF web service.

WebService (.asmx)

First the web service:

1. Add a new class called Person to the project and enter the following class definition:

```
public class Person
{
    public string Name { get; set; }
    public string Age { get; set; }
}
```

2. Add a new .asmx web service to the project called GetData.asmx.

3. Add the following using directive to GetData.asmx.cs:

```
using System.Web.Script.Services;
```

4. Uncomment the following attribute in the GetData class:

```
[System.Web.Script.Services.ScriptService]
```

5. Now create a new method to return a list of people. Note the call to System.Threading.Sleep(); it slows down the service so you can see the results appear (you might want to remove the sys-template style to see the effect latency can have):

```
[WebMethod]
[System.Web.Script.Services.ScriptMethod]
public List<Person> GetPeople()
{
    System.Threading.Thread.Sleep(2000);

    List<Person> People = new List<Person>();

    People.Add(new Person { Name = "Alex Mackey", Age = "28" });
    People.Add(new Person { Name = "Matt Lacey", Age = "31" });
    People.Add(new Person { Name = "Barry Dorrans", Age = "78" });
```

```
        People.Add(new Person { Name = "Craig Murphy", Age = "33" });
        People.Add(new Person { Name = "Chris Hay", Age = "32" });
        People.Add(new Person { Name = "Andy Gibson", Age = "21" });

        return People;
    }
```

6. Copy the file dataviewProgrammatic.htm and rename the new copy as dataviewAsmx.htm.

7. Replace the existing script block with the following code:

```
<script type="text/javascript">

        Sys.require([Sys.components.dataView, Sys.scripts.WebServices], function () {

        Sys.create.dataView('#peopleView',
        {
            dataProvider: "GetData.asmx",
            fetchOperation: "GetPeople",
            autoFetch: "true"

        });
    });
</script>
```

8. Right-click dataviewAsmx.htm and select View in Browser. After about two seconds, you should see the results of the web service bound to the template.

WCF Binding

Binding to a WCF service is accomplished in a very similar way. In this example, you will pass in a name parameter as well as retrieve a single person.

1. Add a new AJAX-enabled WCF service (similar to standard WCF service, but has some additional attributes to enable JavaScript methods calls) to the project called GetDataFromWCF.svc.

2. Now add the following method to the new web service:

```
[OperationContract]
public Person GetPerson(string Name)
{
    //System.Threading.Thread.Sleep(2000);

    List<Person> People = new List<Person>();

    People.Add(new Person { Name = "Alex Mackey", Age = "28" });
    People.Add(new Person { Name = "Matt Lacey", Age = "31" });
    People.Add(new Person { Name = "Barry Dorrans", Age = "78" });
    People.Add(new Person { Name = "Craig Murphy", Age = "33" });
    People.Add(new Person { Name = "Chris Hay", Age = "32" });
    People.Add(new Person { Name = "Andy Gibson", Age = "21" });

    return People.FirstOrDefault(p => p.Name == Name);
}
```

3. Replace the current `script` block in `webserviceWCF.htm` with the following code:

```
<script type="text/javascript">

//We need Sys.scripts.WebServices in order to interact with the WCF service
Sys.require([Sys.components.dataView, Sys.scripts.WebServices], function () {

Sys.create.dataView('#peopleView',
{
    dataProvider: "GetDataFromWCF.svc",
    fetchOperation: "GetPerson",
    fetchParameters: { Name: "Alex Mackey" },
    autoFetch: "true"

});
});
</script>
```

JSONP

The latest release of the AJAX libraries contains support for working with JSONP services. JSONP (or JSON with padding) is a bit of a hack that allows you to make AJAX calls to external domains (not allowed with standard XHTTP requests and utilized by Flickr and Bing). JSONP works by exploiting the fact that you can reference a script file on a different server. This script then calls a function in the calling page to return the data.

DataView contains support for binding to JSONP services such as those offered by Flickr and Bing. The Microsoft AJAX site has an example of how to call a JSONP service at `http://www.asp.net/ajaxlibrary/HOW%20TO%20Use%20JSONP%20to%20Request%20Data%20from%20Remote%20Websites.ashx`.

For more information on JSONP, please refer to the following links:

- `http://ajaxian.com/archives/jsonp-json-with-padding`

- `http://www.west-wind.com/Weblog/posts/107136.aspx`

Advanced Binding

Hopefully, by now you are excited about how easy the Microsoft AJAX libraries can make client-side data binding. The ASP.NET AJAX libraries also contain a number of other useful features that you will look at now:

- Conditional rendering

- Converters

- Two-way data binding,

- Implementation of the observer pattern

Conditional Rendering

Sometimes you will want to apply logic to the rendering of your content—perhaps in a medical application to highlight abnormal lab results. The Microsoft AJAX libraries allow you to do this by embedding conditional logic within your markup.

■**CAUTION** Be careful when using this approach. You are polluting the UI with business logic, which will be harder to maintain and is more easily corrupted by designers.

Let's look at the different conditional logic statements you can utilize.

sys:if

The sys:if condition applies only if a condition is true. Suppose that you want to render a warning div if a particular person's name comes up in the bound data. This is easily achieved as follows:

```
<div sys:if="$dataItem.Name == 'Barry Dorrans'">Warning do not approach!</div>
```

$dataItem

In the preceding example, you needed to reference data in the bound set. To do this, you used the $dataItem object. This allows you to access individual properties with the following syntax:

```
$dataItem.MyPropertyName
```

$index

You can also apply code based on the index position of the item by querying the $index pseudo property:

```
<div sys:if="$index == 0">first</div>
```

sys:codebefore and sys:codeafter

Sometimes you want to render HTML before or after the element you are binding. The codebefore and codeafter statements allow you to do this:

```
<div
    sys:if="$index == 0"
    sys:codebefore="$element.innerHTML='I get placed first'"
    sys:codeafter="$element.innerHTML='I get placed second'"
    >
</div>
```

sys:innertext and sys:innerhtml

Finally it can be useful to output text or HTML (similar to JavaScript's innerText or innerHtml properties):

```
<div sys:innertext="{{ foo }}"></div>
<div sys:innerhtml="{{ foo }}"></div>
```

Binding Converters

When you bind data you might want to perform some processing on a value before rendering it. For example, maybe you don't need the level of precision the data has, or you want to convert it to a different measurement or format it to the user's current locale. This can be accomplished with a converter that is simply a standard JavaScript function.

This example creates a function to uppercase a string:

```
function ToUpper(Input) {
  return Input.toUpperCase();
}
```

This function can then be used in binding like so:

```
<div class=""> {binding Name, convert=ToUpper} </div>
```

Two-way Binding

Until now, you have bound items using one-way binding. One-way binding is used automatically when you declare your binding using two curly brackets, one on each side of the data item:

```
{{ Name }}
```

ASP.NET AJAX also allows you to implement two-way data binding—if an item is updated, any other page elements bound to the same data item will also be updated. You will also soon learn how to bind to a WCF service and persist changes back. To use two-way binding, simply use one curly bracket instead of two when you define the template:

```
{binding Name}
```

If you want to be more verbose/explicit about your intentions you can also specify the binding mode:

```
{binding Name mode=oneWay} or {binding Name mode=twoWay}
```

Let's take a look at this in action now:

1. Copy the file dataviewProgrammatic.htm and rename the new file as dataviewTwoWay.htm.

2. Modify the template tag to the following:

```
<body>
    <div id="peopleView" class="sys-template">
    <div class="dataItem">
    <input type="text" sys:value="{binding Name}" />
    <input type="text" sys:value="{binding Name}" />
    <hr />
    </div>
    </div>
</body>
```

3. Now run the application, edit one of the text boxes, and tab out of it, noting that the new value is updated automatically (see Figure 11-2).

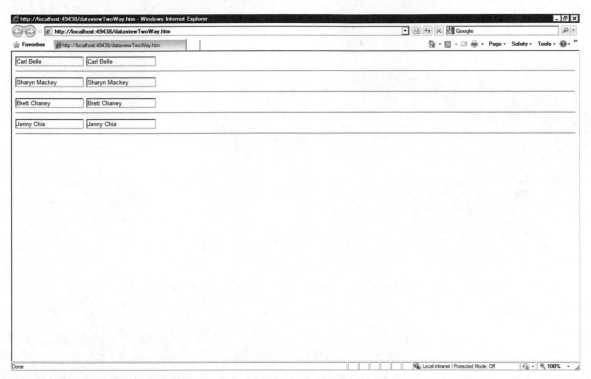

Figure 11-2. *Two-way data binding*

Sys.Observer

A common problem when designing web applications is the need to refresh the UI in response to changes in an underlying data source. You might have accomplished this by polling an object or service for changes, but you now have a better option with the Sys.Observer functionality. Sys.Observer functionality is Microsoft AJAX libraries' implementation of the popular Observer pattern.

You will now write some example code to tell ASP.NET AJAX to monitor an array of numbers and refresh the template if anything changes to the array. You will then create a function that adds a random number to the array and note how the result is returned:

1. Copy and paste the file dataviewDeclarative.htm and rename the copy to observer.htm.

2. Replace the existing script block with the following code:

```
<script type="text/javascript">
Sys.require(Sys.components.dataView);
var dataArray = [];

Sys.Observer.makeObservable(dataArray);

function NewRandom() {
    var newRand = Math.random();
    var newItem = { MyRandom: newRand };
    dataArray.add(newItem);
}
</script>
```

3. Replace the body section with the following HTML:

```
<div id="peopleView" class="sys-template"
sys:attach="dataview"
dataview:data="{{dataArray}}"
>
    <div class="dataItem">
        {{ MyRandom }}
        <hr />
    </div>
</div>
```

Note that you make a call to the method Sys.Observer.makeObservable(dataArray) that tells ASP.NET AJAX libraries that you are interested in any changes to this object and that it needs to refresh any templates.

WCF Data Services Data Context

The ASP.NET AJAX libraries can be easily integrated with WCF Data Services. If you are unfamiliar with WCF Data Services, please refer to Chapter 9 for more in-depth details of how to create a service.

■NOTE As described in Chapter 9, WCF Data Services used to be called ADO.NET Data Services, which is reflected in the names of the templates used in this exercise.

The steps to integrate with a data context are described as follows:

1. Add a new ADO.NET entity data model to the project called book.edmx that contains the Films table from the demo database with pluralization options switched on.

2. Now add a new ADO.NET data service called BookService.

3. Modify BookService's InitializeService() method to the following to enable full read/write access (don't do this in a production application):

```
public static void InitializeService(DataServiceConfiguration config)
{
    config.SetEntitySetAccessRule("*", EntitySetRights.All);
    config.SetServiceOperationAccessRule("*", ServiceOperationRights.All);
    config.DataServiceBehavior.MaxProtocolVersion = DataServiceProtocolVersion.V2;
}
```

4. Copy dataviewProgrammatic.htm and rename the new copy as dataviewAdo.htm.

5. Modify the script block to the following code:

```
<script type="text/javascript">

var dataContext;
Sys.require([Sys.components.dataView, Sys.components.adoNetDataContext], function () {

dataContext = Sys.create.adoNetDataContext({
    serviceUri: "BookService.svc"
});

var master = Sys.create.dataView("#peopleView",
{
    dataProvider: dataContext,
    fetchOperation: "Films",
    itemRendered: detailRendered,
    autoFetch: true
});

function detailRendered(dataView, ctx) {
    Sys.bind(Sys.get("#txtFilmTitle", ctx), "value", ctx.dataItem, "Title");
}

});

function SaveChanges() {
    dataContext.saveChanges();
}

    </script>
```

6. Finally, modify the body section to the following:

```
<body>
    <input type="button" onclick="javascript:SaveChanges();" value="Save Changes" />

    <div id="peopleView" class="sys-template">
    <div class="dataItem">
    <input id="txtFilmTitle" type="text" sys:value="title" />
    <hr />
    </div>
    </div>
</body>
```

Run the project up; you will find that the films list is bound to the DataView, and you can update the films by clicking the Save Changes button.

Conclusion

This release of the Microsoft AJAX libraries introduces some compelling new features that should interest all web developers.

Prior to this release, I did not recommend the Microsoft AJAX libraries as a general-purpose JavaScript framework because jQuery was better documented, supported, and easier to use.

However, the great news is that in this release the Microsoft AJAX libraries are integrated very nicely with jQuery. So you don't have to make this choice anymore; you have the best of both worlds.

It is worth considering what Microsoft's motivation behind open sourcing the AJAX libraries is. Does this indicate that Microsoft is starting to pull out from its development? I'm not sure; perhaps this is unlikely given all the recent enhancements, but it is something to bear in mind.

One thing for certain, however, is that there are some fantastic features in this release that should interest all web developers, whatever platform they are developing for.

Further Reading

- http://ajax.codeplex.com/

- http://www.asp.net/ajaxlibrary/

- http://www.jamessenior.com/

- http://weblogs.asp.net/fredriknormen/archive/2009/09/11/asp-net-ajax-4-0-preview-5-available.aspx

CHAPTER 12

■ ■ ■

jQuery

Availability: Any IntelliSense Support from Visual Studio 2008 Onward

> *"jQuery is a fast and concise JavaScript Library that simplifies HTML document traversing, event handling, animating, and AJAX interactions for rapid web development. jQuery is designed to change the way that you write JavaScript."*

`http://jquery.com/`

In a surprising but excellent move, late 2008 Microsoft announced that it would be integrating jQuery into Visual Studio. jQuery is used by some very big names such as Amazon, Google, Dell, IBM, and Slashdot (for a full list, please refer to `http://docs.jquery.com/Sites_Using_jQuery`).

JavaScript is a very powerful language and can produce some amazing results in the right hands. But let's be honest; writing JavaScript can be a painful process. There is nothing intrinsically wrong with JavaScript (apart from unhelpful error messages), but few take the time to learn and understand its intricacies.

If you are involved in web development, you will work with JavaScript at some point. jQuery can make your life much easier by providing easy-to-use methods to perform common tasks in a cross-browser friendly manner.

jQuery or Microsoft AJAX libraries?

There is certainly overlap in the functionality provided by jQuery and the Microsoft AJAX libraries. Theoretically, there is nothing stopping you from using both (especially because now Microsoft AJAX libraries work very well with jQuery), but you don't want your users to have to download unnecessary additional scripts.

Each set of libraries has its own strength; the Microsoft AJAX Libraries (discussed in Chapter 11) contain rich data binding functionality and make it very easy to communicate with .NET web services and AJAX-enabled methods (as you will see, this is also possible with jQuery). In this release, Microsoft has done some work to integrate the two (see Chapter 11).

On the other hand, jQuery has arguably better support for manipulating and querying the DOM, and is better supported with many examples and extensions or plug-ins.

My own preference is certainly jQuery over the Microsoft AJAX libraries for a general purpose framework.

jQuery Overview

jQuery is a lightweight (18 KB at time of writing) JavaScript library, first released in 2006 by John Resig. jQuery provides the following:

- Numerous ways to select, traverse, and manipulate elements on the page

- "Chainability "of functions that allows the results of one function to be fed into another

- Functionality to separate code from design

- Utilities for performing common tasks such as AJAX calls and browser capability checks

- Special effects, such as fades and glides, and easy manipulation of CSS

- Easy to extend plug-ins

Figure 12-1 shows a high-level view of the jQuery architecture. Antonio Lupetti has produced a much more detailed diagram that I would encourage you to take a look at here: http://www.box.net/shared/as4xkezd6a.

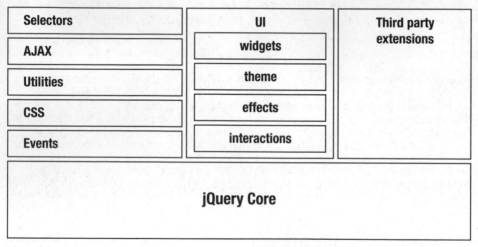

Figure 12-1. *Overview of jQuery libraries*

Downloading jQuery

jQuery scripts (version 1.3.2) are included out of the box with ASP.NET web site and application projects and MVC projects. The latest release is always available from jQuery's home page at http://jquery.com/. You can also obtain the latest development version from http://github.com/jquery/jquery.

IntelliSense

Visual Studio provides intellisense support for jQuery from Visual Studio 2008 onward (see Figure 12-2). To provide intellisense support, a special file with the ending –vsdoc is used that describes jQuery's functionality to Visual Studio. This file shouldn't be used in production and is automatically referenced by the IDE. The use of an external file means that if you want intellisense support, you probably will not be using the latest version of jQuery until the vsdoc file is produced for it.

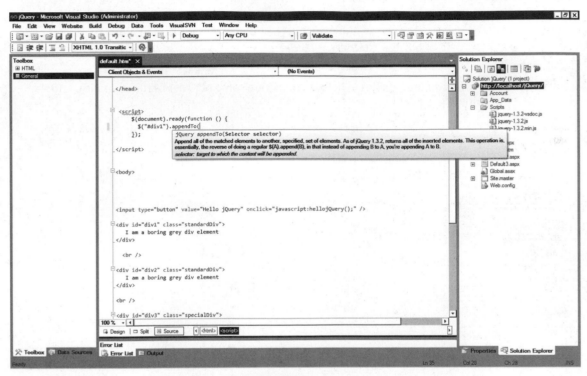

Figure 12-2. *Visual Studio intellisense support for jQuery*

Script Hosting

You can utilize Microsoft and Google's extensive content delivery networks to host jQuery libraries for free. Content delivery networks through DNS trickery serve content from a server as near to the user as possible, resulting in a very fast download and saving bandwidth costs.

For information on Microsoft's service (which also hosts Microsoft AJAX libraries), please refer to http://www.asp.net/ajax/cdn/; for Google's service, please refer to http://code.google.com/apis/ajaxlibs/documentation/.

Hello jQuery

Enough talk; let's get into some jQuery:

Create a new C# web site project called Chapter12.

Delete ~/default.aspx.

Add a new HTML page called default.htm.

We need to reference the jQuery libraries before we can use them, so either drag the jQuery script file from the Solution Explorer to the code window or add the following to the header element of your page (this line will change depending on the jQuery version you are using):

```
<script src="Scripts/jquery-1.3.2-vsdoc.js" type="text/javascript" ></script>
```

We will now add a couple of inline styles to help demonstrate some of jQuery's functionality. Add the following styles inside the header tag:

```
<style>

    .standardDiv
    {
        background:#cccccc;
        width:300px;
        height:200px;
    }

  .specialDiv
    {
        background:#00ff00;
        width:300px;
        height:200px;
    }

</style>
```

We will now need some HTML elements to manipulate so add the following inside the body tag:

```
<input type="button" value="Hello jQuery" onclick="javascript:hellojQuery();" />

<div id="div1" class="standardDiv">
   I am a boring grey div element
</div>

  <br />

<div id="div2" class="standardDiv">
   I am a boring grey div element
</div>

<br />

<div id="div3" class="specialDiv">
   I am a special div!
</div>
```

At the bottom of the page, add a script block containing a very simple jQuery function (you will see at a better way of wiring up this script to the click of a button shortly):

```
<script language="javascript">

    function hellojQuery() {
      $("#div1").html("hello jQuery");
    }

</script>
```

Press F5 to run your application and click the Hello jQuery button; the text of the first div should change to "hello jQuery".

How Does It All Work?

Probably the only weird looking bit of code is this line:

```
$("#div1").html("hello jQuery");
```

Let's dissect it:

- The $ sign is an alias that tells the browser to use the jQuery namespace. You could instead replace it with jQuery("#div1") if you want, but that would involve more typing, so don't be silly.

- The text "#div1" tells jQuery to select all elements with an ID of div1. jQuery will return a wrapped set of all elements matching the selector. Note that even if your selector returns just one element, you will be working with a wrapped set. jQuery also allows you to utilize CSS type selectors and adds a few of its own that you will look at shortly.

- The .html() function is jQuery's version of the innerHTML property and it applies the change to all elements in the returned set.

USING .HTML()

Warning: note the difference when using .html() and .innerHTML:

```
.html("hello jQuery")
.innerHTML="hello jQuery"
```

Selecting Elements

jQuery's strength is the ease with which you can select and manipulate elements on the page. We have used a selector method already to select all div elements that have an ID of div1:

```
$("#div1").html("hello jQuery");
```

jQuery supports many different ways to select an element or elements that should meet all but the most awkward requirements. Table 12-1 lists examples of other selection methods you might want to use.

Table 12-1. *Example selection methods*

Selector	Selected
$("#div1")	Select a div with ID of div1.
$("div")	Select all divs.
$("div.standardDiv")	Select all divs with a class of standardDiv.
$(".standardDiv")	Select all elements with a class of standardDiv.
$("#div4 #div5")	Select a div with ID of div5 nested inside a div with id of div4.
$(".standardDiv")[0].innerHTML= "hello jQuery";	Select the first element of a group of divs with class of standardDiv and set innerHTML property to "hello jQuery". Note that the use of traditional properties and jQuery selectors is sometimes possible.

CSS Selectors

In addition to the previous standard selectors, more modern selectors are also available (browser support may differ, but you are probably safe with IE 7+ and Firefox 3+):

Table 12-2. *CSS Selectors*

Selector	Selected
$("div:first")	First div
$("div:last")	Last div
$("div:even")	Even-numbered divs
$("div:odd")	Odd-numbered divs
$("div:first-child")	First child element
$("div:last-child")	Last child element
$("div:nth-child(3)")	Third child element
$("a[href^=http://]")	Any hyperlink starting with the text http://

Selector	Selected
$("a[href$=.zip /]")	Any hyperlink ending with .zip
$("a[href*=Microsoft")	Any hyperlink with the text Microsoft in it
$("input[type=button]")[0].innerText="hello jquery2"	Selects first input element of type button and changes innerText property to "hello jquery2"
$(":checked")	Gets all check boxes that are checked
$(":disabled")	All disabled elements
$(":enabled")	All enabled elements

jQuery Selectors

jQuery also has provides some inbuilt selectors of its own:

Table 12-3. *jQuery selectors*

Selector	Effect
$(":button")[0].innerText="hello jquery2";	Change innerText property of first button element
$(":contains(alex)")	All elements containing text alex
$(":hidden")	All hidden elements
$(":selected")	All selected elements
$(":visible")	All visible elements
$("div:not(.standardDiv)")	Select all div elements that do not have a class of standardDiv

Working with Sets

So you have used one of the preceding selector methods and now have a collection of matching elements. How can you work with them? jQuery has a number of different methods to work with collections.

Table 12-4. *Different ways to manipulate sets.*

Example	Meaning
$("div").get(0)	Get first element in set
$("div")[0]	Get first element in set
$("div").get()	Gets all elements in set
$("div").size()	Gets size of set

.each() method

The .each() method works similar to the foreach statement in C# or Visual Basic and allows you to iterate through a set of elements. The following example iterates through a set of divs, modifying the innerHTML property on each element.

```
function showDivNumber()
{
    $("div").each(function(index) {
        this.innerHTML = "I am div number " + index;
    });
}
```

Of course if you just wanted to set the same text to each div element you could apply the change to the wrapped set as follows:

$("div").html("I am a div");

Working with Attribute Values and CSS

jQuery provides methods to read, set and remove attributes on page elements.

Table 12-5. *Examples of working with attributes*

Example	Meaning
alert($("#div1").attr("id"));	Retrieving id attribute from div
$("#div1").attr("title", "hello");	Sets the title attribute to "hello"
$("#div1").removeAttr("title")	Removes title attribute
$("#div1").addClass("specialDiv");	Adds specialDiv CSS class to element

Writing Elements Dynamically

jQuery allows you to easily insert elements on a page. The following code appends a p tag to the div with id of div1:

```
<script>$("<p>hello I am dynamically added text</p>").appendTo("#div1")</script>
```

You can also insert an element after the target element with the .insertAfter() method:

```
<script>$("<p>hello I am dynamic text</p>").insertAfter("body")</script>
```

Remember that adding elements dynamically works slightly differently in IE than Firefox. While researching this chapter, I was playing around with the following script:

```
<script>$("<p>hello I am dynamic text</p>").appendTo("body")</script>
```

This works fine in Firefox but will give you a strange error when run in IE 7 (see Figure 12-3). Can you guess why?

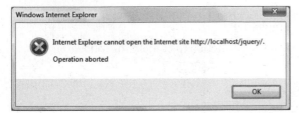

Figure 12-3. *Internet explorer error*

Why does this work fine in Firefox and not IE? Well it is quite simple really; the problem is that the document was not fully rendered yet, so the script couldn't find the element when it ran. This is a common problem with JavaScript. So how can we specify that a script should run only when the document is fully loaded?

Running a Script on Page Load

One solution to the previous problem is to run the script inside the window.onload() function, but the script will not be run until the entire page including images is loaded.

jQuery offers a neat solution with the ready event:

```
$(document).ready(function() {
    $("<p>hello I am dynamic text</p>").appendTo("body");
});
```

This is a good way to ensure that the page is loaded before the script and will resolve the earlier issue. You must ensure that you have added any elements to the page before running code that manipulates them.

Adding Functions

A common problem many designers and developers encounter is the separation of design from code. Many developers (in fact, I got you to do this in the very first example) if asked to call a JavaScript function when a button is clicked will write something such as this:

```
<input id="cmdTest" type="button" value="Hello jQuery"
       onclick="javascript:hellojQuery();" />
```

However this is not the best way because it is very vulnerable to polo neck, snowboarding designer corruption and isn't standards compliant.

jQuery offers a neat solution with the .bind() method. The following code binds the hellojQuery() function to the click of the cmdTest button:

```
$("#cmdTest").bind('click', hellojQuery());''
```

Animation/Effects

Many people become aware of jQuery through seeing one of its many impressive graphical effects. Let's check out the fadeOut effect using our original example.

1. Go back to default.htm and change the helloJQuery() function to contain the following:

   ```
   $("#div1").fadeOut();
   ```

2. Press F5 to run your application,

3. Click the Hello jQuery button,

4. The div should then fade out of view.

Effect Overloads

Most of the effects in jQuery are overloaded, allowing fine-grained control (see Table 12-6).

Table 12-6. *Different overloads of fadeOut method*

Example	Meaning
`$("#div1").fadeOut();`	Basic effect with default options
`$("#div1").fadeOut(10000);`	Effect time specified in milliseconds
`$("#div1").fadeOut('slow');`	Specifies the time the effect will take to run: slow, normal, or fast

You can also specify a callback function to be executed when the effect has completed:

```
function hellojQuery()
{
    $("#div1").fadeOut('slow',funtionToCall);
}

Function functionToCall()
{
…
}
```

Core Library Effects

Table 12-7 lists jQueries core effects.

Table 12-7. *Core libary effects*

Example	Meaning
`$("#div1").hide();`	Hides element.
`$("#div1").show();`	Shows element.
`$("#div1").fadeOut();`	Fades out element.
`$("#div1").fadeIn();`	Fades in element.
`$("#div1").toggle();`	Toggles display of element. If it is hidden, it will become visible. If it is visible, it will be hidden.
`$("#div1").slideDown();`	Animates element to become visible like a vertical blind sliding down.
`$("#div1").slideUp();`	Animates element to become hidden like a vertical blind sliding up.
`$("#div1").animate({`	Powerful function that animates an element to specified CSS property values over time span in milliseconds specified.

`width: "100%",`
`fontSize: "100px"`
`}, 1500 );`
`$("#div1").stop();`
	Stops any animation or effects in progress.

Additional Effects

In addition to the previous effects, a number of additional effects can be downloaded: fold, pulsate, puff, bounce, and explode (my personal favorite). For more details on these effects please go to `http://docs.jquery.com/UI/Effects`.

Glimmer

If you don't want to hand-code your jQuery effects, you can use a great tool called Glimmer produced by Microsoft that offers a wizard-based approach (see Figure 12-4). Refer to `http://visitmix.com/lab/glimmer`.

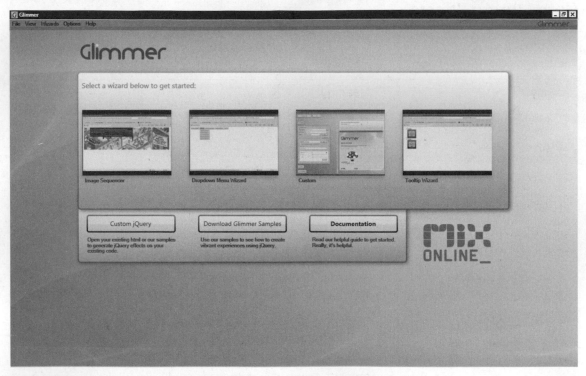

Figure 12-4. *Glimmer allows you to easily construct jQuery effects*

Glimmer allows the construction of simple effects such as rotating images, drop-down menus, and animation.

jQuery Tools

jQueryPad ((`http://www.paulstovell.com/jquerypad`) and `http://jsbin.com/` can be very useful tools for prototyping and playing with jQuery.

Chaining Events

The real power of jQuery comes from its capability to chain functions together. Imagine that we wanted to fade our div in and out a number of times. This procedure can be easily accomplished with the following code:

```
$("#div1").fadeOut().fadeIn().fadeOut().fadeIn().fadeOut();
```

Customizing jQuery

You can add your own functions to the jQuery library. For example, to create a simple function that will pop up an alert box, you can do so with the following code:

```
//don't use $ alias in case user overrides it
jQuery.fn.say = function (message) {
    alert("jQuery says " + message);

    return this;
}
```

You can then call the new function with the following code:

```
$.fn.say("hello").say("good bye");
```

And there is, of course, no reason why you couldn't write a new effects function and use it as part of a chain of effects.

For more information, please refer to http://docs.jquery.com/Plugins/Authoring.

AJAX Methods

It is very common for performance optimization to need to retrieve data or code from an external source after a page is loaded. jQuery makes this very easy.

Load and Run JavaScript File

The following code loads an external JavaScript file called test.js and then executes it:

```
$.ajax({
    type: "GET",
    url: "test.js",
    dataType: "script"
});
```

The test.js file consists of just the following line:

```
alert('hello');
```

Submitting Data

You often need to submit data to another web page. This can easily be done with the following code:

```
$.ajax({
    type: "POST",
    url: "myForm.aspx",
    data: "firstname=Alex&lastname=Mackey",
    success:
    function() {
        alert("form submitted");
    }
});
```

You will use this functionality in the ASP.NET MVC example (see Chapter 13) to submit your form data:

```
//Submit client side
$.ajax({
    type:
    "POST",
    dataType: "json",
    url: "Edit",
    data: { Description: InputDescription, Length: InputLength,
            DateShowing: InputDateShowing },
    success: function(result) {
        alert(result.Message +  " adding film at " + result.DateShowing);
    },
    error: function(error) {
        alert('error ');
    }
});
```

Getting the Latest Version of a Page

We can retrieve the contents of a page in the same domain as the calling page with a few lines of code. This could be useful in AJAX scenarios in which you want to load content behind the scenes:

```
$.ajax({
    url: "default2.aspx",
    cache: false,
    success: function(returnHtml) {
        $("#div1").append(returnHtml);
    }
});
```

Retrieving a JSON Object

JSON is a compact format for representing data. jQuery contains support for working with JSON objects. We will first create a page called default2.aspx that will return a JSON-formatted string (you will soon look at a better way of doing this).

1. Right-click your solution and add a new page called default2.aspx and select the place code in a seperate file option.

2. Remove all the code on default2.aspx except for the page declaration.

3. Add the following code to default2.aspx.cs:

```
protected void Page_Load(object sender, EventArgs e)
{
    Response.Buffer = true;
    Response.Clear();
    Response.ContentType = "application/json";
    Response.Write("{firstName: \"Alex\",lastName: \"Mackey\"}");
}
```

4. Open default.htm and alter the helloJQuery() function to the following (note that we pass a URL to which we send the query and then a function to be called when the query is completed):

```
$.getJSON("default2.aspx",
    function (data) {
        alert(data.firstName);
    }
);
```

5. Press F5 to run the project.

6. Click the Hello jQuery button.

You should see an alert box displaying "Alex" (the firstName property from the JSON object).

A Better Way

Visual Studio 2008 (and later) offers a better way:

1. Create a new page called default3.aspx and then open default3.aspx.cs.

2. Add the following using statement:

```
using System.Web.Services;
```

3. Add the following class to represent our returned object:

```
public class Person
{
    public string firstName {get; set;}
    public string lastName { get; set; }
}
```

4. Now add a new method to your page marked with the [WebMethod] attribute to expose it to the client script:

```
[WebMethod]
public static Person GetFirstname()
{
    Person p = new Person();
    p.firstName = "Alex";
    p.lastName = "Mackey";

    return p;
}
```

5. Now amend the existing jQuery code to the following:

```
$.ajax({
    type: "POST",
    url: "Default3.aspx/GetFirstname",
    data: "{}",
    contentType: "application/json",
    dataType: "json",
    success: function (input) {
        alert(input.d.firstName);
    }
});
```

Much easier—and safer. Note that we had to access the d property in order to access the firstName property. This is to prevent the execution of the returned string as a script. For more information, please refer to: http://encosia.com/2009/02/10/a-breaking-change-between-versions-of-aspnet-ajax/.

Utility Methods

Browser detection is notoriously unreliable, but jQuery provides a number of methods to assist you with detecting the capabilities of your visitors' browsers. For example, the following code will return true or false depending on whether the browser supports the box rendering model:

```
alert($.support.boxModel);
```

For the full list of functionality you can query, please see http://docs.jquery.com/Utilities/jQuery.support.

jQuery Additions

In addition to the core jQuery functionality, a number of additional jQuery libraries and add-ons exist that you might find useful. Note some of these are not produced by the core jQuery team but are excellent nevertheless:

*   Drag and drop elements (http://docs.jquery.com/UI/Draggable)

*   Sorting (http://docs.jquery.com/UI/Sortable)

*   Selecting (http://docs.jquery.com/UI/Selectable)

- Resizing (http://docs.jquery.com/UI/Resizable)

- jqgrid (http://www.trirand.com/blog/)

jQuery also provides a number of UI elements (called widgets) that you might want to utilize:

- Accordian

- Data picker

- Dialog

- Progress bar

- Slider

- Tabs

For more information, please refer to http://docs.jquery.com/Main_Page.

Summary

It is fantastic to see Microsoft not reinventing the wheel and choosing to integrate and provide support for jQuery. jQuery is a lightweight framework, and you would be crazy not to use it in your own projects.

Further Reading

- http://jquery.com/

- http://github.com/jquery/jquery

- http://weblogs.asp.net/scottgu/archive/2009/09/15/announcing-the-microsoft-ajax-cdn.aspx

- http://www.andy-gibson.co.uk/

- http://encosia.com/

For a more in-depth read on jQuery functions, I don't think you can do much better than *jQuery in Action* by Bear Bibeault and Yehuda Katz, published by Manning.

CHAPTER 13

ASP.NET MVC

Availability: Framework: 3.5sp1 Onward

ASP.NET MVC is Microsoft's implementation of a tried and tested architectural pattern. MVC separates out an application's user interface, logic, and data, and makes it easier to test, extend, and maintain. MVC stands for Model, View, Controller. If you were to map these terms to a traditional ASP.NET/database application (and they don't map exactly) you might consider the following:

- **Model** would be the database.

- **View** would be the pages and controls.

- **Controller** would manage the interaction between the pages/controls (view) and the database (model).

So is MVC a replacement for web forms that you know and mostly love? Although some people will argue that ASP.NET MVC will replace the web forms model, I don't think this is true or is Microsoft's intention. Both web forms and MVC have their own advantages and, judging by the enhancements made to ASP.NET in this release, web forms are still going to be around for the foreseeable future. So at the moment MVC is *another way* not *the* way of creating web applications on the Microsoft .NET platform.

I would argue that ASP.NET MVC is a bad choice for some types of applications. If you are designing an application with a rich and complex user interface, development with web forms is much easier with inbuilt handling of state and events. Of course, you could develop such an application with ASP.NET MVC, but I expect it would take longer.

MVC History

The MVC design pattern has been around since 1979 when it was first described by Trygve Reenskaug, who was working on a language called Smalltalk at Xerox. Trygve called his idea "Thing Model View Editor," which I think we can all agree really wasn't as catchy as MVC. Although Trygve's vision was quite different from ASP.NET's implementation of MVC, most people agree that Trygve's vision kicked everything off. You can read Trygve's original idea at: `http://folk.uio.no/trygver/1979/mvc-1/1979-05-MVC.pdf`.

So Why MVC?

MVC is about dividing up your applications. This separation of concerns has a number of advantages:

- *Division/testability*: Traditionally, ASP.NET web applications were difficult to test because ASPX and ASCX controls often end up containing code related to user interface and business logic. In ASP.NET, MVC classes called *controllers* manage the interaction between the UI and data (model). This separation also makes it much easier to write tests for your application. You can test controller classes directly instead of having to create complex ways of simulating ASP.NET's UI.

- *Flexibility*: Because all the layers are decoupled, it should be easy to swap out any individual layer without affecting the others. The ASP.NET MVC framework itself is very flexible and allows customization of many components. Perhaps you want to change your UI/view or use a different database?

- *Maintainability*: Although ASP.NET MVC is inherently customizable, it enforces a project to be constructed in a specific way and can help keep an application's code tidy. Additionally, because the project structure is relatively rigid, new developers arriving on the team should be able to quickly understand its architecture.

MVC is a lean mean fighting machine; it doesn't contain much ASP.NET functionality. This makes it quick (no parsing or sending of viewstate info) and also means no interference with rendered HTML. This makes MVC a great choice for high-volume web sites or where complete control over rendered HTML is vital.

An Existing MVC application

I think it is useful to start by looking at what a popular application built using MVC looks like. You might be familiar with the Stack Overflow (SO) site.

SO is a popular programming web site in which users can ask programming questions to be answered by other users. Other users then answer the questions. These answers are then voted on by other users; those with the most votes (hopefully the best ones!) move to the top of the answer list.

Let's take a look at SO now:

1. Open up a browser and go to http://www.stackoverflow.com.

2. Take a look around the site, paying particular attention to the URL of each page.

3. Imagine that you were creating an application similar to SO but were writing it using web forms. How might you construct it?

At a very simple level in a traditional ASP.NET application, you would probably have two pages: one to list all the questions users have asked and another page to display the actual question and answers.

From the question list page, you would then pass a question ID in the query string through to the detail page and retrieve the relevant answers. For example when a user clicks on a question the URL might look something like `http://www.stackoverflow.com/questionDetail.aspx?id=3434`.

Now click any question in SO and take a look at the URL. You will see something similar to `http://stackoverflow.com/questions/294017/visual-studio-2005-freezes`.

This URL is superior to the query string version for a number of reasons:

- Search engines index it better than a query string version. At the time of writing, Google seems to give a higher precedence to pages with the search term in the URL.

- It's more readable to humans. If you had a product site it's a lot easier for users to remember an address like `http://www.microsoft.com/vs2010/` than `http://www.microsoft.com/product/productDetail.aspx?id=4563432234`.

- The URL can assist other developers integrating with your application to understand how it works. For example, if you examine the question detail page (as shown in Figure 13-1), you will see the answer posts to `/questions/740316/answer`. You can probably figure out that 740316 is an ID for the question, and it wouldn't be too tricky to develop an addition to post answers.

Figure 13-1. *Stack Overflow web site—an example of an ASP.NET MVC application*

This facility is called *routing* and although it isn't specific to ASP.NET MVC, it is an important concept.

■**TIP** Routing is available in ASP.NET 4.0 and net 3.5sp1 (see Chapter 10 for more details), so don't think you have to use ASP.NET MVC to take advantage of this.

ASP.NET MVC uses the requested URL to decide how to route users' requests to a special class called a controller that in turn interacts with your applications model.

Before you get started with creating a simple application, you should also be aware of the following:

- MVC has no Viewstate.

- Type initialization syntax.

What a State

ASP.NET MVC does not use viewstate. Viewstate is used in ASP.NET WebForm applications to maintain the state of controls such as the item that is selected in a drop-down menu between page posts.

By default in ASP.NET, all controls have viewstate, which can bloat pages and slow an application down. Viewstate is often unnecessary; by removing it you can reduce page size and increase the speed of the application because the web server no longer has to parse it and load control state.

Partly due to the lack of viewstate (and because it is kind of missing the point of ASP.NET MVC), you probably should not be using standard ASP.NET controls such as <asp:hyperlink /> in your MVC application. That's not to say these controls and tags will not work (although many such as DataGrid might give you issues), but it is not keeping with the clean ASP.NET MVC way of doing things, so don't do it! As you will see later in the chapter, ASP.NET MVC offers many ways of writing HTML.

As you can imagine, the lack of view state can be problematic—after all, ASP.NET's developers did not add it without reason! Imagine, for example, creating a new data paging, orderable data grid control without viewstate and you can see that ASP.NET MVC also has the potential to complicate your life!

Type Initialization

ASP.NET MVC makes frequent use of type initializers, a feature added in C# version 3. Following is an example of this syntax:

```
public class person
{
    public string FirstName{get;set;}
    public string LastName{get;set;}
}

person Alex=new person{FirstName="Alex", LastName="Mackey"};
```

This is just a shorthand way to instantiate an object and set properties. In ASP.NET MVC, you will find this syntax frequently used when working with the HtmlHelper classes. For example, the following code generates a text box called LastName, bound to the LastName property of the model, and sizes the text box to 50 pixels.

```
<%= Html.TextBox("LastName", Model.LastName, new {@class="textbox", size=50} )%>
```

■**NOTE** Note the use of the @ sign as an escape character next to class to set the class property. The @ sign is used as an escape character because class is obviously a keyword in .NET.

Installing MVC

Visual Studio 2010 has ASP.NET MVC 2 functionality included out of the box but Visual Studio 2008 users can download it as a separate install from: http://www.asp.net/mvc/download/.

When you want to deploy your application, the method will differ depending on whether you are installing to IIS 6 or IIS 7. For instructions on installing MVC please refer to http://www.asp.net/learn/mvc/tutorial-08-cs.aspx.

Creating the MVC Application

In the example, you will create an MVC site for Bob who owns a movie theatre. Bob has a movie theatre imaginatively called "Bob's Movie Theatre". Bob's movie site will display lists of films, a detail page for each film, and also the skeleton of an administration interface.

1. In Visual Studio, select File➤New Project.
2. Expand the C# node, and click Web.
3. Choose ASP.NET MVC 2 Web Application. Give the project the name Chapter13.BobsMoviesMVC and click OK.
4. Visual Studio will ask you if you want create a unit test project; click Yes.
5. Visual Studio will now create your ASP.NET MVC project.

Project Structure

Visual Studio has divided the project up into a number of directories (see Figure 13-2):

- Content
- Controllers
- Models
- Scripts
- Views
- Shared (nested inside views)

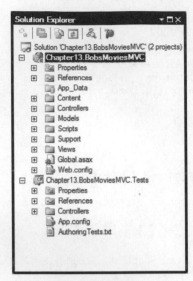

Figure 13-2. *MVC project structure*

When your application gets bigger, you might want to separate your model and controllers into another project, but you will keep with this structure in the example.

Take a look through the directories:

- The Content directory contains any non code files such as images and CSS.

- The Controllers directory contains all the classes that are managing the interaction between the view and model.

- The Models directory contains classes that interact with the underlying database. Models can be created in a number of different ways, and there is no one answer for what constitutes a model. For example, the Models directory might contain items such as LinqToSQL, EF, NHhibernate, classes, and so on. In a real world project you would probably want your model to be in a different project to facilitate reuse etc.

- The Scripts directory includes commonly used JavaScript libraries (ASP.NET AJAX and jQuery). As you will see, ASP.NET MVC works very well with JavaScript.

- The Views directory is where the UI is contained. Within the directory is a shared directory that contains the master page file for laying out your application.

Changing the Layout of MVC Pages

The default ASP.NET MVC project contains a master page at: `~/Views/Shared/Site.Master`

In this chapter, you will use the jQuery libraries, so let's add a reference to it in the master page. Add the following in the header tag:

```
<script type="text/javascript" src="../../Scripts/jquery-1.3.2.js">
</script>
```

You won't win any design awards with this, so you might be interested in the gallery of free MVC design templates at `http://www.asp.net/MVC/Gallery/default.aspx?supportsjs=true`.

Creating the Model

Bob's business revolves around films, so you will need a way of storing this data. In the example, you will utilize EF because it is very easy to get up and running. Please refer to chapter 8 for further details of Entity Framework.

First, you have to connect to sample data:

1. In Visual Studio, select View➤Server Explorer.

2. On the Data Connections node, right-click and select Add Connection.

3. Select Microsoft SQL Server when Visual Studio asks you to choose a data source.

4. Enter the connection details to where you restored/created the example database.

5. Click OK.

Creating EF Entities

Now that you have a database connection, you need to create the EF classes:

1. Right-click the Models directory and select Add New Item.

2. Select ADO.NET entity data model (under the Data tab) and call the file `BobsMovies.edmx`.

3. Select Generate from database.

4. Select the connection you created earlier or enter new connection details.

5. Check the Tables box to add all the tables to the application.

6. Set the model namespace as `Chapter13.BobsMoviesMVC.Model`.

7. Open `BobsMovies.designer.cs`.

8. By default, Visual Studio will generate a context class with the same name as the example database. Expand the region where it says `Contexts` and rename the existing context class and its constructors to `TheatreEntities`.

Repository Pattern

When you query the model, you are using EF, which accesses the database. This can pose an issue if you want to write unit tests because you have to ensure that the database is set up the same each time. Querying a database can also slow down large unit tests. An alternative is to use a repository pattern. For more information, please refer to `http://martinfowler.com/eaaCatalog/repository.html`. The repository pattern allows you to use a technique called *dependecy injection* that allows you to give it a different mechanism to retrieve data.

■**NOTE** For more information on patterns I highly recommend the very readable *Head First Design Patterns* by Eric and Elisabeth Freeman et al., published by O'Reilly.

Let's see this in action.

1. Right-click the Models folder and select Add New Item➤Class. Call the class IFilmRepository and enter the following code:

```
namespace Chapter13.BobsMoviesMVC.Models
{
    public interface IFilmRepository
    {
        bool Add(Film film);
        void Delete(int ID);
        IEnumerable<Film> GetAll();
        Film GetFilm(int ID);
        void Save();
        bool Update(Film film);
    }

}
```

2. Add another class called FilmRepository and add the following code:

```
using System;
using System.Collections.Generic;
using System.Linq;
using System.Web;

namespace Chapter13.BobsMoviesMVC.Models
{
    public class FilmRepository : BobsMoviesMVC.Models.IFilmRepository
    {
        private BobsMoviesMVC.Models.TheatreEntities dbContext =
            new BobsMoviesMVC.Models.TheatreEntities();

        public IEnumerable<Film> GetAll()
        {
            return dbContext.Films;

        }

        public Film GetFilm(int ID)
        {
            return dbContext.Films.Single(f => f.FilmID == ID);
        }


        public bool Add(Film film)
        {
            if (film.GetErrors().Count == 0)
            {
```

```
            dbContext.Films.AddObject(film);
            Save();
            return true;
        }
        else
        {
            return false;
        }

    }

    public bool Update(Film film)
    {
        if (film.GetErrors().Count == 0)
        {
            var ExistingFilm =
              dbContext.Films.Single(f => f.FilmID == film.FilmID);
            ExistingFilm.Title = film.Title;
            ExistingFilm.Description = film.Description;
            ExistingFilm.Length = film.Length;

            Save();
            return true;
        }
        else
        {
            return false;
        }
    }

    public void Delete(int ID)
    {
        dbContext.Films.DeleteObject(dbContext.Films.Single(f => f.FilmID == ID));
        Save();
    }

    public void Save()
    {
        dbContext.SaveChanges();
    }
    }
}
```

Note this code will not work until we create our GetErrors() method so let's get onto that now.

Creating Validation for Data Model

Usually you will want to validate data before saving it back to the database (or you should). In this simple example, you will want to ensure that film entries have a title before inserting them into the database.

One method of creating validation rules, as suggested in Wrox's *Professional ASP.NET MVC*, is using partial classes (an excellent ASP.NET MVC introduction). You will utilize a very similar method to that suggested in the book as it is easy to understand and very effective.

1. Right-click Models directory, select Add New Item➤Class, and call it Error.cs.

2. Enter the following code:

```
public class Error
{
    public string Description { get; set; }
    public string Property { get; set; }
}
```

3. You now want to utilize this in the Film class. Right-click Models directory, select Add New Item➤Class, and call it Film.cs.

4. Enter the following code:

```
using System;
using System.Collections.Generic;
using System.Linq;
using System.Web;

namespace Chapter13.BobsMoviesMVC.Models
{
    public partial class Film
    {
        public bool IsValid()
        {
            if (this.GetErrors().Count == 0)
            {
                return true;
            }
            else
            {
                return false;
            }
        }

        public List<Error> GetErrors()
        {
            List<Error> Errors = new List<Error>();

            if (String.IsNullOrEmpty(this.Title)) {
                Errors.Add(
                  new Error { Description = "Title cannot be blank", Property = "Title"
});
            }
            return Errors;
        }
    }
}
```

Creating a Controller

You have now completed the model that you will utilize shortly, so let's create a simple view.
You first need to create a controller class for the application to handle incoming users' requests.

5.   Right-click the Controllers directory and add a controller. Call the controller `FilmController`.

■**WARNING** Naming is very important in MVC because it is used to infer where to send requests. It is important you enter the names *exactly* as specified.

---

6.   Make sure that the option to create action methods for create, update, and delete scenarios is unchecked (you will create them in this example, but this is a useful option to quickly put an application together). Click Add.

7.   Replace the method Index with the following code:

```
public ActionResult Index()
{
    ViewData["Message"] = "Hello and welcome to MVC!";
    return View();
}
```

Adding a View

1.   Let's add a View now.

2.   In the Views folder, add a new folder called Film.

3.   Right-click the ~/Views/Film directory you just created and select Add➤View.

4.   Name the View Index. Make sure that the option to select a master page is selected. This will create the view at ~/Views/Film/Index.aspx.

5.   Replace the content tag with ID Content2 with the following code:

```
<asp:Content ID="Content2" ContentPlaceHolderID="MainContent" runat="server">
  <%= ViewData["message"] %>
</asp:Content>
```

6.   You will now modify this page to make navigation around the example easier. Open the view file ~/Views/Home/Index.aspx.

7.   Replace the content tag with the following code:

```
<asp:Content ID="indexContent" ContentPlaceHolderID="MainContent" runat="server">
  <%= TempData["Message"] %>

    <a href="Film">Example 1 - Hello MVC</a> <br />
    <a href="Film/All">Example 2 - All Films</a> <br />
    <a href="Film/Detail/1">Example 3 - Film Detail</a> <br />
    <a href="Film/Edit/1">Example 4 -  Edit Strongly Typed</a> <br />
    <a href="Film/EditJSON/1">Example 5 - Edit using JSON</a> <br />

</asp:Content>
```

■**NOTE** You will look at other ways to create HTML shortly.

Running the application

Press F5 to run the application and accept the option to modify web.config to Allow Debugging. The home page will open with all the links on it. Click the link labelled Example 1—Hello MVC. You should be taken to a page with the message "Hello and welcome to MVC!" (see Figure 13-3).

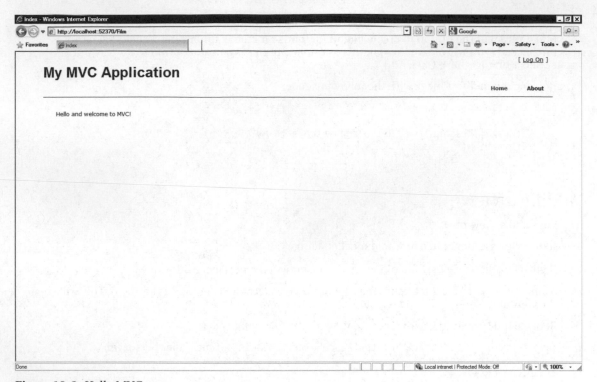

Figure 13-3. *Hello MVC page*

Exciting stuff (okay, not really). Let's recap what you did here:

- You defined a Film controller that would handle requests to URL's containing Film.

- Inside the controller you created an action called Index to be called when the user enters a URL such as ~/Film/ or ~/Film/Index.

- Inside the Index action, you set the ViewData Message property to "Hello MVC!".

- When the user requested a URL containing Film, the request was routed to the Film controller.

- The Film controller then passed this request to method Index in FilmController.cs.

- The Index method set the ViewData Message property to "Hello and welcome to MVC!".

- This view was then displayed to the user.

300

Notice that you did not have to link the Film Controller and ~/Views/Film/Index.aspx page. ASP.NET MVC inferred this relationship because you followed a naming convention. By following this convention, you can avoid having to write additional code.

A Closer Look at Routing

Let's look at this process in more detail. Figure 13-4 shows how a request in ASP.NET MVC is processed.

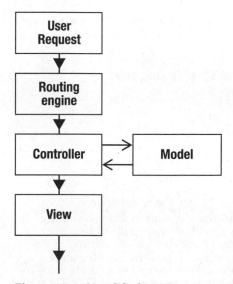

Figure 13-4. *Simplified MVC routing process*

A typical MVC URL might be something like http://www.myshop.com/Product/Detail/1. This URL would be handled as follows:

1. The request is received and sent to the ASP.NET MVC routing engine.

2. The routing engine looks at the URL and compares it with its mapping rules (you will look at these shortly, but for now know that they are defined in global.asax).

3. The default ASP.NET MVC rules say the first part of the URL indicates which controller class will deal with this request (in this case, Product).

4. The Product Controller class would then receive the request and look for a method (action in MVC terminology) named Detail.

5. The Detail action receives the (optional) parameter 1.

6. This parameter would then be used to retrieve a product from the application's model.

7. The model would then pass the individual product to the controller class, which would then return it to the view.

8. The view would then be rendered to the user.

Figure 13-5 shows how a URL is divided up and processed with MVC's default rule set:

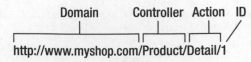

Figure 13-5. *How MVC separates URLs*

Returning Views

In the first example, you returned a view that matched the action name (Index). Views don't necessarily have to match the URL, although it is not a bad idea because it makes your intention clearer and reduces how much code you have to write.

If you wanted to return the Index view you just created when the user navigates to an arbitrary address such as ~/Film/IWillAlsoReturnIndex, you can do this with the following code:

```
public ActionResult IWillAlsoReturnIndex()
{
    ViewData["Message"] = "I am using Index view";
    return View("Index");
}
```

ViewData and TempData

So what is this ViewData thing you just used? You can think of ViewData as a place to store objects that you will use in your view. For example, you might store a Film class in ViewData and then bind to its properties. The syntax used to access items from ViewData is similar to working with ViewState.

Many developers don't like using ViewData because it is not strongly typed and involves some tedious casting operations when working with objects. My recommendation would be to avoid using it as much as possible. You will shortly look at a better way of binding data to a page.

Related to ViewData is TempData. TempData is very similar except data added to it will be saved for only one post. TempData can be useful for storing and displaying items such as error messages that you don't want to maintain between posts. TempData is another controversial area that some developers dislike because they feel it is not in keeping with MVC's ideals.

Displaying a List of Data

You will now create a page to display a list of all the films. You need to add this functionality to the controller.

1. Open the file ~/Controllers/FilmController.cs.

2. Add the following code at the top of the class to get an instance of the FilmRepository:

    ```
    BobsMoviesMVC.Models.IFilmRepository filmRepository;

    public FilmController()
    {
        filmRepository = new BobsMoviesMVC.Models.FilmRepository();
    }
    ```

3. You might think there are easier ways of doing this (and you would be right), but this sets you up nicely for testing the application. Now add the following action to retrieve a list of all the films:

```
public ActionResult All()
{
        return View(filmRepository.GetAll());
}
```

4. Right-click the ~/Views/Film directory and select Add New View. Name the view All and click OK (ASP.NET MVC does have some nice functionality to automate creation of CRUD operations such as list and edit forms, which you will look at shortly).

5. Replace the Content2 Content tag with the following code:

```
<asp:Content ID="Content2" ContentPlaceHolderID="MainContent" runat="server">

<a href="<%= "Create/" %>">Create</a>

<br /><br />

<%
    foreach (Chapter13.BobsMoviesMVC.Models.Film Film in
(IEnumerable<Chapter13.BobsMoviesMVC.Models.Film>)Model)
    {
%>

<a href="<%= "Detail/" + Film.FilmID %>">
    <%= Film.Title %>
</a>

   
  <%= Html.ActionLink("[Edit]", "Edit", new { id = Film.FilmID })%>

 

  <%= Html.ActionLink("[Edit JSON]", "EditJSON", new {id=Film.FilmID})%>

 

  <%= Html.ActionLink("[Delete]", "Delete", new {id=Film.FilmID})%>

<br />

<%
    }
%>

</asp:Content>
```

6. Press F5 to run your application.

7. Click the Example 2—All Films link. You should see a list of film hyperlinks like those shown in Figure 13-6.

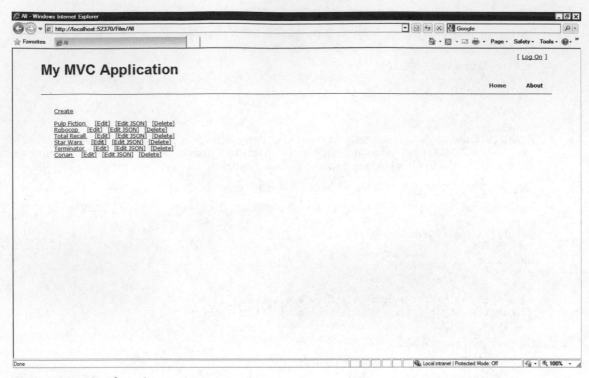

Figure 13-6. *List of movies*

Have We Gone Back to 1998?

I think you will agree that the code in this view looks a bit unpleasant when compared with ASP.NET. Readers who have worked with classic ASP are probably scratching their heads asking whether we have gone back in time. Well, personally I don't find ASP.NET MVC code as readable as ASP.NET, either, but ASP.NET MVC does give you full control over the rendered HTML. (ASP.NET 4.0 does have some improvements in this area—see Chapter 10.) ASP.NET MVC can create smaller, quicker web pages that can better meet web site standards and accessibility requirements.

In ASP.NET MVC, sometimes it is necessary to embed code as in the previous examples, but there are also HtmlHelper classes that can make writing the views more readable. Let's take a look at these next by creating a simple detail page to display more information about each movie.

Creating a Detail Page

Users of your site will probably want to know more than just the title of a film so you can create a page they can click through to display more detailed film information.

When creating views, there are two types you can create:

- Standard/looseley typed views

- Strongly typed views

You will create a loosely typed view first to show the basic concepts:

1. Right-click the ~/Views/Film/ folder and click Add View.

2. Enter the name Detail.

3. Replace the Content2 tag with the following code:

```
<asp:Content ID="Content2" ContentPlaceHolderID="MainContent" runat="server">

<%= ViewData["Title"] %> <br /> <br />

Description: <br />
<input type="text" value='<%= ViewData["Description"] %>' style='width:300px' /> <br
/>

Length: <br />
<%= Html.TextBox("Length") %> <br />

</asp:Content>
```

4. Open the Films controller and enter the following code:

```
public ActionResult Detail(int ID)
{
    Models.Film Film = filmRepository.GetFilm(ID);
    ViewData["Title"] = Film.Title;
    ViewData["Description"] = Film.Description;
    ViewData["Length"] = Film.Length.ToString();

    return View();
}
```

5. Press F5 to run the application.

6. Click the Example 3—Film Detail link. You should now see a page similar to Figure 13-7.

Let's run through again what happened when you clicked a film. The URL probably looked something like this: http://localhost:51857/Film/Detail/1.

1. Request is made by user.

2. MVC knows request is intended for the FilmController and Detail action.

3. Request sent to following method:

```
public ActionResult Detail(int ID)
```

4. The number at the end of the URL (1) was then mapped to the parameter ID in the action:

```
public ActionResult Detail(int ID)
```

5. The ActionDetail method then retrieved the film matching this ID from the model and passed it into the ViewData collection.

6. View is returned.

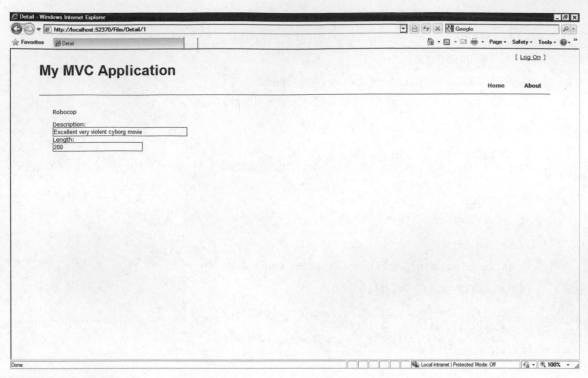

Figure 13-7. *Film detail*

Microsoft folks are no fools (most of the time) and knew that displaying an item with an ID parameter was a very common thing to do so by default. If you specify a parameter called ID in your function, it will automatically be mapped to the last value in the URL.

HtmlHelper Methods

In the last example, you used a number of different ways of constructing HTML on the page. You will now take a closer look at them.

In the ~/Film/Detail.aspx view, you used a number of different methods to render HTML elements:

- Writing into the HTML directly (which offers the greatest flexibility and allows you to construct the HTML exactly as you wish):

  ```
  <input type="text" value='<%= ViewData["Description"] %>' style='width:300px' />
  ```

- Using HtmlHelper methods:

  ```
  <%= Html.TextBox("Length") %> <br />
  ```

- You can also use HtmlHelperMethodswith property initializers:

  ```
  <%= Html.TextBox("txtDateShowing", ViewData["DateShowing"], new { Style =
  "width:300px" })%> <br />
  ```

It is your choice of which method to use, although I believe that HtmlHelper methods look a bit neater and are easier to use. A very commonly used HtmlHelper is ActionLink. ActionLink can be used to render a hyperlink, and I would argue is a bit more readable than embedding code in an href tag.

The following code will render a hyperlink labelled "All films" to the film controller ViewAll action:

```
<%= Html.ActionLink("All Films", "All", "Film") %>
```

This results in the following HTML:

```
<a href="/Film/All/>All Films</a>
```

Sometimes it is necessary to pass parameters into a link, and for this you can use the following syntax:

```
<%= Html.ActionLink("Film Detail", "Detail", new {Controller="Film", id = 1 })%>
```

This will render the following:

```
<a href="/Film/Detail/1>Film Detail</a>
```

Strongly Typed Views

The second type of view you can create is called a *strongly typed view*. Strongly typed views offer a number of advantages over standard views:

- You don't have to go through the laborious process of setting properties in ViewData. Values can instead be retrieved from ViewData.Model.

- Intellisense.

- Type safety.

- No unnecessary casting between types in ViewData.

- Compile time checks.

So why wouldn't you use strongly typed views?

Creating a Strongly Typed View

You will use a strongly typed view to create an edit page for the movies:

1. Right-click the Views/Film folder.

2. Click Add, then select View.

3. Call the view Edit.

4. Check the box that says Create a strongly-typed view, and on the drop down menu select Chapter13.BobsMoviesMVC.Models.Film.

5. In the View content drop-down menu, select the Edit option to have Visual Studio create a basic edit template for you. Click Add.

6. Open ~/Controllers/FilmController.cs.

7. Add two Edit methods (one for loading the view and one for handling the submission of data):

```
[AcceptVerbs("GET")]
public ActionResult Edit(int ID)
{
    return View(filmRepository.GetFilm(ID));
}


 [AcceptVerbs("POST")]
public ActionResult Edit(BobsMoviesMVC.Models.Film Film)
{
    if (Film.IsValid() == true)
    {
        filmRepository.Update(Film);

        return RedirectToAction("All");
    }
    else
    {
        foreach (BobsMoviesMVC.Models.Error error in Film.GetErrors())
        {
            ModelState.AddModelError(error.Property, error.Description);
        }

        return View(filmRepository.GetFilm(Film.FilmID));
    }
}
```

8. Press F5 to run the application.

9. Click the Example 4—Edit Strongly Typed link (this is hard-wired to take you to a specific film).

10. Delete the title of the film and click Submit. You should see a screen similar to Figure 13-8.

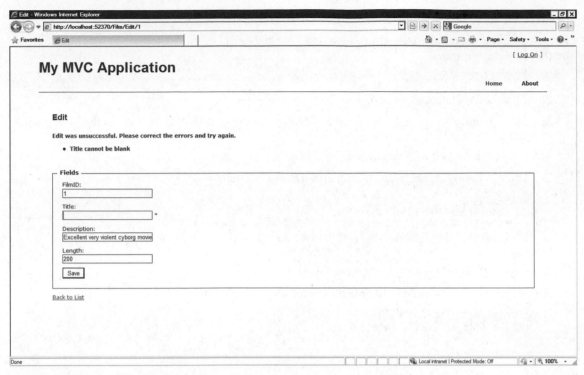

Figure 13-8. *ASP.NET MVC validation*

Note that MVC will not allow you to save a film with a blank title (because of the validation rules created earlier). Enter a new title, click Save, and note that you were redirected back to the All Films page with the updated data.

Whew, we covered a lot here:

- You created two actions with the same name that were differentiated by GET and POST attributes (covered in the next section).

- You did not allow a user to save a film with no title because you utilized the Film.IsValid method on the film class. If the film was not valid, you then displayed the returned error messages to the user by using the ModelState.AddModelError(error.Property, error.Description) method.

Because you have two Edit ActionResults, you used an attribute to tell ASP.NET MVC to use one method when the page is loaded (AcceptVerbs["GET"]) and another when the user submits data (AcceptVerbs["POST"]).

The AcceptVerbs attribute refers to the method in the HTTP protocol that is used when the browser communicates with the server. The use of the AcceptVerbs attribute can assist with making the code a bit neater, but some developers might prefer having a load and edit controller action instead.

Creating an Add New and Delete Functionality

Let's finish off the skeleton administration interface by adding the facility for users to create new movies and delete existing movies:

1. Right-click View folder.

2. Click Add➤View. Call it Create.

3. Select to create a strongly typed view and select BobsMoviesMVC.Models.Film as the View data class.

4. Select Create as the View content.

5. Open ~/Views/Film/Create.aspx. Remove the FilmID field code:

    ```
    <p>
      <label for="ID">ID:</label>
      <%= Html.TextBox("ID") %>
      <%= Html.ValidationMessage("ID", "*") %>
    </p>
    ```

6. Open ~/Controllers/Film/FilmController.cs.

7. Add the following code to handle the create and delete actions:

    ```
    [AcceptVerbs("GET")]
    public ActionResult Create()
    {
        return View();
    }

    [AcceptVerbs("POST")]
    public ActionResult Create(BobsMoviesMVC.Models.Film film)
    {
        filmRepository.Add(film);
        return RedirectToAction("All");
    }

    public ActionResult Delete(int ID)
    {
        filmRepository.Delete(ID);
        return RedirectToAction("All");
    }
    ```

■**CAUTION** In a real-life application, be very careful with creating a delete method like this. I am taking shortcuts to avoid tedious steps. It is bad practice for methods that modify data to be activated by a GET method—imagine if a search engine crawled your site and accidently deleted data!

---

8. Press F5 to run the application.

9. Click the Example 2—All Films link. You should now be able to delete movies by clicking the Delete link and create new movies by clicking the Create link.

Accepting Data from Users

In the previous example, you let ASP.NET MVC infer how to bind the submitted data back to the model. However, what if you did not want users to be able to alter all the properties of Film? For example in the previous page you exposed the ID property? There are a couple of methods to restrict this:

Specify individual properties

You can specify the individual form elements that you will accept in your controller methods (make sure that the name of the variable matches the name of the form element that is getting submitted) in your edit method. MVC will then bind these properties accordingly:

```
[AcceptVerbs("POST")]
public ActionResult Edit(string Title, string Description)
{
    return RedirectToAction("All");
}
```

Form Collection

Instead of binding to a strongly typed object, you can work with the raw form submission like this:

```
[AcceptVerbs("POST")]
public ActionResult Edit(FormCollection FormValues)
{
    String Title="" + FormValues["Title"] ;
    return RedirectToAction("All");
}
```

Bind Attributes

Bind attributes allow you to specify a white-and-black list of form elements to accept and reject. The following will only allow the Title property to be modified. ID and Description will be null if requested:

```
public ActionResult Edit(
  [Bind(Include = "Title",Exclude="ID, Description")]BobsMoviesMVC.Models.Film Film
)
```

CREATE A CUSTOM BINDER

You can also create your own binder methods to work with data. For more information on this please refer to the following:

```
http://www.hanselman.com/blog/SplittingDateTimeUnitTestingASPNETMVCCustomModelBinders.aspx
```

Attributes

You have already utilized a number of attributes such as AcceptVerbs and Bind. Attributes extend ASP.NET MVC's functionality and you can even create your own. Let's take a quick look at some important attributes.

AcceptVerbs

You have already used the AcceptVerbs attribute to distinguish between load and update methods in the Film controller.

OutputCache

OutputCache is perhaps one of the most useful attributes to reduce load on the server. If your data is changing infrequently, consider using OutputCache. The duration is specified in minutes. To use it, simply add above your action method:

```
[OutputCache(Duration = 20, VaryByParam = "None")]
public ActionResult News()
{
    return View();
}
```

Authorization

Another important attribute is Authorization. It is used in conjunction with the standaed security providers and allows you to restrict access to a function. The standard template ASP.NET MVC project shows you how to use this. To use it, simply add above your method as follows:

```
[Authorize(Roles="Admin")]
public ActionResult All()
{
    return View(filmRepository.GetAll());
}
```

ASP.NET MVC and JavaScript

ASP.NET MVC is very much set up for easy integration with popular JavaScript frameworks such as jQuery. For more information on jQuery, please refer to Chapter 12.

You will create a new edit page that utilizes the jQuery libraries to send the contents of a form to the edit controller. To do this, you will format the data as JSON. JSON stands for JavaScript Object Notation and is a very lightweight format to pass around simple classes and properties.

In the film example, a film class formatted as JSON might look something like this:

```
{ID:"1",Title:"Kung Fu Panda"}
```

JSON is very easy to construct and has the advantage that JavaScript frameworks understand JSON objects, allowing you to easily access properties with code like this:

```
alert(Film.Title);
```

JSON is also a lot less verbose than a typical SOAP request, which might look like this:

```xml
<?xml version="1.0" encoding="utf-8"?>
<soap:Envelope xmlns:xsi="http://www.w3.org/2001/XMLSchema-instance"
xmlns:xsd="http://www.w3.org/2001/XMLSchema"
xmlns:soap="http://schemas.xmlsoap.org/soap/envelope/">
  <soap:Body>
    <AddFilm xmlns="http://tempuri.org/">
      <objFilm>
        <FilmID>1</FilmID>
        <Title>Kung Fu Panda</Title>
      </objFilm>
    </AddFilm>
  </soap:Body>
</soap:Envelope>
```

Currently, JSON support in .NET is a bit limited (although expect this to be an area Microsoft develops in the future). The ASP.NET MVC framework, however, has a special action type for working with the JSON requests you will use in the next example.

Let's see how to submit a form using JQuery.

1. Right-click the Views folder and add a loosely typed view called EditJSON.

2. Replace the Content2 place holder with the following code:

```
<asp:Content ID="Content2" ContentPlaceHolderID="MainContent" runat="server">

<script>

    function submit() {

        //Get values from form
        var InputFilmID = $("#FilmID").val();
        var InputTitle = $("#Title").val();
        var InputDescription = $("#Description").val();

        //Submit client side
        $.ajax({
            type:
"POST",
            dataType: "json",
            url: "EditJSON",
```

```
                    data: { FilmID: InputFilmID, Title: InputTitle, Description:
        InputDescription },
                success: function (result) {
                    alert(result.Message + " updating film " + result.Title);
                    window.location = "../All";
                },
                error: function (error) {
                    alert('error ');
                }

            });
        }


    </script>


    <form>

    ID: <br />
    <%= Html.TextBox("FilmID")%>

    <br /> <br />

    Title: <br />
    <%= Html.TextBox("Title")%>

    <br /> <br />

    Description: <br />
    <%= Html.TextBox("Description")%>


    <br />
    </form>

    <input type="button" onclick="javascript:submit();" value="Update" />

    </asp:Content>
```

■**NOTE** The JavaScript code $("#Description").val just means retrieve the value of the element with ID Description.

---

3. Open the file ~/Controllers/FilmController.cs and add the following code:

```
[AcceptVerbs("GET")]
public ActionResult EditJSON(int ID)
{
    return View(filmRepository.GetFilm(ID));
}
```

```
    [AcceptVerbs("POST")]
    public JsonResult EditJSON(BobsMoviesMVC.Models.Film film)
    {
        filmRepository.Update(film);

        //Return a very simple JSON response
        return Json(new { Message = "Success", Title = film.Title });
    }
```

■**NOTE** The return type of this function is of type `JsonResult` instead of `ActionResult` because you are passing back a JSON object.

---

4. Click F5 to run the application.

5. Click the Example 5—Edit JSON Link. This will open the film with ID 1. (If you have already deleted this film, update the Index view.)

6. Modify some details and then click Update.

The film should now have been updated (if it hasn't, ensure that you have referenced the jQuery libraries in your master page as described in the section "Changing the layout of ASP.NET MVC pages"). Note that you passed back the `film` property in the JSON object returned. That is how easy it is to update the model using client script.

Custom Routing

By now, you should have a basic understanding of URL routing in MVC and how important it is. Routing is very flexible, and the default can be modified by changing the rules in `global.asax`. Right-click `global.asax` (it handles global events within your application) and select View Code. Your code will look similar to the following:

```
public static void RegisterRoutes(RouteCollection routes)
{
    routes.IgnoreRoute("{resource}.axd/{*pathInfo}");

    routes.MapRoute(
        "Default",                                          // Route name
        "{controller}/{action}/{id}",                       // URL with parameters
        new { controller = "Home", action = "Index", id = "" } // Parameter defaults
    );

}

protected void Application_Start()
{
    RegisterRoutes(RouteTable.Routes);
}
```

But what's this code doing? I will tackle the line routes.MapRoute first. This maps the default route the user will be sent to (in this case, ASP.NET MVC will send them to ~/home/index) if they do not enter a controller or action. Thus, if you want to alter the default view that ASP.NET MVC will serve up when the user goes to the root of your site, this is the place to do it.

The line routes.IgnoreRoute tells ASP.NET MVC to ignore any requests ending in the .axd extension, which is used by IIS to route incoming requests to HTTP modules and handlers. This is often done in order to generate something dynamically, such as a thumbnail image or chart. You don't want ASP.NET MVC to interfere with these types of requests, so this line tells ASP.NET MVC to ignore requests for any files ending in .axd.

You will want to create custom routes sooner or later. For example, in the movie theatre example it would be useful if users could access information about a popular film by going to www.bobsMovies.com/kungFuPanda/ rather than something less memorable like www.bobsMovies.com/film/detail/2.

To implement this, all you need to do is add the route with the routes.MapRoute method. Add the following route before the existing call to MapRoute:

```
routes.MapRoute(
    "PopularFilm",                                      // Route name
    "KungFuPanda",                                      // URL with parameters
    new { controller = "Film", action = "Detail", id = 1 } // Parameter defaults
);
```

This code tells MVC that if it receives a request with KungFuPanda in it (such as www.bobsMovies.com/KungFuPanda) to send it to the Film controller's Detail action passing in an ID of 1.

Check that this works by pressing F5 to run up the application. Change the URL to ~/KungFuPanda/. You should be taken to the film detail view of film ID 1 (although the URL will appear Film/KungFuPanda).

■TIP When you define routes, they are processed in the order in which they are declared. Make sure that you declare routes in order of specificity because a more general route could hide a specific route.

ASP.NET MVC and Security

In any web application, it is important not to trust user input and to limit as much as possible the areas the attacker can exploit. Validation and strong typing can assist with this. One of the biggest dangers facing any web application is cross-site scripting (XSS).

XSS occurs when an application allows a user to submit code that is then rendered un-encoded on a page. Malicious users can submit JavaScript code to an application that will then be run when a page is loaded up. Imagine if a user were to post JavaScript code on a forum that would then be run by all users viewing the page. At best, this could be annoying, but the bad code could also be performing tasks such as stealing other user's session identifiers that would allow an attacker to log in to the application. (For more information, please refer to http://www.owasp.org/index.php/XSS.)

In a traditional ASP.NET application, entering a script such as the following and submitting it would cause ASP.NET to throw an exception because the ASP.NET engine has detected potentially dangerous input*:

```
<script>alert('XSS waiting to happen');</script>
```

ASP.NET MVC will not throw an exception, so be sure any output is encoded when rendered in the browser using the `Server.HtmlEncode` method (you should be doing this in ASP.NET anyway because the detection is pretty poor):

```
<%= Server.HtmlEncode(strMyValue) %>
```

You could also use the new HTML encode syntax (see Chapter 10 for more details):

```
<%: strMyValue %>
```

■**TIP** Look into the Microsoft Anti XSS library at `http://www.codeplex.com/AntiXSS`.

Another problem that can occur with web applications is Cross-Site Request Forgery (CSRF). CSRF attacks occur by a user being authenticated to a particular site and then activating code that is constructed to perform a request on the logged-in site. For example, I could be logged into my bank account, open an e-mail that has an embedded image with a URL such as `http://www.bank.com?withdraw=10000&to=badPerson`. Because I am logged in to the site, this action would then be performed. MVC contains support for preventing these attacks by generating a secure token. For more information on this please refer to `http://blog.codeville.net/2008/09/01/prevent-cross-site-request-forgery-csrf-using-aspnet-mvcs-antiforgerytoken-helper/`.

Extending MVC

ASP.NET MVC is very easy to customize and extend. You don't like how the View engine works? No problem—you can override it. ASP.NET MVC is a framework practically begging for customization.

Extension Methods

One of the easiest ways to extend the existing ASP.NET MVC functionality is by writing extension methods on some of the `HtmlHelper` classes. For example, you might need to render a home page link to a specific page throughout your application. To accomplish this, you can create an extension method.

Let's do so now. Create a new class called `UrlHelperExtension.cs`:

```
using System;
using System.Collections.Generic;
using System.Linq;
using System.Web;
using System.Web.Mvc;
```

```
namespace Chapter13.BobsMoviesMVC.Controllers
{
    public static class UrlHelperExtension
    {

        public static string AllFilms(this UrlHelper helper)
        {
            return helper.Content("~/Film/All");
        }
    }

}
```

You can then use this as follows:

```
<a href="<%= Url.AllFilms() %>">All Films</a>
```

Filters

ASP.NET MVC allows the creation of reusable blocks of code called filters that intercept and process various types of requests. Common uses of filters include authorization and logging. For information on overriding controller classes and views, see the "Further Reading" section at the end of the chapter.

Testing

Of course, one of the biggest advantages of MVC is its testability, and no overview of ASP.NET MVC would be complete without looking at this functionality. Note that this functionality is not available in all versions of Visual Studio. An alternative is to use an open source framework such as NUnit (which is arguably much better supported and documented, anyway).

Creating a Fake Film Repository

To avoid accessing the database, you will create a fake class to return films:

1. Create a new folder in the project called Support.

2. Add a new class called FakeFilmRepository.

3. Replace the code in FakeFilmRepository.cs with the following:

    ```
    using System;
    using System.Collections.Generic;
    using System.Linq;
    using System.Web;
    using Chapter13.BobsMoviesMVC.Models;
    ```

```
namespace BobsMoviesMVC.Support
{
    public class FakeFilmRepository : IFilmRepository
    {

        public List<Film> Films = new List<Film>();

        #region IFilmRepository Members

        public bool Add(Film film)
        {
            throw new NotImplementedException();
        }

        public Film Create()
        {
            throw new NotImplementedException();
        }

        public void Delete(int ID)
        {
            throw new NotImplementedException();
        }

        public IEnumerable<Film> GetAll()
        {
            return Films;
        }

        public Film GetFilm(int FilmID)
        {
            return Films.Single(f => f.FilmID == FilmID);
        }

        public void Save()
        {
            throw new NotImplementedException();
        }

        public bool Update(Film film)
        {
            throw new NotImplementedException();
        }

        #endregion
    }
}
```

Creating a Test

When you first created the project, Visual Studio asked whether you wanted to created a test project. Hopefully, you selected Yes, so you should have two projects in your solution.

1. Open the project named Chapter13.BobsMoviesMVC.Test.

2. Right-click the Controllers folder and select Add New Item➤Class. Call it FilmControllerTest.

3. Enter the following code for the test:

```
using System;
using System.Collections.Generic;
using System.Linq;
using System.Text;
using System.Web.Mvc;
using Microsoft.VisualStudio.TestTools.UnitTesting;
using BobsMoviesMVC;
using Chapter13.BobsMoviesMVC.Controllers;
using Chapter13.BobsMoviesMVC.Models;

namespace BobsMoviesMVC.Tests.Controllers
{
    [TestClass]
    public class FilmControllerTest
    {

        [TestMethod]
        public void All_Action_Should_Return_All_View()
        {
            FilmController controller = new FilmController(GetFakeRepository());
            ViewResult result = controller.All() as ViewResult;
            Assert.IsNotNull(result);
        }

        [TestMethod]
        public void Test_To_Show_What_Failed_Test_Looks_Like()
        {
            Assert.IsTrue(1 == 2);
        }

        [TestMethod]
        public void Detail_Action_Should_Return_Specific_Film_Matching_ID()
        {

            FilmController controller = new FilmController(GetFakeRepository());
            ViewResult result = controller.Detail(1) as ViewResult;
            Assert.IsTrue(result.ViewData["title"].ToString() == "Test film");
        }

        [TestMethod]
        public void Film_Should_NotValidate_With_No_Title()
        {
            Film Film= new Film();
            Film.Title = "";
            Assert.IsTrue(Film.IsValid() == false);
        }

        private BobsMoviesMVC.Support.FakeFilmRepository GetFakeRepository()
        {
```

```
                    //Set up pretend repository
                    BobsMoviesMVC.Support.FakeFilmRepository PretendRepository =
                      new BobsMoviesMVC.Support.FakeFilmRepository();

                    //Add a film to pretend repository
                    PretendRepository.Films.Add(new Film { FilmID = 1, Title = "Test film" });

                    return PretendRepository;
                }
            }
        }
```

Modify Film Controller

You now need to tell the `Film` controller to make use of the `FakeFilmReposiory`. Open `FilmController` and add the following constructor to allow you to inject the fake repository:

```
public FilmController(BobsMoviesMVC.Models.IFilmRepository Repository)
{
    filmRepository = Repository;
}
```

Running Tests

You can run tests in a number of ways. One way is to open the test window:

1. Select Test on the main menu; then choose Windows➤Test View.

2. Select the test `Film_Should_NotValidate_With_No_Title`.

3. Right-click it and select Run selection.

    After the test has run, a dialog indicating the current status will be displayed (see Figure 13-9).

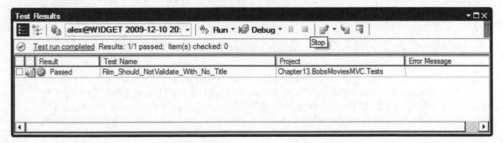

Figure 13-9. *Visual Studio test results dialog*

ASP.NET MVC V2

At the time of writing, VS2010 includes a preview of ASP.NET MVC V2, the second generation of ASP.NET MVC. Microsoft says that the final release of ASP.NET MVC 2 is expected to contain the following new features:

- Areas that allow you to group controllers and views

- New annotation attributes for validation logic

- New `Html.EditorFor` and `Html.DisplayFor` methods

ASP.NET MVC in the real world

I asked a few developers about their experiences with using the ASP.NET MVC. Below is Jeremy Skinner's (a member of the MVC contrib project) experience with developing a site for college applications using ASP.NET MVC:

> *Although we have now developed several systems with ASP.NET MVC, one of the most successful is the online application form that allows students to apply to our college via the web and then subsequently track the progress of their application. Despite being given short notice for the development of this project, we were able to implement it quickly thanks to the simplicity of the framework. The system was a resounding success and received over 1200 applications within the first 15 minutes of going live.*

> *I've been working with the ASP.NET MVC framework since its first public preview in late 2007. Since that time I've developed several intranet applications and two public facing websites with the framework. While ASP.NET MVC may not be suitable for everyone, I personally have found the framework's lightweight and stateless approach to web development a much more natural way of working than the pseudo-stateful approach used by ASP.NET Web Forms.*

> *However, using the framework so early in its development cycle had several problems. Firstly, the early previews contained a lot of breaking changes from release to release as its API evolved. This caused a lot of frustration as it constantly meant re-writing sections of our applications, but this is the price of being an early adopter. On top of this, there was initially a lack of publicly available documentation on the framework but thankfully the source code was available which made it possible to diagnose issues with relative ease.*

The MVC framework's simplicity was also somewhat of a curse—its focus on lightweight HTML-driven views (rather than the control-centric model of Web Forms) meant that the majority of existing ASP.NET controls and components were not reusable with ASP.NET MVC. However, a community quickly sprang up to address this issue and I contributed several components to the open source MvcContrib project (http://mvccontrib.org).

Despite these initial shortcomings the experience has been largely positive. The MVC framework has helped to address some of the pain points that I encountered when working with Web Forms. For example, being a practitioner of Test Driven Development, I have found the framework's focus on testability has meant that we could be easily integrate it into our development process without the need to write layers of abstraction to ease testing. In addition, the framework's relatively open nature has meant that we have been able to extend and replace areas of functionality where the default behavior has been unsuitable for our needs. I plan to continue using the MVC framework for developing web applications on the Microsoft platform going forward.

You can view the finished site at `http://www.farnborough.ac.uk/`.

Jeremy Skinner

`http://www.jeremyskinner.co.uk`

What's Next?

When you start writing real-world MVC applications you will probably find you have a number of questions about the best way to design your applications (which is somewhat ironic given that MVC stresses convention over configuration).

When dealing with design decision, it can help to bear the following ideals in mind:

- Aim for a thin controller and fat model—the controller is just responsible for interacting with the View and Model, and should never contain any logic! Okay, you haven't been that strict in this chapter, but you should because it will make your applications much easier to test.

- Consider whether your application could be easily split or load-balanced across a number of servers easily. If it can, the chances are good that your architecture is pretty clean. If, however, you are storing data in session, you might want to reconsider your approach.

- ASP.NET MVC is a framework to be built on. It allows you access to the raw metal but this comes at a price: lack of inbuilt functionality! You will want to take a look into the MVC Contrib project that adds some very useful additional functionality: `http://www.codeplex.com/MVCContrib`.

- In the example, you used dependency injection techniques. Read up on this and IOC containers such as Castle Windsor.

ASP.NET MVC Highlights

Here are some of the highlights of ASP.NET MVC:

- ASP.NET MVC's seperation of concerns eases testability.

- Complete control over rendered HTML.

- If you adhere to MVC's guidlines, you have the flexibility of being able to alter your UI, business logic, or database without affecting other layers.

- Control over your application's URL, which can aid with search engine indexability and can make your application easier to navigate (note routing functionality is available in ASP.NET 4).

- ASP.NET MVC offers better performance than ASP.NET.

- ASP.NET MVC follows the stateless nature of the Web, which can make it easier to scale out applications and for integration purposes.

- Works well with a test-driven development approach.

- Integrates well with JavaScript frameworks.

Considerations

Take the following into account before choosing ASP.NET MVC:

- ASP.NET MVC is a radically different approach to web development, so do not underestimate the time it will take developers to adapt to it. Additionally, developers will need familiarity and be able to understand some more advanced concepts such as loosely coupled applications and IOC.

- ASP.NET MVC is a framework to build upon; it will probably not contain all the functionality you require.

- ASP.NET MVC is unsuitable if your existing code makes extensive use of ViewState.

- ASP.NET can make creating custom controls much harder.

- Many third-party ASP.NET controls will not be compatible with ASP.NET MVC (note that some vendors have released ASP.NET MVC control suites already).

- ASP.NET MVC can increase application development time.

- Developers coming from a winforms background might find ASP.NET easier to similarities in event models.

- Some developers feel that ASP.NET MVC is going back to the days of ASP classic and do not like the "tag soup" that pages can become.

- ASP.NET MVC is still in its infancy, and other more mature alternatives exist. Perhaps the most popular is on the .NET platform is MonoRail (http://www.castleproject.org/monorail/ (note the similarities between ASP.NET MVC and Monorail). Another rising star is OpenRasta (http://www.openrasta.com), which is "an MVC framework with a focus on REST."

- People get really religious about ASP.NET versus MVC approaches!

Summary

Developers seem to either love or hate MVC. Both MVC and ASP.NET have a number of advantages for different scenarios. Learn when each is appropriate.

Further Reading

A number of links and books to further explore MVC include the following:

- *Pro ASP.NET MVC Framework*, by Steven Sanderson (Apress). A great in depth look at ASP.NET MVC utilizing Castle suite and delves deep. Also take a look at the author's site at http://blog.codeville.net/.

- *Professional ASP.NET MVC* by Scott Hanselman (Wrox). This is a very readable introduction to ASP.NET MVC that I very much enjoyed. Advanced users might find this book doesn't delve deep enough, however, and be better served by Steven Sanderson's book.

- `http://haacked.com/`. Phil Haack is a program manager at Microsoft, currently working on ASP.NET MVC framework. He often posts ASP.NET MVC–related articles.

- `http://folk.uio.no/trygver/1979/mvc-1/1979-05-MVC.pdf`. Original document that lead to MVC.

■ ■ ■

Silverlight Introduction

Availability: Framework 3.5sp1 Onward

> *"Silverlight is a new web presentation technology that is created to run on a variety of platforms. It enables the creation of rich, visually stunning and interactive experiences that can run everywhere: within browsers and on multiple devices and desktop operating systems (such as the Apple Mac)."*

http://silverlight.net/content/GetStarted.aspx

Some might say that Silverlight is Microsoft's version of Adobe's Flash and Flex products. This doesn't really do it justice, though. Silverlight has a number of compelling features that make it an ideal choice for creating web applications with the functionality traditionally only found in desktop applications. These applications are known as Rich Internet Applications (or RIA to its friends).

Silverlight offers the following:

- Ability to use the .NET development tools you know and love

- Utilize *many* of the .NET framework libraries in your applications (for security reasons, not everything is available)

- An easy-ish path to convert web applications to desktop (WPF) applications if required in the future (also check out Silverlight 3's offline capabilities in Chapter 15)

- Great media-streaming capabilities

- Support for designers (more prevalent in Blend)

Although Silverlight was available for earlier versions of .NET and Visual Studio, I decided to include a brief introduction because Silverlight was released between VS2008 and VS2010, and I suspect that many developers are not aware of how easy it is to use. I believe Silverlight will grow in importance and is something that all .NET developers should at least be aware of.

Silverlight versus Flash

When Silverlight was first released, it was inevitable that it would be compared to Adobe Flash (and Flex) due to its similar function. Although there is overlap between the two products, I don't think Microsoft's primary intention was to just launch a competing product.

Silverlight's development was the obvious offshoot of WPF, and there was no satisfactory technology for the Microsoft developer to create RIAs prior to its release. Options such as ActiveX controls or embedded Windows forms suffered from being difficult to develop and debug, were not cross-platform, and had security and deployment issues.

For a taste of just what is possible using Silverlight, take a look at the upcoming Microsoft Office Online application (`http://channel9.msdn.com/posts/PDCNews/First-Look-Office-14-for-Web/`). Office Online utilizes Silverlight to provide online versions of Word, Excel, and PowerPoint.

Perhaps the biggest advantage offered by Silverlight is that applications can be written using the .NET framework and existing Microsoft tools such as Visual Studio. This immediately lowers the entry barrier to new developers and gives them access to much more functionality.

Although Flash is almost certainly installed on more browsers than Silverlight, at the time of writing, Microsoft is in a strong position to encourage uptake of Silverlight (subject to future possible antitrust legislation!).

It is hard to get accurate statistics about Silverlight uptake, but the sites `http://www.riastats.com/` and `http://www.statowl.com/silverlight.php` are well worth a look. At the time of writing, they indicate that roughly 25 percent of browsers have some version of Silverlight installed. Adobe indicates that it has a much higher uptake, which is to be expected with a more mature product: `http://www.adobe.com/products/player_census/flashplayer/`.

Silverlight in the Real World

An impressive example of a Silverlight application is "Descry: A Website Named Desire" that was created for the Mix conference. This web site illustrates the web site development process (see Figure 14-1) and is available online at `http://www.visitmix.com/labs/descry/awebsitenameddesire/`.

Figure 14-1. *Descry example project from Mix team* (`http://www.visitmix.com/labs/descry/awebsitenameddesire/`)

One of the earliest but still very impressive uses of Silverlight is on the Hard Rock Café's memorabilia page. If you haven't seen it, go to it now at (http://memorabilia.hardrock.com/). The page shows rock memorabilia items owned by the Hard Rock café (see Figure 14-2). The user can fluidly zoom in and out to display more detail of any individual item. This site was created with Silverlight and a technology called Deep Zoom.

■**NOTE** Deep Zoom is freely available for your use if you want to create a similar application: http://msdn. microsoft.com/en-us/library/cc645050(VS.95).aspx.

Although a relatively new technology, Silverlight has already been put to the test when it was used very successfully to stream coverage of the Beijing Olympics for NBC. Brian Goldfarb (group product manager) said Silverlight streamed more than 250TB of data over this period (http://www.eweek.com/ c/a/Application-Development/Microsoft-Proving-Ground-Silverlight-at-the-Olympics/).

Interested? You should be. Take a look at the technology stack Silverlight is built on.

Figure 14-2. *Hard Rock Café memorabilia page* (http://memorabilia.hardrock.com/)

WPF

As part of.NET framework version 3.0, Microsoft released Windows Presentation Foundation (WPF): a new way of creating UIs for applications. Silverlight uses a subset of the full WPF and .NET framework. You will find some classes and methods unavailable, and anything with the `SecurityCritical` attribute cannot be used.

Why not use the full WPF and .NET framework?

- Silverlight is a browser plug-in, so it needs to be small.

- Some WPF functionality might present a security risk when run in the browser.

- Not all WPF functions are cross-platform.

XAML

Silverlight applications are developed using eXtensible Application Markup Language (XAML). XAML is an XML-based language that is used to describe objects. XAML is used in other areas of .NET such as WPF and WCF. You can expect to see Microsoft making increasing use of XAML for many different purposes in the future.

Silverlight Requirements and Installation

To develop Silverlight applications, you will require one of the following:

- Visual Studio 2008 and Silverlight Tools for Visual Studio and .NET 3.5sp1

- Visual Studio 2010

Expression Blend

The design time support for WPF and Silverlight applications is greatly improved in Visual Studio 2010 (see Chapter 17), but for serious Silverlight development a separate product called Expression Blend is almost essential.

Expression Blend (written using WPF) is very much aimed at designers and eases tasks such as layout, animation, and customization of controls. You will still need to edit code in Visual Studio, but Visual Studio and Blend play well together so you can have both open at the same time and skip between them.

When a designer and a developer work at the same time on an application, there can be issues as one developer's changes overwrite the others. Microsoft has tried to address this with a declarative data binding syntax and design of Blend. I am not sure they have fully achieved this lofty aim, but it is a step in the right direction. If you want to see whether Blend is worth using for you, download the free trial version of Blend from the main Silverlight.net site at `http://silverlight.net/GetStarted/`.

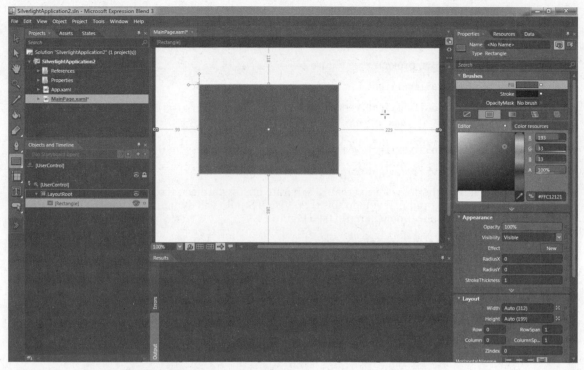

Figure 14-3. *Expression Blend Designer*

Creating a New Silverlight Project

Get started creating a new Silverlight project.

1. Open Visual Studio.

2. Select File▶New Project.

3. Select the C# node and then the Silverlight node.

4. Select Silverlight Application.

5. Call your project Chapter14.HelloSilverlight.

6. Make sure the "Host the Silverlight application in a new Web site" option is selected (this will be essential later on).

7. Click OK.

Visual Studio will now create a Silverlight solution for you to use.

Project Structure

Visual Studio has created two projects (see Figure 14-4):

- Chapter14.HelloSilverlight
- Chapter14.HelloSilverlight.Web

Why two projects?

- Chapter14.HelloSilverlight.Web acts as a host or test harness for the application.
- Chapter14.HelloSilverlight contains the Silverlight code.

In the future, you might not want to create a separate hosting project. If so, don't check the add a new ASP.NET web project option. If you do this then Visual Studio will dynamically generate a page to display your Silverlight application when run (see Figure 14-4).

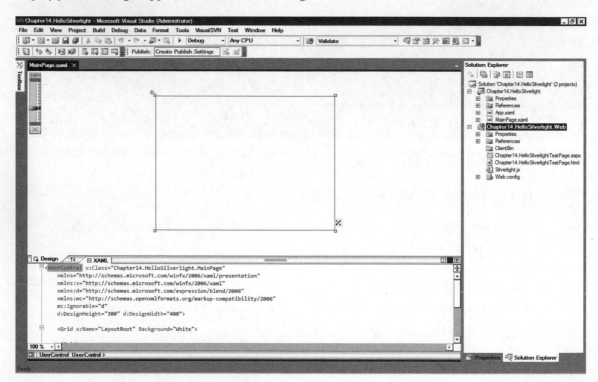

Figure 14-4. *Silverlight default project setup*

Hi Yo, Silver!

Let's create a Hello World (or Hi yo Silver) application:

1. Open the file ~\MainPage.xaml.

2. By default, `MainPage.xaml` will contain a `Grid` tag like the following:

   ```
   <Grid x:Name="LayoutRoot" Background="White"> </Grid>
   ```

   Silverlight and WPF allow you to nest tags inside one another. Enter the following between the `Grid` tags:

   ```
   <TextBlock>Hi yo Silver</TextBlock>
   ```

   You should now have something like the following:

   ```
   <UserControl x:Class="Chapter14.HelloSilverlight.MainPage"
       xmlns="http://schemas.microsoft.com/winfx/2006/xaml/presentation"
       xmlns:x="http://schemas.microsoft.com/winfx/2006/xaml"
       xmlns:d="http://schemas.microsoft.com/expression/blend/2008"
       xmlns:mc="http://schemas.openxmlformats.org/markup-compatibility/2006"
       mc:Ignorable="d"
       d:DesignHeight="300" d:DesignWidth="400">

       <Grid x:Name="LayoutRoot" Background="White">
           <TextBlock>Hi yo Silver</TextBlock>
       </Grid>
   </UserControl>
   ```

3. Press F5 to run your application. You should see the text `Hi yo Silver` displayed on a page.

Understanding the Basics

Let's run through the lines of code to understand what they do. The following line tells the compiler which class to inherit from. (It is similar to ASP.NET's inherits property in an `.aspx` or `.ascx` file.)

```
x:Class="Chapter14.HelloSilverlight.MainPage"
```

The lines beginning with `xmlns` import a number of WPF- and Silverlight-related namespaces (such as a `using` or `imports` statement).

The following line creates a `TextBlock` on the page and sets the text to `Hi yo Silver`:

```
<TextBlock>Hi yo Silver</TextBlock>
```

■**NOTE** Hi yo, Silver was a line said by the Lone Ranger as he rode away on his horse. It was on a TV/radio series that I am too young to remember, but it was the only Silver-related reference I could think of.

Note the line `xmlns:x`—x is a prefix you can use to refer to this namespace. You then use this prefix in the line `x:name`, which is similar in function to ASP.NET's ID property.

Adding Content

Content can be added either declaratively or programmatically. If you wanted to create the previous example programmatically, you could do so in `MainPage.xaml.cs` in the constructor as follows:

```
TextBlock TextBlock = new TextBlock();
TextBlock.Text = "Hi yo Silver";
LayoutRoot.Children.Add(TextBlock);
```

Note that the TextBlock control is added as a child element to the LayoutRoot control. Elements in a XAML page are maintained in a hierarchy like HTML's document object model (DOM). The Children property is similar to ASP.NET's Controls property.

This hierarchy allows you to do some strange things such as nesting text boxes inside buttons that wouldn't be possible with Windows forms. I can't wait to see some of the appalling uses this feature will no doubt be used for. Let's create an example to demonstrate this now:

```
<Button Width="200" Height="100">
  <TextBox Width="150" Height="20"></TextBox>
</Button>
```

Figure 14-5. *Text box inside a button*

Adding Silverlight to your Application

So back to the Hi yo Silver application. How did this end up being rendered in the browser? In Silverlight 3.0, applications are displayed using the object tag. Previous versions of Silverlight utilized an ASP.NET Silverlight tag that has since been depreciated (although still available on Codeplex).

Object Tag

Select the `Chapter14.HelloSilverlight.Web` project and open the file `~/Chapter14.HelloSilverlightTestPage.html`. The page will contain an object tag similar to the following:

```
<object data="data:application/x-silverlight-2," type="application/x-silverlight-2"
        width="100%" height="100%">
    <param name="source" value="ClientBin/Chapter14.HelloSilverlight.xap"/>
    <param name="onError" value="onSilverlightError" />
    <param name="background" value="white" />
    <param name="minRuntimeVersion" value="3.0.40818.0" />
    <param name="autoUpgrade" value="true" />
```

```
    <a href="http://go.microsoft.com/fwlink/?LinkID=149156&v=3.0.40818.0"
        style="text-decoration:none">
        <img src="http://go.microsoft.com/fwlink/?LinkId=161376"
            alt="Get Microsoft Silverlight" style="border-style:none"/>
    </a>
</object>
```

Note the following from the preceding code:

- An object tag is used to embed the Silverlight plug-in in the web page.

- The object tag has a param value that references the JavaScript function onSilverlightError() to return any errors from Silverlight to the user via JavaScript.

When you compile your Silverlight application, all the XAML, resources, references, and so forth get compressed into an XAML Application Package (XAP) file. The object tag has a property called Source that contains the location of the XAP file.

Also note that the test page contains the following line:

```
<script type="text/javascript" src="Silverlight.js"></script>
```

Silverlight.js contains lots of functionality such as error handling, loading, and displaying the plug-in; routing messages to JavaScript; and upgrading the plug-in. If you want to customize how the Silverlight application is displayed, you can modify the parameters passed into Silverlight.js (or even Silverlight.js itself).

Pages in Silverlight

Silverlight allows you to divide your application up into a number of XAML pages. However, you cannot just move between pages as you do in ASP.NET with functions such as Response.Redirect or Server.Transfer.

A popular way of implementing navigation between pages is to create one page with a container control that you then load other XAML files into.

■**TIP** Silverlight 3.0 introduced an easier way (NavigationApplication) that you will examine in Chapter 15.

You will create this paging functionality now because it will make it easy to navigate through the examples:

1. Right-click Chapter14.HelloSilverlight solution.

2. Select Add Class.

3. Call the class PageNavigator.

4. Enter the following code:

   ```
   using System;
   using System.Net;
   using System.Windows;
   using System.Windows.Controls;
   ```

```
using System.Windows.Documents;
using System.Windows.Ink;
using System.Windows.Input;
using System.Windows.Media;
using System.Windows.Media.Animation;
using System.Windows.Shapes;

namespace Chapter14.HelloSilverlight
{
    public class PageNavigator
    {
        private static Grid RootLayoutElement;

        static PageNavigator()
        {
            RootLayoutElement = Application.Current.RootVisual as Grid;
        }

        public static void LoadPage(UserControl NewControl)
        {
            //Get reference to old control
            var OldUserControl = RootLayoutElement.Children[0] as UserControl;

            //Add new control
            RootLayoutElement.Children.Add(NewControl);

            //Remove old control
            RootLayoutElement.Children.Remove(OldUserControl);
        }
    }
}
```

Creating a Silverlight User Control

You will now create a menu page with a number of buttons to take you to the examples you will create:

1. Right-click the Chapter14.HelloSilverlight solution and select Add➤New Item.

2. Select Silverlight User Control.

3. Enter the name MainMenu.

4. Note that at the top of the XAML code is a control declaration:

```
<UserControl x:Class="Chapter14.HelloSilverlight.MainMenu"
    xmlns="http://schemas.microsoft.com/winfx/2006/xaml/presentation"
    xmlns:x="http://schemas.microsoft.com/winfx/2006/xaml"
    xmlns:d="http://schemas.microsoft.com/expression/blend/2008"
    xmlns:mc="http://schemas.openxmlformats.org/markup-compatibility/2006"
    mc:Ignorable="d"
    d:DesignHeight="300" d:DesignWidth="400">
```

You want the menu control to span the whole page, so remove this code:

```
d:DesignHeight="300" d:DesignWidth="400"
```

5.   Enter the following XAML inside the LayoutRoot Grid to create buttons to navigate to the test pages:

```
<TextBlock  FontSize="40" Canvas.Left="200" Canvas.Top="25" >Silverlight
Demo</TextBlock>

<StackPanel Canvas.Left="300" Canvas.Top="150"  Orientation="Vertical"
            VerticalAlignment="Top">
  <Button x:Name="cmdStackPanel" Content="Stack Panel"></Button>
  <Button x:Name="cmdGrid" Content="Grid"></Button>
  <Button x:Name="cmdAnimation" Content="Animation"></Button>
  <Button x:Name="cmdCallJS" Content="Call JS"></Button>
  <Button x:Name="cmdMediaTest" Content="Media"></Button>
  <Button x:Name="cmdDataBind" Content="Data Binding"></Button>
</StackPanel>
```

Okay, nearly done. But when the Silverlight application is first loaded, you want to load MainMenu.xaml rather than MainPage.xaml. You can do this by editing a file called App.xaml.

App.xaml

App.xaml handles global events in a manner similar to Global.asax.
   Open ~/App.xaml.cs. By default, App.xaml.cs has code such as the following:

```
private void Application_Startup(object sender, StartupEventArgs e)
{
    this.RootVisual = new MainPage();
}
```

This loads the MainPage.xaml file when the application starts. You want to alter this to load the MainMenu.xaml file instead. Change the Application_startup method to the following:

```
private void Application_Startup(object sender, StartupEventArgs e)
{
    Grid root = new Grid();
    root.Children.Add(new MainMenu());
    this.RootVisual = root;
}
```

Styles

Silverlight allows you to define set styles for objects in a manner that is a cross between CSS and ASP.NET themes. You will create a simple style that will format the page title on the menu page.

6. Open up ~/App.xaml.

7. Inside the `<Application.Resources>` block, enter the following:

```
<Style x:Key="MyStyle" TargetType="TextBlock">
  <Setter Property="FontFamily" Value="Comic Sans MS"/>
  <Setter Property="FontSize" Value="54"/>
  <Setter Property="Foreground" Value="#FF0000FF"/>
</Style>
```

8. Now go back to `MainMenu.xaml` and find the line where it says the following:

```
<TextBlock FontSize="40" Canvas.Left="200" Canvas.Top="25">Silverlight
Demo</TextBlock>
```

9. Add the following attribute to this tag to reference the style you created in `App.xaml`:

```
Style="{StaticResource MyStyle}"
```

Your tag should now look like this:

```
<TextBlock  FontSize="40" Canvas.Left="200" Canvas.Top="25"
Style="{StaticResource MyStyle}">Silverlight Demo</TextBlock>
```

APPLICATION.RESOURCES

The `Application.Resources` section allows you to hold much more complex styles than you have just created. It can be used to hold pretty much any set of properties you might want to reuse. For example, you could include colors, gradients, or even control templates.

Positioning Elements

One of the most confusing parts of Silverlight and WPF is element positioning. When you start working with Silverlight and WPF, it is quite common to find yourself wondering why an element is not displaying. This is normally due to the following:

- You haven't set the width or height.

- Your element is obscured by another element.

- You have positioned the element off the screen.

- Your element is transparent.

Silverlight positions elements using two axes running from the top-left corner of the screen called Left (horizontal axis) and Top (vertical axis). The top-left corner is referred to as coordinates 0, 0 (see Figure 14-6).

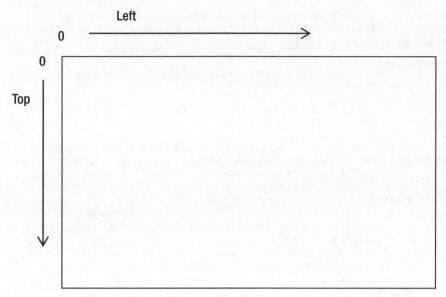

Figure 14-6. *Silverlight screen coordinates system*

You are probably expecting to be able to position elements in Silverlight similar to the following code:

```
<TextBlock Left="10" Top="20"></TextBlock>
```

However, elements are positioned using the Canvas.Left and Canvas.Top properties (unless positioned through some other means such as a Grid):

```
<TextBlock Canvas.Left="10" Canvas.Top="20"></TextBlock>
```

Canvas.Left and Canvas.Top are a special type of property called an *attached property*. The Left and Top properties are actually attached to the Canvas element. This means you are positioning the TextBlock relative to the Canvas element. This is an important concept to understand and brings you to the subject of attached and dependency properties.

Attached and Dependency Properties

When you set a property of an object in ASP.NET such as Width on a TextBox, you would usually write something like this:

```
<asp:TextBox Width="300" Runat="server" />
```

Behind the scenes, the Width value is retained in a private field. If you were to retrieve the Width property, it would be the same as when it was first set. However, when working with dependency properties, this is not necessarily true.

Consider how a browser works out where to display an item on the screen. It is not as straight forward as it first sounds. There are actually a number of things that need to be taken into account when calculating where an item will be positioned on a page:

- Other elements on the page

- Runtime settings (e.g., screen and browser settings)

- Styles

- Templates

That's quite a lot to consider. You could say the positioning is *dependent* on lots of other factors. *Dependency properties* are properties that are dependent on other property values. It's as simple as that and it saves you lots of work, and not just for tasks such as positioning elements. Dependency properties are also used for tasks such as data binding where Silverlight needs to know to redraw an item if the underlying data source were to change.

A predefined order exists that determines how dependency properties will be evaluated, which is intuitive for the most part. For more information on how dependency properties are evaluated, please refer to http://msdn.microsoft.com/en-us/library/ms743230.aspx.

Attached properties are a type of dependency property, but attached properties do not necessarily exist in the object they are set on. They are easy to spot because are written in this format:

```
AttachedPropertyProvider.PropertyName
```

With the theoretical stuff out the way let's look at the controls that allow you to position elements on a page.

Layout Controls

The main layout controls in Silverlight are the following:

- Canvas

- StackPanel

- Grid

Canvas

Canvas is the simplest of all the layout controls. You can think of it as a rectangle or div tag in which you put content. Content added to a canvas is normally then positioned absolutely by setting the Canvas.Left and Canvas.Top properties. Canvas is unique from the other layout controls in that it is the only layout control that allows you to modify the Z index (or which elements on top of which).

Stack Panel

Stack panels allow you to set items positioned within them to flow horizontally or vertcially by setting a property called Orientation to either Vertical or Horizontal (see Figure 14-7).

Vertical Alignment   **Horizontal Alignment**

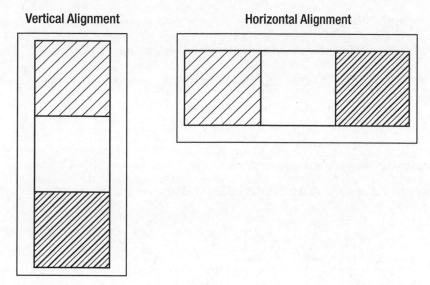

Figure 14-7. *Diagram of a stack panel set to vertical and horizontal alignment*

Let's create an example stack panel now:

1. Right-click the project and add a new folder called Layout.

2. Right-click and select Add►New Item.

3. Select Silverlight User Control.

4. Name the control StackPanelTest.

5. Add the following XAML inside the LayoutRoot Grid tag (make sure to alter the width and height, or you will not see the whole column):

```
<StackPanel  Orientation="Vertical" Width="200" Height="500">
  <Rectangle Fill="blue"  Width="100" Height="100"></Rectangle>
  <Rectangle Fill="Red"  Width="100" Height="100"></Rectangle>
  <Rectangle Fill="Yellow"  Width="100" Height="100"></Rectangle>
  <Rectangle Fill="Green"  Width="100" Height="100"></Rectangle>
</StackPanel>
```

You now need to modify the MainMenu control to enable it to take you to the stack panel page you have just created.

Wiring up a button in Silverlight is similar to performing the same task in ASP.NET or Windows forms. You need to wire up an event in the page loaded event because the button won't be created until this point.

1. Open `MainMenu.xaml.cs`.

2. Add an event handler for when the `MainMenu` is loaded in the `MainMenu` constructor:

```
public MainMenu()
{
    InitializeComponent();
    this.Loaded += new RoutedEventHandler(MainMenu_Loaded);
}
```

3. In `MainMenu_Loaded()` add the following code:

```
void MainMenu_Loaded(object sender, RoutedEventArgs e)
{
    this.cmdStackPanel.Click += new RoutedEventHandler(cmdStackPanel_Click);
}
```

4. Now create a method to be called when `cmdStackPanel` is clicked:

```
void cmdStackPanel_Click(object sender, RoutedEventArgs e)
{
    PageNavigator.LoadPage(new Layout.StackPanelTest());
}
```

Your code should now look similar to the following:

```
public partial class MainMenu : UserControl
{
    public MainMenu()
    {
        InitializeComponent();
        this.Loaded += new RoutedEventHandler(MainMenu_Loaded);
    }

    void MainMenu_Loaded(object sender, RoutedEventArgs e)
    {
        this.cmdStackPanel.Click += new RoutedEventHandler(cmdStackPanel_Click);
    }

    void cmdStackPanel_Click(object sender, RoutedEventArgs e)
    {
        PageNavigator.LoadPage(newLayout.StackPanelTest());
    }
}
```

Now press F5 to run the application. Click the Stack Panel button and you should see a screen similar to Figure 14-8.

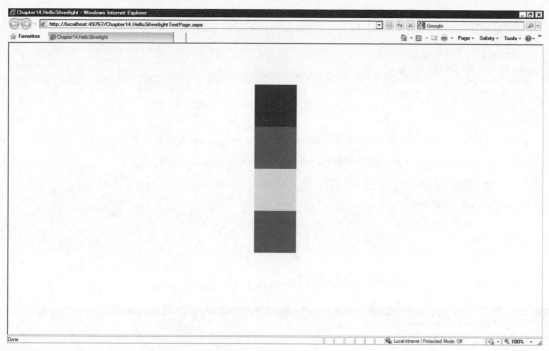

Figure 14-8. *Laying out items with the StackPanel*

Try changing the Orientation of the StackPanel to Horizontal to see how it affects the positioning of the squares. StackPanel is a very useful control and is very flexible. It is used extensively to perform tasks such as laying out lists of elements and creating menus.

Grid

The Grid layout control allows you to define a grid strucure to place individual elements within and is in some ways similar to an HTML table. You will create a 2 x 2 grid and some colored rectangles and then position them within the grid:

1. Right-click the Layout folder and select Add➤New Item➤Silverlight User Control.

2. Name it GridTest.

3. Enter the following XAML between the Grid tags (note that the Grid was defined first, and then the Grid.Row and Grid.Column attached properties are added to position the elements):

```
<Grid.RowDefinitions>
  <RowDefinition Height="150"></RowDefinition>
  <RowDefinition Height="150"></RowDefinition>
</Grid.RowDefinitions>
<Grid.ColumnDefinitions>
  <ColumnDefinition Width="300"></ColumnDefinition>
  <ColumnDefinition Width="300"></ColumnDefinition>
</Grid.ColumnDefinitions>
```

```
<Rectangle Fill="blue" Grid.Row="0" Grid.Column="0" Width="100"
Height="100"></Rectangle>
<Rectangle Fill="Red" Grid.Row="0" Grid.Column="1" Width="100"
Height="100"></Rectangle>
<Rectangle Fill="Yellow" Grid.Row="1" Grid.Column="0" Width="100"
Height="100"></Rectangle>
<Rectangle Fill="Green" Grid.Row="1" Grid.Column="1" Width="100"
Height="100"></Rectangle>
```

4. Let's add the ability to navigate to this page on the main menu. Open ~/MainMenu.xaml.cs.

5. Add the following code to the MainMenu_Loaded() method:

    ```
    this.cmdGrid.Click += new RoutedEventHandler(cmdGrid_Click);
    ```

6. Add the following event handler:

    ```
    void cmdGrid_Click(object sender, RoutedEventArgs e)
    {
        PageNavigator.LoadPage(new Layout.GridTest());
    }
    ```

7. Press F5 to run the application you should see a page like Figure 14-9.

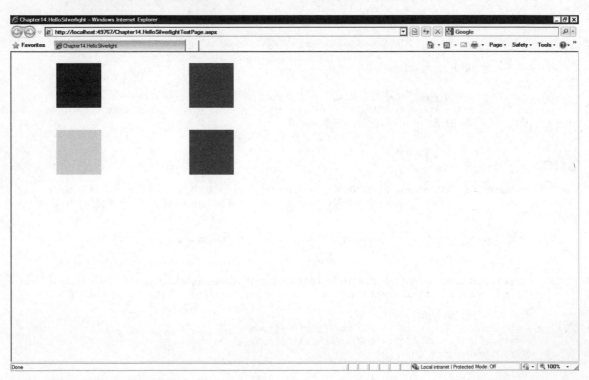

Figure 14-9. *Grid Layout control*

Simple Animation

Silverlight allows you to animate objects both declaratively and programmatically. Animation is perhaps easier to understand programmatically, so you will create a very simple animation to move a rectangle across a screen and at the same time change its transparency by modifying its opacity.

You will use a Storyboard class to create an animation. The Storyboard defines what will happen within the animation (the story) and contains features to start, stop, and repeat the animation.

The storyboard has a property called Interval that is a timer that allows you to perform the animation. In the example when the storyboard interval occurs, you will increment the x and y position of the rectangle and increase the opacity.

Creating Animation Programmatically

Let's start the example:

1. Create a new folder called Animation within your project.

2. Right-click this folder➤Add➤New Item➤Silverlight User Control.

3. Call it Animation.

4. Remove the d:DesignHeight="300" d:DesignWidth="400" properties from the user control tag.

5. Replace the Grid tags with the following XAML:

```
<Canvas Width="900" Height="700" Background="AliceBlue">
  <Rectangle Width="52" Height="52" Stroke="#FF000000" Opacity="0" Fill="Red"
             x:Name="rectAnimation" RadiusX="10" RadiusY="10" />
</Canvas>
```

6. Open ~/Animation/Animation.xaml.cs and enter the following code:

```
public partial class Animation : UserControl
{
    Storyboard StoryBoard = new Storyboard();
    int Count = 0;

    public Animation()
    {
        this.Loaded += new RoutedEventHandler(Animation_Loaded);
        StoryBoard.Completed += new EventHandler(StoryBoard_Completed);
        InitializeComponent();
    }

    public void Animation_Loaded(object sender, RoutedEventArgs e)
    {
        StoryBoard.Duration = TimeSpan.FromMilliseconds(10);
        StoryBoard.Begin();
    }

    void StoryBoard_Completed(object sender, EventArgs e)
    {
        Canvas.SetTop(rectAnimation, Count);
        Canvas.SetLeft(rectAnimation, Count);
        rectAnimation.Opacity = 0.001 * Convert.ToDouble(Count);
```

```
            Count += 1;

            StoryBoard.Begin();

            if (Count == 100)
                StoryBoard.Stop();
        }
    }
}
```

7.   Now edit MainMenu so you can navigate to this page. Open ~/MainMenu.xaml.cs.

8.   In the `MainMenu_Loaded()` method add a handler for the animation button:

```
this.cmdAnimation.Click += new RoutedEventHandler(cmdAnimation_Click);
```

9.   Add the code to load `Animation.xaml` when the animation button is clicked:

```
void cmdAnimation_Click(object sender, RoutedEventArgs e)
{
    PageNavigator.LoadPage(new Animation.Animation());
}
```

10. Press F5 to run the application.

When the page is loaded you should see a rectangle move diagonally across the screen. Note that you incremented the `Opacity` value using the following code:

```
rectAnimation.Opacity = 0.001 * Convert.ToDouble(Count);
```

However, when you incremented the `Left` and `Top` properties, you had to increment the values using the following syntax:

```
Canvas.SetTop(rectAnimation, Count);
Canvas.SetLeft(rectAnimation, Count);
```

This is because `Opacity` is not an attached property, but `Top` and `Left` are.

Responding to User Events

You will now detect the user clicking the rectangle and then perform a different animation:

1.   In `Animation_Loaded()`, add the following code:

```
rectAnimation.MouseLeftButtonDown +=
    new MouseButtonEventHandler(rectAnimation_MouseLeftButtonDown);
```

2.   Let's add another storyboard for an animation that will start when the rectangle is clicked. You will change the rectangle's color to yellow to indicate that it has been clicked and then move it horizontally instead of diagonally acrosss the screen—Pixar has nothing to fear. Add a new `Storyboard` object within the `Animation` class:

```
Storyboard StoryBoard2 = new Storyboard();
```

3. Create the methods rectAnimation_MouseLeftButtonDown() and StoryBoard2_Completed():

```
void rectAnimation_MouseLeftButtonDown(object sender, MouseButtonEventArgs e)
{
    rectAnimation.Fill = new SolidColorBrush(Colors.Yellow);
    rectAnimation.Opacity = 1;
    StoryBoard.Stop();

    StoryBoard2.Completed += new EventHandler(StoryBoard2_Completed);
    StoryBoard2.Duration = TimeSpan.FromMilliseconds(10);
    StoryBoard2.Begin();
}

void StoryBoard2_Completed(object sender, EventArgs e)
{
    Canvas.SetLeft(rectAnimation, Count);
    Count += 1;
    StoryBoard2.Begin();
}
```

4. Press F5 to run your application and then click the rectangle. The rectangle should change to yellow and then move across the screen.

Declarative Animation

Animation can also be declared declaratively. Following is an example produced by Blend 3 for moving a rectangle horizontally across the screen in two seconds (not the sort of thing you will be writing yourself):

```xml
<UserControl.Resources>
  <Storyboard x:Name="Storyboard1">
    <DoubleAnimationUsingKeyFrames BeginTime="00:00:00" Storyboard.TargetName="rectangle"
      Storyboard.TargetProperty="(UIElement.RenderTransform).(TransformGroup.Children)[3].
(TranslateTransform.X)">
      <SplineDoubleKeyFrame KeyTime="00:00:00" Value="0"/>
      <SplineDoubleKeyFrame KeyTime="00:00:02" Value="258"/>
    </DoubleAnimationUsingKeyFrames>
  </Storyboard>
</UserControl.Resources>

<Grid x:Name="LayoutRoot" Background="White">
  <Rectangle Height="80" HorizontalAlignment="Left" Margin="34,123,0,0"
           VerticalAlignment="Top" Width="91" Fill="#FFE24646" Stroke="#FF000000"
           x:Name="rectangle" RenderTransformOrigin="0.5,0.5">
    <Rectangle.RenderTransform>
      <TransformGroup>
        <ScaleTransform/>
        <SkewTransform/>
        <RotateTransform/>
        <TranslateTransform/>
      </TransformGroup>
    </Rectangle.RenderTransform>
  </Rectangle>
</Grid>
```

Although the preceding XAML is not as readable as animating the item programmatically, it is arguably easier to produce. Blend allows you to define key frames for your object and will then animate between them. For more information about Blend, check out the great tutorial videos available at http://silverlight.net/learn/videocat.aspx?cat=2#HDI2Basics.

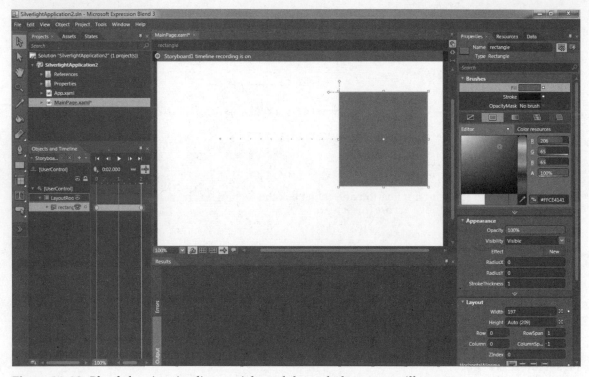

Figure 14-10. *Blend showing timeline on right and the path the square will move to*

HTML Integration

Silverlight has some great functionality that allows you to interact with the web page through something called the *HTML bridge*. The HTML bridge allows you to modify DOM elements and call JavaScript functions from within your Silverlight application. The reverse is also possible, allowing you to call Silverlight functions from within JavaScript. Note that Silverlight utilizes parts of the DLR (refer to Chapter 3) to perform some of this functionality (Silverlight was one of the first applications to benefit from the DLR).

Calling a JavaScript Function from Silverlight

Select the Chapter14.HelloSilverlight.Web project:

1. Open ~\Chapter14.HelloSilverlightTestPage.aspx.

2. Add the following code within the page's head tag to show an alert box with the message parameter you will shortly pass in:

    ```
    <script type="text/javascript">

    function ShowMessage(Message) {
        alert(Message);
    }

    </script>
    ```

3. Open ~/MainMenu.xaml.cs.

4. In the MainMenu_Loaded() method, add the following event handler to the cmdCallJS button:

    ```
    this.cmdCallJS.Click += new RoutedEventHandler(cmdCallJS_Click);
    ```

5. Now add the following code:

    ```
    void cmdCallJS_Click(object sender, RoutedEventArgs e)
    {
        System.Windows.Browser.HtmlPage.Window.Invoke(
            "ShowMessage", "This function was called from Silverlight");
    }
    ```

6. Press F5 to run your application and click the Call JS button.

You should receive the message "This function was called from Silverlight".

Changing DOM Element Values from Silverlight

You can manipulate any aspect of the DOM from Silverlight. To demonstrate this feature, add a text box with ID txtHelloFromSilverlight to Chapter14.HelloSilverlightTestPage.aspx and utilize the following code:

```
System.Windows.Browser.HtmlPage.Document
.GetElementById("txtHelloFromSilverlight")
.SetProperty("value", "Hello from Silverlight");
```

Calling a Silverlight Function from JavaScript

It is also possible to call Silverlight functions from JavaScript. Because this has some security risks, you have to tell Silverlight you want to expose functions to JavaScript:

1. Add the following function to ~/MainMenu.xaml.cs, which you will shortly expose:

    ```
    public string CallMeFromJS()
    {
        return "Silverlight function called from JS";
    }
    ```

2. Add the following attribute to the `CallMeFromJS()` method:

```
[System.Windows.Browser.ScriptableMember()]
```

Your function should look like this:

```
[System.Windows.Browser.ScriptableMember()]
public string CallMeFromJS()
{
    return "Silverlight function called from JS";
}
```

■**NOTE** You can also add the [`System.Windows.Browser.ScriptableType`] attribute to the whole class to make all public methods accessible via JavaScript. Be careful with this, though, because it can have security implications.

Before you can call this function, you need to register the function for JavaScript's use.

1. Add the following code at the end of the `Application_Startup` event in ~\App.xaml.cs.

```
//Set up client side access to function within Main Menu
System.Windows.Browser.HtmlPage.RegisterScriptableObject("MainMenu", new MainMenu());
```

2. Add the following code inside the head tag in `Chapter14.HelloSilverlightTestPage.aspx` to call the method when the Silverlight plug-in is loaded:

```
<script type="text/javascript">
function Silverlight_PluginLoaded(sender)
{
    silverlightControl = document.getElementById("silverlightObject");
    alert(silverlightControl.Content.MainMenu.CallMeFromJS());
}
</script>
```

3. Add an `id` property to the Silverlight object tag:

```
id="silverlightObject"
```

4. Add a new parameter to tell the Silverlight plug-in the JavaScript function to call when it is loaded:

```
<param name="onLoad" value="Silverlight_PluginLoaded" />
```

5. Press F5 to run your application; you should see an alert box pop up with the text "Silverlight function called from JS".

Unless you want an alert box popping up throughout the rest of this chapter (which would be pretty irritating), it is probably a good idea to remove the `onLoad` param from the Silverlight control now.

Silverlight has extensive functionality for interacting with the web page. For more information, refer to Mike Taulty's excellent blog at http://mtaulty.com/CommunityServer/blogs/mike_taultys_blog/archive/2008/10/15/10836.aspx.

Passing Parameters into Silverlight

There are a number of different methods for passing parameters into Silverlight:

- Query string
- InitParams property
- JavaScript function calls (as explained previously)

InitParams

The easiest way to pass parameters into a Silverlight application is with the InitParams property on the Silverlight control. Values passed in using this method need to be represented in the format *Name=Value* and separated by commas. For example:

```
Name=Alex,Age=28,Country=Australia
```

To use the IntitParams property, just add params to the object tag like so:

```
<param name="InitParams" value="name=alex,sex=male" />
```

Input values can then be retrieved by iterating through the InitParams keys collection in App.xaml.cs:

```
//Initialization parameters.
foreach (String key in e.InitParams.Keys)
{
    string strKey = key;
    string strValue=e.InitParams[key];
}
```

Query String

Another method of passing paramaters to a Silverlight is with the query string. The following code shows you how to iterate through all the query string values:

```
//URL Params
foreach (String key in System.Windows.Browser.HtmlPage.Document.QueryString.Keys)
{
    string KeyName = key;
    string strValue=System.Windows.Browser.HtmlPage.Document.QueryString[key];
}
```

Embedding Content in a Silverlight application

If you want to utilize content such as images within your Silverlight application, you have a number of options, two of which are shown here:

- Relative rath + resource:

    ```
    <Image Source="myImage.jpg"></Image>
    ```

- Full URL:

```
<Image Source="http://www.mysite.com/myImage.jpg"></Image>
```

■**NOTE** Silverlight currently displays only JPG or PNG images. This means that GIF images *do not* display. The Silverlight team apparently left this out to reduce the size of the plug-in (not to mention GIF becoming a paid standard), but it does seem to be a weird omission. On a related note, if you are interested in manipulating images, you might be interested in checking out `http://www.codeplex.com/imagetools`.

The steps to include an image in your project are as follows:

1. Add the image to the Silverlight project.

2. Select properties of the image.

3. Change the Build action to Resource.

Figure 14-10. *Bundlling an image file in a Silverlight Project*

4. You can then reference the image as follows:

```
<Image Source="myImage.jpg"></Image>
```

Loading XAML Dynamically

Silverlight allows you to load XAML at runtime. You might want to do this to reduce your application size, spread out loading through your application's lifetime or dynamically load content. When you have retrieved your XAML content as a string, you need to pass it into the `XamlReader.Load()` method. All that is then necessary to do is cast the results of `XamlReader.Load()` to the type of object the XAML represents.

When constructing the XAML, be sure to add the `xmlns` namespace property to your objects; otherwise, Silverlight will be unable to determine the type of object you are trying to create. Following is a simple example illustrating loading a TextBlock from a string that would be placed in the code behind of a XAML file (and assumes an element called LayoutRoot exists):

```
string XAMLContent=@"<TextBlock xmlns=""http://schemas.microsoft.com/winfx/2006/xaml/
presentation""  Canvas.Left=""200"" Canvas.Top=""100"" Text=""Hello""></TextBlock>";

TextBlock TextBlock=(TextBlock) System.Windows.Markup.XamlReader.Load(XAMLContent);
LayoutRoot.Children.Add(TextBlock);
```

■**TIP** Unless you are creating just one XAML object, you probably want to load your XAML within a layout control such as Canvas. You can then easily cast the result of the Load() method to a Canvas object.

Media

One of Silverlight's biggest strengths is its media functionality. Silverlight has been used to stream media content on a number of high-profile sites such as the 2008 Beijing Olympics on NBC, Blockbuster Video, Netflix, and UK TV channel ITV.

Silverlight supports these formats:

- Windows Media audio and video
- MP3 audio
- AAC
- AVC
- H.264/MPEG
- HD formats (introduced in Silverlight 3.0)

Silverlight also supports a great feature called adaptive streaming that varies the quality (bit rate) of the media stream depending on the user's available bandwidth to obtain the best experience possible.

It's very easy to add video functionality to your application, so let's create a simple video player:

1. Create a new folder called Media in your project.

2. Right-click and select Add➤New Item.

3. Select Silverlight User Control and call it MediaPlayerTest.

4. Add the following XAML within the Grid tags:

```
<Canvas Width="800" Height="600" Background="White">

    <MediaElement x:Name="MediaPlayer" Width="400" Height="300"
                Source="/Robotica_720.wmv"></MediaElement>

    <Button x:Name="cmdPlay" Canvas.Left="50"  Canvas.Top="300" Width="150" Height="50"
            Content="Play"></Button>
```

```xml
    <Button x:Name="cmdStop" Canvas.Left="250"  Canvas.Top="300" Width="150" Height="50"
          Content="Stop"></Button>
    <Button x:Name="cmdPause" Canvas.Left="450"  Canvas.Top="300" Width="150"
Height="50"
          Content="Pause"></Button>
</Canvas>
```

5. Open ~/Media/MediaPlayerTest.xaml.cs and replace the existing code with the following:

```csharp
public partial class MediaPlayerTest : UserControl
{
    public MediaPlayerTest()
    {
        InitializeComponent();
        this.Loaded += new RoutedEventHandler(MediaTest_Loaded);
    }

    void MediaTest_Loaded(object sender, RoutedEventArgs e)
    {
        this.cmdPlay.Click += new RoutedEventHandler(cmdPlay_Click);
        this.cmdStop.Click += new RoutedEventHandler(cmdStop_Click);
        this.cmdPause.Click += new RoutedEventHandler(cmdPause_Click);
    }

    void cmdPause_Click(object sender, RoutedEventArgs e)
    {
        MediaPlayer.Pause();
    }


    void cmdStop_Click(object sender, RoutedEventArgs e)
    {
        MediaPlayer.Stop();
    }

    void cmdPlay_Click(object sender, RoutedEventArgs e)
    {
        MediaPlayer.Play();
    }
}
```

6. If you don't have a WMV file on hand (you will need to update the Source property of the media element), download a test file from the following URL (remember to unzip it) and place it in the media directory you created in the solution:

http://download.microsoft.com/download/4/1/b/41b10a4f-f4f4-4692-aa44-a458d0047e91/Robotica_720.exe

7. You now need to include this media file with the application or reference it. If you were developing a real-world application, you would want to reference it because it will make your Silverlight application smaller. In this example, to reduce the setup, just set the build action to Resource.

8. All that remains is to wire up the Media button on MainMenu to take you to the player page: open MainMenu.xaml.

9. Add an event handler for the click of the Media button in MediaTest_Loaded:

```
this.cmdMediaTest.Click += new RoutedEventHandler(cmdMediaTest_Click);
```

10. Add the event handler code:

```
void cmdMediaTest_Click(object sender, RoutedEventArgs e)
{
    PageNavigator.LoadPage(new Media.MediaPlayerTest());
}
```

11. Press F5 to run your application and click the Media button. You should see the WMV file playing. You can click the buttons to pause/play and stop the media player.

Silverlight contains rich media functionality allowing you to jump to specific points on the video, alter playback speed, and so on.

■**TIP** You can even use media files as a brush to fill in XAML elements.

Additional Controls

In addition to the standard Silverlight controls such as TextBox, Image, and ComboBox additional controls such as a DataGrid, Slider, and Calendar are available. The easiest way to use controls such as DataGrid is to drag them from the toolbar and have VS sort out the references for you.

Data Binding

There are few applications that do not have to work with data. Silverlight offers a rich binding model that makes it very easy to work with data. Let's create a simple example to bind data to a text box:

1. Add a new folder called DataBinding to the example project.

2. Right-click and Add➤New Item➤Silverlight UserControl. Call it DataBindingTest.

3. In the XAML, you need to add a namespace reference to the assemblies you're going to use. Add the following line in the UserControl tag of DataBindingTest.xaml:

```
xmlns:Data="clr-
namespace:System.Windows.Controls;assembly=System.Windows.Controls.Data"
```

4. Between the layout root tag add the following:

```
<StackPanel Orientation="Vertical">
  <TextBlock>Bound programmatically:</TextBlock>
  <TextBox x:Name="txtBoundProgrammatically" Width="300" Height="20"></TextBox>

  <TextBlock>Bound declaratively:</TextBlock>
  <TextBox x:Name="txtDeclaration" Width="300" Text="{Binding Title, Mode=OneWay}"
           Height="20" ></TextBox>
</StackPanel>
```

5. Open ~/DataBinding/DataBindingTest.xaml.cs and add the following using directive:

`using System.Windows.Data;`

6. You need something to bind the controls to. You will create a class called Movie that will have two properties: Title and Length. Add the Movie class to the DataBindingTest.xaml.cs code:

```
public class Movie : System.ComponentModel.INotifyPropertyChanged
{
    // implement the required event for the interface
    public event System.ComponentModel.PropertyChangedEventHandler PropertyChanged;
    private string _title;
    private string _length;

    public string Title
    {
        get
        {
            return _title;
        }

        set
        {
            _title = value;
            //Tell Silverlight Title property has changed
            NotifyChanged("Title");
        }

    }

    public string Length
    {
        get
        {
            return _length;
        }

        set
        {
            _length = value;
            //Tell Silverlight Length property has changed
            NotifyChanged("Length");
        }

    }
```

```
//This procedure raises the event property changed
//so Silverlight knows when a value has changed
public void NotifyChanged(string PropertyName)
{
    if (PropertyChanged != null)
    {
        PropertyChanged(this,
                    new
System.ComponentModel.PropertyChangedEventArgs(PropertyName));
    }
}
}
```

7. Change the DataBindingTest class code to the following:

```
public partial class DataBindingTest : UserControl
{
    public List<Movie> MoviesList = new List<Movie>();

    public DataBindingTest()
    {
        InitializeComponent();
        this.Loaded += new RoutedEventHandler(DataBindingTest_Loaded);
    }

    void DataBindingTest_Loaded(object sender, RoutedEventArgs e)
    {
        //Create items for binding
        PopulateItems();

        //Create binding programmatically
        CreateBinding_programmatically();

        //Set binding declaratively
        txtDeclaration.DataContext = MoviesList [0];
    }

    public void PopulateItems()
    {
        //Create a list of items
        Movie Movie1 = new Movie();
        Movie Movie2 = new Movie();
        Movie Movie3 = new Movie();

        Movie1.Title = "Terminator";
        Movie1.Length = "120";

        Movie2.Title = "Conan the barbarian";
        Movie2.Length = "124";

        Movie3.Title = "Robocop";
        Movie3.Length = "130";
```

```
        MoviesList.Add(Movie1);
            MoviesList.Add(Movie2);
            MoviesList.Add(Movie3);
        }

        public void CreateBinding_programmatically()
        {
            //Creates a binding programmatically
            Binding NewBinding = new Binding("Now");
            NewBinding.Source = System.DateTime.Now;
            NewBinding.Mode = BindingMode.OneWay;
            txtBoundProgrammatically.SetBinding(TextBox.TextProperty, NewBinding);
        }
    }
```

8. All you now need to do is link MainMenu to the data binding test page. Open ~/MainMenu.xaml.cs.

9. Add the following code to the MainMenu_Loaded() method in MainMenu.xaml.cs:

```
this.cmdDataBind.Click += new RoutedEventHandler(cmdDataBind_Click);
```

10. Add a method to the click event of the data bind button:

```
void cmdDataBind_Click(object sender, RoutedEventArgs e)
{
    PageNavigator.LoadPage(new DataBinding.DataBindingTest());
}
```

11. Press F5 to run the application. You should see two text boxes: the first displays the current time and date, and the other displays "The Terminator" (item 0 in MoviesList).

So what have you done here? First, you created a binding programmatically:

```
//Creates a binding programmatically
public void CreateBinding_programmatically()
{
    //Creates a binding programmatically
    Binding NewBinding = new Binding("Now");
    NewBinding.Source = System.DateTime.Now;
    NewBinding.Mode = BindingMode.OneWay;
    txtBoundProgrammatically.SetBinding(TextBox.TextProperty, NewBinding);
}
```

You then set the source (value) to today's date and then linked the binding to the txtBoundProgrammatically text box. To bind the TextBox txtDeclaration declaratively, first set the data context with the following code:

```
txtDeclaration.DataContext = MoviesList[0];
```

Set the Text property of the text box as follows:

```
<TextBox x:Name="txtDeclaration" Width="300" Text="{Binding Title, Mode=OneWay}"
        Height="20" ></TextBox>
```

DataBinding Modes

In the preceding example, you bound a TextBox to the Title property of Movie and defined the binding mode as one way:

```
<TextBox x:Name="txtDeclaration" Width="300" Text="{Binding Title, Mode=OneWay}"
        Height="20" ></TextBox>
```

Silverlight offers three binding modes:

- OneTime: This is the lightweight option and should be used if the value will never change from what it is initialized as.

- OneWay: If the item the object is bound to is changed, the bound property will be updated as well. If you change the bound property, it will not affect the object it is bound to.

- TwoWay: Like OneWay binding, but any changes to the bound property will also alter the bound object.

Data Binding and Dependency Properties

As mentioned earlier, data binding uses dependency properties to maintain the relationship between the object and datasource. If you change an item that is databound then any other controls bound to the data item will change as well. Let's create an example to demonstrate this.

1. Open ~/DataBinding/DataBindingTest.xaml.

2. Add the following XAML after the TextBox that has the x:name set to txtDeclaration:

   ```
   <TextBlock>Change an object in list:</TextBlock>
   <Button x:Name="cmdChangeTitle" Width="100" Height="20" Content="Change
   Title"></Button>
   ```

3. Open DataBindingTest.xaml.cs and add a click event handler:

   ```
   this.cmdChangeTitle.Click+=new RoutedEventHandler(cmdChangeTitle_Click);
   ```

4. Add a method to handle the click:

   ```
   void cmdChangeTitle_Click(object sender, RoutedEventArgs e)
   {
       //Change an item in the list
       MoviesList[0].Title = "Title Changed";
   }
   ```

5. Press F5 to run the application. Click the button to change the movie title. The text box that was bound to this item will then change.

Note that the contents of the text box that is bound was automatically updated when you changed the class it was bound to.

Two-Way Binding

You will now create an example to demonstrate two-way data binding.

1. Open `DataBindingTest.xaml`.

2. Add the following XAML after the `cmdChangeTitle` button (note that the binding mode is set to TwoWay now):

    ```
    <TextBlock>Two way binding:</TextBlock>
    <TextBox x:Name="txtTwoWay" Width="300" Text="{Binding Title, Mode=TwoWay}"
    Height="20" >
    </TextBox>
    ```

3. Open `DataBindingTest.xaml.cs`. In `DataBindingTest_Loaded()()`add the following code (after the call to `PopulateItems()`) to bind the text box `txtTwoWay` to the first item in the movie list:

    ```
    //Set up two way binding
    txtTwoWay.DataContext = MoviesList[0];
    ```

4. Press F5 to run your application.

5. Click the DataBinding button and select the text box labelled `txtTwoWay`.

6. Change the text to "The Terminator 2".

7. Click another text box.

Notice how all the other items bound to this movie were updated. The other bound items were updated in the example when the focus changed to another control. But you don't even need to change the item's focus because Silverlight will update other bound properties automatically after about 20 seconds.

Binding ListBox

You will now bind a `ListBox`:

1. Open `DataBindingTest.xaml` and add the following XAML (note the use of the `DisplayMemberPath` property, which tells it which item to bind to; in this case Title):

    ```
    <TextBlock>List of items:</TextBlock>
    <ListBox x:Name="lstItems" Width="300" DisplayMemberPath="Title"
    Height="100"></ListBox>
    ```

2. Open `DataBindingTest.xaml.cs`. In `DataBindingTest_Loaded()` after the call to `PopulateItems()`, add the following:

    ```
    //Bind listbox
    lstItems.ItemsSource = MoviesList;
    ```

3. Press F5 to run the application. You should see a list box populated with the movies in the list.

DataTemplates

Silverlight supports templating for data bound items. Let's see a simple example of templating:

1. Open DataBindingTest.xaml and add the following after the Listbox lstItems:

```
<TextBlock>List of items with data template:</TextBlock>
<ListBox x:Name="lstItemsWithTemplate" Width="300"  Height="100">
  <ListBox.ItemTemplate>
    <DataTemplate>
      <StackPanel Orientation="Horizontal">
        <TextBlock Text="{Binding Title}"></TextBlock>
        <TextBlock Text="{Binding Length}"></TextBlock>
      </StackPanel>
    </DataTemplate>
  </ListBox.ItemTemplate>
</ListBox>
```

2. In DataBindingTest_Loaded()(), bind lstItemsWithTemplate:

```
//Bind listbox with template
lstItemsWithTemplate.ItemsSource = MoviesList;
```

3. Press F5 to run your application and click the DataBinding button.

You should now see a list box with the movie's title and length displayed.

DataGrid

One of the most-used controls in ASP.NET is undoubtedly the DataGrid control. Silverlight has its own version of DataGrid that contains some great built-in functionality such as the following:

- Column ordering
- Two-way data binding
- Column resizing
- Column positioning
- Highlighting selected rows

Let's look at the DataGrid control in Silverlight:

1. Open DataBindingTest.xaml and drag a data grid from the toolbox to beneath the ListBox lstItemsWithTemplate:

```
<Data:DataGrid x:Name="dgSimple"></Data:DataGrid>
```

2. In DataBindingTest_Loaded() somewhere after the call to PopulateItems(), bind the DataGrid to the list of movies:

```
dgSimple.ItemsSource = MoviesList;
```

3. Press F5 to run the application and click the Data Binding button. You should see a screen like Figure 14-12.

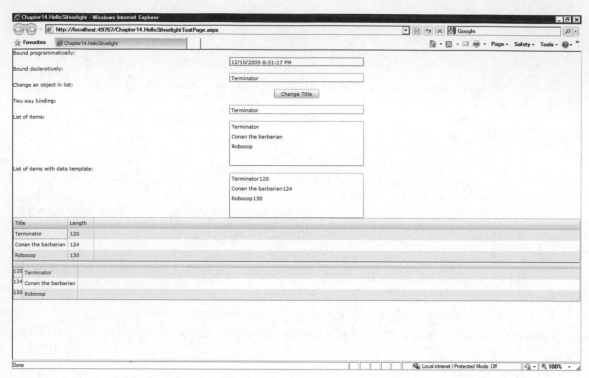

Figure 14-12. *Silverlight DataGrid*

In the previous example, you let Silverlight automatically determine the columns that would be bound in the DataGrid. Normally, however, you will want more control over how the data is displayed—for which you will use DataTemplates. Let's modify the DataGrid to use a template:

1. Open DataBindingTest.xaml and add the following code beneath the dgSimple DataGrid:

```
<Data:DataGrid x:Name="dgSpecify" AutoGenerateColumns="False">
  <Data:DataGrid.Columns>
    <Data:DataGridTemplateColumn>
      <Data:DataGridTemplateColumn.CellTemplate>
        <DataTemplate>
          <TextBlock Text="{Binding Length}" />
        </DataTemplate>
      </Data:DataGridTemplateColumn.CellTemplate>
    </Data:DataGridTemplateColumn>

    <Data:DataGridTextColumn Binding="{Binding Title, Mode=TwoWay}">
    </Data:DataGridTextColumn>

  </Data:DataGrid.Columns>
</Data:DataGrid>
```

2. Open `DataBindingTest.xaml.cs`. In `DataBindingTest_Loaded()`, add the following after the call to `PopulateItems()`:

   `dgSpecify.ItemsSource = MoviesList;`

3. Press F5 to run the application and then click the Data Binding button.

Note that you switched the order of the columns around (not very creative, but you get the idea).

Network Communications

Normally in an ASP.NET application you retrieve data from the database server using the `System.Data` classes. In Silverlight, because your application is running on the user's machine you cannot (and should not) connect directly to your SQL Server. Data is instead retrieved using calls to a web service.

When retrieving data, you don't want your application to pause execution, so all web service calls from Silverlight must be made asynchronously. For more information about Silverlight and communications, please refer to `http://silverlight.net/learn/videocat.aspx?cat=2#HDI2WebServices` and `http://www.west-wind.com/weblog/posts/546995.aspx`.

Summary

One of the greatest aspects of Silverlight is its flexibility. If an existing control doesn't provide the functionality you required then you can customize it to do so (although the Silverlight toolkit is definitely worth a look first: `http://www.codeplex.com/Silverlight`). All Silverlight controls can be broken down into primitive shapes such as rectangles and ellipses that can then be modified.

Think more about the functionality that the control provides more than what it looks like. At a presentation I attended at VBug (a UK user group), EMC/Conchango suggested adapting radio buttons to create a tab control. The tab control is perfect for this situation because only one can be selected at a time.

For more information on this subject please refer to `http://silverlight.net/quickstarts/controltemplates.aspx`.

Some of the things to consider about Silverlight include the following:

- It utilizes the .NET framework (take that, Adobe Flash!).

- It makes use of existing .NET development skills.

- It has excellent media playback/streaming capabilities.

- It creates cross-platform .NET applications.

- It can be a better choice for creating a complex UI than JavaScript/AJAX.

- It has good third-party control support already.

- Silverlight/HTML integration has interesting possibilities.

- Because Silverlight is based on WPF, it is possible to convert Silverlight applications to the desktop (also consider Silverlight's offline support, as discussed in Chapter 15).

- It is supported in some mobile devices.

Finally, there are some considerations when choosing Silverlight:

- Silverlight requires a separate plug-in and is available on most (but not all) major operating systems. (Wikipedia has a good list at http://en.wikipedia.org/wiki/Silverlight.)

- Sandboxed hosting environments could pose some problems.

- No printing or support for external devices (until Silverlight 4), which makes creating a line of business applications difficult.

- Some layout issues across different platforms.

- Adoption is lower than Flash, although this is changing.

- Silverlight files tend to be larger than Flash.

- Current web site design trends prefer clean HTML sites rather than slower Flash/Silverlight applications.

- XAML has a steep-ish learning curve, but is becoming an important language within the .NET sphere.

- Silverlight is running on the client's browser, so it is open to manipulation. Do not store any sensitive data in the plug-in and carry all validation out on the server side.

Further Reading

The next topics you will probably want to look at in your Silverlight studies include the following:

- Customization of Silverlight controls

- Silverlight network communications

Microsoft has produced a very good Silverlight site that contains a huge number of examples and video tutorials: http://www.silverlight.net.

Josh Smith has an excellent WPF/Silverlight tutorial series: http://joshsmithonwpf.wordpress.com/a-guided-tour-of-wpf/.

The Silverlight toolkit contains a number of additional controls, such as docking and graphs, which look very promising: http://www.codeplex.com/Silverlight.

Apress has a couple of Silverlight books:

- *Beginning Silverlight 3*, by Robert Lair

- *Pro Silverlight 3 in C#*, by Matthew MacDonald

CHAPTER 15

WPF 4.0 and Silverlight 3.0

WPF and Silverlight developers get some great new features in this release and will benefit from a more stable and feature-rich IDE, fine-grained control over text rendering, multitouch APIs, ability to cache any part of the visual tree, support for Windows 7 features such as jump lists, and much more.

Some of the WPF 4.0 changes were influenced and overlap with Silverlight 3.0 so in this (rather lengthy) chapter you will be covering WPF 4.0 first, then the highlights of Silverlight 3.0, and then briefly touching on some of the Silverlight 4.0 announcedments from PDC 09.

IDE Enhancements

The IDE support in VS2008 for WPF and (particularly) Silverlight developers was not fantastic; in fact, for Silverlight developers it sucked because the design view was read only! Although some readers will no doubt be happier working in pure XAML, the design view can be very useful. The improvements make it easier than ever to develop WPF and Silverlight applications.

VS2010 WPF/Silverlight Designer

VS2010 contains a much improved designer that offers the same full design time experience in both WPF and Silverlight projects. The new VS2010 WPF/Silverlight designer supports WPF 3.5, WPF 4.0, and Silverlight 3.0 project types and is constructed in an extensible manner so will also work with future releases—which is important with Silverlight 4.0 just around the corner!

It is worth noting that Silverlight SDK is included with VS2010, so it is no longer necessary to install the Silverlight tools to receive IDE support.

Sort by Property Source

The Properties window in VS2010 for XAML applications has a new view mode that prioritizes the properties that you have defined above all the others.. This allows you to easily amend and change properties you are interested in rather than scroll through a lengthy list.

Let's say you wrote the following XAML (and you would probably write something much more witty and interesting):

```
<TextBlock Text="Hello" FontFamily="Arial"></TextBlock>
```

In VS2010 you can now open the Properties window, click the Sort by property source button (the third one along), and you will find the properties that you just defined appear at the top of the list (see Figure 15-1).

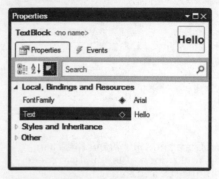

Figure 15-1. *Sort by property source*

Property Icons

Determining how a property gets set can sometimes be quite difficult in WPF. The Properties window now appends a small icon after each property to indicate their source. Figure 15-1 shows how FontFamily and Text are prefixed with a black diamond (this indicates a locally set item). A small blue sun indicates a style setter, and a brush indicates a resource. You can also view further information about how a property gets set by hovering the mouse over the icon.

Style

The designer in VS2010 makes it much easier to create and manage styles with the new enhancements to the Properties window. Let's take a look at this fab feature now.

1. Add the following style to app.xaml:

   ```
   <Style x:Key="MyStyle" TargetType="TextBlock">
   <Setter Property="FontFamily" Value="Comic Sans MS"/>
   <Setter Property="FontSize" Value="54"/>
   <Setter Property="Foreground" Value="#FF0000FF"/>
   </Style>
   ```

2. Now add a TextBlock to your page:

   ```
   <TextBlock>Hello WPF</TextBlock>
   ```

3. Make sure that the TextBlock is selected and then open the Properties window.

4. Inin the Properties window scroll down to where it says Style.

5. Click the text box on the right labeled Resource; this will open a new window. The new window will show various styles available within the current project (see Figure 15-2). Note this window also offers a text box–based search as larger projects can obviously contain many styles.

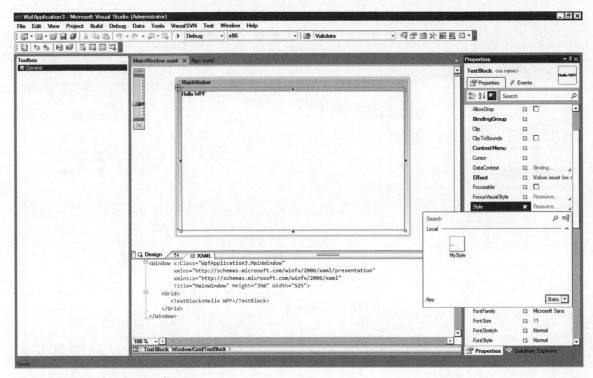

Figure 15-2. *Style selection box*

6. Finally select the style MyStyle that defined earlier by clicking it to apply it to the element. The XAML will then be updated to the following:

```
<TextBlock Style="{StaticResource MyStyle}">Hello WPF</TextBlock>
```

Brushes

The Properties window contains new functionality to make it easier to create brushes:

1. To see this, select the window or grid and then go to the Properties window.

2. Select the button next to the background text box and a new color picker dialog will appear, as shown in Figure 15-3 (this color picker window is new).

Figure 15-3. *New color picker dialog*

3. Select a color (I choose a murky swamp-like green).

4. Right-click the Background text box in the Properties window and select the Extract Value to Resource option from the context menu to bring up a new resource window.

5. Give the resource a name, and note you are going to save it in the only option currently available (`app.xaml ()`; if you had resource dictionaries, they would be available here as well).

6. Now select the grid in the design view and then on the Properties pane right-click the Background option and select Apply Resource.

7. A new window will pop up showing the resources you can apply. Click the local selection bar to expand it and select the resource you created earlier. You should then see something similar to Figure 15-4.

Figure 15-4. *Using the newly created brush to commit crimes against graphic design*

Binding Window

VS2010 makes creating bindings very much easier with a new Binding window. To see this window open the Properties window; then right-click any property that supports data binding (e.g., a dependency property) and select the Apply Data Binding option on the context menu.

A window similar to Figure 15-5 will then appear that allows you to easily create and modify bindings. Note that you can modify the source and path, specify converters, and define various other advanced options.

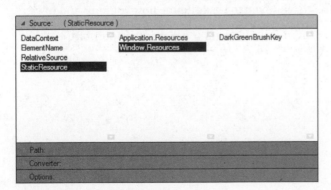

Figure 15-5. *Binding window*

Design Time Data Binding

You can now define a new data source setting that is used just in design view. This could be useful to allow designers to see how formatting changes would look. At the time of writing I have no information on this feature.

New Image Picker

A new image picker dialog has been added that allows you to easily select images and will take care of formatting the returned path for you (see Figure 15-6).

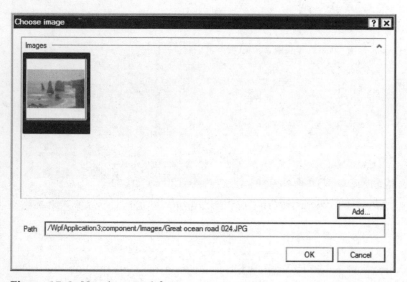

Figure 15-6. *New image picker*

Improved Grid Designer

VS2010 adds a new option to the DataGrid control to allow you to easily define how columns and rows should be sized. This window will appear when you define columns and rows and then hover over it. The menu allows you to choose the following options: Fixed (e.g. 200), Star (* weighted proportion), or Auto (where the size is determined by the contents). See Figure 15-7.

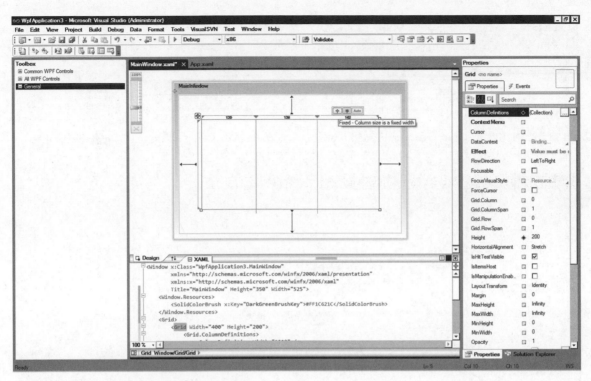

Figure 15-7. *New grid designer feature*

Improved Error Handling for User Controls

In VS2008, if you added a control to a page that contained an error, it would not appear and you would be left with no clue about what the error could be. This improves in VS2010 because the editor will now give you a detailed exception message allowing you to easily debug the problem (see Figure 15-8). Note that until the exception is fixed, the designer will be read only.

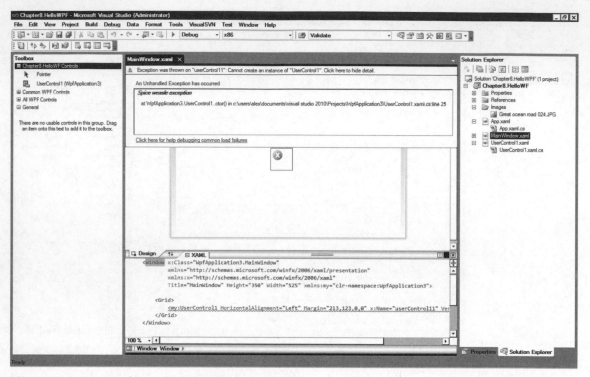

Figure 15-8. *Improved error handling for user controls*

Static Resource and Designer Fix

Previously, if a static resource was declared in app.xaml, you could not use it in the designer. In VS2010, you can.

Drag-and-Drop Data Binding

I'm not a big fan of drag-and-drop data binding and I think it's fair to say that most programmers will rightly scorn such functionality. However, this type of feature can be very useful for quickly putting together simple data entry forms and prototyping applications.

VS2010 includes new functionality to easily create data forms and creates some pretty clean XAML. It seems likely that Microsoft might have brought in this feature to encourage some winforms developers to move over.

You will now learn about this feature by creating a simple master detail form.

1. Select Data ➤ Show Data Sources.

2. Click the Add New Data Source button on the Data Sources window, and the Choose a Data Source Type window will appear (see Figure 15-9).

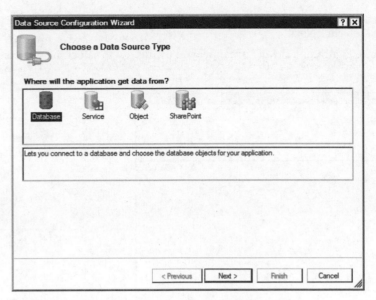

Figure 15-9. *Choose a Data Source Type dialog*

3. Select Database and then click Next. The Choose a Database Model screen will appear (see Figure 15-10).

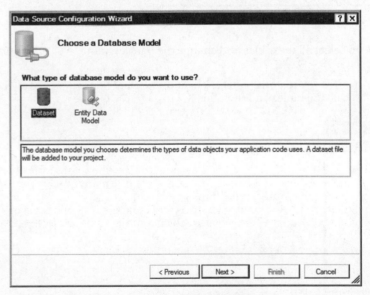

Figure 15-10. *Choose a Database Model dialog*

4. Select Dataset (you could also use an entity data model for this feature) and then click Next.

5. In the next screen, select the connection to the example database connection (or create it if you haven't already) and then click Next.

6. A new screen (similar to Figure 15-11) will now appear, allowing you to select the objects you want to use.

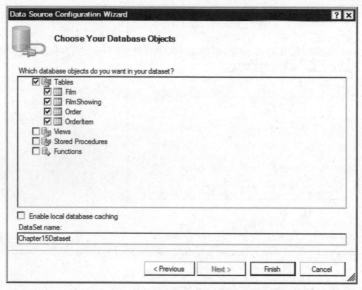

Figure 15-11. *Choose your poison (sorry) database objects*

7. Select the Tables node to select all the tables and change the dataset name to `Chapter15Dataset` before clicking `Finish`.

8. You now have the data source set up and if you look over to the Data Sources window (see Figure 15-12), you will see all the tables and their fields.

Figure 15-12. *Data Sources window after configuring the data source*

9. You will now create a data grid to show all the films. You don't want the field FilmID to appear, so click the FilmID beneath the Film table node. A drop-down menu will then appear, allowing you to select different types of UI to be generated for the field. In this case, you don't want it to appear, so select None.

10. Now drag the Film table node onto the designer surface to create a DataGrid of films (see Figure 15-13). If you run your project now, you will find a fully working DataGrid. However, you're not done yet; VS2010 also supports the ability to easily create master detail forms.

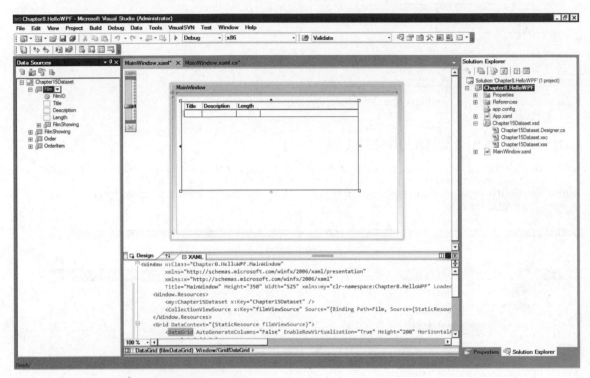

Figure 15-13. *Data grid linked to Data source*

11. You will now create a details panel to show more details of the film. Click FilmID (beneath the Film node) and change the type to Textbox.

12. Now click the Film node itself and on the drop-down menu change it to Details before dragging it to the right of the data grid (you might want to reposition the grid).

13. You also want to display all the film showings, so click the FilmShowing node and change the drop-down menu to List, and then drag it to the page beneath the grid.

14. Now press F5 to run your application and you will have a fully functional master details view similar to Figure 15-14.

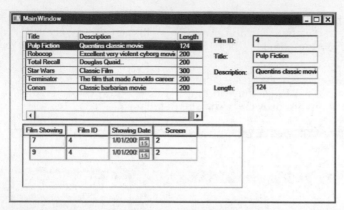

Figure 15-14. *The final product of the drag-and-drop binding*

Improved XAML Intellisense

XAML Intellisense has been tweaked. Now when you enter the curly bracket for a binding expression, Intellisense will add the other curly bracket for you and pop up a dialog with available options (see Figure 15-15). It seems a shame the team didn't go further with this feature and show you different objects you could bind to.

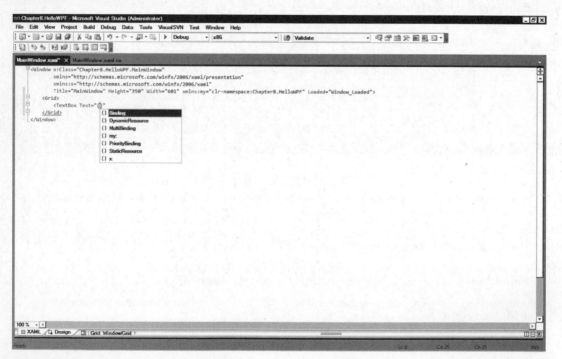

Figure 15-15. *Improved XAML intellisense*

New Controls

WPF 4.0 now contains the DataGrid, Calendar, and DatePicker controls that were previously available as part of the WPF toolkit. Microsoft says that these controls are nearly 100 percent compatible with their Silverlight relations. Figure 15-16 shows the new Calendar and DatePicker controls; Figure 15-17 shows the DataGrid control in action.

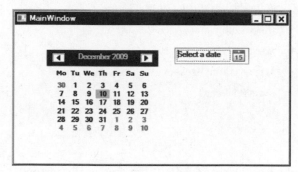

Figure 15-16. *Calendar and DatePicker controls*

Film ID	Title	Description	Length▲
4	Pulp Fiction	Quentins classic movie	124
7	Robocop	Excellent very violent cyborg movie	200
8	Total Recall	Douglas Quaid...	200
10	Terminator	The film that made Arnolds career	200
11	Conan	Classic barbarian movie	200
9	Star Wars	Classic Film	300

Figure 15-17. *DataGrid control*

The easiest way to create these controls is to drag them from the toolbox or add them manually with the following XAML:

```
<Calendar></Calendar>
<DatePicker/>
<DataGrid></DataGrid>
```

Ribbon Control and Bag O'Tricks

Microsoft says that shortly after the release of VS2010 it will introduce a new WPF Ribbon control. The Ribbon control could work particularly well in conjunction with the new touchscreen APIs. A CTP of the Ribbon control is available at `http://wpf.codeplex.com/Release/ProjectReleases.aspx?ReleaseId=29117`.

Microsoft will also be making an out-of-band release that will contain the following controls under the collection name "Bag O'Tricks" (sorry, no information is available at time of writing, although judging by the control names you can have a pretty good guess at what they do):

- `AnimatingTilePanel`
- `ColorPicker`
- `InfoTextBox`
- `ListPager`

- `NumericUpDown`
- `Reveal`
- `TransitionsPresenter`
- `TreeMapPanel`

Windows 7 Integration

Windows 7 has some great new UI features such as jump lists, taskbar overlays, and progress indicators. WPF 4.0 allows you to add these features to your applications. It is also worth noting that in this release WPF dialogs now have the same feel of Vista and Windows 7 (depending what they are running on).

Jump Lists

Jump lists, which allow you to easily perform common tasks, are activated by right-clicking an application on the task bar. Figure 15-18 shows the jump list for Windows Live Messenger.

Figure 15-18. *Jump list in Windows 7*

Like most things in WPF/Silverlight, jump lists can be created programmatically and declaratively. The following code shows how to create a jump list to open Internet Explorer and Notepad that you would define in your `MainWindow.xaml`:

```
using System.Windows.Shell;

...

JumpList appJumpList = new JumpList();

//Configure a JumpTask
JumpTask jumpTask1 = new JumpTask();
jumpTask1.ApplicationPath = @"C:\Program Files (x86)\Internet Explorer\iexplore.exe";
jumpTask1.IconResourcePath = @"C:\Program Files (x86)\Internet Explorer\iexplore.exe";

jumpTask1.Title = "IE";
jumpTask1.Description = "Open IE";

JumpTask jumpTask2 = new JumpTask();
jumpTask2.ApplicationPath = @"C:\Windows\System32\notepad.exe";
jumpTask2.IconResourcePath = @"C:\Windows\System32\notepad.exe";

jumpTask2.Title = "Notepad";
jumpTask2.Description = "Open Notepad";

appJumpList.JumpItems.Add(jumpTask1);
appJumpList.JumpItems.Add(jumpTask2);

JumpList.SetJumpList(App.Current, appJumpList);
```

Task Bar

Windows 7 applications can communicate progress and application status via the task bar. For example, Figure 15-19 shows IE indicating download progress.

Figure 15-19. *IE indicating download progress*

WPF 4.0 Windows 7 task bar APIs give you control over the following:

- Progress bar overlay (refer to Figure 15-19).

- Icon overlay through the `Overlay` property (e.g., a small picture).

- Thumbnail window (a window that pops up showing a miniview of the application's window). Note that you can pick which bit of the window is shown using the `ThumbnailClipMargin` property.

Let's take a look at how to work with the progress bar. The progress bar allows you to specify a double value between 0 and 1 to indicate your application's progress with the `ProgressValue` property. You can also indicate different types of status by specifying the `ProgressState` property. This has five different settings that change the color of the bar:

- Error (red)
- Indeterminate (green)
- None (not shown)
- Normal (green)
- Paused (yellow)

You will now see how to work with this by setting a progress bar at 50% for the application:

1. Create a new WPF application called Chapter15.ProgressBar.

2. Open MainWindow.xaml.cs and add the following using statement:

   using System.Windows.Shell;

3. Amend the code to the following:

```
public MainWindow()
{
    InitializeComponent();
    this.Loaded += new RoutedEventHandler(MainWindow_Loaded);
}

void MainWindow_Loaded(object sender, RoutedEventArgs e)
{

    TaskbarItemInfo taskBarItemInfo = new TaskbarItemInfo();

    taskBarItemInfo.ProgressState = TaskbarItemProgressState.Normal;
    this.TaskbarItemInfo = taskBarItemInfo;
    taskBarItemInfo.ProgressValue = 0.5d;

}
```

4. If you now run your application, you should find the progress bar at 50%.

Multitouch Functionality

Probably one of the most interesting features in WPF 4.0 is multitouch functionality. Multitouch allows your application to work with touch input and gestures (e.g., you can spin an image around by rotating your hand).

Multitouch support is Windows 7 only and is enabled by setting the IsManipulationEnabled property on an element to true and then handling the various events that the APIs expose. It's worth noting that multitouch functionality is compatible with Surface SDK 2.0 (the world's most expensive but cool table).

ContentElement, UIElement, and UIElement3D elements support the following events:

- PreviewTouchDown
- TouchDown
- PreviewTouchMove
- TouchMove

- PreviewTouchUp

- TouchUp

- GotTouchCapture

- LostTouchCapture

- TouchEnter

- TouchLeave

Besides simple touch-related events WPF4.0 also supports various gestures. You can restrict the manipulations that can be performed in the ManipulationStarted event by specifying the ManipulationMode.

WPF4.0 supports the following gesture-related events:

- ManipulationStarted

- ManipulationDelta

- ManipulationInertiaStarting

- ManipulationCompleted

- ManipulationBoundaryFeedback

At present, hardware support for multitouch is a bit limited and expensive (and who wants grubby fingerprints on their monitors?), but expect this to rapidly change in 2010.

Probably the best known multitouch device is the Dell Latitude XT2 and HP touchsmart. If you don't want to fork out for one of these devices you could give the clever work around with two mice here: http://blog.wpfwonderland.com/2009/06/29/developing-win-7-multi-touch-apps-without-multi-touch-screen/.

MSDN has a good simple example demonstrating WPF's touch functionality: http://msdn.microsoft.com/en-us/library/ee649090(VS.100).aspx.

Binding Changes

Besides the very welcome new Binding window in VS2010, there are a number of other changes in the exciting world of binding.

Run.text

Run.text is now a dependency property, which means you can now bind to it (one way) unlike previous releases of WPF.

Dynamic Binding Support

WPF4.0 supports binding to properties implementing the IDynamicMetaObjectProvider interface such as ExpandoObject and anything inheriting from DynamicObject ((see Chapter 3).

Input Bindings Now Support Bindings

In previous releases of WPF, it was quite tricky to set binding to input keys using the InputBinding class. This was because the Command property was not a dependency property and also didn't inherit the parent's data context. This could make certain scenarios such as implementing the MVVM pattern difficult.

This is resolved in WPF 4.0. InputBinding, MouseBinding, and KeyBinding now inherit from Freezable and various related properties are now made dependency properties. This should then allow you to write input binding XAML such as the following:

```
<Window.InputBindings>
<KeyBinding
Modifiers="Control" Key="L"
Command="{Binding MyCustomCommand}" />
</Window.InputBindings>
```

Text-Rendering Improvements

In previous releases of WPF, text could sometimes appear a bit blurry. This is fixed in WPF 4.0 (possibly driven by the need for clear text in VS2010 IDE) and you now have much finer-grained control over how text is rendered with the new TextFormattingMode and TextRenderingMode properties.

TextOptions.TextFormattingMode

TextFormatting mode allows you to set the text metrics that WPF will use for formatting text. TextFormatting mode has two settings:

- Ideal (as per previous versions)

- Display (ensures that every glyph's position and width is not fractional, which is very similar to how the GDI renders text)

The following code demonstrates setting text to use the Display setting:

```
<TextBlock TextOptions.TextFormattingMode="Display">
Hello I am using new Display mode formatting
</TextBlock>
```

Setting text to Display mode will in many cases make the text look darker and clearer. In Figure 15-20 the first paragraph uses the old Ideal setting; the second uses the new Display setting (yes, the difference is subtle, especially in print, but try it for yourself).

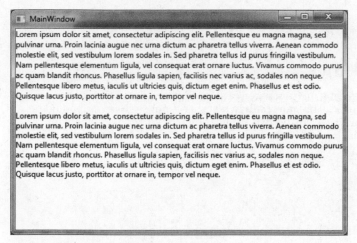

Figure 15-20. *Display mode property*

Ideal mode works well for situations when you have large fonts or perform transformations/zoom into the text but can look a bit blurry at small font sizes. In these cases you would probably be better off using the Display setting.

TextOptions.TextRenderingMode

The TextRendering setting, which allows you to control how text is anti-aliased, has four settings:

- Auto (uses clear type unless disabled)
- Aliased (disables anti-aliasing)
- Grayscale (uses grayscale anti-aliasing)
- Cleartype (uses clear type anti-aliasing)

The following code shows how to apply the Grayscale rendering mode:

```
<TextBlock TextOptions.TextRenderingMode="Grayscale">
I am rendered using  Grayscale
</TextBlock>
```

Figure 15-21 shows how these settings effect the output.

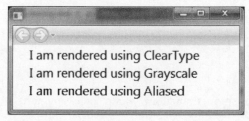

Figure 15-21. *Demonstration of TextRendering setting*

Microsoft recommends that for most scenarios Auto is the best setting to use because it takes advantage of ClearType where available.

RenderOptions.ClearTypeHint

In some rendering situations (such as rendering on transparent areas), ClearType functionality will be disabled and Grayscale rendering will be used. This can result in text that is not as sharp as it could be. WPF 4.0 contains a new option called ClearTypeHint to force applications to utilize ClearType. The following code illustrates how to apply this to a TextBlock:

```
<TextBlock RenderOptions.ClearTypeHint="Enabled">
I will use cleartype
</TextBlock>
```

East Asian Bitmap font support

Some non-English alphabet characters can be quite complex (think Chinese glyphs), and when rendered at smaller sizes can appear very blurry using vector transformations. WPF now uses bitmaps for smaller text size (if available) which can result in crisper text. Microsoft say this feature is supported for the following languages and fonts such as:

- Japanese (MS Gothic)
- Korean (Gulium)
- Korean (Batang)
- Traditional Chinese (MingLiu)
- Simplified Chinese (SimSun)

Layout Rounding

When positioning elements in WPF you can sometimes end up with fractional values. For example, splitting a grid 100 pixels wide into 3 columns of equal size gives each column a nasty width of 33.333333. These fractional properties can result in images and objects with blurry edges and other horrid rendering artifacts. To see many examples, see this excellent site that visually demonstrates the affects of subpixel layouts: http://blogs.msdn.com/text/archive/2009/08/27/layout-rounding.aspx.

Silverlight 2.0 introduced a new property called UseLayoutRounding that offers a solution to this issue by forcing the layout to use whole pixel values only. UseLayoutRouting is now supported in WPF. Using this feature can result in crisper images and layouts, but your layout might not be pixel perfect. This XAML demonstrates how to use this property:

```
<Grid UseLayoutRounding="True" >
</Grid>
```

Cached Composition

Arguably one of the best additions to WPF 4.0 is cached composition, that allows you to cache any part of the visual tree. Complex effects can take time to render, which results in a jerky experience for your users and uses vast amounts of CPU and memory. WPF 4.0 allows you to cache elements as a bitmap, reducing this rendering time and resource usage with the new BitmapCache and BitmapCacheBrushes classes. The BitmapCacheBrushes class is used when you will reuse the same content multiple times.

Cached composition supports dirty regions, so it is clever enough to re-render only the parts that have changed. Re-rendering can occur when WPF detects the visual tree changes or any cache-related properties are modified. Note that the maximum dimensions the bitmap cache supports are 2048 by 2048 pixels.

There is an excellent demo by Lester Lobo that shows the difference cached composition can make: http://blogs.msdn.com/llobo/archive/2009/11/10/ new-wpf-features-cached-composition.aspx.

CacheMode can be turned on with the following XAML (applied to a Canvas element in this example):

```
<Canvas.CacheMode>
<BitmapCache />
</Canvas.CacheMode>
<Canvas x:name="myCanvas" CacheMode="BitmapCache"/>
```

Or programmatically:

```
myCanvas.CacheMode = new BitmapCache();
```

And turned off with the following code:

```
myCanvas.CacheMode = null;
```

Animation Easing

WPF contains new effects for creating nonlinear movements using complex mathematical formulas to produce effects such as bouncy spring animations. You will look at how to utilize these in Silverlight 3.0 later in the chapter, but know that WPF 4.0 provides the following effects:

- BackEase
- BounceEase
- CircleEase
- CubicEase
- Elasticease
- ExponentialEase
- Quadraticease
- QuarticEase
- Quinticease
- PowerEase
- SineEase

Pixel Shader 3.0 Support

Previous releases of WPF supported Pixel Shaders version 2.0. WPF 4.0 now supports Pixel Shader version 3.0. Note that the hardware the application is running on must also support the Pixel Shader capabilities. To query this, use the static methods on the `RenderCapability` class such as `RenderCapability.IsPixelShaderVersionSupported`.

Visual State Manager Integration

Visual State Manager (VSM)) allows you to define a set of states for your controls (e.g., normal, mouse over, mouse down) and then define a different look for each of these states. VSM will automatically animate the transitions between states; for example, if you have a black button with a mouse down state that highlights it blue, the button can gradually be highlighted blue as the user hovers the mouse. In WPF 4.0, the `VisualStateManager` and related classes are added to the main framework.

HTML-XBAP Script Interop

HTML-XBAP applications can use the new `BrowserInteropHelper` class to interact with the hosting web page. `BrowserInteropHelper` provides full DOM access and can handle DOM events.

Full-Trust XBAP Deployment

In previous releases of WPF, it was quite difficult to create a fully trusted XBAP application. That changes with this release; XBAP applications that require full trust that are run from intranet or trusted site zones will now give users the `ClickOnce` elevation prompt. This allows users to easily grant the necessary privileges for your application.

Client Profile

It is worth mentioning the client profile (a cut-down version of the full .NET Framework) aimed at reducing application size and installation time is also used for WPF applications. For more information about the client profile, please refer to Chapter 4.

Miscellaneous Changes

You have barely touched the surface with all the new functionality available in WPF 4 but4.0 before you leave this area I would like to mention a number of other additions that were made:

- New XAML parser

- Many additions to XAML 2009 language such as support for Generics

- `RichTextBox` now supports custom dictionaries rather than just using the OS-provided dictionary (http://blogs.msdn.com/text/archive/2009/10/02/custom-dictionaries.aspx)

- Text selection can be customized for `TextBox`, `RichTextBox`, `FlowDocumentPageViewer`, `FlowDocumentScrollViewer`, `FlowDocumentReader`, and `PasswordBox` with the new Selection Brush API

- Many changes to API and refactoring of XamlSchemaContext for performance improvements

- System.Xaml.dll no longer has a dependency on WindowsBase.dll

- The same XAML stack is utilized by WCF, WF, and WPF

- Performance optimizations in Baml2006Reader class

- New class XamlXmlReader

- Improved localization support

- Baml2006Writer class might be available with this release, which could potentially allow the obfuscation of BAML

Silverlight 3.0

Silverlight developers are in for a treat with the latest version of Silverlight which offers the ability to run your applications offline, deep linking for content and much more.

■**NOTE** This chapter assumes a basic knowledge of Silverlight and WPF. If you haven't used Silverlight before you might want to take a look at Chapter 14 where I introduce Silverlight.

Upgrading from Silverlight 2

Before you look at the new changes in Silverlight 3.0, note that upgrading can potentially break existing applications. This URL lists breaking changes: http://msdn.microsoft.com/en-us/library/cc645049(VS.95).aspx.

And this URL provides guidance on how to upgrade your Silverlight 2.0 applications: http://msdn.microsoft.com/en-us/library/cc645049(VS.95).aspx.

Offline Applications

Probably the best feature of Silverlight 3.0 is the ability it offers to run your applications offline. Offline Silverlight applications run with the same permissions as their web counterparts, so they do not require additional permissions to install. Offline applications also work on both PC and Mac platforms, providing a very easy way to create cross-platform .NET applications.

Creating an Offline Application

To enable your Silverlight applications to run offline is very easy and involves making a simple change to the AppManifest file. Try it now:

1. Create a new Silverlight application called Chapter15.Offline.

2. Add some content (e.g., an image).

3. Open the project properties (see Figure 15-22).

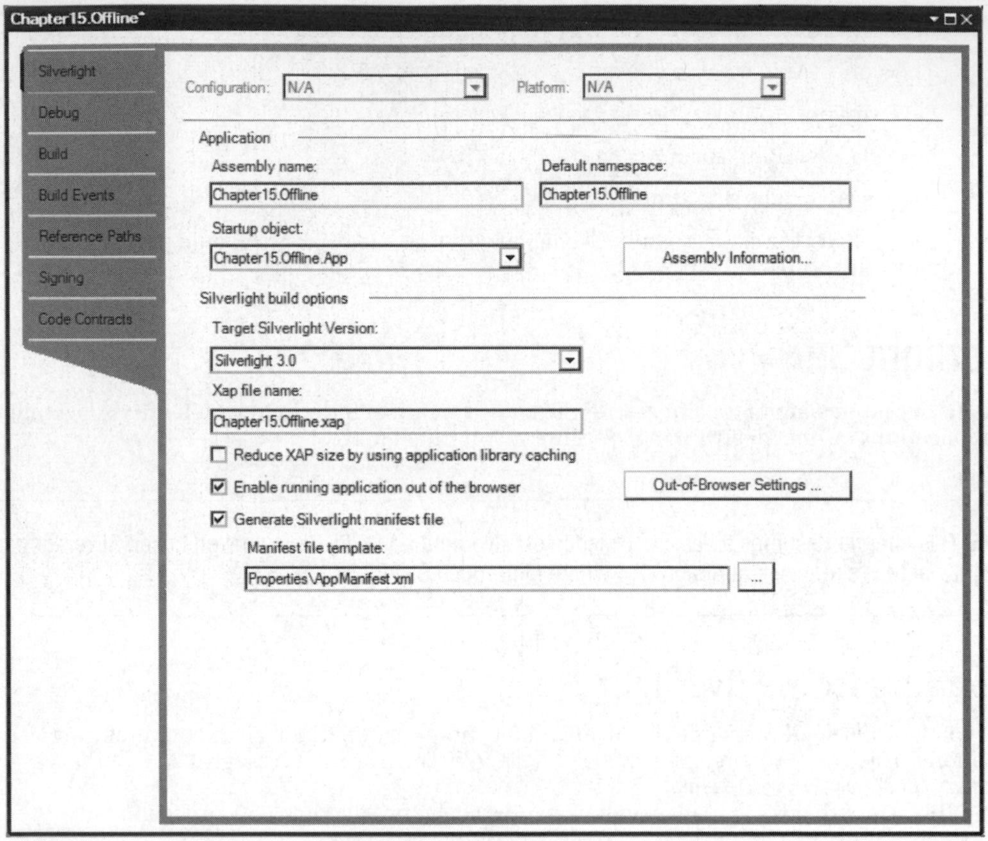

Figure 15-22. *Enabling offline application in project properties*

4. Check the box marked "Enable running application outside of browser".

5. Click the Out-of-Browser Settings button and note that you can set properties such as images, window size, and application title.

6. Press F5 to run your Silverlight project and then right-click the Silverlight app. The Silverlight menu will open up.

7. Select the "Install Chapter15.Offline Application onto this computer" option (see Figure 15-23).

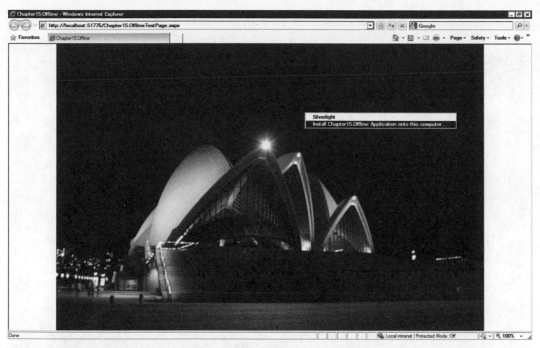

Figure 15-23. *Installing a Silverlight application onto the computer*

8.   Silverlight will then ask you to confirm where you want to place shortcuts to your application: Start menu and/or Desktop (see Figure 15-24).

Figure 15-24. *Offline Silverlight application*

9.   Check both the Start menu and Desktop options.

10. Close the browser.

11. Now click one of the short cuts that has been created, and your application will load up running offline (see Figure 15-25):

Figure 15-25. *Running a silverlight app offline*

Uninstalling Offline Silverlight Applications

If you want to uninstall an offline Silverlight application, simply right-click the window when it is running locally and select the "Remove this application" option.

Detaching Manually

You probably don't want to explain these steps to end users, so the Silverlight API contains an `Application.Current.Install()`method that performs the same functionality. `Application.Current.Install() method` returns a Boolean value indicating whether the detachment was possible or not.

Retrieving Attachment State

To query whether your application is running online in a browser or detached, use the `Application.Current.IsRunningOutOfBrowser` method.

Detecting Connection Status

Now that you have the ability to run applications offline, it is very useful to be able to determine whether the user is connected to the Internet. This can be accomplished through the GetIsNetworkAvailable method that returns true if the user is connected:

```
System.Net.NetworkInformation.NetworkInterface.GetIsNetworkAvailable()
```

■**CAUTION** If the user has chosen to work in offline mode, this method will still return true.

You also have the ability to monitor network address changes through the NetworkAddressChanged event:

```
System.Net.NetworkInformation.NetworkChange.NetworkAddressChanged()
```

Autoupdate

When offline applications are run, Silverlight automatically checks to see whether a later version is available. If it is, it is downloaded.

Deep Linking and Browser History

A major problem with Silverlight applications is that you cannot directly link to content within the application in the same way you can with web pages. This makes it difficult for users to share or bookmark content and makes search engine indexing impossible. Silverlight 3.0 attempts to solve this issue by making use of HTML bookmark syntax in your application's URL.

Navigation Application

Navigation Application is a new type of project in Silverlight 3.0. If you say Navigation Application quickly it sounds like gangsta rap, argued Silverlight MVP Chris Hay, and he was right. But that doesn't have much to do with anything, so let's take a look at Navigation Application now:

1. Create a new Silverlight Navigation Application project called Chapter15.NavigationApplication.

2. Press F5 to run the application and you will see the default Navigation Application project (see Figure 15-26).

3. Click the about button and notice how the URL changes to something similar to this:

   ```
   http://localhost:51951/Chapter15.NavigationApplicationTestPage.aspx#/About
   ```

You can use this URL to refer directly to the about page—try navigating to a different page and then pasting the URL into the address bar. This new URL format allows the browser to maintain a history of pages the user navigated through, which means the back and forward browser buttons can be used to move around your applications.

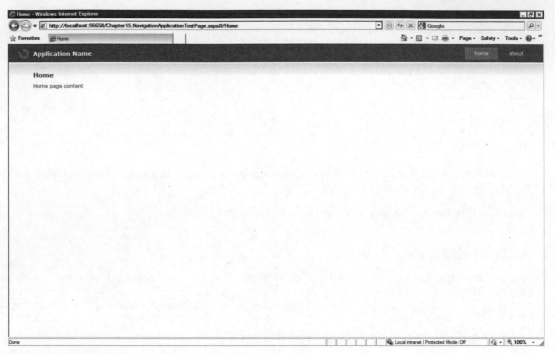

Figure 15-26. *Default Navigation Application*

Local Connections

Some page designs utilize two separate Silverlight controls and need a way to pass information between them. Previously, this could only be accomplished using the HTML DOM methods. Silverlight 3.0 makes this much easier with the local connection API. Let's create a simple example and send some text from one Silverlight control to another:

1. Open Visual Studio and create a new Silverlight application called `Chapter15.Sender`.

2. Add another Silverlight application to the solution called `Chapter15.Receiver` (opt not to create another web hosting project).

3. Open `Chapter15.SenderTestPage.aspx`.

4. You want to display the `Chapter15.Receiver` project on the same page, so add another Silverlight control beneath the existing one by copying the object block and modifying the `source` parameter to display the `Chapter15.Receiver` project`.xap` file:

```
<object data="data:application/x-silverlight-2," type="application/x-silverlight-2"
width="100%" height="100%">
   <param name="source" value="ClientBin/Chapter15.Receiver.xap"/>
   <param name="onError" value="onSilverlightError" />
   <param name="background" value="white" />
```

```
    <param name="minRuntimeVersion" value="3.0.40818.0" />
    <param name="autoUpgrade" value="true" />
    <a href="http://go.microsoft.com/fwlink/?LinkID=149156&v=3.0.40818.0"
style="text-decoration:none">
        <img src="http://go.microsoft.com/fwlink/?LinkId=161376" alt="Get Microsoft
Silverlight"
style="border-style:none"/>
    </a>
</object>
```

5. Open `MainPage.xaml` in the sender project and add a button with the following XAML:

```
<Button x:Name="cmdSendMessage" Content="Send Message" Width="200"
Height="200"></Button>
```

6. Open `MainPage.xaml.cs` in the sender project and import the following namespace:

```
using System.Windows.Messaging;
```

7. Amend the code in `MainMenu.xaml.cs` to the following:

```
public partial class MainPage : UserControl
{
    LocalMessageSender Channel1 = new LocalMessageSender("Channel1");

    public MainPage()
    {
        this.Loaded += new RoutedEventHandler(MainPage_Loaded);
        Channel1.SendCompleted +=
          new EventHandler<SendCompletedEventArgs>(Channel1_SendCompleted);
        InitializeComponent();
    }

    void Channel1_SendCompleted(object sender, SendCompletedEventArgs e)
    {
        //Code to run after message is sent
    }

    void MainPage_Loaded(object sender, RoutedEventArgs e)
    {
        this.cmdSendMessage.Click += new RoutedEventHandler(cmdSendMessage_Click);
    }

    void cmdSendMessage_Click(object sender, RoutedEventArgs e)
    {
        Channel1.SendAsync("Hello from sender project");
    }
}
```

8. Open the receiver project `MainPage.xaml` and add a text box to display the received messages:

```
<TextBlock>Received messages:</TextBlock>
<TextBox x:Name="txtMessage"></TextBox>
```

9. You now need to add code to receive the messages and update the text box with the messages you have received. To receive messages, handle the MessageReceived event on an instance of LocalMessageReceiver. Open MainPage.xaml.cs in the receiver project and import the following namespace:

```
using System.Windows.Messaging;
```

10. Amend MainPage.xaml.cs to the following:

```
public partial class MainPage : UserControl
{
    LocalMessageReceiver Channel1Receiver = new LocalMessageReceiver("Channel1");

    public MainPage()
    {

        Channel1Receiver.MessageReceived +=
            new
EventHandler<MessageReceivedEventArgs>(Channel1Receiver_MessageReceived);
        Channel1Receiver.Listen();
        InitializeComponent();
    }

    void Channel1Receiver_MessageReceived(object sender, MessageReceivedEventArgs e)
    {
        txtMessage.Text="" + e.Message.ToString();
    }
}
```

■**NOTE** The LocalMessageReceiver constructor sets the parameter to Channel1 (the same channel that messages are being sent on).

11. Press F5 to run the project.

12. Click the Send Message button. A message should then be sent using the local connection API and the results displayed in the text box in the receive project.

Styles

Styles in Silverlight 3.0 can now be modified at runtime and support inheritance.

Applying Styles Dynamically

The following code shows how to apply a style to a button at runtime:

```
myButton.Style=(Style)Application.Current.Resources["MyHorridFuciaStyle"];
```

Style Inheritance

Silverlight 3.0 allows you to create styles that inherit from another style (sort of like CSS) by specifying a parent style in the BasedOn property. The following code creates a style inheriting from MyHorridFuciaStyle:

```
<Style x:Key="HybridStyle" TargetType="Button"
BasedOn="{StaticResource MyHorridFuciaStyle}"></Style>
```

Merge Dictionary Support

It is now possible to refer to external resource dictionary files within your application:

```
<ResourceDictionary>
  <ResourceDictionary.MergedDictionaries>
    <ResourceDictionary Source="myExternalResources.xaml" />
  </ResourceDictionary.MergedDictionaries>
</ResourceDictionary>
```

Save File Dialog

A major issue in previous versions of Silverlight was that there was no capability of transferring files to a user. Silverlight 3.0 has a new file save dialog that allows users to save content to their local machine rather than to isolated storage. This example creates a text file and then gives the user the option to save it:

```
void cmdSave_Click(object sender, RoutedEventArgs e)
{
    SaveFileDialog SaveDialog = new SaveFileDialog();
    if (SaveDialog.ShowDialog() == true)
    {
        System.IO.Stream fs = null;

        try
        {
            fs = SaveDialog.OpenFile();
            byte[] info =
              (new System.Text.UTF8Encoding(true)).GetBytes("Test text to write to file");
            fs.Write(info, 0, info.Length);
        }
        finally
        {
            fs.Close();
        }
    }
}
```

Filtering Files in SaveDialog

Files shown in the SaveDialog window can be filtered by type using the Filter and FilterIndex properties. The Filter property allows you to specify a pipe-delimitated list of file types and FilterIndex (0 based) sets the default filter to use.

This example shows how to show two filter options with the default filter option set to all files:

```
SaveDialog.Filter = "Text Files (.txt)|*.txt|All Files|*.*";
//Set default filter to All Files
SaveDialog.FilterIndex = 1;
```

Element to Element Binding

In Silverlight 3.0 and WPF4.0, you can now bind directly to another element. This example binds a TextBlock's Text property to the Text property of the text box txtValue:

```
<TextBox x:Name="txtValue" Width="200" Canvas.Top="50" ></TextBox>
<TextBlock Text="{Binding Text, ElementName=txtValue}"></TextBlock>
```

Effects and Transformations

WPF 4.0 and Silverlight 3.0 introduce some great new effects functionality. Let's take a look at these now.

Plane Projection

Plane Projection is a new effect that allows you to rotate XAML elements around a 3D axis. Figure 15-27 shows the results of a Plane Projection transformation:

Figure 15-27. *RotationY transformation to an image*

The effect was created with this XAML:

```xaml
<Image Source="/pic1.jpg">
    <Image.Projection>
        <PlaneProjection RotationY="130"></PlaneProjection>
    </Image.Projection>
</Image>
```

Note the transformation effect simulates rotating elements around the X, Y, or Z axis, but does not apply light or shading effects.

THE RESULT OF A ROTATIONX TRANSFORM?

You might have expected Figure 15-27 to be the result of a X rather than Y axis rotation. It can help to imagine that the Y axis is like a vertical pole, and the image is placed in front of this pole (see Figure 15-28). When the transformation is applied the image is rotated around whichever pole is specified (in this case, the Y pole).

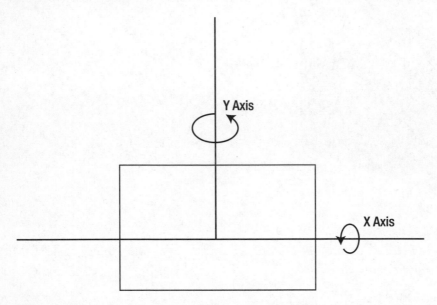

Figure 15-28. *How Silverlight 3.0 views rotation transformations*

Don't think that perspective transforms can be used only on images. Perspective transformations can also be applied to any WPF element allowing you to create some really weird and cool animation effects—and the best part is that the control will still function as per normal, detecting clicks and events! This can be used for some silly (and unfriendly UI design), as Figure 15-29 shows.

Figure 15-29. *Projection transform applied to stack panel*

Easing Effects

Earlier, I discussed some of the new easing effects in WPF4.0. Let's take a look at the BounceEase effect, which animates an element to makes it look like a ball bouncing up and down that gradually loses height with each bounce.

The level of springiness can be controlled through the adeptly named Bounciness property, in which lower numbers are more bouncy (e.g., a rubber ball) than higher numbers (e.g., a cricket ball). This XAML shows how to apply a BounceEase effect to an image (note you will have to start this storyboard to see the animation):

```
<Canvas>
    <Canvas.Resources>
        <Storyboard x:Name="bounceyAnim">
            <DoubleAnimation
                        Duration="0:0:3"
                        From="0"
                        To="300"
                        Storyboard.TargetName="myPic"
                        Storyboard.TargetProperty="(Canvas.Top)">
                <DoubleAnimation.EasingFunction>
                    <BounceEase Bounciness="2" Bounces="5"
                                EasingMode="EaseOut"></BounceEase>
                </DoubleAnimation.EasingFunction>
            </DoubleAnimation>
        </Storyboard>
    </Canvas.Resources>

    <Image Source="/pic1.jpg" Width="200" Height="200" Canvas.Left="50" Canvas.Top="50"
            x:Name="myPic"></Image>

</Canvas>
```

Pixel Shaders

Pixel shaders manipulate a rendered element at the pixel level and can be used to apply cool effects such as shadows and blurs. Figure 15-30 shows the shadow effect applied to an image.

Figure 15-30. *Shadow pixel shader*

This effect was created with the following code:

```
<Image x:Name="myPic" Source="sydney2.jpg">
    <Image.Effect>
        <DropShadowEffect ShadowDepth="15"></DropShadowEffect>
    </Image.Effect>
</Image>
```

Silverlight contains another great built-in pixel shader called Blur (shown in Figure 15-31).

Figure 15-31. *Blur pixel shader effect*

Applying the Blur effect is very similar to applying DropShadow:

```
<Image Source="/pic1.jpg" Width="700" Height="500" Canvas.Left="50" Canvas.Top="20"
x:Name="myPic">
    <Image.Effect>
        <BlurEffect Radius="15"></BlurEffect>
    </Image.Effect>
</Image>
```

■**TIP** Although you cannot apply two pixel shader effects to the same element, you can wrap an element with another element (e.g., add a Canvas element) and then apply effects to the outer element.

■**TIP** Pixel shader effects are always rendered on the CPU, so they do not benefit from GPU acceleration.

Creating Your Own Pixel Shaders

You can create your own pixel shaders by utilizing a language called High Level Shader Language (HLSL).).

Renew Schulte created an excellent filter that simulates an old movie tape effect. For more information on how René created this effect and an example of this applied to a movie please refer to http://kodierer.blogspot.com/2009/08/ye-olde-pixels-silverlight-3-old-movie.html.

Media

One of Silverlight's strengths has always been its rich media capabilities (indeed version 1.0 wasn't good for much else). Silverlight 3.0 now contains support for a number of new formats and smooth streaming when used in conjunction with IIS Media Services (http://www.iis.net/media).

New Formats

Silverlight 3.0 supports the following additional formats:

- HD (720p+)
- MPEG-4–based H.264/AAC Audio (known as HD TV)
- HD playback to full screen by utilizing GPU

Silverlight DRM

Silverlight 3.0 contains built-in DRM support using PlayReady with AES encryption.

■**NOTE** To utilize PlayReady-protected content, you will need access to a PlayReady licensed server.

Performance

Microsoft has been hard at work tweaking Silverlight 3.0's performance. Let's look at what has changed.

Binary XML Support

Silverlight 3.0 has support for Binary XML, allowing you to communicate with WCF binary XML endpoints. Binary XML format is much smaller than regular XML and results in less data being transferred over the network and ultimately better performance for your applications.

Enhanced Deep Zoom performance

DeepZoom is now much quicker than ever before (not that it was slow before).

Improved XAP Compression

XAP files are now compressed more efficiently, and Microsoft says you should see a 10–30 percent decrease in size compared with previous versions.

Silverlight.js

The JavaScript file Silverlight.js in Silverlight 3.0 is compressed and is now just 7k in size (previous versions were 57k). To obtain the uncompressed version, go to http://code.msdn.microsoft.com/silverlightjs/.

Assembly Caching

Silverlight applications can be reduced in size by utilizing a new feature called *assembly caching*. When assembly caching is turned on, core .NET assemblies used by your app will not be included in the Silverlight XAP file that is downloaded by the client. If clients don't have these assemblies on their machine, then they will be downloaded directly from Microsoft.

Enabling assembly caching is very easy:

1. Open the Properties dialog of the Silverlight project

2. Check the Reduce XAP size by using application library caching check box (see Figure 15-32).

3. Recompile your Silverlight application, and you're done.

■**CAUTION** Cached assemblies will be cleared if the browser cache is cleared.

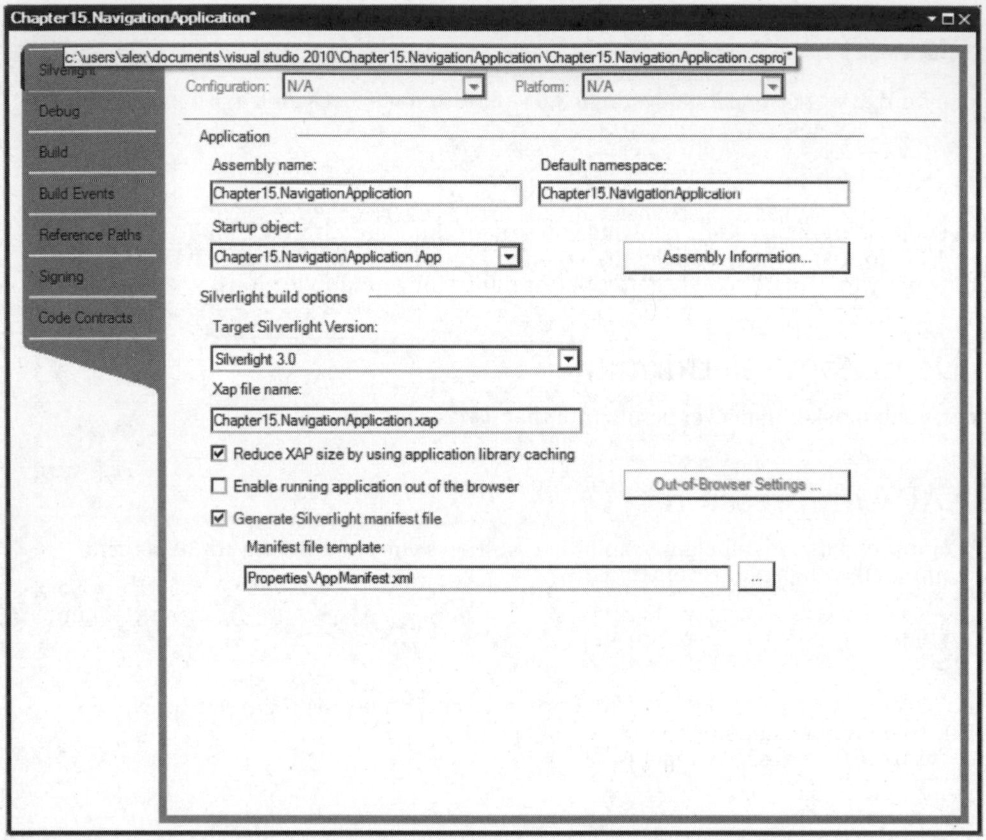

Figure 15-32. *Enabling cached assemblies*

GPU Acceleration

Silverlight 3.0 allows you to shift resource-intensive tasks such as clipping and transformations to the GPU. GPU acceleration must first be enabled at the application level.

1. Open Chapter15.OfflineTestPage.aspx and add the following parameter:

   ```
   <param name="EnableGPUAcceleration" value="true" />
   ```

2. Add the CacheMode property to controls that you want to implement caching and set it to BitmapCache:

   ```
   <Image Source="sydney.jpg" CacheMode="BitmapCache" ></Image>
   ```

■**NOTE** Some effects such as pixel shaders, render transforms, and plane projections do not benefit from GPU acceleration because the calculations for them are always carried out on the CPU.

■**TIP** Silverlight can highlight elements on your page that are utilizing caching if you set the EnableCacheVisualization property in app.config to true. When this setting is enabled, Silverlight will use the cache to tint elements a light red color so you can see what's cached.

Miscellaneous Enhancements

Silverlight 3.0 has a number of other minor tweaks and enhancements.

Controls

There are more than 60 new controls in Silverlight 3.0 (many originally part of the Silverlight Toolkit) and to go through them would require several chapters. However, I will tell you that Silverlight now contains charting, docking, auto-complete, time, accordion, and tree view controls.

Listbox

The Silverlight Listbox control now supports multiselection.

TextBox Cursor Styling

The TextBox caret can now be styled in WPF 4.0 and Silverlight 3.0 with the CaretBrush property. This code example changes the caret to a yellow color:

```
<TextBox x:Name="txtValue" Width="400" CaretBrush="Yellow"  Canvas.Top="50">
</TextBox>
```

Accessibility

Silverlight 3.0 is the first browser plug-in that allows you to utilize any color in the system palette. This can assist partially sighted people by allowing them to view controls in high-contrast schemes.

Browser Zoom Support

Silverlight 3.0 now supports browser zoom requests.

Slsvcutil.exe

The Silverlight SDK contains a new command-line utility for generating proxy classes. This script demonstrates how to use this utility: slsvcutil.exe http://myservice.com/myendpoint.svc?WSDL.

WCF RIA Services

Not really a Silverlight 3.0 change, but I want to make you aware of a new framework called WCF RIA Services. Many Silverlight applications need to perform simple add, update, delete, and call functions, and it can be very tedious to write web service methods to fulfill these requirements.WCF RIA Services will meet these needs and many more; see http://code.msdn.microsoft.com/RiaServices.

Blend 3/SketchFlow

Although VS2010 contains excellent design time support for WPF and Silverlight, if you make many aesthetic changes or are a designer you are probably better off using Blend 3. Blend 3 also contains a great feature called SketchFlow that allows you to produce prototype applications (see Figure 15-33):

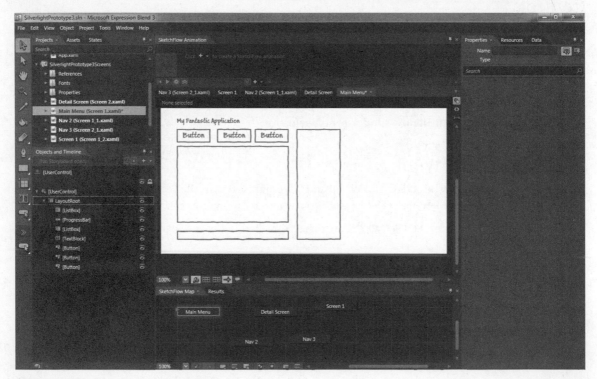

Figure 15-33. *Blend 3 and SketchFlow*

Silverlight 4.0

At the time of writing the first beta of Silverlight 4.0 has just been released. (I don't envy Silverlight authors; their books must have the shortest lifespan in the world.)

I have summarized some of the important changes here:

- Printing support (yay!)

- MEF support

- New controls: TextBox with hyperlink, masked TextBox, DataGrid with copy/paste functionality

- Webcam and microphone support

- Copy-and-paste functionality

- Mouse wheel support

- Google Chrome support

- Performance optimizations

- Multitouch support

- For trusted applications, read/write to documents folders, run other desktop programs (e.g., Microsoft Office suite)

- New interface for requesting more privileges for applications

- Localization enhancements (right-to-left text and complex scripts)

For more information, please refer to http://silverlight.net/getstarted/silverlight-4-beta/.

Silverlight in the Real World

Some developers consider Silverlight little more than a toy at present and argue that it is not suitable for serious line of business applications. Can Silverlight really be used to produce a line of business application? I talked to Rusty and Andy at SharpCloud about their experiences of developing a Silverlight application.

Rusty Johnson and Andy Britcliffe, SharpCloud

SharpCloud (http://www.sharpcloud.com) is currently developing a "project risk assessment application." The application carries out complex calculations to determine the optimum order for carrying out projects. The application is built using Silverlight and WCF, and it runs on the Windows Azure (see Chapter 16). It is shown in Figure 15-34 and Figure 15-35.

Figure 15-34. *SharpCloud's Silverlight application*

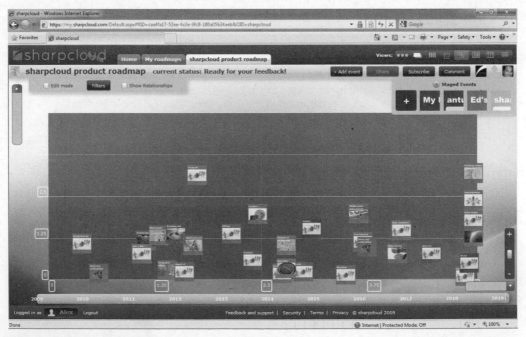

Figure 15-35. *SharpCloud's Silverlight application*

Rusty and Andy summarized their experiences here:

- They developed a usable application from scratch in about four months ("startup" days, not 9–5!).

- It is quite easy for .NET developers to get up to speed with Silverlight (although Andy did have a lot of Silverlight experience). Andy mentioned that some developers might struggle to understand the async event model.

- Don't load your entire application at once, but be prepared to use dynamic loading facilities (Andy recommended looking at PRISM and the following URL: http://www.sparklingclient.com/prism-silverlight/.)

- Be prepared to do much work tweaking the performance of your application.

- Utilize third-party components (graphing in particular) because Silverlight's current toolkit is lacking.

- Some third-party Silverlight control vendors are not taking full advantage of Silverlight's capabilities and producing controls that run in Silverlight but work like an ASP.NET control.

- Much of the layout work was hand-coded rather than using designer features.

- Blend 3 seems slower than Blend 2, but contains some great features such as SketchFlow.

Summary

There are some fantastic new features in WPF 4.0 and Silverlight 3.0. And the release of Silverlight 4.0 is just around the corner. If you are beginning a new project should you create it using Silverlight or WPF?

Pete Brown (Developer Community Program Manager for Windows Client) has the following to say on his blog:

> *"In the future, it is very likely that both Silverlight and WPF will be a single technology with a single codebase. After all, Silverlight was originally known as WPF/E (E as in Everywhere), and in an amazing 180 degree reversal of our usual approach, we took an ugly codename and created a great product name (Silverlight) from it."*

http://community.irritatedvowel.com/blogs/pete_browns_blog/archive/2009/12/01/The-Future-of-Client-App-Dev-_3A00_-WPF-and-Silverlight-Convergence.aspx

Whatever happens (and it's likely this merge won't happen overnight), it is clear that WPF and Silverlight have a very bright future ahead and are certainly technologies to invest io invest in.

Further Reading

- http://msdn.microsoft.com/en-us/library/bb613588(VS.100).aspx
- http://blogs.msdn.com/llobo/
- http://blogs.windowsclient.net/rob_relyea/

- http://weblogs.asp.net/scottgu/archive/2009/10/26/wpf-4-vs-2010-and-net-4-0-series.aspx

- http://community.irritatedvowel.com/blogs/pete_browns_blog/

- http://silverlight.net/getstarted/silverlight3/

- http://timheuer.com/blog/archive/2009/03/18/silverlight-3-whats-new-a-guide.aspx

- http://blogs.windowsclient.net/rob_relyea/archive/2009/03/25/xaml-in-net-4-update.aspx

Windows Azure

Availability: Framework 3.5+

The research company Gartner defines cloud computing as:

> *"A style of computing where massively scalable IT-related capabilities are provided as a service"*

http://www.gartner.com/it/page.jsp?id=707508

Windows Azure is Microsoft's entry into the cloud-computing arena and competes with offerings from established heavyweights such as Amazon and Google. Windows Azure applications are created using standard .NET technologies and developers will be glad they will not need to learn many additional techniques to get up and running.

The complexity of the Azure infrastructure is hidden from the developer and managed by Microsoft, allowing you to concentrate on developing your application without having to worry about maintaining the platform your application runs on. Once your application's development is complete, you can then deploy it to Windows Azure, taking as much or as little of Microsoft's massively powerful infrastructure as you need. Unlike traditional hosting, you can instantly scale up the infrastructure your application runs on to meet demand.

Hosting applications and services within the cloud environment poses a number of challenges to the developer, such as how to authenticate requests, store data, and route messages, so in addition to the core Azure offering, Microsoft offers a number of services or building blocks to assist you with conquering these problems.

WARNING: AZURE IS WORK IN PROGRESS

At the time of writing, Windows Azure was not finalized, so functionality and screenshots may differ upon release. This chapter was written with Windows Azure Tools VS2010 Beta 2.

Azure Overview

Microsoft's cloud computing offering can be divided into a number of stand-alone modules or services:

- Windows Azure Platform
- Microsoft .NET Services
- SQL Azure (formally SQL Data Services)
- Live Services

Books could be written on each of these areas (and will be) so in this chapter we will be looking only at the core building block services to get you started. We will be looking at

- Windows Azure Service Platform
- Azure Storage

And we will be taking a brief look at

- SQL Azure
- Microsoft .NET Services

RANDOM TRADEMARK FACT

In 2007 computing manufacturer Dell tried to trademark the term "cloud computing."

http://tarr.uspto.gov/servlet/tarr?regser=serial&entry=77139082

Architecture

Windows Azure is made up of a huge number of connected virtualized servers running Windows 2008 64-bit edition and a hypervisor (at the simplest level, a hypervisor allows multiple instances of an operating system to run on a single machine at the same time) optimized for Windows Azure and based on Hyper V technology. This collection of servers is referred to as the fabric, in that its usage should appear seamless to the developer.

Currently there are two Azure data centers in North America with plans to open additional centers in Chicago (USA) and Dublin (Ireland).

An individual server runs a number of virtual machines, which, in turn, host a number of roles (or instances of an Azure application). Each Azure instance has dedicated an individual virtual machine, which does not have access to the other virtual machines for security and resource allocation purposes.

Individual servers are connected by the fabric controller and Windows Agent (see Figure 16-1). The fabric controller additionally provisions, deploys, and monitors service health. It is important to note that an instance of Azure is never accessed directly but routed through a load balancer.

When you request more than one role instance, Windows Azure physically allocates them in the safest, most redundant manner possible. This means your application will run on a server in a different rack and subnet than other roles you may have.

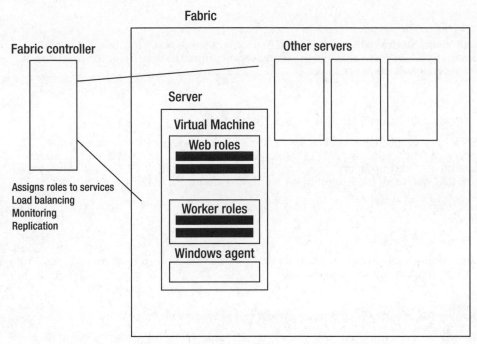

Figure 16-1. *Azure architecture*

Will I Be Able to Install My Own Version of Windows Azure?

Currently no, although a number of people have made this request. Arguably you may be missing one of the major benefits of cloud computing—outsourcing infrastructure management. Do, however, expect to see some of the advances on the Azure platform, such as the hypervisor and virtualization, creeping their way into Windows Server in the future.

Before You Begin

Although you can work through many of the examples locally, it's more fun, if you can, to deploy them to the cloud—even if your application just prints out "Hello Azure"!
So before you do anything else, sign up for an Azure account at
http://www.microsoft.com/windowsazure/account/.

■**TIP** MSDN subscriptions now come with Azure time.

Installation

If you are working with Visual Studio 2008, you will need to download and install the Azure SDK and Tools. At the time of writing, when you create a new Cloud Service project in VS2010 for the first time, it will download the latest version of the Azure tools.

Web Roles

The first type of application we will create is called a web role. In Windows Azure the term web role refers to an application that is accessible over HTTP (which in our example is an ASP.NET application) although it is also possible to create other types such as ASP.NET MVC, Delphi, PHP, Ruby, or even a C++ application (through a CGI web role). It's also probably worth mentioning that Azure applications operate in full trust.

Hello Azure

We will now create and deploy a very simple application that reads a value from a configuration file and prints it to the screen with the current time and date.

1. Load up Visual Studio.

2. Create a new Windows Azure Cloud Service project called Chapter16.HelloAzure.

3. Visual Studio will now ask you what roles you want to create within your project (Figure 16-2).

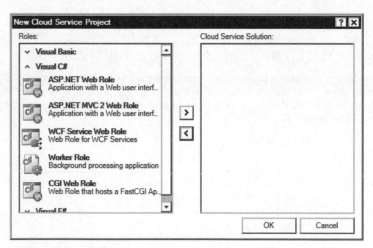

Figure 16-2. *Adding a web role to project*

4. Select ASP.NET Web Role and click the > button to add it into your solution.

5. Right-click on the role in the right-hand pane, select Rename on the context menu, and call it Chapter16.WebRole.

6. Click OK.

7. Visual Studio will now create two projects within the solution (Figure 16-3):

Chapter16.HelloAzure

Chapter16.WebRole

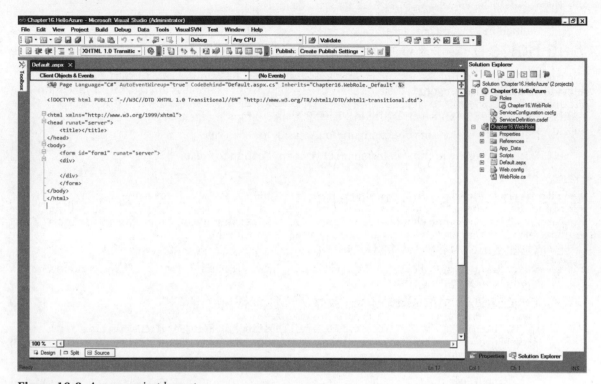

Figure 16-3. *Azure project layout*

Chapter16.WebRole

This is a standard ASP.NET project that references some Azure-specific functionality.

Chapter16.HelloAzure

The Chapter16.HelloAzure project describes our application to Windows Azure and allows us to configure it for the Azure platform. We will use the output from this project when we deploy our application. Chapter16.HelloAzure contains two (annoyingly similarly named) configuration files you will not have come across before:

- ServiceDefinition.csdef

- ServiceConfiguration.cscfg

ServiceDefinition.csdef

`ServiceDefinition.csdef` is responsible for

- Describing your application's requirements
- Defining configurable settings that your application will use (the actual values are defined in `ServiceConfiguration.cscfg`)
- Configuration settings applicable to all instances of your application

ServiceConfiguration.cscfg

`ServiceConfiguration.cscfg` is responsible fors responsible for

- Defining the values of your configuration settings for each role
- Determining the number of instances of your application to create

Azure and Configuration Settings

Most applications have some element of configuration. In our example application, we will define a configurable value that we will be read in the `Page_Load` event with the `RoleManager.getConfigurationSetting()` method.

1. Select the `Chapter16.HelloAzure` project and open `ServiceDefinition.csdef`. The contents should look something like this:

```
<?xml version="1.0" encoding="utf-8"?>
<ServiceDefinition name="Chapter16.HelloAzure"
xmlns="http://schemas.microsoft.com/ServiceHosting/2008/10/ServiceDefinition">
  <WebRole name="Chapter16.WebRole">
    <InputEndpoints>
      <InputEndpoint name="HttpIn" protocol="http" port="80" />
    </InputEndpoints>
    <ConfigurationSettings>
      <Setting name="DiagnosticsConnectionString" />
    </ConfigurationSettings>
  </WebRole>
</ServiceDefinition>
```

2. Add the following inside the `ConfigurationSettings` element to tell Azure that we will be creating a setting called `Message`:

```
<Setting name="Message"/>
```

3. Your `ServiceDefinition.csdef` file should now look like the following:

```
<?xml version="1.0" encoding="utf-8"?>
<ServiceDefinition name="Chapter16.HelloAzure"
xmlns="http://schemas.microsoft.com/ServiceHosting/2008/10/ServiceDefinition">
  <WebRole name="Chapter16.WebRole">
    <InputEndpoints>
      <InputEndpoint name="HttpIn" protocol="http" port="80" />
    </InputEndpoints>
```

```
    <ConfigurationSettings>
      <Setting name="DiagnosticsConnectionString" />
      <Setting name="Message"/>
    </ConfigurationSettings>
  </WebRole>
</ServiceDefinition>
```

4. We will now define the actual value of this setting, so open `ServiceDefinition.cscfg` and add a new setting inside the `ConfigurationSettings` element:

```
<Setting name="Message" value="Hello Azure"/>
```

5. While we are working with `ServiceDefinition.cscfg`, find the element that reads

```
<Instances count="1"/>
```

and change it to

```
<Instances count="5"/>
```

6. Changing the instances count tells Azure to create five instances of our application and simulates scaling our application to use five Azure nodes (you will need to set this back before deployment depending on your pricing structure). This setting can be easily amended online; note how easy it is to quickly scale up your application depending on demand. Microsoft recently announced Azure supports an API that allows you to do this programmatically. Your `ServiceDefinition.cscfg` should now look like

```
<?xml version="1.0"?>
<ServiceConfiguration serviceName="Chapter16.HelloAzure"
xmlns="http://schemas.microsoft.com/ServiceHosting/2008/10/ServiceConfiguration">
  <Role name="Chapter16.WebRole">
    <Instances count="5" />
    <ConfigurationSettings>
      <Setting name="DiagnosticsConnectionString" value="UseDevelopmentStorage=true"
/>
      <Setting name="Message" value="Hello Azure"/>
    </ConfigurationSettings>
  </Role>
</ServiceConfiguration>
```

Open `Default.aspx.cs` and enter the following code:

```
using Microsoft.WindowsAzure.ServiceRuntime;

protected void Page_Load(object sender, EventArgs e)
{
    string GreetingString = "" +
RoleEnvironment.GetConfigurationSettingValue("message");
    Response.Write(GreetingString + " at " + DateTime.Now.ToString());
}
```

7. Press F5 to run the application and you should see the greeting value we defined output to the screen with the current time and date.

Logging and Debugging

When running your Azure applications locally, you can make full use of standard Visual Studio debugging facilities. However, when applications are deployed to the cloud, debugging and logging support is a bit limited at the time of writing.

At the time of writing the logging APIs are in a state of flux (`http://blogs.msdn.com/windowsazure/archive/2009/10/03/upcoming-changes-to-windows-azure-logging.aspx`) so expect the final version to have performance monitoring features and integration with Azure storage (see the following).

Note that the `RoleManager.WriteToLog()` method that was present in preview versions has been removed.

Testing Azure Applications

We have now finished our application's development, so we need to test it. Development would be very slow if we had to deploy to the cloud each time to test it, so Microsoft provides a local version of Azure called the development fabric that simulates how our applications will function in the cloud.

Before we can run Azure our application, we will need to create the development storage database (which is just a SQL Server database). This seems to be used for deployment and testing of Azure applications. It can also be quite useful for debugging Azure storage issues (discussed later in the chapter).

Creating Development Storage

To create development storage, open the Windows Azure SDK command prompt (on the Windows menu under the Windows Azure SDK v1.0 folder) and then enter the following command replacing `INSTANCENAME` with the name of your SQL Server instance (if you don't want to use an instance just enter a dot to refer to the machine itself):

```
DSInit /sqlinstance:INSTANCENAME
```

After you press return, the `DSInit` utility will start creating the development storage database (Figure 16-4):

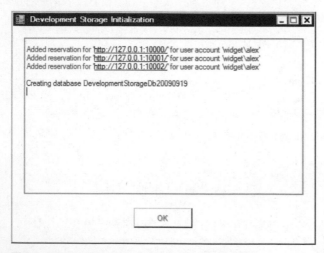

Figure 16-4. *Creation of development storage*

Now press F5 to run your application and you should see an exciting screen like Figure 16-5:

Figure 16-5. *Hello Azure application*

Well done—you have created your first Azure application—but don't close the web browser window just yet. Take a look at the Windows taskbar (you have to click Show hidden icons if you are using Windows 7) where there will be a small blue Windows Azure flag showing. Left-clicking on this will show you the current Azure storage and development fabric status (Figure 16-6).

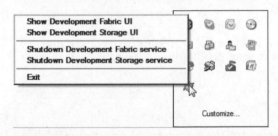

Figure 16-6. *Azure storage*

Now right-click on the blue flag and notice how you can shut down the development storage and fabric here as well. This time, however, select the option to show the development fabric UI, and you should see a screen similar to Figure 16-7:

419

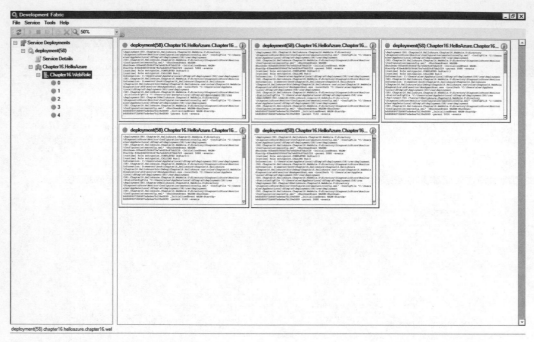

Figure 16-7. *Development Fabric UI*

The window is split into two panes. On the left-hand side is a tree structure that allows you to view details of the service and individual web roles, while over on the right is the logging output from the various Azure instances.

Service Details Node

Click the Service Details node to show you details of where your service is running.

Chapter16.HelloAzure Node

Right-click on the `Chapter16.HelloAzure` node and you will see options for starting, suspending, and restarting the services. You can further configure the project restart configuration by right-clicking and selecting Settings.

Chapter16.WebRole Node

Right-click the web role node and you will see options for clearing the logs and changing the logging level. Left-clicking the web role node will expand it to show all instances of the application running, which are represented by a number of green globes. The black screens on the left show the output from the individual nodes.

Green Globes

If you right-click a green globe (web role) you will see options to attach a debugger and view the local store.

Viewing Azure Logs

To view the log file of your application, click one of the black screens to see the output. If you right-click on the green globe you have the options to filter the message types displayed by selecting the logging level (Figure 16-8).

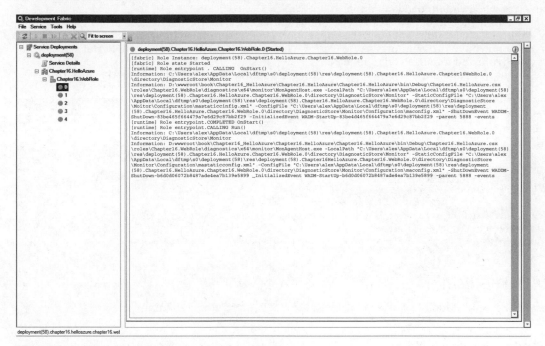

Figure 16-8. *Viewing Azure log on development storage*

■**TIP** For applications that will be deployed to both standard web servers and Azure it can be useful to determine whether you are running in the fabric. The `RoleEnvironment.IsAvailable()` method returns a Boolean value indicating this.

Deployment

To deploy your application to the cloud you will need a Windows Azure account. If you do not have one yet, what are you waiting for? Go and sign up for one now at http://www.microsoft.com/windowsazure/account/.

Deploying Hello Azure Application

Before you deploy your application, check whether you have reset the instance count in the .cscfg file of the Hello Azure application from five to one, as depending on your price plan; otherwise, you may receive an error when you upload your application.

OK, let's deploy the project we created earlier by right-clicking on the HelloAzure project and selecting Publish. Visual Studio will build the application, open the publish directory folder in Windows Explorer and send you to the Windows Azure platform login page. The Windows Azure Portal allows you to deploy, configure and manage your applications.

Once you have logged into the services portal and you should see a screen similar to Figure 16-9:

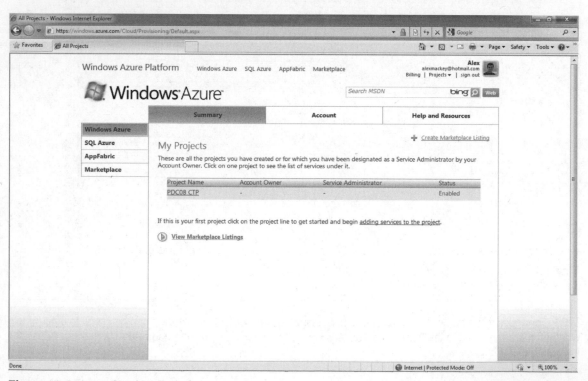

Figure 16-9. *Azure Services Portal*

This page lists all the projects associated with this user. If you haven't created a project yet, click the adding services to the project link. In the previous example, I have a project called PDC08CTP; click this and you will then be taken to the project services screen (Figure 16-10).

Here, if you haven't already, click the New Service link and add a new hosted service (in the screen shot mine is called Introducing VS2010). Then click on it.

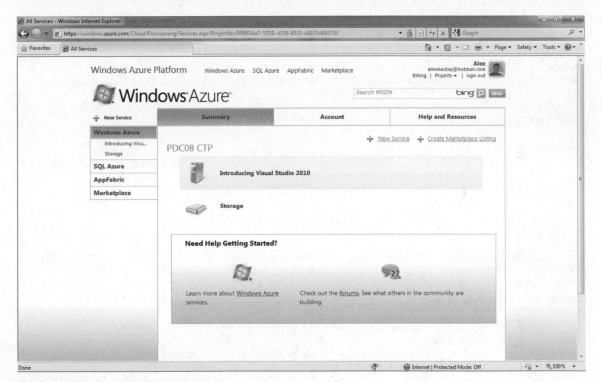

Figure 16-10. *Project services screen*

You should then be taken to a screen that shows the current status of your Azure roles (Figure 16-11).

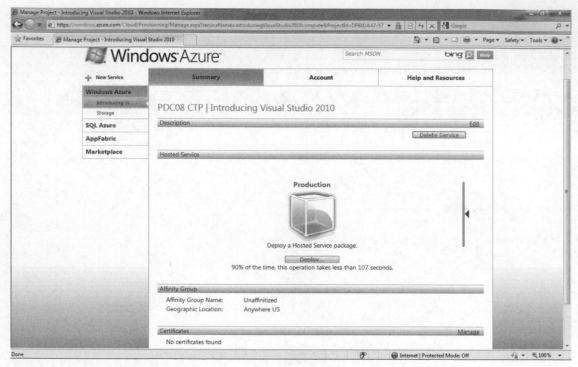

Figure 16-11. *Inactive web role*

Notice at the moment this screen shows only the production instance (see the following section for how to upload to staging instance). We want to upload our application to Windows Azure, so click the Deploy button beneath the staging cube and you will be taken to the Staging Deployment screen.

We now need to upload our application itself and its service configuration file.

Application Package Section

On the Application Package section, click the Browse button and select the compiled application's cspkg file (by default this is built at: ~\bin\Debug\Publish\). See Figure 6-12.

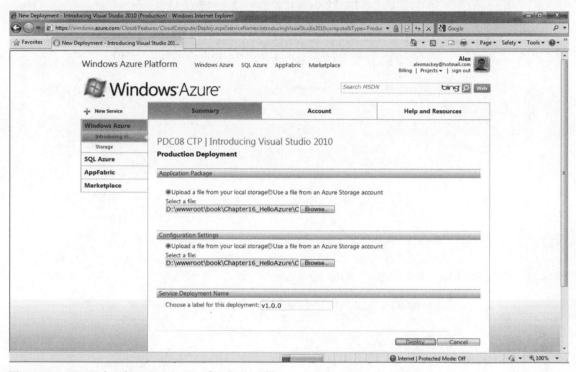

Figure 16-12. *Uploading ServiceConfiguration files*

Configuration Settings Section

On the Configuration Settings section, click the Browse button and select the **ServiceConfiguration** file (default location: **~\HelloAzure\bin\Debug\Publish\ServiceConfiguration.cscfg**). Now give the deployment a descriptive label (e.g., v1.0.0) and click Deploy. Your service will now be deployed to the cloud (Figure 16-13). This is not the quickest process so you may want to go and do something else for five minutes.

Once your application has been uploaded, a number of new options will appear beneath the cube enabling you to configure and run it (Figure 16-14).

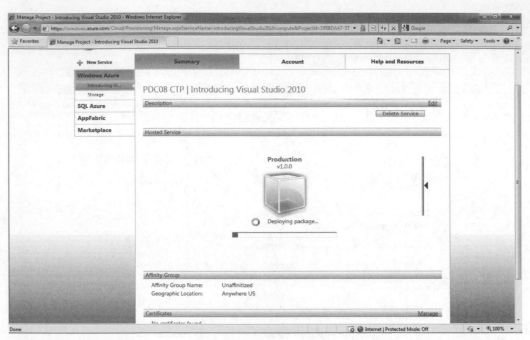

Figure 16-13. *Screen after uploading an application*

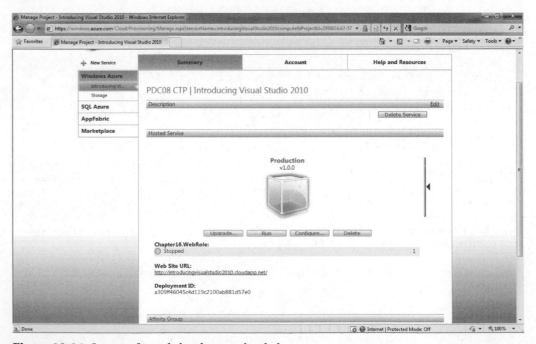

Figure 16-14. *Screen after role has been uploaded*

Click the Run button to start your Azure application up. Azure will chug away for a bit and then your application should be running (Figure 16-15). Notice that beneath the cube is a URL that you can click to be taken to your running application.

Figure 16-15. *Our web role running in the cloud*

Staging

Normally you will want to test your changes before moving them to production (or you probably should), so Windows Azure allows you to deploy applications to a staging deployment as well. To access the staging deployment, click the arrow on the right of the manage project screen to show the staging options and upload in a similar manner similar to what we just did.

When you want to promote your staging application to production, click the blue sphere with the two white arrows in the middle. After accepting a confirmation that you really want to do this, Windows Azure will then move your staged application into production.

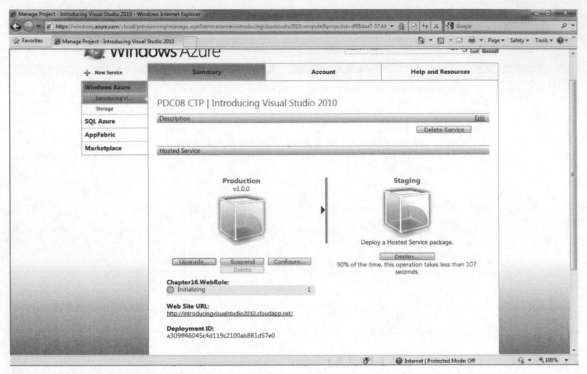

Figure 16-16. *Azure allows production and staging environments*

Production URLs

Obviously you will want to configure your application to run at your own domain name. At the time of writing there was no easy facility to do this (apart from by domain forwarding), so please consult the Azure online documentation for details of how to do this.

Analytical Data

A big omission in my opinion is the current lack of analytical data available in Azure, which is crucial given its pay-per-use pricing model. In the future it is likely Microsoft will add this (indeed earlier previews contained an analytical tab).

Local Storage

LocalStorage is an area to which you can temporarily save files and it can be useful for caching, uploading, and serialization. Warning—you should not save anything here you want to keep since local storage will be cleared if your application restarts.

To use LocalStorage, simply add a new entry to ServiceDefinition.csdef to define the storage area:

```
<LocalStorage name="MyStorage"/>
```

Once you have defined the storage you can now use the RoleEnvironment.GetLocalResource() method to return a LocalResource object that allows you to utilize the file. The following example shows how to save a file to local storage:

```
LocalResource resource = RoleEnvironment.GetLocalResource("MyStorage");
string Path = resource.RootPath + "messages.txt";
string FileContents = "Hello Azure";
System.IO.File.WriteAllText(Path, FileContents);
```

If you want to see items that have been saved in the development fabric's local storage with the previous code, then you can right-click on the web role and select Open local storage option and browse to Directory/MyStorage.

Worker Roles

A worker role is Azure's version of a Windows service. Worker roles are used for continual or long-running tasks, such as processing data held in an Azure queue (we will look at Azure queues shortly). Worker roles cannot be accessed directly like a web role or ASP.NET page, but they do allow the creation of HTTP-based endpoints for inter-role communication. Please see the Azure samples November training kit (http://www.microsoft.com/downloads/details.aspx?FamilyID=413e88f8-5966-4a83-b309-53b7b77edf78&displaylang=en), which contains a thumbnail image generator example.

In many Azure projects you will want to use both web and worker roles. To add a web or worker role to an existing project, just right-click on the ~/Roles/ directory and then select to add a new worker role. You may remember you also had the option to add a role when creating a project.

Let's take a quick look at worker roles.

1. Right-click on the Roles directory and select Add➤New Worker Role Project.

2. Call it Chapter16.WorkerRole.

3. Open WorkerRole.cs if it is not already open, and you should see code similar to the following (shortened to save space). Note how a worker role at its most basic level is little more than a big loop for you to put your code inside.

```
public override void Run()
{
    Trace.WriteLine("WorkerRole1 entry point called", "Information");

    while (true)
    {
        Thread.Sleep(10000);
        Trace.WriteLine("Working", "Information");
    }
}
```

```
public override bool OnStart()
{
    ServicePointManager.DefaultConnectionLimit = 12;
    DiagnosticMonitor.Start("DiagnosticsConnectionString");

    RoleEnvironment.Changing += RoleEnvironmentChanging;
    return base.OnStart();
}
}
```

Storage in Azure

For storing data in Windows Azure there are three main options:

- Azure Storage

- SQL Azure

- Other external storage mechanism accessible over HTTP

So what's the difference?

Azure storage is very fast and intended for storing files or data with a simple structure, and it is also cheaper than its SQL counterpart. In contrast, SQL Azure is better suited to working with complex data relationships and should be an easier option for application migration but is slower and more expensive. SQL Azure is built on top of SQL Server but has a few important limitations, most notably a 10gb size limit. SQL Azure also has a reduced set of functionality to normal SQL Server (although if you are using only the basic/standard features of SQL Server, then your application will probably run fine on SQL Azure). Note that initially SQL Azure (formally SQL Data Services) was similar to Azure table storage, but due to customer feedback, it was changed to a more traditional SQL Server model.

The differences between the two services are summarised here:

- Azure Storage:

    - More scalable than SQL Azure

    - Stores Blobs, Queues, and Entities (a type of .NET objects)

    - Cheaper than SQL Azure

    - Does not use SQL Server (the development version does, though)

    - Is not relational and doesn't use SQL

    - Access is provided by the REST API

- SQL Azure

    - SQL Server you know and love, offering an easier migration path for existing applications

    - Supports complex relational queries

    - More expensive than Azure Storage

    - Access is similar to standard SQL Server apart from using an Azure-specific connection string

Before you jump to automatically using SQL Azure you may want to consider whether a traditional relational database is scalable for very high traffic applications and whether you would be better served using Azure Storage.

Azure Storage

Azure Storage holds three different types of data:

- Blobs - for files or large amounts of textual data

- Queues - messages retrieved in a first-in, first-out manner

- Tables - hold objects (called entities in Azure terminology) and bear little resemblance to traditional storage mechanisms

Azure storage can be accessed by any application that can send an HTTP request, so don't think that you are confined to using this service with just .NET applications. Azure storage can also be tested locally by using the development storage. To access the development storage control panel, right-click on the Windows Azure blue flag and select the show development fabric UI option.

The Development Storage management screen should then appear, showing the end points each of the storage service is running at (Figure 16-17):

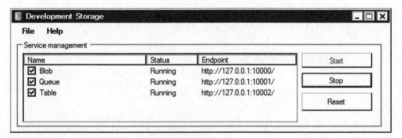

Figure 16-17. *Development Storage UI*

You can see that Azure Storage is divided into three different services of type: Blob, Queue, and Table. The management screen shows each service's current status and end points. Tables differ in that they can be subdivided into containers.

Working with Azure Storage

To work with Azure storage there are two options:

- Make a request to the REST API directly

- Utilize the Windows Azure API, which makes REST requests behind the scenes

So you can see that ultimately you will be using the REST API or er... the REST API.

Azure API or REST Requests?

The Azure APIs will be more than suitable for most applications, but for integration purposes or where performance is paramount you may want to use the REST API directly, as it will give you full control over your requests. However, before you rush off to develop your own REST API, here is a word of warning—don't underestimate the amount of work involved. Producing a class with enough functionality to work with a single type of Azure storage data will mean creating many different methods and can be quite boring, fiddly work.

Let's REST for a Minute

REST stands for Representational State Transfer and is a style of architecture introduced by a guy named Roy Fielding (one of the main authors of HTTP). You can read about what Roy proposed at `http://www.ics.uci.edu/~fielding/pubs/dissertation/top.htm`.

Applications implementing Roy's proposed architecture are sometimes described as RESTful. I don't want to get into a debate about what exactly constitutes a RESTful system (some people that probably need to get out a bit more feel scarily passionate about this) but the important points to note are

- Everything is abstracted into a resource that is accessible by a unique address.

- REST applications don't maintain state between requests.

These two characteristics might not seem like a big deal, but are essential for cloud-based applications since they allow us to:

- Easily scale applications by taking advantage of features such as caching and load balancing. There is no difference at an HTTP level between a request to Azure storage and a web page request.

- Write inter-platform applications that integrate easily.

Azure Storage Names

Everything in Azure has to be accessible using HTTP, so Azure has a number of rules regarding naming of objects that must be adhered to (basically anything that would form a valid URL address):

- Names must start with a letter or number.

- Names can only contain letters, numbers, and dashes.

- Every dash character must be preceded and followed by a letter.

- All letters must be lowercase.

- Names must be 3–63 characters in length.

Blobs (Binary Large Object)

Blobs are for storing binary data such as images, documents, and large strings. There are two types of blobs in Windows Azure, block and page blobs. Block blobs are refined for streaming operations while page blobs are used to write to a series of bytes. A block blob can be up to 200gb in size and is uploaded in 64mb increments. Should your blob exceed 64mb then it will be split into individual *blocks*, which are then reassembled. Page blobs can be up to 1 TB in size.

Blob Example

We will create a program to add, delete, and display blobs. Our application will allow the user to upload images with the FileUpload control, which will then store them as a Blob. We will then bind the stored Blobs to a DataList to check we have actually uploaded something.

1. Open Visual Studio and create a new Windows Azure Cloud Service called Chapter16.BlobTest and add a web role called Chapter16.BlobTestWebRole.

2. Open Default.aspx and add the following code inside the form tag:

```
<asp:FileUpload ID="uploadFile" runat="server" /> <asp:Button ID="cmdUpload"
runat="server"
Text="Upload"  />

<br /><br />

<asp:repeater ID="images" runat="server">
<ItemTemplate>
<asp:Image ID="image" runat="server" ImageUrl='<%# Eval("Url") %>' />
 </ItemTemplate>
</asp:repeater>
```

3. Open Default.aspx.cs.

4. Add the following using statements:

```
using Microsoft.WindowsAzure;
using Microsoft.WindowsAzure.ServiceRuntime;
using Microsoft.WindowsAzure.StorageClient;
```

5. Add the following code. Here, when the user uploads an image, an instance of the BlobClient is created. The BlobClient then checks if a container called pictures exists and creates one if not. Next we create a permission object to allow everyone to view our uploaded image before saving the image. We then call the bindImages() method to display our uploaded images:

```
protected void Page_Load(object sender, EventArgs e)
{
    this.cmdUpload.Click += new EventHandler(cmdUpload_Click);
    bindImages();
}

void cmdUpload_Click(object sender, EventArgs e)
{
    CloudStorageAccount.SetConfigurationSettingPublisher((configName, configSetter) =>
    {
        // Provide the configSetter with the initial value
        configSetter(RoleEnvironment.GetConfigurationSettingValue(configName));
    });

    var storageAccount =
      CloudStorageAccount.FromConfigurationSetting("DataConnectionString");
```

```
        CloudBlobClient blobClient = storageAccount.CreateCloudBlobClient();
        CloudBlobContainer blobContainer = blobClient.GetContainerReference("pictures");

        blobContainer.CreateIfNotExist();

        var permissions = blobContainer.GetPermissions();
        permissions.PublicAccess = BlobContainerPublicAccessType.Container;
        blobContainer.SetPermissions(permissions);

        blobContainer.GetBlockBlobReference(
          Guid.NewGuid().ToString()).UploadFromStream(uploadFile.FileContent
        );

        bindImages();
    }


    public void bindImages()
    {
        CloudStorageAccount.SetConfigurationSettingPublisher((configName, configSetter) =>
        {
            // Provide the configSetter with the initial value
            configSetter(RoleEnvironment.GetConfigurationSettingValue(configName));
        });


        var storageAccount =
          CloudStorageAccount.FromConfigurationSetting("DataConnectionString");

        CloudBlobClient blobStorage = storageAccount.CreateCloudBlobClient();
        CloudBlobContainer blobContainer = blobStorage.GetContainerReference("pictures");

        blobContainer.CreateIfNotExist();

        images.DataSource = from blob in blobContainer.ListBlobs()
                            select new { Url = blob.Uri };
        images.DataBind();
    }
```

6. The last step is that we need to tell Azure how to access the storage. Open
    `ServiceDefinition.csdef` and add the following inside the `ConfigurationSettings` block:

    `<Setting name="DataConnectionString" />`

7. Add the following settings in the `ServiceConfiguration.cscfg` configuration block:

    `<Setting name="DataConnectionString" value="UseDevelopmentStorage=true" />`

8. Press F5 to run your project.

9. Click Browse, select a JPG or GIF image, and click Upload and you should then see your picture
    displayed like in Figure 16-18.

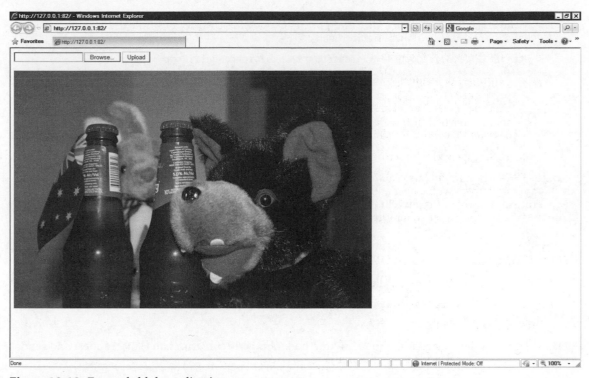

Figure 16-18. *Example blob application*

If you right-click on the image to examine its URL, notice how the URL is made up of a number of properties we defined in our ServiceConfiguration: AccountName, pictures container, and the GUID we used for the ID (this URL is made up of IP:PORT/account/container/blobID) (e.g., http:// 127.0.0.1:10000/devstoreaccount1/pictures/4d5eee66-162e-4fb1-afcb-197f08384007).

Accessing REST API Directly

Now that we have worked with the StorageClient, however, I think that it is useful to understand what is happening behind the scenes. In our previous example we created a container to store our images, called pictures. We will now create an application to list all the containers in our local Azure Storage by constructing the raw HTTP request.

How Do We Work with the REST API?

To interface with the Azure Storage REST API, we will construct a request using the WebRequest classes. We need to do the following:

1. Make an HTTP request to a URL and port. The following URL, for example, is used to retrieve a list of containers held in Azure Storage:

    ```
    http://127.0.0.1:10000/devstoreaccount1/devstoreaccount1?comp=list
    ```

2. Set a number of headers in the request.

3. Set the HTTP verb of the request to describe what we are doing (e.g., GET, PUT).

4. Calculate a hash of the headers we added and a hidden key. This ensures no one can modify the request and allows Azure Storage to authenticate us.

5. Azure Storage will then return our results as XML.

Azure Storage authenticates each user by hashing the headers (using SHA 256) with a shared secret key. If anyone tampers with a header or the wrong key is used, then the hash will not match what Azure is expecting and it will return an HTTP 403 error (not authenticated). Note that, for additional security, Azure messages expire after 15 minutes and will be rejected.

Working with Azure Storage with Raw HTTP Requests

Create a new Console application called Chapter16.AzureRawHttp.

1. Add the following using directive:

    ```
    using System.Net;
    ```

2. Add the following code to the Main() method. This code constructs an HTTP request and sends it to Azure local storage to list containers:

    ```
    //Gets a list of containers
    string AccountName = "devstoreaccount1";
    string AccountSharedKey = "<YOUR_SHARED_KEY";
    string Address = "http://127.0.0.1";
    string Port = "10000";

    //Action to perform e.g. ?comp=list
    string QueryString="?comp=list";

    string uri = Address + ":" + Port + "/" + AccountName + QueryString;
    string MessageSignature = "";

    //Build Request
    HttpWebRequest Request = (HttpWebRequest)HttpWebRequest.Create(uri);
    Request.Method = "GET";
    Request.ContentLength = 0;
    Request.Headers.Add("x-ms-date", DateTime.UtcNow.ToString("R"));
    ```

```
                        //Create signaure of message contents
                        MessageSignature+="GET\n"; //Verb
                        MessageSignature+="\n"; //MD5 (not used)
                        MessageSignature+="\n"; //Content-Type
                        MessageSignature+="\n"; //Date optional if using x-ms-date header
                        MessageSignature += "x-ms-date:" + Request.Headers["x-ms-date"] + "\n"; //Date
                        MessageSignature+="/"+AccountName+"/"+AccountName+QueryString; //resource

                        //Encode signature using HMAC-SHA256
                        byte[] SignatureBytes = System.Text.Encoding.UTF8.GetBytes(MessageSignature);

                        System.Security.Cryptography.HMACSHA256 SHA256 =
                          new System.Security.Cryptography.HMACSHA256(
                            Convert.FromBase64String(AccountSharedKey)
                          );

                        // Now build the Authorization header
                        String AuthorizationHeader =  "SharedKey " + AccountName + ":"
                          + Convert.ToBase64String(SHA256.ComputeHash(SignatureBytes));

                        // And add the Authorization header to the request
                        Request.Headers.Add("Authorization", AuthorizationHeader);

                        //Get response
                        HttpWebResponse Response = (HttpWebResponse) Request.GetResponse();

                        using (System.IO.StreamReader sr =
                          new System.IO.StreamReader(Response.GetResponseStream()))
                        {
                            Console.WriteLine(sr.ReadToEnd());
                        }
                        Console.ReadKey();
```

3. Press F5 to run your application.

You should have a response like the following (in my example I have two blob containers: blobs and pictures):

```
<?xml version="1.0" encoding="utf-8"?>
<EnumerationResults AccountName="http://127.0.0.1:10000/devstoreaccount1">
<Containers>
<Container>
<Name>blobs</Name>
<Url>http://127.0.0.1:10000/devstoreaccount1/blobs</Url>
<LastModified>Mon, 16 Nov 2009 02:32:13 GMT</LastModified>
<Etag>0x8CC347C240E3FE0</Etag>
</Container>
<Container>
<Name>pictures</Name>
```

```
<Url>http://127.0.0.1:10000/devstoreaccount1/pictures</Url>
<LastModified>Mon, 16 Nov 2009 09:16:40 GMT</LastModified>
<Etag>0x8CC34B4A41BA4B0</Etag>
</Container><Container>
<Name>wad-control-container</Name>
<Url>http://127.0.0.1:10000/devstoreaccount1/wad-control-container</Url>
<LastModified>Mon, 16 Nov 2009 09:16:21 GMT</LastModified>
<Etag>0x8CC34B498B195D0</Etag>
</Container>
</Containers>
<NextMarker />
</EnumerationResults>
```

If you want to know more about working with the REST API directly, please refer to the SDK documentation directly, which specifies the format of requests. David Lemphers also has a good series of articles on working with Azure storage (based on preview versions, so they may be a bit out of date now): http://blogs.msdn.com/davidlem/archive/2008/12/20/windows-azure-storage-exploring-blobs.aspx.

Queues

Queues are an important concept in Azure storage, and they are made up of an unlimited number of messages that are generally read in the order they are added (Azure documentation says this is not guaranteed). Messages are removed as they are read, so if you don't want this to occur make sure you use the peek method instead.

Messages can be up to 8kb in size each, so if you need more space than this you can use a blob field and link the two by using the blob's meta data. Messages added to queues have a default time-out of seven days (called time to live). After that passes, then they will be destroyed.

We will create a new application to add and read items from a queue:

1. Create a new Azure project called Chapter16.QueueTest with a web role called Chapter16.QueueTestWebRole.
   Open Default.aspx and add the following code inside the form tag:

   ```
   <asp:TextBox ID="txtMessage" runat="server" Width="300"></asp:TextBox>
   <asp:Button ID="cmdAddToQueue" Text="Add" runat="server" />

   <asp:Button ID="cmdShowQueue" Text="Show Queue" runat="server"  />
   <br /><br />

   Queue contents:
   <br />
   <asp:Literal ID="litQueueContents" runat="server"></asp:Literal>
   ```

2. Open Default.aspx.cs and add the following using statements:

   ```
   using Microsoft.WindowsAzure;
   using Microsoft.WindowsAzure.StorageClient;
   using Microsoft.WindowsAzure.ServiceRuntime;
   ```

3. Add the following code to Default.aspx.cs:

```
protected void Page_Load(object sender, EventArgs e)
{
    cmdAddToQueue.Click += new EventHandler(cmdAddToQueue_Click);
    cmdShowQueue.Click += new EventHandler(cmdShowQueue_Click);
}

void cmdShowQueue_Click(object sender, EventArgs e)
{
    CloudStorageAccount.SetConfigurationSettingPublisher((configName, configSetter) =>
    {
        // Provide the configSetter with the initial value
        configSetter(RoleEnvironment.GetConfigurationSettingValue(configName));
    });


    var storageAccount =
      CloudStorageAccount.FromConfigurationSetting("DataConnectionString");

    CloudQueueClient queueStorage = storageAccount.CreateCloudQueueClient();
    CloudQueue queue = queueStorage.GetQueueReference("testqueue");
    queue.CreateIfNotExist();

    string queueContents = "";

    while (queue.PeekMessage() != null)
    {
        queueContents += queue.GetMessage().AsString + "<BR>";
    }

    litQueueContents.Text = queueContents;

    CloudQueueMessage readMessage = queue.GetMessage();
}

void cmdAddToQueue_Click(object sender, EventArgs e)
{
    CloudStorageAccount.SetConfigurationSettingPublisher((configName, configSetter) =>
    {
        // Provide the configSetter with the initial value
        configSetter(RoleEnvironment.GetConfigurationSettingValue(configName));
    });

    var storageAccount =
      CloudStorageAccount.FromConfigurationSetting("DataConnectionString");

    CloudQueueClient queueStorage = storageAccount.CreateCloudQueueClient();
    CloudQueue queue = queueStorage.GetQueueReference("testqueue");
    queue.CreateIfNotExist();
```

```
CloudQueueMessage message = new CloudQueueMessage(txtMessage.Text);
queue.AddMessage(message);

txtMessage.Text = "";
```

}

4. The last step is to again tell Azure how to access the storage. Open ServiceDefinition.csdef and add the following inside the ConfigurationSettings block:

   `<Setting name="DataConnectionString" />`

5. Add the following settings in the ServiceConfiguration.cscfg configuration block:

   `<Setting name="DataConnectionString" value="UseDevelopmentStorage=true" />`

6. Press F5 to run the application.

7. You will see a textbox and a button. Enter something like "Message1" in the text box, then click the "Add" button.

8. Click "Show Queue" to display the contents of the queue. The queue should show your message.

9. Click "Show Queue" again. No items should be returned as they have been read already.

10. Enter another item into the textbox and click Add.

11. Enter a further item into the textbox and click Add.

12. Click Show Queue, noting all the items displayed (Figure 16-19).

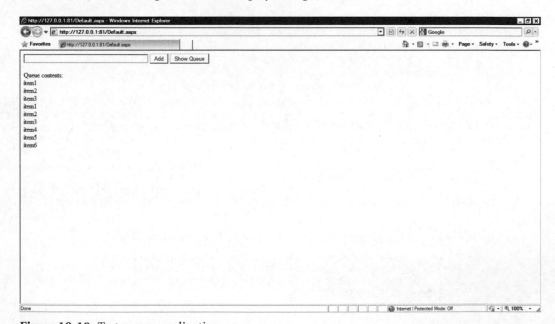

Figure 16-19. *Test queue application*

Table Storage

Azure table storage is the third Azure storage option and allows you to store .NET objects (entities in Azure terminology) and access them in a manner compatible with WCF Data Services. Azure table storage also requires that your entities have three additional fields:

- PartitionKey
- RowKey
- TimeStamp

PartitionKey and RowKey are combined as a composite key to uniquely identify a row, so it is important the combination of the two must be unique (Figure 16-20). The PartitionKey can be used by Azure to divide data up onto different servers for load-balancing purposes, while TimeStamp is used for conflict resolution.

Client Table

Timestamp	Partitionkey	Rowkey	Properties
2009-03-01 14:00:00,	Partition1,	1,	Bill, Gates, Microsoft US
2009-04-02 14:00:00,	Partition1,	2,	Eric, Nelson, Microsoft UK
2009-05-03 14:00:00,	Partition1,	3,	Scott, Guthrie, Microsoft US
2009-06-04 14:00:00,	Partition2,	1,	Larry, Page, Google
2009-07-05 14:00:00,	Partition2,	2,	Sergey, Brin, Google

Figure 16-20. *Visualization of an Azure table*

I think it's fair to say that table storage is probably not the most intuitive technology ever invented, but it is very flexible and easy to use once you get over the initial, "What the heck is this?". Items stored in table storage are created as standard .NET classes that inherit from TableServiceEntity. Another context class that inherits from TableServiceContext is also created that is used to interact with table storage.

This is actually simpler than it sounds, so let's create an example of table storage now to save and retrieve a Film entity.

1. Create a new Cloud Service project called Chapter16.TableStorage, adding a single ASP.NET web role to it.

2. In the WebRole1 project add a reference to System.Data.Services.Client.

3. Open the ServiceDefinition.csdef file and add the following entry to the ConfigurationSettings section:

   ```
   <Setting name="DataConnectionString" />
   ```

4. Open ServiceConfiguration.cscfg and add the following entry to ConfigurationSettings:

   ```
   <Setting name="DataConnectionString" value="UseDevelopmentStorage=true" />
   ```

441

5. Add a new class to the project called AzureDataServiceContext and add the following using directives:

```
using Microsoft.WindowsAzure.StorageClient;
using Microsoft.WindowsAzure;
```

6. Now enter the following code in AzureDataServiceContext.cs:

```
public class AzureDataServiceContext : TableServiceContext
{
    public AzureDataServiceContext(string baseAddress, StorageCredentials credentials)
            : base(baseAddress, credentials)
    {
    }

    public IQueryable<Film> FilmTable
    {
        get
        {
            return this.CreateQuery<Film>("Films");
        }
    }
}
```

7. Add a new class to the project called Film with the following using directive:

```
using Microsoft.WindowsAzure.StorageClient;
```

8. Now add the following code to define the class:

```
public class Film : TableServiceEntity
{
    public int FilmID { get; set; }
    public string Title {get; set; }
}
```

9. Open Default.aspx.cs and add the following using statements:

```
using Microsoft.WindowsAzure;
using Microsoft.WindowsAzure.ServiceRuntime;
using Microsoft.WindowsAzure.StorageClient;
```

10. Now enter the following code:

```
CloudStorageAccount.SetConfigurationSettingPublisher((configName, configSetter) =>
{
    // Provide the configSetter with the initial value
    configSetter(RoleEnvironment.GetConfigurationSettingValue(configName));
});

var storageAccount =
CloudStorageAccount.FromConfigurationSetting("DataConnectionString");
var tableStorage = storageAccount.CreateCloudTableClient();
tableStorage.CreateTableIfNotExist("Films");
```

```
AzureDataServiceContext svc =
  new AzureDataServiceContext(storageAccount.TableEndpoint.ToString(),
                              storageAccount.Credentials);

Film f1 = new Film();
f1.FilmID = 777;
f1.Title = "Commando";
f1.Timestamp = System.DateTime.Now;
f1.PartitionKey = "UK";
f1.RowKey = Guid.NewGuid().ToString();

svc.AddObject("Films", f1);
svc.SaveChanges();
Film film = svc.FilmTable.Where(f => f.FilmID == 777).FirstOrDefault();

Response.Write(film.Title);
```

11. Press F5 to run your application and you should have the film title Commando printed out to the screen.

Other Azure Services

In addition to Windows Azure Services and SQL Azure, Microsoft offers a number of other services such as Microsoft.NET Services and Windows Live Services.

Microsoft.NET Services

Microsoft.NET Services is made up of a number of services aimed at providing integration and authentication:

- Service Bus. The Service Bus is a message broker used for connecting applications across networks and through firewalls.

- Access Control Service. This provides a centralized access control mechanism exposed as a web service.

- WorkFlow Service (not currently available). The original previews of Windows Azure contained a workflow service, but this has since been removed. It is likely that at some point this will be re-introduced.

Windows Live Services

Windows Live Services is a collection of pretty much any other web-based service Microsoft has ever provided and is now held under the umbrella of Windows Live Services and accessed using the Live SDK. At the time of writing the SDK documentation and Azure site listed the following services (some of which are not yet complete):

- Advertising

- Alerts

- Live Messenger

- FeedSync

- Live Search
- Live Spaces
- Media Streaming
- Mesh
- Photo gallery
- Silverlight Streaming
- User-Data Storage services
- Writer
- Virtual Earth and Geospatial services

For more information please refer to http://msdn.microsoft.com/en-us/library/bb264574.aspx.

Pricing and SLA

Most cloud computing platforms only charge you for what you use, and Windows Azure is no exception. Microsoft says that free trials will be on offer for developers to experiment with Azure and preview accounts will be cancelled in January. Table 16-1 lists the prices. I've also included a brief summary of the current SLA agreement.

Alan Dean (one of the organizers of the UK Alt Net conference and REST architecture expert) suggested to me this could lead to financial reviews being carried out on code (as if you didn't have enough to worry about without accountants as well). For example, unnecessary use of ViewState could result in a big bill at the end of the month.

Table 16-1. *Summary of Windows Azure Pricing*

Service	Pricing
Windows Azure	Compute @ $0.12 / hour
	Storage @ $0.15 / GB stored
	Storage Transactions @ $0.01 / 10K
	Bandwidth $0.10 in / $0.15 out / GB
SQL Azure	Web Edition – Up to 1 GB relational database @ $9.99
	Business Edition – Up to 10 GB relational database @ $99.99
	Bandwidth – $0.10 in / $0.15 out / GB
.NET Services	Messages @ $0.15/100K message operations, including Service Bus messages and Access Control tokens
All	Bandwidth across all three services will be charged at $0.10 in / $0.15 out / GB

Source: http://www.microsoft.com/azure/pricing.mspx

Azure employs a pricing model similar to other cloud-computing suppliers such as Amazon. I was a little disappointed that Microsoft was not more innovative in this respect, and, as you can see, it could be quite tricky to work out how much your application will actually cost you (particularly with limited analysis support at present).

The Windows Azure site lists the following regarding SLA agreement:

"Windows Azure has separate SLAs for compute and storage. For compute, we guarantee that when you deploy two or more role instances in different fault and upgrade domains your Internet facing roles will have external connectivity at least 99.95% of the time. Additionally, we will monitor all of your individual role instances and guarantee that 99.9% of the time we will detect within two minutes when a role instance's process is not running and initiate corrective action. For storage, we guarantee that at least 99.9% of the time we will successfully process correctly formatted requests that we receive to add, update, read and delete data. We also guarantee that your storage accounts will have connectivity to our Internet gateway."

```
http://www.microsoft.com/azure/pricing.mspx
```

Real World Azure

I talked to a couple of developers about their experience of working with Windows Azure:

Ray Booysen

```
http://vistasquad.co.uk/blogs/nondestructive/default.aspx
```

Ray Booysen has developed two Windows Azure applications. The first is a proof of concept/ demonstration project to visually display how articles are linked in Wikipedia (http://www.dotnetsolutions.co.uk/evidence/wikiexplorer/, shown in Figure 16-21) and the second is an application for providing financial risk assessment.

Ray had the following tips:

- When working with Azure storage stop thinking normalization—this is not a normal database.

- Carefully consider your partition and row keys as cross partition searching is very slow (in his Wikipedia explorer example the first letter of the article was used as the partition key).

- Consider duplicating data for performance reasons.

Ray felt that Azure could be improved by

- Better logging and analytics

- Performance counters and some kind of query analyzer for Azure table storage

- Option to use the distributed cache system velocity

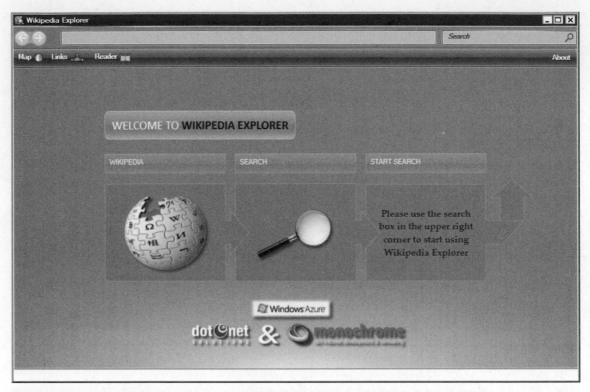

Figure 16-21. *DotNetSolutions Wikipedia explorer* http://www.dotnetsolutions.co.uk/
evidence/wikiexplorer/

Rusty Johnson and Andy Britcliffe, SharpCloud

(www.sharpcloud.com)

SharpCloud is currently developing a Silverlight/Azure project risk assessment application (discussed in Chapter 15 as well). The application carries out many complex calculations (using Azure worker roles) and suggests the optimal project selection.

Rusty and Andy had the following to say:

- The move to Azure was very easy (previously they were using Amazon's cloud services).

- Azure Table storage can take a bit of getting used to but is quite intuitive once you start using it.

- Azure is about **scalability not performance**—this is an important difference and you will have to do additional performance work.

Advantages

Here is a summary of the main advantages of Windows Azure and cloud computing:

- Low entry cost and ability to quickly scale up your applications infrastructure for peaks of demand

- No infrastructure expertise necessary—let Microsoft take care of this for you

- Potentially cheaper than dedicated data center although a detailed analysis would be necessary to determine this

- Greener computing

- Allows you to utilize existing .NET skills

- No hardware compatibility issues due to abstraction of hardware (although I would question how much of a problem this currently is)

Disadvantages

Here is a summary of the main disadvantages of Windows Azure and cloud computing:

- Cloud computing has many potential security issues that may make it unsuitable for some applications. You can obviously not be sure who has access to data and cannot ensure true deletion.

- There are governance/data protection issues with data being held around the world. Microsoft will in the future allow you to specify the hosting location.

- Poor debugging and logging support for deployed applications

- Untested compared to Google and Amazon's offerings

- Less control

- Pricing could and likely will change over years.

- How are you going to import large amounts of data?

- Vendor lock in—although unlikely Microsoft could terminate service in the future; where would this leave you?

- Learning curve

- Note: With regard to security concerns, it is worth keeping an eye on developments in a field known as "Homomorphic encryption." This could allow data to be encrypted in such a way that calculations can be conducted on it without un-encrypting it. Recently Craig Gentry at IBM made advances in this area: http://www.forbes.com/forbes/2009/0713/breakthroughs-privacy-super-secret-encryption.html

Conclusion

Windows Azure looks very promising but is currently hampered by poor logging and analytics. In time, however, these issues will no doubt be resolved. Microsoft has a big advantage over its competitors by integrating Azure into its development product portfolio, so expect to see Windows Azure becoming a major if not dominant player in the cloud computing sky.

Further Reading

- http://smarx.com/

- http://blogs.msdn.com/jnak/default.aspx

- http://silverlightuk.blogspot.com/

We have covered a huge amount of technologies over the last 400 or so pages and it is my hope that I have given you a good overview of all the cool stuff that awaits you in VS2010 and .net 4.

It is very likely that you now have many more questions than before you started reading–great!

Now that you have an overview of what's new then it is up to you to explore VS2010 and .net 4 further and hopefully share your experiences with the development community.

Probably both the best and most annoying aspect of .net (and programming) is that it is continually evolving - you have to work hard to keep up to date but there is always more to learn to keep you interested. :-)

Index

■ B

■P

U

You Need the Companion eBook

Your purchase of this book entitles you to buy the companion PDF-version eBook for only $10. Take the weightless companion with you anywhere.

We believe this Apress title will prove so indispensable that you'll want to carry it with you everywhere, which is why we are offering the companion eBook (in PDF format) for $10 to customers who purchase this book now. Convenient and fully searchable, the PDF version of any content-rich, page-heavy Apress book makes a valuable addition to your programming library. You can easily find and copy code—or perform examples by quickly toggling between instructions and the application. Even simultaneously tackling a donut, diet soda, and complex code becomes simplified with hands-free eBooks!

Once you purchase your book, getting the $10 companion eBook is simple:

❶ Visit **www.apress.com/promo/tendollars/**.

❷ Complete a basic registration form to receive a randomly generated question about this title.

❸ Answer the question correctly in 60 seconds, and you will receive a promotional code to redeem for the $10.00 eBook.

THE EXPERT'S VOICE™

233 Spring Street, New York, NY 10013

Offer valid through 11/10.